BIG
BUSINESS
AND
PRESIDENTIAL
POWER

BIG BUSINESS AND PRESIDENTIAL POWER

From FDR to Reagan

KIM McQUAID

William Morrow and Company, Inc.
New York   1982

Library of Congress Cataloging in Publication Data

McQuaid, Kim.
  Big business and presidential power.

  Bibliography: p.
  Includes index.
  1. United States—Economic policy. 2. Industry and state—United States—History—20th century. 3. Business and politics—United States—History—20th century. I. Title.
  HC106.M36   322'.3'0973   82–6332
  ISBN 0–688–01313–9   AACR2

Printed in the United States of America

First Edition

1 2 3 4 5 6 7 8 9 10

BOOK DESIGN BY BERNARD SCHLEIFER

To the memory of
the Roman historian
P. Cornelius Tacitus

PREFACE

THIS IS A BOOK about patterns of interaction between big businessmen and the federal government during the past half century. It was
written on the assumption that the primary responsibility of the
historian is to tell a good story about what happened and why it
happened, in as brief a fashion as possible. The work, therefore, is
comparatively free of technical jargon. As information regarding
high-level interaction between corporate and governmental leaders
is often extremely hard to come by, notes have been included to
direct particularly interested readers to the relevant source materials.

A few caveats are in order. This book is primarily about economic policy, foreign and domestic—with the emphasis upon the
latter. Those interested in corporate reactions to social issues such
as civil rights and women's liberation are advised to look elsewhere.
Nor will the work try to resolve all of the debates among left, right,
and center regarding the place occupied by giant corporations in
America's political and economic order. The author does not believe
in hero worship or devil theory. Those who want to hear about
plutocrats pulling strings with politicos dangling from them, or peer-
less entrepreneurs defending the market system from the depreda-
tions of a monster state, will not like this book. Other readers,
however, may at least come away with a belief that their opinions and
concerns have been addressed in some significant way. If this hap-
pens, the author can rest content that he has done his job.

This book is an intellectual child whose birth was assisted by
many individuals worthy of regard and mention. First I must thank

my parents, Mr. Frank McQuaid and Mrs. Margaret McQuaid of Edgecomb, Maine, for raising me so that I was later able to complete this work. Acknowledgments are also due to Antioch College, from which I graduated in 1970, and especially to Dr. Louis Filler of that school's faculty, a man who taught me more about the craft of history than anyone else whom I am ever likely to meet. Thanks also go to Professor Bill Domhoff of the University of California, Santa Cruz. Though we agreed to disagree on many things, Bill responded to my ideas and encouraged me at a crucial early stage in the book's creation. Dan Fenn of the John F. Kennedy Library, Bryce Harlow of Harper's Ferry, West Virginia, Leonard Silk of the *New York Times,* and Ed Berkowitz, formerly of the University of Massachusetts in Boston, also gave unselfishly of their time and suffered more than the usual share of foolish questions. Ed, in addition, is a good friend with whom it has been a pleasure to work over the years. He and his wife, Emily Frank, have often welcomed me to their home, as have others including Marc Gaynes and Leslie Landis of Chicago, Illinois, Sid and Helene Amster of Kitchener, Ontario, Joel and Margalit Mokyr of Skokie, Illinois, and Kamran and Brenda Ahmadkorour of Painesville, Ohio. I thank them all for hospitality that made the necessary loneliness of the writer much easier to bear. I must also express my appreciation to Ms. Patricia Dussaux of Cleveland, Ohio, for her excellent organizational, typing, and proofreading skills. Three other people deserve special mention: Professor William Appleman Williams very kindly helped me get a literary agent. Literary agent Gerry McCauley, in turn, promptly won a publisher over to my manuscript's cause. And Senior Editor Maria Guarnaschelli of William Morrow & Company used all of her considerable skills to turn that manuscript into a successful book. I owe them all big favors in return.

CONTENTS

RENDERING
UNTO CAESAR

SEPTEMBER 1, 1938, was not a good day for Edward R. Stettinius, Jr. Stettinius, who had just succeeded financier Myron C. Taylor as chairman of the board of the United States Steel Corporation, was scheduled for an off-the-record meeting with the President of the United States. Political bargaining of the toughest kind was the major, indeed the only, item on the agenda.

Stettinius and his corporation faced problems that had been developing for some time. In the summer of 1937, a sharp drop in business activity had ended four years of steady economic recovery from the depths of the Great Depression. Democratic leaders, who had helped bring on this new economic downturn through a misguided decision to cut back federal spending in an effort to balance the budget, winced as their political enemies bemoaned the miseries of the "Roosevelt recession."

One Democratic leader in particular was quick to act. By the fall of 1937, President Franklin D. Roosevelt had begun to sound out businessmen about the possibility of their taking actions aimed at restoring both unsteady markets and his own wobbling political fortunes.

Among the business leaders whom Roosevelt approached was Myron C. Taylor of U.S. Steel. The White House message to Taylor's giant and symbolically important corporation was simple: cut prices, but do not cut wage rates. Taylor, as he later telegraphed to his successor Stettinius, then "explained carefully to number one [FDR] . . . our desire to readjust price [levels] but made clear [that this] could not be done without wage changes, to which many times the

11

reply [from the President] has been to let [the] US government review [the steel corporation's] price and cost structure." Taylor, not to put too fine a point on it, turned Roosevelt down cold. Roosevelt thereupon informed U.S. Steel that cutting wage levels without his approval might lead to serious consequences.[1]

The threatened consequences quickly materialized. High-level administration spokesmen led by Secretary of the Interior Harold Ickes and Assistant Attorney General Robert Jackson began making speeches attacking large corporations and their plutocratic, even "fascist," works. Allegations flew that the recession was a consequence of a strike of capital against a liberal Democratic regime that it despised. The White House strongly opposed moves to reduce corporate tax rates as a means of spurring economic recovery. In the spring of 1938, with the recession worsening, 4 million people thrown out of work, and industrial indexes hovering at the worst levels since the Hoover era, Roosevelt made a well-publicized move to strengthen the Antitrust Division of the Justice Department by bringing lawyer Thurman Arnold to Washington to put teeth into the agency. By June, congressional Democrats had gotten involved by establishing the Temporary National Economic Committee (TNEC) to conduct a wide-ranging investigation into the extent of monopoly power in the United States. The United States Steel Corporation was prominently rumored to be the number one target on the new antimonopoly committee's list.

U.S. Steel leaders realized that the wind was blowing against them. On June 11, 1938, Taylor telegraphed Stettinius that he "must do nothing to put U.S. Steel Corporation of Delaware or subsidiaries in the front of the whole [antimonopoly] investigation contemplated," but went on to add that "readjustment" (i.e., lowering) of both prices and wages was still the strategy that the corporation should try to follow.[2]

Telling Stettinius what he should not do was a good deal easier than helping him get out of the hole that Taylor's policies had put him in. Angling for advantage, U.S. Steel's new chairman trod the path of compromise. First, the corporation announced that it would lower prices without cutting wage rates for its employees, who had only fifteen months before been unionized by the Congress of Industrial Organizations (CIO). Roosevelt immediately congratulated the corporation for its "statesmanship" in a nationally broadcast fireside chat.

Amid all of the *pro forma* good cheer emanating from the White House, Stettinius then journeyed to Washington to try to make the best deal possible for himself and his company. On June 13, he and fifteen other corporate leaders including Walter C. Teagle (Standard Oil of New Jersey), Marion B. Folsom (Eastman Kodak), Donald M. Nelson (Sears, Roebuck), and W. Averell Harriman (Union Pacific Railroad and Brown Brothers, Harriman) met with a blue-ribbon group of federal officials. Among these were antitrust chief Thurman Arnold, Robert Jackson, presidential advisers Benjamin V. Cohen and Gerald Frank, and the Undersecretaries of the Treasury and Commerce departments.

Although the topic of the meeting was how to keep general wage rates up, Stettinius was informed of administration appreciation for his corporation's price and wage policies. In the words of a confidential diary Stettinius kept during the negotiations, Democratic officials present intimated that "if the Government diverted to the Steel Corporation all its available steel tonnage [orders then being placed for an expanded defense program], this might bring about a sufficient volume of business immediately to increase our activities to a point where it would be unnecessary for the United States Steel Corporation to make a wage cut."[3]

Throughout the meeting, Stettinius remained wary of accepting any such deal. He merely promised to study the matter with his associates in Pittsburgh and New York. Perhaps because of fears that well-publicized government favoritism would incense the managements of other steel firms and business generally, U.S. Steel's leadership deemed acceptance of federal largesse "extremely unwise," and so informed Washington on June 28.

Matters did not rest there for long. Throughout the summer of 1938, back-door contacts between the White House and U.S. Steel were maintained. Finally, on September 1, Stettinius met with Roosevelt to negotiate an agreement at the highest level.

At Roosevelt's request, Stettinius brought with him confidential corporate price, profit, and cost-of-production statistics. The figures, Stettinius argued, demonstrated that U.S. Steel's sales and shipments had declined in the wake of its price cuts of the preceding June. Sales, Stettinius added, might start rising slowly in future months, barring any further worsening of the economy's problems.

Costs were also much on Stettinius' mind. Showing Roosevelt a chart depicting the relationship between prices and wage levels at

U.S. Steel for the twelve years from 1926 to 1938, Stettinius remonstrated that Roosevelt's refusal to countenance wage cuts was costing his corporation $36 million a year. Some relief from these burdens was required. Nor was John L. Lewis of the CIO helping matters by rejecting the suggestions of his associate Sidney Hillman to applaud the steel corporation for refusing to lower wage rates, and to consider the possibility of the steelworkers' union agreeing to wage cuts in the event that the industry continued depressed. U.S. Steel was in the worst of all possible worlds, squeezed between poor sales and high wage costs.

After further verbal sparring, the participants in the meeting started getting down to the real business at hand. Roosevelt stated his opinion that any wage cuts by so strategic and powerful a corporation as U.S. Steel would "spread like wild fire throughout the country" and make upcoming contract talks in other key industries, especially the railroads, extremely difficult. Two red herrings were then introduced into the discussion. First, Roosevelt suggested that any discontent in the rail industry caused by wage cuts might lead to an immediate federal takeover of the railroads. When this prospect failed to alarm Stettinius, Roosevelt threatened to attack the "basing-point" pricing system then used by the American steel industry. When Stettinius responded that the abolition of this system would only harm U.S. Steel slightly, while causing widespread dislocation among relatively small steel-transportation and -fabrication firms, Roosevelt quickly dropped this second line of argument.

Finally, the gloves came off. Roosevelt calmly asked, "What is your time schedule on this whole [wage-cutting] business?" Stettinius responded that no "precipitous" action was in the offing, due to previous presidential assurances that had been delivered to U.S. Steel through White House intimate Harry Hopkins. Roosevelt, it appears, had promised to ensure that U.S. Steel would not be inconvenienced by the Congress' ongoing antimonopoly investigation.

Stettinius continued to edge his way through verbal thickets by suggesting that it was essential that U.S. Steel's board of directors be allowed to reassume control over the pricing policies of the corporation. Roosevelt quickly cut to the heart of the matter by interjecting: "Of course, Ed, I understand your position. You have all been most cooperative and reasonable—of course our big problem now is to figure out a face-saving plan for John Lewis and his group. But in releasing you from your obligation [not to cut wages], it is my hope that you will see your way clear not to act for a certain period of time."

By "a certain period of time," Stettinius noted, Roosevelt was indirectly but clearly referring to the upcoming 1938 mid-presidential-term congressional elections. Stettinius, equally obliquely, then asked Roosevelt if it was perfectly clear that U.S. Steel would be allowed to cut wages after Election Day without reprisals. "Perfectly," Roosevelt replied, and the meeting closed.[4]

U.S. Steel had struck a bargain. Wage rates would not be reduced before the 1938 elections in return for amnesty on the antitrust front. Stettinius' problem now, however, was to make sure that the agreement held. During the next two months, Stettinius returned to Washington several times to test the political waters. FDR intimate Tommy Corcoran provided initial reassurances. On September 30, newly appointed Attorney General Robert Jackson arranged meetings with highly placed Justice Department officials Thurman Arnold and William O. Douglas as well as Leon Henderson, the director of the TNEC's investigative division. All said they bore no animus whatsoever toward U.S. Steel regarding antitrust matters. Antitruster Arnold went a good deal further. The aluminum industry, he suggested to Stettinius, was giving the Democrats a lot of trouble. Would U.S. Steel like to help out by entering that field in order to end the virtual monopoly enjoyed by the Aluminum Corporation of America?

After evading this and other friendly requests, Stettinius was finally reassured by Arnold that

> confidentially to you, it looks as though the whole [TNEC investigation] might be a flop. . . . Leon [Henderson] has no answers; [Senator Joseph] O'Mahoney [the chairman of the TNEC] is cooling off, and between you and myself, I don't know whether or not the boys are going to get to first base. I am much more interested in proper antitrust procedure than I am in any damn fool monopoly investigation. [But] I am going to put on a show regardless, and give the American public what they expect and demand.

A week after these events, Congress itself was heard from when Senator O'Mahoney informed Stettinius, "with a wink of the eye," that the TNEC investigations shouldn't "take very long" as far as U.S. Steel was concerned.[5]

Given backstairs political bargaining like that detailed here, it comes as no surprise that the most ambitious investigation of the structure and operations of large corporations in U.S. history was eventually without substantive effect. In John Kenneth Galbraith's words, the TNEC was "unable to approve of the economy it found but, equally . . . [proved] unable to endorse any alternative."[6]

U.S. Steel, then, met the antimonopoly challenge. The steps necessary, however, were neither cost-free nor pleasant. In effect, the corporation had to purchase antitrust protection from the White House. Bargaining of the sort necessary to make such back-door deals was deeply unsettling to large segments of the big-business community in the United States. Corporate leaders, of course, had long experience in asking for specific political favors—and in delivering them. They were not, however, used to dealing with activist leaders of a national government who had both the power and the will to compel them to engage in horse trading on important economic and industrial issues, whether they wished to or not.

The fundamental problem, then, was one of power. During the Great Depression, the federal government came of age in the United States. By the late 1930's, Washington had been armed with an expanded and strengthened arsenal of regulatory, tax, and fiscal weapons. A new generation of leaders in the Congress, the judiciary, and the executive branch was determined to use these weapons to achieve national economic and social recovery; they would use them in cooperation with business leaders where possible, but in opposition to them if necessary.

The change here was profound. For the first time in American history, the national leadership of a major political party staked its chances on an alliance of political forces among which no important segment of the nation's business community figured publicly. The Democrats, who had nominated Wall Street lawyer John W. Davis as their presidential candidate as recently as 1924, were now being flayed again and again by their enemies for being "antibusiness," and in an important sense they were. A party that had seriously considered drafting Owen D. Young, the chairman of the board of General Electric, as its presidential nominee in 1932 was, during the domestic reform phase of the New Deal era, led by a President who could describe himself as welcoming the hatred of most of the major organized business groups in the country.

Here was the stuff of high political drama. The Roosevelt administration's creation of the Temporary National Economic Committee in 1938 and its later use of this antimonopoly agency as a bludgeon to force one of the largest corporations in the nation to act in a "statesmanlike" fashion provides only one illuminating example of the processes of change that began during the Depression decade. In the chapters that follow, we will examine the most important currents of challenge and response that have affected the course of government-business relationships in the United States during the past half century. We will also demonstrate how the compromises and conflicts that have resulted from this lengthy and complicated process have survived to influence the political economy of the present.

1

BIG BUSINESS AND THE DOMESTIC REFORM PHASE OF THE NEW DEAL, 1933–1938

A Basis for Discussion

ANY SURVEY OF business-government relationships in modern America must necessarily begin with the wrenching economic catastrophe called the Great Depression. For the nation's business leaders, the Depression was a rip in time, a seminal event from which most of their present-day relationships with federal power derived.

The purpose of this chapter is to provide an overview of the corporate community at the time of the New Deal. Here a problem presents itself. Generally, when trying to understand what business leaders thought or did about something, observers focus on the statements of individuals, trade associations like the American Iron and Steel Institute, specific corporations, or well-known national business organizations including the National Association of Manufacturers (NAM) and the United States Chamber of Commerce. An important difficulty with this approach is that of representativeness. Looking at an individual company or a specific trade association does not allow us to understand what "big business" generally thought. Public statements issued by the chief executive officers (CEOs) of major companies are often drafted by public relations departments and have very little if anything to do with what the CEO is actually thinking or doing. And, lastly, thoughts or actions of panindustrial groups such as the U.S. Chamber of Commerce emerge from organizations that are a melange of small-, medium-, and large-sized companies with wildly divergent interests. It would be helpful, then, if we could concentrate our attention on an organization that represents *only* big-business interests, instead of big *and* small interests. It would also be useful to find a group composed entirely of corporate chief executive officers (chairmen or presidents) and their closest aides, whose deliberations were undertaken as confidentially as possible. Thus, the historical record that we look at would not be one created for us by public relations personnel or trade association executives whose job was to make their corporate clients look as good as possible.

Fortunately, such an organization exists, and will be used as a focus of discussion throughout this chapter. The Business Council, created in 1933, has—from that day to this—been a blue-ribbon assembly of just over sixty chief executive officers of the largest corporations in the country. Though only rarely noticed—and almost never investigated—by historians of any type, the Business Council is a barometer of big-business thought and action that can allow us to make sense of a complicated historical transition in the nation's economic and political life.

Roosevelt Arrives

What Americans call the New Deal was a long, drawn-out, and none too polite struggle regarding the responsibilities and powers of the federal government. Central to the discussion was a disagreement concerning the scope of Washington's activities as a guarantor of last resort in the midst of an unprecedented peacetime emergency.

Nobody doubted that the federal government had important and necessary guarantor responsibilities in time of war. Even the nation's hardiest frontier individualists never hesitated to call upon the United States cavalry to secure Indian lands for their own use. Nor did they oppose the creation of a federally administered reservation system to house those Indians the cavalry didn't kill. The same underlying logic of naked self-interest applied to the considerably more numerous and threatening British, Mexican, Confederate, and continental European enemies that the nation faced during the first century and a half of its history. When military crises arose, Americans normally granted their central authorities emergency powers, and then allowed these powers to lapse once the crises had passed.

Grants of emergency powers to deal with peacetime economic catastrophe, however, were another matter entirely. The Great Depression was not a secessionist movement, foreign invasion, or Indian uprising that could be dealt with by centralized military might. It was, instead, an emergency that arose from the economic structure of the society itself.

A goodly number of business leaders, like their peers in other political clienteles, were shocked by the disaster that had befallen the economy. Fundamental institutions, however, would certainly stand any strain. To help ensure this, businessmen moved to do their part to repair the damage, using whatever economic and political technology they possessed. But as institutions buckled and broke throughout the desperate years of 1930, 1931, and 1932, business leaders became increasingly nervous—so nervous that the threat of widespread panic loomed.

Panic, of course, would not do. Eventually, to strengthen the rescue efforts, a wide spectrum of corporate leaders reluctantly called upon Washington to assume unheard-of peacetime powers. In particular, the federal government was entreated to become a guarantor of last resort—for businessmen alone. The Reconstruction Finance Corporation (RFC) created during the final year of Herbert Hoover's plagued presidency embodied the first hesitant political response to businessmen's desires.

The businessmen, however, were by no means satisfied. When Hoover's Democratic successor arrived in Washington in March of 1933, businessmen redoubled their pleas for preferential assistance. Eventually they got it in the form of the National Recovery Administration (NRA) and a reorganized RFC capable of serving as a multibillion-dollar lender and investor of last resort. The Democrats, however, did not confine their expanded guarantor role to businessmen alone. The nation's farmers—via the Agricultural Adjustment Act (AAA)—were the next important economic interest group to receive a share of federal attention.

Initially, such expansion of federal guarantor responsibilities beyond the corporate realm did not alienate business leaders. Farmers, after all, could be seen as rural entrepreneurs, small businessmen that occupied a relatively modest part in a neoclassical economic world. But as the scope of federal guarantees tendered to other discontented groups grew, businessmen began to balk.

Three groups, in particular, posed problems to businessmen: the unemployed, the organized labor movement, and the nation's elderly. As we shall see, the eventual extension of permanent, long-term, statutory federal guarantees to the latter two groups via the Wagner Act of 1935 and the Social Security Act of the same year alienated most important segments of the nation's big-business leadership. Only a few unusual businessmen realized that the federal government's guarantor role could not realistically be limited to themselves and those interest groups that posed few direct threats to their power or their status. This due to the simple fact that groups businessmen considered dangerous (most notably the millions of hitherto-unorganized workers streaming into new industrial unions) were forcing the federal government to act in their interests in order to preserve itself—and the nation—from the threat of revolutionary conditions.

Such unusual businessmen existed. Moreover, their actions and influence in important policy arenas helped them and corporate capitalism as a whole to bridge a necessarily reformist political transition without suffering a catastrophic decline in power and influence. In assisting this transition, CEOs such as Edward Stettinius, W. Averell Harriman, and several score less well known men helped to set the stage for American capitalism in the modern era.

From Black Thursday to the NIRA

The task of the W. Averell Harrimans of the corporate world was hardly an easy one. Worsening economic conditions frightened the nation's businessmen; but fear did not cause the vast majority of them to move very far beyond the previously established limits of the nation's curiously dogmatic capitalist creed.

By the fall of 1931, for example, no sane individual could argue that the Depression was normal in either severity or extent. Unemployment had doubled from the year before: 16 percent of the labor force—8 million people—were jobless. Over thirteen hundred banks had closed their doors, and the prices of the blue-chip stocks composing the Dow Jones list had fallen to just under one half of the levels that they had reached in 1929. Financiers and bankers, however, generally remained loyal to the staples of classical economic theory and waited for "natural forces" to set off an economic revival. But industrialists and merchants were not convinced of traditionalist revelation. Their problem was that they did not know what to replace it with. Only a handful of corporate leaders were more ambitious,

ambitious enough to slowly begin moving beyond the voluntaristic capitalist rhetoric of the 1920's to propose relatively activist forms of "partnership" between organized business and the state.

Preeminent among this small group of men was Gerard Swope, the president of the General Electric Company. In September of 1931, Swope unveiled what became known as the Swope Plan, a proposal for industrial recovery which argued that the nation's larger corporations must organize themselves for recovery under the auspices of the federal government.

The heart of Swope's proposal was cartelization. Washington should suspend the antitrust laws to allow industries—acting through national trade associations—to stabilize markets through price fixing and production limitations. Once this process of voluntary cartelization was complete, industry would provide increased employment and income possibilities for the masses.

That much of Swope's proposal was basic trickle-down economics. However, he appended recommendations for a corporate welfare state. He proposed, in effect, that all industries that chose to cartelize pay for the privilege. The payments, in this case, would be for industry-specific unemployment compensation, retirement pensions, life insurance, and disability programs for the workers in those industries.

If we recall that in 1931 almost no workers anywhere in U.S. industry had such benefits as Swope was suggesting, we can understand why mainstream business opinion wanted little to do with Swope's ideas. The U.S. Chamber of Commerce and the National Association of Manufacturers, for example, thought that "modification" of the antitrust laws and voluntary price-fixing schemes were wonderful ideas. They were not, however, about to advocate paying anything to achieve them. Not even to reassure workers that they, too, were likely to gain something from economywide price-fixing.

Swope, however, had not finished. GE's president went on to make proposals that—in a 1931 setting—were even more unsettling. Washington, he suggested, should establish a "federal supervisory body" to oversee the employee welfare schemes he proposed that industry trade associations create. Administration of these welfare programs would remain in the hands of the various associations, but federal representatives would have the power to approve or disapprove of particular industry-specific norms, and to set minimum accounting and reporting requirements. Further, to help insure that all firms would go along with the welfare standards, Swope proposed that all companies within a particular industry "with fifty or more employees and doing an interstate business" would be *required* to adopt *all* unemployment, retirement, insurance, and disability standards drawn up by their trade association within three years, unless the time limit was extended by federal officials. Washington, in short, would be an umpire of last resort in dealing with "free-rider" problems. It could compel any firm in a cartelized industry to go along with industrywide employee-welfare provisions whether it wanted to or not.[1]

This final element of Swope's scheme was the one furthest outside the pale of established corporate thinking. Depression-era businessmen previously acclimated to the soothing ideological balm of Herbert Hoover's New Era were not accustomed to thinking about government-industry "partnership" in the activist fashion popularized by General Electric's president.

The differences between Hoover and Swope were ones of degree. Herbert Hoover basically viewed Washington as an expediter instead of an umpire or a referee. The federal government, in his unremittingly conservative opinion, was analogous to a hotel and convention center. Private groups from across the country met at the hotel, discussed their problems, and returned home with solutions in their briefcases. The government ran the hotel, encouraged—but never forced—people to attend meetings, and was not responsible for interests left unattended to or questions left unaddressed. Washington basically helped businessmen and others to arrive at—and depart with—private understandings.

Whereas Hoover looked at the federal government's rightful role as a mixture of hotel manager and midwife, Gerard Swope proposed a more activist role for Washington. Federal bureaucrats, Swope affirmed, should be umpires enforcing economic rules and regulations drawn up largely by organized business itself. Even this careful effort to enlist federal enforcement power in the recovery effort, however, was not widely attractive to big businessmen weaned on a steady diet of New Era voluntarism. Further, time—and economic decay—were necessary before big businessmen began to make a noticeable shift in ideology or action.

Instances of corporate reticence are not hard to find. Later in the fall of 1931, a cross section of the leaders of the largest corporations in the nation appeared in Washington to testify before a Senate committee regarding a proposal put forward by a group of congressmen and liberal economists to establish a National Economic Council. The idea was not very revolutionary. A purely advisory body of fifteen members representing industrial, financial, agricultural, transportation, and labor interests was being proposed to conduct fact-finding surveys of economic problems and to forward recommendations to Congress.

Even so benign a form of federal activity, however, was not pleasing to the nation's business establishment. CEOs like Alfred P. Sloan (General Motors), James A. Farrell (U.S. Steel), Daniel Willard (Baltimore and Ohio Railroad), and Albert H. Wiggin (Chase National Bank) agreed that Washington should relax the antitrust laws, but believed it should do little or nothing else to hasten economic recovery. In particular, it should not seek to supervise or sponsor the efforts of industry to police itself through price and output limitations. Government, Alfred Sloan intoned, must not try "getting into business." It was as if Sloan preferred that Washington exist on the moon.

Other big-business spokesmen including Gerard Swope, Henry I. Harriman (a utility executive then serving as the president of the U.S. Chamber of Commerce), and Melvin A. Traylor (First National Bank of Chicago) went only slightly further—arguing that any National Economic Council that might be created should be a "business cabinet" not directly tied to any branch of the federal government. This cabinet would function, instead, through a voluntary network of national industrial trade associations, as in the Swope Plan. Only CEOs such as George J. Anderson (Consolidation Coal), Ralph M. Flanders (Jones and Lamson), Henry P. Kendall (a Boston textile manufacturer), and newspaper publisher John H. Fahey (a former president of the Chamber of Commerce) went so far as to state that the federal government had a necessary part to play in coordinating, and if necessary enforcing, the economic recovery efforts undertaken by organized industry. Even these most liberal employers, however, opposed the creation of an economic mobilization authority like the War Industries Board through which businessmen had organized themselves under federal auspices during the industrial emergency called the First World War. Concerns about federal "meddling" were quite evident.[2]

Only months after the businessmen had spoken, however, their reluctance to support anything smacking of government-sanctioned emergency planning was overwhelmed by the onrush of events. The year 1932 started out dreadfully for American capitalism and quickly worsened. By the end of the year, stock prices had fallen to one tenth of their 1929 levels. Exports and farm prices had decreased to 40 per cent of their pre-Depression levels. Industrial production was only half of what it had been in 1929. The nation's banking system was reeling and unemployment had risen to an official total of 15 million people—one quarter of the labor force. Even 1931 looked like a good year by comparison. In such an emergency, businessman Henry S. Dennison wrote, people who wanted to keep the government out of business were "Canutes ordering the tides to stop."[3]

As Dennison indicated, business opposition to federal action was evaporating. Guarantees from Washington began to look very good indeed, provided that federal umpires confined themselves to enforcing those standards—and only those standards—that the nation's business leaders were able to formulate for themselves. Any other approach, businessmen reasoned, would be equivalent to the tail wagging the dog.

Businessmen, however, found themselves wielding progressively less clout with the Republican President. Herbert Hoover resolutely opposed cartelization as an answer to the nation's economic woes. The limit of his administration's activism was represented by the Reconstruction Finance Corporation, established in January of 1932 to serve as a lender of last resort to tottering banks and railroads. The RFC's loans, however, were only as good as the underlying stability of the economy on which the recipients of its largesse depended. By 1932, such stability was nowhere to be found.

In their search for salvation, then, increasingly impatient businessmen started to look to the Democratic party, and corporate donations consequently flowed into the campaign chest of presidential candidate Franklin D. Roosevelt. Herbert Hoover, as Harriman of the Chamber of Commerce commented disgustedly to a friend, simply "would not take advice." Roosevelt, on the other hand, was likely to be more amenable, a man who would "surround himself with advisors of good judgement and follow their advice." It was a comforting thought while it lasted.[4]

The battle for the mind of the incoming Roosevelt administration began in earnest after the Democratic party's resounding victory in the November elections. Roosevelt's mandate for change was clear.

Fifty-seven percent of the popular vote went to him, as did majorities in forty-two of the forty-eight states. In the House, Democrats outnumbered Republicans by 312 to 123, and in the Senate by 59 to 37. The GOP, to all intents and purposes, had temporarily ceased to exist as a national political force. A defeated Hoover might mutter that government-sanctioned cartelization proposals were Frankenstein monsters that were both fascist and monopolistic in tendency, but such proposals were increasingly on the corporate agenda. Implementing them, business activists hoped, would be easy.[5]

But such business leaders had a good deal to learn about the nuances of political access and influence. Initially, men like Henry I. Harriman appear to have looked upon the incoming President as a pliant individual who would do little but follow their suggestions. They soon learned otherwise. Roosevelt had been running for the presidency for most of the preceding eight years, and had many political constituencies to answer to. He realized well enough that corporate support for his candidacy had been more a matter of economic panic than of long-term political loyalty. Corporate proposals for cooperative action within and among industries were only one among many types of economic recovery plans circulating through the corridors of power, seeking political legitimization at the highest levels. Throughout the winter of 1932–1933, Roosevelt and his top advisers juggled cartelization, public works, currency inflation, wage-and-hour, reemployment, and quick-fix recovery recommendations as if they were so many oranges. Roosevelt knew—if historians have often forgotten—that a successful President can only lead after he knows which way the wind is blowing.

By the first week in April, the wind started blowing in earnest. Liberal senators and representatives, impatient with White House delays, gave decisive support to a proposal to cut the work week to a maximum of thirty hours as a means of spreading employment. Weekly wage rates, however, were not to be decreased. Roosevelt opposed this intended remedy as inflationary, and ordered aides to come up with something better. During the ensuing five weeks, frenetic bargaining aimed at short-circuiting the hours-reduction approach to economic recovery took place.

On May 17, 1933, the President finally had a program to send to Congress. The administration's National Industrial Recovery Act (NIRA) was a polyglot solution to Roosevelt's political problems— one that gave the business establishment most of the favors it was seeking, at the price of providing relatively modest guarantees to other groups, notably industrial workers and the unemployed, whose fate especially concerned congressional progressives in both parties.

As passed into law by Congress on June 16, 1933, NIRA was a clear victory for the many prominent businessmen who were backing cartelization as a solution to the nation's industrial problems. The act suspended the antitrust laws to allow industries to create "codes of fair practice." These codes were national cartel agreements that enabled corporations in particular trades to set prices, restrict output, and increase profits. The essence of the NIRA, then, was to place dominant industrial trade associations in charge of a nationwide restructuring of the peacetime United States economy.

Cartels, however, were not the whole story. Like almost all bills that have ever survived a conflict-ridden passage through the congressional labyrinth, NIRA was modified and added to in order to meet the requirements of a variety of interest groups.

First, NIRA was a temporary piece of legislation with a legislative mandate that ran for only two years. Congressional renewal of the mandate was possible, but the act could also be rescinded by the President or by a joint resolution of Congress at any time if, in their opinion, the state of industrial emergency had passed. This element of the bill was meant to reassure conservatives that socialism was not even a remote possibility on the Democratic agenda. Second, nothing in the administration of the act was to forward "monopoly." Writing this reassurance into the act lessened the objections of those moderates and liberals whose distrust of big businessmen generally manifested itself in support for strong enforcement of the antitrust laws. Large corporations might cartelize, but they would merge with each other—or otherwise "cooperate" to the detriment of their smaller competitors—at their peril. Third, Roosevelt was granted the temporary right—which he never exercised—to force codes on industries that were unable or unwilling to organize themselves. Such legislative language reassured Democratic liberals that codes could be used as sticks as well as carrots.

Liberals also received other, more *pro forma* reassurances. First, the National Industrial Recovery Act stated that a presidentially appointed director would oversee cartelization efforts and uphold the "public interest" at each stage of the process. Second, labor and consumer groups were given vague guarantees of representation in code-making and enforcement procedures. Two advisory boards were created to serve as bases for this hoped-for exercise of labor and consumer influence.

Other efforts to placate liberal opinion, however, were considerably more substantial. First, all industries formulating codes had to agree to abide by the terms of minimum-wage, maximum-hour, and child labor standards if they wanted shelter under the federal cartel umbrella. The logic here was precisely that contained in the Swope Plan of two years earlier: businessmen had to pay something, in terms of enhanced employee-welfare standards, for the privilege of avoiding competition. Businessmen grudgingly accepted these terms for salvation, but only companies operating in oligopolistic markets, with opportunities to pass along added costs to consumers, felt much enthusiasm for this new breed of federally mandated minimum standards that the Depression emergency had made possible.

With even less enthusiasm, businessmen accepted an unprecedented authorization for a peacetime, federally financed, public-works jobs program as an element of the National Industrial Recovery Act. Even Roosevelt himself was initially resistant to congressional desires for a public works element in the NIRA. But he eventually agreed to the necessity of an initial two-year appropriation of just over $3 billion, to be granted to federal, state, and local agencies to enable them to serve as employers of last resort for the nation's unemployed.

Subject to various fits and starts, public-sector jobs programs benefited a total of 8 million people, 20 percent of the labor force, during the remainder of the Depression decade. Strong efforts were made to keep public works projects from competing directly with goods or services provided by the private sector. Streets were repaired, murals were painted, and leaves were raked, but federally paid workers did not build automobiles, construct private residences, or dig for precious metals. For all such attention to corporate sensibilities, however, a vast majority of businessmen were never really reassured that the mere existence of federal jobs programs was not a threat to capitalist survival. When asked, businessmen found themselves in the position of arguing that government, instead of providing jobs, should, at most, content itself with passively subsidizing the unemployed with cash grants—a "dole"—until such time as the private sector could reabsorb them. This, of course, put businessmen in the rather unusual position of arguing that it was better for the federal treasury to subsidize indolence rather than productive work.

Such an intellectual irony—added to the fact that businessmen generally knew a good deal when they saw one—led most to mute their early opposition to public-sector jobs programs in order to obtain the benefits that NIRA cartels promised them.[6]

A final element of NIRA that nettled corporate sensibilities was a vague right of collective bargaining tendered to employees. Under the terms of Section 7-A of the act, all employers that participated in federally sanctioned cartels had also to agree that workers possessed the prerogative to "organize and bargain collectively through representatives of their own choosing," and that workers might select such representatives as they desired in a fashion free from managerial interference or restraint.

Section 7-A, then, reassured the established leaders of American trade unions that they, too, might benefit from emergency peacetime industrial mobilization. Specifically, they gained an indistinct promise of federally sanctioned access to the workers in mass production trades that had been largely closed to union penetration. As we shall see, not all big businessmen feared the prospect of increased trade-union organizing activity within their firms or industries. But strains within the business establishment regarding collective-bargaining issues went a long way toward destroying the ability of corporate leaders to unilaterally design or implement a workable recovery program.

The National Industrial Recovery Act, then, was not "industrial self-government" pure and simple. Aside from its minimum-standards and public works components, however, NIRA was very largely the Swope cartelization program with a loosely worded fringe of guarantees to workers, labor unions, and consumers. Subject to these latter constraints, which were still to be worked out, the federal government had become a guarantor of last resort for the business community as a whole and was assisting organized business to take the clear lead in industrial reconstruction.

NRA and the Effort to Achieve a Corporate Self-regulatory Order

Business leaders were not slow to follow through upon the opportunities tendered to them by the industrial recovery legislation. Throughout the hectic New Deal summer of 1933, cartelization proceeded under the benign oversight of a National Recovery Ad-

ministration established to administer the code-making and enforcement elements of the act.

Cartelization was only part of the story, however. Simultaneously, businessmen also moved to expand the scope of their powers
within NRA's administrative structure, and to make use of these
expanded powers in order to further more ambitious corporate
efforts to restore industrial and social stability. Federal help was an
important element in this political process.

By the time the National Industrial Recovery Act was being
frenetically drawn up and passed into law, the nation's corporate
leadership was considerably more interested in creating long-term
economic mobilization and "planning" authorities on a nationwide
basis than it had been only two short years before. Such "planning"
as took place, however, was to be a corporate, not a governmental,
responsibility. As Henry Harriman put it in a letter to FDR in May,
"The psychology of the country [i.e., of businessmen like Harriman]
is now ready for self-regulation of industry with government approval of agreements reached either within or without trade conferences." Washington must be an umpire in a game in which organized
business set the rules.[7]

To create such rules as Harriman had in mind, he and a small
group of business leaders including Gerard Swope, Walter Teagle of
the Standard Oil Company of New Jersey, and Louis Kirstein of
Federated Department Stores collaborated with FDR's newly appointed Secretary of Commerce, Daniel C. Roper, to create a "business cabinet." This, its corporate sponsors hoped, would first marry
corporate expertise to federal power, and then serve as a long-range
economic planning council with primary responsibility for formulating industrial recovery strategy.

The agency that was established through these efforts was the
Business Council, surely one of the more unusual efforts ever made
to associate the nation's corporate elite with the federal government.
Traditional American concepts of governmental structure, in fact,
had very little relevance when applied to this organization.

Fundamentally, the Business Council was a group of between
forty and sixty-five active chief executive officers from a cross section
of the largest firms in the country. These CEOs were serving on a
quasi-public advisory agency that was *in* the government, but not
of it. No executive order formally establishing the Business Council
was ever drawn up, nor did federal officials have any significant say

regarding the selection of the membership of the group. The latter task was turned over to "business statesmen" Gerard Swope, Walter Teagle, Henry Harriman, Louis Kirstein, and their eventual successors. These men formed an executive committee that initially selected, for Council membership, corporate leaders including Alfred Sloan of GM, Pierre S. du Pont of E. I. du Pont de Nemours, Myron C. Taylor of U.S. Steel, Thomas J. Watson of IBM, W. Averell Harriman of the Union Pacific Railroad, Winthrop W. Aldrich of the Chase National Bank, Robert E. Wood of Sears, Roebuck, the Chicago banker Melvin Traylor, and the articulate New England capitalists Ralph Flanders, Henry Kendall, and Henry Dennison. Secretary of Commerce Roper hoped that these business leaders were the germ of a national economic parliament that would one day include "representatives of all groups in the economic and social structure of the country" and would bring them into "constant relationships" with one another.[8]

One reason that businessmen of such stature readily accepted membership on the newly formed Business Council was that the group's advisory and planning mandate was exceedingly broad. From its beginning, the Council drew up scores of confidential reports for executive-branch consideration on a wide variety of issues affecting the domestic and foreign economic relationships of the United States. Such ambitious advisory activity was not a strange phenomenon, given that the group was a self-governing body. Agendas for Council meetings, for example, were not drawn up by Commerce Department officials, even though the Council was officially a Commerce agency. Nor did high Commerce Department bureaucrats attend Council meetings, except when specifically invited. Such invitations were rare indeed, and the organization's affairs were generally carried on with no direct federal administrative oversight whatsoever.

Nor did federal ministrations to corporate sensibilities end there. Business Council staff members were regularly provided with free offices by the Commerce Department in Washington despite the fact that such staff assistants were not federal employees. Staff expenses —like all other Council expenses—were, indeed, never a matter of federal concern, as the organization raised all its revenues and paid all its bills through membership levies and corporate donations.

Finally, the Business Council was allowed to be extremely secretive. Council minutes, reports, and policy statements (all of which were confidential) were stored on government property, but were not subject to public or congressional review. Journalists fared no better. None were ever allowed access to Council meet ings, including the two to four black-tie gatherings which were— and still are—held with Cabinet officers and other bureaucratic barons each year. Abbreviated reports on the Council's views, how- ever, appeared regularly in the *New York Times.* The Business Council, then, was created as a powerful forum of corporate lead- ers with privileged access to the highest levels of the executive branch of the federal government. If any organization could be called the executive committee of the nation's corporate elite dur- ing and after the formative stages of the New Deal, the Business Council was surely it.

Once in existence, the Business Council did not have to wait long for highly placed federal officials to find uses for it. On June 26, 1933, the Council's members held their first general meeting in Washing- ton. Among the bureaucrats in attendance was Hugh S. Johnson, an articulate and hard-drinking former general and aide to Democratic party gray eminence Bernard Baruch. Ten days earlier, Johnson had been appointed director of the National Recovery Administration, upon which the Roosevelt administration was depending to success- fully cartelize the American economy. Johnson realized that massive amounts of industrial expertise were necessary to accomplish NRA's goals, and proposed to obtain such assistance from the membership of the Business Council.

In the Business Council's first chairman, Gerard Swope, Johnson found a receptive audience. During the First World War, GE's presi- dent had served as an assistant to General Johnson, who was then managing the U.S. Army's purchases of gargantuan amounts of strategic commodities. None other than wartime mobilization head Bernard Baruch had been the one to bring Swope to Johnson's attention, advising the newly minted general that Swope was "so suave and smooth and discerning that he could seduce a house fly," an opinion that Johnson came to share enthusiastically.

Hugh S. Johnson and Gerard Swope, then, were exactly alike in their experience of industrial emergency planning. They spoke each other's language. Therefore, when Johnson proposed to Swope that Business Council members staff an Industrial Advisory Board that Johnson was creating within NRA to iron out problems in the cartel- ization process, Swope and his fellow corporate leaders were more than happy to oblige. Cooperation was, after all, a matter of stark necessity on both sides.

The frantic pace of early NRA procedures put a premium on the advice of the Business Council and allowed those Council members selected for service on the Industrial Advisory Board to exercise great influence in setting overall NRA policies and in assisting trade associations in formulating and ratifying national cartel agreements. Their work was made all the easier by the repeated, calming assurances of NRA Director Johnson and his chief assistant, Donald M. Richberg, that the emergency agency that they headed was not going to "dictate" to business. Instead, the code-making process that the CEOs of the Business Council were expediting was aimed at allowing "almost complete self-government" to organized industry "excepting where the action of any one [trade] will interfere with the other." The Business Council and the Industrial Advisory Board both existed in order to ensure that such interindustry friction would not get out of hand and spoil the cartelization effort.

Frictions there indeed were, and plenty of entrepreneurial leverage was necessary to force recalcitrant corporate interest groups into line. But, in general, the Business Council built well. Codes for most major industries passed through NRA's administrative structure rapidly, and efforts made by consumer and trade union representatives within that structure to significantly involve themselves in the cartelization process were very largely contained.[9]

The labor movement generally, however, presented Business Council leaders with a much less tractable problem. Whatever most of the established leadership of American industry or trade unions might have preferred, the nation's industrial workers, with the active support of John L. Lewis and Sidney Hillman, were voting with their feet. Throughout the summer of 1933, strikes surged upward in number and intensity. Workers in hitherto open-shop industries including steel, automobiles, rubber, and chemicals organized. Industrial-union organizations on the grass roots level clamored for the organizational and financial support of the uneasy conservatives who led the crafts-dominated American Federation of Labor (AFL). Employers in affected industries generally responded with lockouts, firings, and vigorous efforts at creating company unions. The outlook for labor peace was bleak. A clear danger existed that the loosely worded grant of employee-organizing and collective-bargaining rights contained in Section 7-A of the National Industrial Recovery

Act might allow trade unions to substantially increase the scope of their power within America's industrial economy.

Business Council leaders on the Industrial Advisory Board of the NRA quickly responded to this growing challenge. In August of 1933, the entire membership of a shadowy but important group known as the Special Conference Committee (SCC) was reconstituted as an industrial-relations advisory committee for the Business Council. Ever since its creation in 1919 by executives of the General Electric Company and Standard Oil of New Jersey, the Special Conference Committee had served as a forum where the top managers of about a dozen of the nation's largest corporations had gathered to discuss their respective labor strategies. In 1933, the SCC roster included American Telephone and Telegraph, Bethlehem Steel, Du Pont, General Electric, General Motors, Goodyear Tire and Rubber, International Harvester, Standard Oil of New Jersey, and Westinghouse. Using the SCC as a base, CEOs like GE's Swope and Jersey Standard's Teagle had led the way in the creation of company unions, employee pension and insurance programs, and other "welfare capitalist" initiatives during the 1920's. Not all SCC members were very receptive to the "experiments" undertaken by these two corporate CEOs. General Motors, in particular, copied very few of General Electric and Jersey Standard's initiatives. In incorporating the Special Conference Committee within the Business Council, however, Council leaders Gerard Swope and Walter Teagle sought to more firmly establish their influence in the resolution of labor disputes, and to convince a wider circle of big-business leaders that company unions and other employee-welfare programs were necessary and important techniques for CEOs to adopt in their collective efforts to restore stability inside the factory gates.[10]

Nor did Gerard Swope and Walter Teagle's efforts to restore stability stop here. On August 3, 1933, these men, joined by other Business Council and Industrial Advisory Board activists, hosted a private meeting with the members of the NRA's Labor Advisory Board in Washington. The purpose of the occasion was to achieve a workable national compromise on the vexing problems of strikes and organizing drives.

The participants in the conference were well equipped to speak with authority on such matters. Labor was represented by AFL President William Green, United Mine Workers President John L. Lewis, Amalgamated Clothing Workers President Sidney Hillman,

George L. Berry of the Typographer's Union, labor economist Leo Wolman, and a handful of high AFL officials, including John Frey of the AFL's important Metal Trades Department. Industry's roster included Jersey Standard's Teagle, GE's Swope, Federated Department Stores' Kirstein, and Edward Stettinius (who was then employed as General Motors President Sloan's contact man in Washington).

Business Council leader Teagle opened the secret meeting by proposing a "truce" between organized labor and organized business. Teagle stated that he had no personal complaint about "what was being done to organize labor. . . . It was only natural," he continued, "for labor to try to use this opportunity to organize and for employers to resist." Business and labor leaders alike, however, had to control the activities of their less-enlightened brethren. So, until such time as NRA's cartelization efforts were fully completed, labor and business statesmen should agree to preserve the status quo regarding wages, hours, and collective-bargaining rights in order to halt strikes that threatened short-term industrial recovery. To ensure this result, the Labor and Industrial advisory boards of the NRA must make some effort to arbitrate difficulties caused by conflicting interpretations of Section 7-A of the National Industrial Recovery Act. Big business and organized labor should stop fighting and make a deal.

Labor participants Wolman, Hillman, and Frey got Teagle's message and agreed that a truce was required. Hillman, however, was skeptical of proposed arbitration machinery, whose purpose was limited to preserving the status quo. Labor's right to organize should, Hillman added, be explicitly recognized. This logic was not persuasive to Teagle, who reiterated that organizing drives were irritating employer sensibilities and should be halted during the NRA's formative stages. The meeting was starting to uncover deep conflicts.

The focus of discussion then shifted to AFL President Green. He expressed his willingness to "sign a statement to instruct [workers], if he could, that they must not go on strike" pending the settlement of all NRA codes, but continued that "he could not say to his people [in the AFL] that they must stop organizing for the present." Strikes and organizing drives, then, were separate issues. Agreement to halt the former did not imply agreement to halt the latter. Teagle's proposal was too extreme. The AFL president had buckled, but not broken. Silence ensued.

Swope then stepped in to achieve a compromise. His credentials for the task were excellent. During the late 1920's, he had unsuccessfully tried to persuade lackluster AFL leaders, including Green, to undertake extensive industrial-union-organizing drives in the electrical manufacturing industry and had even implied that General Electric might go so far as to provide financial assistance to the effort. Green, Frey, and their peers had proved unwilling to challenge the crafts tradition of the AFL, but Swope's comparative enlightenment on labor matters was known to them.[11]

Swope proposed that a small subcommittee meet privately to draw up a combined declaration on labor policy for presentation to President Roosevelt and NRA Director Johnson. Green, Wolman, Teagle, and Swope were quickly selected, and reported back after a short recess with a proposal for a bipartisan arbitration board composed of an equal number of Business Council and Labor Advisory Board members and headed by a chairman representing "the public." The organizing-drive issue was not even mentioned. To further reassure labor leaders about big businessmen's intentions, Swope deftly proposed Senator Robert F. Wagner of New York, a friend of the AFL, as chairman—an idea that was promptly seconded by the AFL's Green. A compromise seemed to be in the making.

At this point, the negotiations hit another snag. Two labor leaders started backing away from the deal. The United Mine Workers' Lewis confined himself to florid oratory that communicated little as to his opinions or intentions. But Hillman of the Amalgamated, a liberal industrial union not affiliated with the AFL, clearly expressed a skeptical outlook. Hillman repeated his opinion that the "right to organize on the part of labor" should be unambiguously announced as the centerpiece of overall labor policy.

This was too much for Green, who moved to isolate Hillman by declaring that Hillman's views were as "extreme" as Teagle's proposal to halt all organizing drives for the duration. Where Hillman preferred clear definition, Green, like Swope, sought to maintain a "cooperative spirit" by leaving the crucial issue of organizing rights suspended in midair.

The meeting then began to close. Kirstein somewhat ingenuously "wondered if the small employer had not been overlooked" by the Business Council and trade union representatives. (Of course he had.) Lewis remained uncommunicative. Finally, Swope, Teagle, Frey, and Green indicated their willingness to support a national arbitration board. The suggestion to appoint Senator Wagner the board's chairman received unanimous consent, and the bargaining was concluded.

Within twenty-four hours, the Business Council–AFL proposal had been put into its final form and passed unanimously by the membership of both the Labor and the Industrial advisory boards of the NRA. Senator Wagner was appointed chairman. Green, Lewis, and Wolman were proposed as labor members, while Council leaders Swope, Teagle, and Kirstein composed the employer contingent. Employers and employees alike were urged to cooperate to remove "causes of irritation or industrial discontent . . . so far as possible." President Roosevelt was thereupon notified of the recommendations, and approved of them *in toto* on August 5. In a two-day period, a National Labor Board (NLB) had been created to arbitrate strikes and lockouts, report labor violations, and secure voluntary consent to Section 7-A from all parties concerned. A deal had been cut after all.[12]

The Short, Unhappy Life of "Self-Government of Industry"

The creation of the National Labor Board was a model of the way in which American business leaders thought that they should be allowed to solve their problems. Acting under the loose organizational supervision of a federal umpire, union and business representatives had met together to solve their common problems. Federal leaders then ratified the proposals of these private interest groups rather than trying to formulate any rules of their own.

In acting as they had, businessmen, labor leaders, and federal bureaucrats sought to repeat the labor relations experience of the First World War. During America's abortive Great Crusade, a National War Labor Board of five AFL leaders, five businessmen, and two "public" chairmen had been established to arbitrate employer-employee differences. The National Labor Board mimicked the strategy and structure of its wartime predecessor, and its sponsors hoped that it could repeat its experience as well, particularly in the troublesome area of organizing rights.

During World War I, AFL leaders had made a deal. They had surrendered the right to strike in return for increased corporate tolerance for the right to organize skilled craftsmen in the mass production trades. Unskilled and semiskilled workers that AFL craft unions had little or no interest in organizing could participate in firm-specific "work councils"—which were usually company unions set up by management to represent all the employees in a given factory. Where industrial unionism existed, then, it was very largely a creature of interested businessmen rather than trade union leaders. Articulate corporate leaders like Gerard Swope and Walter Teagle believed that the creation of the National Labor Board would allow William Green and other AFL leaders to renew the cooperative relationships they had enjoyed with big businessmen during the wartime emergency. The AFL would gradually get easier access to the relatively small number of unorganized craftsmen, in return for allowing business to design alternative collective-bargaining institutions for all other workers. The National Labor Board was, in essence, the institutional linchpin of this hoped-for compromise.

Hopes were one thing, the ability to achieve them decidedly another. For the National Labor Board to work, it was essential that big businessmen such as those in the Business Council build a consensus for compromise among themselves—and among larger employers generally. Without such a consensus, the noncoercive mediation, conciliation, and arbitration efforts of the NLB could not succeed, and the compromise worked out between Business Council and AFL leaders would fall apart. If the business establishment failed to accommodate relatively conservative leaders like William Green, labor policy would increasingly be made on the streets and picket lines rather than at secret meetings.[13]

The employer delegates of the National Labor Board sought to achieve exactly such a consensus and accommodation when they helped to work out the so-called Reading formula in the first week of the Board's existence, applying four major principles to the NLB's efforts to resolve Section 7-A disputes. First, they and their opposite numbers representing the AFL agreed, strikes should end pending final NLB arbitration. Second, all striking workers should be reinstated without prejudice. Third, representation elections were to be held under NLB guidelines including secret balloting. Finally, employers and employees should agree to refer all differences they might have regarding NLB-facilitated collective-bargaining agreements back to the Board itself for final resolution.

The Gerard Swopes of the corporate world did everything in their power to ensure that the Reading formula was applied throughout the U.S. industrial economy. In the process, Swope himself on more than one occasion had head-to-head verbal encounters with virulently anti-union employers. Roosevelt's Secretary of Labor, Frances Perkins, described one such run-in that occurred during the first month of the National Labor Board's life. A tough German-American textile manufacturer from Gastonia, North Carolina, had been persuaded to come to Washington:

> Gerard Swope dealt with him in his office. Swope, a patient mediator, tried to reason with him. . . . But that day he merely would not agree to meet the union.
> "I have a suggestion," Swope said. "Let them vote on it. We'll have a free election by secret ballot and every employee of yours can vote whether he wants to be represented by a union or not. That's fair, isn't it? Then you'll know."
> "Vy," replied the mill owner in a thick accent, "vy should they vote?"
> "Because," said Swope quietly, though he was boiling and furious by this time, "this is America and that's the way we do things here."

One week later, an NLB-sponsored secret election was held at this employer's company—over his continuing protests. All the debates regarding the meaning of collective-bargaining rights under 7-A were not, however, as easily resolved.[14]

The issue that proved most troublesome to corporate leaders was a debate concerning "proportional representation" versus "majority rule" interpretations of Section 7-A. Though couched in technical terminology, this debate was hardly a technical matter. Under majority rule, if a majority of the workers in a particular plant voted for, say, an AFL union to represent them, that union would be certified to bargain for *all* workers. Proportional representation, on the other hand, allowed a variety of collective bargaining agents to enjoy a parallel existence within a plant. Each agent bargained for the group of workers that had selected it. AFL unions, company unions or other employee representation plans, and unorganized workers could all exist simultaneously.

Proportional representation was, in fact, precisely the form of open-shop unionism that had been the cornerstone of federal labor policy during World War I, and compromise-minded businessmen such as those on the NLB overwhelmingly preferred it as a solution to labor problems. Proportional representation allowed corporations to attempt to outbid AFL organizers by offering employees—particularly the majority of workers who were not skilled craftsmen—alternative forms of collective bargaining. Primary among such employer-initiated alternatives were new versions of the firm-specific company unions that had arrived on the American industrial scene during the 1917–1918 wartime mobilization.

AFL leaders, for their part, had little initial reason to oppose proportional representation, however vivid their rhetoric on the subject of worker rights and company unionism. So long as it seemed that businessmen in the mass production trades might allow it—or be compelled to allow it—AFL craftsmen could plan on skimming the cream off the top of labor by organizing their traditional constituencies within the ranks of the skilled and leaving the much larger numbers of the unskilled in limbo.

Reacting to the scent of this convergence of interests between AFL craft leaders and compromise-minded businessmen, labor commentator Louis Adamic went so far as to accuse AFL officials of intentionally pushing unskilled and semiskilled workers into the arms of company unions. Adamic continued:

> It was not to the advantage of the old AF of L oligarchy to have their [craft] unions become big organizations. How could they keep out the thousands of [unskilled and semiskilled] workers who, NRA-inspired, wanted to come in? By impressing them with the importance and formidableness of company unionism, by scaring them, and driving them, fear-stricken, into the company unions.
>
> Am I giving the AF of L leaders credit for more brains than they were likely to have? I think not. They were not very intelligent men, but they were desperate. They were fighting for their [traditional craft-oriented] existence. The CIO was not yet in existence, but they knew that sooner or later, probably sooner, something like it was bound to appear. And in such a situation even a normally dull or stupid person or group is apt to develop great cunning.[15]

Whether Adamic was correct about the conscious "cunning" of AFL craft leaders or not, it remained true that these men had little reason to extend themselves to organize workers that most of them considered unorganizable, and little reason to oppose a compromise in which company unions played a significant part.

The AFL leadership, however, could not effectively speak for the unskilled and semiskilled masses whose interests they usually ignored. As time passed, it became increasingly clear that these workers were simply not willing to be governed by the wartime-labor-relations analogies that Business Council and AFL eminences generally assumed should apply to them. Four years of wrenching depression had convinced a growing segment of the nation's industrial work force that industrial unions were a necessary element of their security in an era of economic emergency. These workers, in turn, became the vanguard of industrial-union-organizing drives in key industries like steel, automobiles, textiles, chemicals, and rubber. Gradually, such workers found champions. John L. Lewis, head of the largest industrial union within the AFL, began to put both the organizational and the financial clout of his United Mine Workers Union behind efforts to organize millions of people whom his opposite numbers in the AFL crafts all too often considered unorganizable. A clear possibility existed that such collective-bargaining rights as the masses of the unskilled and semiskilled enjoyed would no longer be a matter of managerial discretion due to craft union default.

Businessmen, then, had a problem. If they wanted to keep unions —especially industrial unions—out of their factories, they had to do something. Workers were not going to turn into passive observers of events just because managers wanted them to. Realizing this simple and undeniable fact, the big-business activists of the Business Council and the National Labor Board enunciated the Reading formula to channel dissent. This formula concerned itself with means rather than ends, with processes rather than precise institutional alternatives. Workers could vote for or against various types of collective bargaining. What precise bargaining approach or mix of approaches was presented to employees depended on how clever businessmen and their opposite numbers in the labor movement were at evolving particular institutions for particular worker clienteles. Company unions, for instance, were as legitimate an alternative as any other under the formula. However, businessmen who did nothing to create workable, attractive, prophylactic company unions and then expected the NLB to protect them from the results of their own corporate caveman psychology vis-à-vis unions were going to be in for a big disappointment.

It was all very well for Business Council and AFL leaders to set forth such formulas. It proved to be another matter entirely to get others to abide by them. The National Labor Board, like so much of the rest of the early New Deal, depended upon voluntary cooperation for its effectiveness. NLB members could suggest, but could not go on to enforce their suggestions.

In the months immediately following NLB's creation, these voluntary schemes started running into trouble. In particular because the nation's business elite proved unable—indeed, often unwilling—to formulate effective compromises on labor questions. It also became increasingly evident that the Council leaders who were willing to compromise had thereby outrun the majority of their own high-echelon corporate peers.

The resulting corporate struggle was not without some behind-the-scenes bloodletting. By November of 1933, for example, Business Council Chairman Swope was busy reiterating the industrial planning proposals that he had unsuccessfully urged two years before, and trying to convince the Council to form a united front to support them. The trade associations administering NRA's industrial codes should, Swope argued, be organized into a National Chamber of Commerce and Industry to "make permanent many of the essentials of the NRA." This Chamber, in turn, would elect the corporate members of an advisory National Economic Council composed of approximately equal numbers of representatives from business, trade unions, agricultural organizations, banks, transportation companies, and "the public" (Cabinet officers and other presidential appointees).

Swope's proposal was an extension of the logic that had led him to propose his Swope Plan of 1931 and, more importantly, an extension of the cooperative inclination that had led him and other Business Council figures to sit down with their counterparts in the AFL to establish and man the National Labor Board. Swope and his corporate allies hoped to forestall social and political unrest by allying the big-business leadership of the nation with all other powerful and *already organized* economic interest groups to negotiate a set of rules for industrial recovery. Once these private interest groups arrived at such decisions, they should invite the federal "umpire" to apply these rules throughout the society. Thereby, the NRA, National Labor Board, and Business Council could all serve as the institutional foundations for a nationalized corporate self-regulatory order.[16]

The problem with Swope's corporatist logic was that it had little place within it for newly emergent industrial interest groups—industrial unionists in particular. As these people hammered on the corporate gates throughout the strife-torn winter of 1933–1934, heads of small and medium-sized businesses became frightened by the prospect of a wide-ranging growth in organized labor's power—particularly after trade unions began making large gains in about three fourths of the early representation elections held under the auspices of the NLB. Such corporate unrest also extended into the ranks of the Business Council itself. As early as October of 1933, important employers like Du Pont, Sloan of GM, and Wood of Sears, Roebuck were becoming extremely anxious about the deals that their peers Swope, Teagle, and Kirstein were trying to make with AFL craft union chieftains.[17]

By December of 1933, employer frustrations began to boil over in the National Labor Board itself. At issue was the still-unresolved question of proportional representation versus majority rule. A trade union composed of slightly over half of the 678 employees who had voted in an NLB-ordered representation election at a streetcar company in Denver, Colorado, came before the NLB to argue that it should be allowed to bargain for all the firm's workers, even though 325 men had voted to retain their membership in a company union that had been in existence for a decade, and an additional 36 employees had cast no ballots at all. An NLB subcommittee composed of Gerard Swope, William Green, and George L. Berry of the Typographer's Union dismissed the union's argument. The union, they said, could bargain for the 353 men who had chosen it and for them alone. Management could also bargain collectively with the company union representing the minority of employee voters, and could deal with the 36 nonvoting workers on an individual basis.

By the time the full membership of the National Labor Board announced its decision in the Denver Tramways case, however, the verdict had changed. Early in February of 1934, the group announced publicly that majority rule should, in fact, be the governing principle in all collective-bargaining elections. It is likely that a good deal of back-room bargaining had taken place, and that impatient AFL members like John L. Lewis had pushed other labor members on the Board and Board Chairman Wagner to attempt an end run around the employer members of the Board. Or perhaps several employer representatives (most likely Gerard Swope and possibly also Louis Kirstein—a longtime friend of Sidney Hillman) had agreed to support majority rule in order to placate Wagner and their opposite numbers from the AFL.

Whatever had in fact transpired, the NLB's change in view in the

Denver Tramways case incensed NLB employer representative
Pierre du Pont and a goodly number of his peers on the Business
Council. Council moderates including Lincoln Filene vainly sought
to convince Du Pont that the political environment was too fluid for
labor and employer members of the NLB to take ironclad positions
on Section 7-A, but Du Pont, speaking for Council conservatives,
continued to demand absolute guarantees against the majority rule
interpretation of the statute as a precondition for their continued
cooperation with the Board. As Du Pont and his supporters stonewalled, NRA Director Johnson weighed in with reassuring statements in favor of proportional representation and multiple
bargaining agents, while President Roosevelt did his best to ignore
the issue entirely.[18]

Throughout the month of February, debate raged within the
Business Council regarding what to do about 7-A. All the while,
events external to Washington were making these corporate deliberations increasingly academic. A nationwide strike wave—the worst in
over a decade—was beginning. Eventually, 1.5 million workers were
involved in almost nineteen hundred work stoppages, including violent general strikes in Minneapolis and San Francisco. Larger employers in the rubber, steel, automobile, and textile industries—
joined by most of the nation's newspaper owners—reacted viscerally.
By March of 1934, Henry Harriman of the Chamber of Commerce
had begun calling upon the Roosevelt administration to squelch
unruly workers for businessmen as an act of political good faith. The
small and medium-sized employers grouped in the National Association of Manufacturers were even more incensed by the reality of an
emergent industrial-union movement. As the spring of 1934 progressed, it became all too obvious that smaller employers generally
were willing to accept *no* form of collective bargaining except *pro
forma* company unions, and that Council members like Swope, Kirstein, Filene, and Dennison were perceived to be radicals for even
supporting genuine forms of proportional representation.

As internal capitalist squabbling racked the NLB, AFL craft
leaders—most of whom were as uncomfortable with the scale of
worker unrest as their corporate counterparts—became increasingly
skeptical of the Business Council's ability to control the anti-union
proclivities of businessmen either within or without the organization.
The likes of William Green and Sidney Hillman wanted action—or
at least tolerance. They got neither, and, as a result, became increas-

ingly supportive of majority rule as a means of preserving their own organizational interests. Discomfort with corporate obtuseness extended to National Labor Board Chairman Wagner, who as a senator started drafting a bill aimed at separating the Board from the NRA administrative structure and reestablishing it as a permanent federal agency staffed by public representatives affiliated with neither corporations nor trade unions. Gerard Swope's visions of a self-policing American industrial order were fading fast.

The author of these visions, political realist that he was, sought to do what he could. In a last-ditch effort to close the widening gap between the management and the labor members of the NLB, Business Council Chairman Swope again came out in support of majority rule in the Denver Tramways case, and went on to reiterate this view in several other NLB cases decided early in March.[19]

The logic of Swope's actions completely escaped employers like Pierre du Pont, who vociferously reiterated their opposition to majority rule while ignoring the political circumstances which made compromise on the issue necessary. Not content with hectoring attacks, Du Pont and his allies on the Business Council withdrew their participation and support from the NLB and prepared to launch an all-out drive to destroy the entire New Deal under the auspices of the red-baiting American Liberty League. The organizational decay which resulted soon killed the object of their wrath, but did nothing whatever to replace the National Labor Board with an agency that could successfully arbitrate employer-employee differences.

Corporate divisiveness on the proper—or the practically necessary—interpretation of Section 7-A presented the White House with a problem. Roosevelt and his advisers had originally ducked the whole issue of collective bargaining by allowing interested private parties (the Business Council and the AFL) to assume major policy-making authority in that area. The Council's inability to maintain a united front for compromise in the wake of widespread worker unrest, however, ruined this nongovernmental effort, and Senator Wagner was pushing legislation aimed at forcing the federal government to accept the primary political responsibility for arbitrating industrial disputes.

The White House had no great desire to accept the responsibilities that Senator Wagner and his allies wanted to give it. To forestall the senator, Roosevelt first tried to reassure Council conservatives like Pierre du Pont and Alfred Sloan. He did this by repudiating the majority rule decision of the moribund National Labor Board. NRA Director Johnson, with Roosevelt's support, worked out a short-lived collective-bargaining agreement for the automobile industry that was based squarely upon the principle of proportional representation. To help assure that the principle would hold, an Automobile Labor Board was created to operate completely independently of the NLB. Not surprisingly, Business Council members started consoling themselves with the thought that the wartime collective-bargaining precedents that the NLB had discarded were going to be restored on an industry-by-industry basis. "Just between you and me and the lamp-post," Walter Teagle wrote Louis Kirstein in April of 1934, "it strikes me that the President's decision in the automobile controversy had put the Labor Board out of the running. I am sure that neither you nor I will shed any tears if such is the case."[20]

Like Roosevelt, the businessmen reckoned without the determination of congressional liberals—and the continuing labor insurgency that made such determination possible. Wagner kept right on pressing for federalization of the National Labor Board throughout the strife-filled spring of 1934, and, once again, Roosevelt was forced to act. In June, with Wagner's cooperation, the NLB was finally replaced with a three-person National Labor Relations Board (NLRB) composed solely of presidential appointees. The three prominent lawyers composing the new labor board operated under a directive that specified their responsibilities very loosely indeed, and gave them no enforcement powers whatsoever. The status of majority rule versus proportional representation interpretations of Section 7-A—the issue that had destroyed the effectiveness of the NLB—was left unresolved. The new NLRB was, in effect, a public labor-arbitration board, an NLB shorn of its Business Council and AFL members. Like the NLB, it tried to persuade rather than compel.

Though initially greeted with some optimism in Business Council circles, the NLRB proved to be as futile an effort as the National Labor Board had been. Strikes and lockouts bloomed as perennially as the grass. Responding in the same fashion as intelligent conservatives like Gerard Swope had earlier done, the moderate lawyers of the NLRB rather quickly enunciated a majority rule interpretation of 7-A to calm labor unrest. Corporate leaders in the auto, steel, textile, chemical, and rubber industries reiterated their opposition to such views, and everything went back to square one. But the widespread violence perpetrated by employer and employed alike continued.[21]

This same reality of violence on the picket lines of industrial America, however, reenergized Senator Wagner and like-minded congressmen. The midterm congressional elections of November, 1934, swept additional reform-minded Democrats into office, firmed up the party's domination of the House and Senate, and convinced Wagner to draft a revised and strengthened collective-bargaining statute—one that gave Washington the power to *enforce* rules, rather than simply expediting such voluntary agreements as might be made by affected parties.

In February of 1935, the final act in this congressional drama began when Wagner introduced his strengthened bill, the National Labor Relations Act, in both houses of Congress. The Business Council was not insensitive to the threat that Congress might replace failed corporate voluntarism with federal compulsion. For the first time, the Business Council joined organizations representing smaller business interests in virulent opposition to a New Deal "experiment." The language of a hurriedly prepared Council position paper showed the extent to which the moderation of Swope, Kirstein, Teagle, Flanders, and Dennison had been undermined by the truculent, reactionary stances of Du Pont, Sloan, and others.

The [Wagner] Bill provides that formal procedure by a quasi-judicial federal labor board be made a substitute for the common-sense method of direct contact and negotiation between employer and employees, whether or not the latter be an organized national labor union, an independent local [industrial] union, an employee representation plan, or a completely or partially unorganized group. Such quasi-judicial procedure will result in delay in the settlement of disputes, will provoke interminable litigation and will require an overwhelming mass of administrative detail to carry out the provisions of the Bill. . . .

[Wagner's bill mandates majority rule and thus] is not . . . impartial. . . . The arguments of proponents indicate clearly that the purpose is to promote a specific kind of labor organization. It is not in the interests of workers generally. By its very nature it opens the door to strife and to action [e.g., court tests of the bill's constitutionality] necessary to protect the legal and public rights of both employee and employer.

After wrapping itself up in the American flag and considerations of individual liberty, the Council concluded its diatribe by announcing that

> the rights of the overwhelming majority of the population are in no way protected in this Bill which, if enacted into law, would strike one of the severest blows at the public interest which the country has ever suffered.[22]

The Business Council's rather too convenient logic, however, failed to persuade Congress. By May 20, the Senate passed the bill by an overwhelming margin of 63 to 12 after its sponsors made a strategic decision to exclude agricultural, migrant, and seasonal laborers from coverage to mollify farm-state senators. Realizing that passage by the House was a certainty, Roosevelt hurriedly met with Senator Wagner again on May 24 to announce his belated conversion to a federal enforcement approach to collective bargaining. Little more than a month later, the National Labor Relations Act of 1935 (or Wagner Act) was signed into law. The Business Council had been handed its first severe public drubbing.[23]

The successful drive to pass the National Labor Relations Act was not an isolated defeat. As corporate fortunes waned on the labor front, the institutional centerpiece of the cooperative industrial order earlier envisioned by Business Council leaders Swope and Teagle was itself falling upon hard times.

Since its birth, the National Recovery Administration had been subject to assaults from diverse points along the political spectrum. Small businessmen opposed to the welfare and price standards promulgated in the NRA's national industrial codes, conservative and liberal antitrusters in Congress, and moderate to radical elements concerned that the NRA marked the beginnings of a fascist "corporate state" combined to subject NRA to a series of withering attacks.

Bureaucratic infighting within NRA's administrative structure did nothing to improve this threatening situation. By June of 1934, a bloc of discontented lawyers and economists on the NRA staff attempted to abolish the price-fixing elements of all NRA codes in all but "emergency" situations. Counterattacks by the Labor and Industrial advisory boards quickly defeated such efforts to restore marketplace pricing, but the agency's internal cohesion and morale sagged badly. Mass resignations of NRA personnel began and, by

August, NRA chief Johnson was fired, to be replaced by a five-man board headed by Business Council member S. Clay Williams of Reynolds Tobacco. Facing midterm congressional elections in the fall, FDR and other important Democratic leaders began a discrete retreat from close connection with the day-to-day affairs of the faltering agency. This process was made all the easier by the fact that the dissolution of the NRA's National Labor Board in March was quickly followed by a rash of bloody strikes that continued throughout the summer. Politicians, in short, had no desire to be tarred with the same brushes that were being applied to businessmen and their works.[24]

As relations between the Democrats and big business worsened, a minority of Business Council members continued to argue that patience was the order of the day and that—in W. Averell Harriman's phrase—business could not expect "to get a good start on NRA" in only one or two years. Corporate leaders, Harriman continued, should concentrate upon improving the self-regulatory institutions they had before impatiently demanding substitutes.[25]

By the late summer of 1934, however, it was becoming clear that the same kind of corporate truculence and disorganization that had killed the Swope-Teagle National Labor Board was also slowly strangling the parent NRA. The minutes of Industrial Advisory Board meetings were filled with a growing number of captious utterances regarding the threats of federal "interference," real or imaginary. As early as July 12, 1934, a majority of the IAB declared suggestively that "until something else is evolved *by industry* to take the place of the NRA, the [Industrial Advisory] Board should be considered a part of the official NRA organization." The scope of corporate disenchantment was clear to all concerned.[26]

While IAB members squabbled and complained, the NRA that Swope, Teagle, and their supporters had done so much to create was unraveling. By the early autumn of 1934, fewer and fewer CEOs attended IAB meetings with any regularity, and the group's responsibilities regarding code revision and enforcement were turned over to lower-level corporate officials. The National Recovery Administration limped along for eight months more, an increasingly hollow shell, until, on May 27, 1935, the Supreme Court finally killed the moribund agency by ruling that its operations and enabling legislation alike were unconstitutional. Only three days before NRA's largely unlamented death, Roosevelt had finally given his support to

Senator Wagner's National Labor Relations Act. For the moment, at least, business-government cooperation had fallen on very hard times indeed.[27]

The Nature of the Problem

The failure of corporate efforts to achieve nongovernmental compromises on labor policy and cartelization procedures during the years from 1933 to 1935 exemplified much of what was wrong with big business' approach to public policy during the domestic reform phase of the New Deal. As the New Deal began, businessmen were still wedded to New Era precedents concerning the virtues of decentralized voluntarism as the preferred solution to national problems. But the emergency gradually allowed the leading edge of corporate opinion, represented by Gerard Swope of General Electric, to successfully advocate centralized planning as a necessary substitute for Hoover-era techniques. Such planning as occurred, however, was to remain largely nongovernmental. Already-organized economic interest groups—among which big businessmen were to be the primary actors—would cooperate with each other to formulate rules that a compliant federal umpire was to enforce. Federal police powers were to be wedded to "self-government of industry" and the results were to apply throughout the nation. Washington was to underwrite enlightened corporate standards such as those worked out by the Business Council.

When the chips were down, however, enlightenment proved to be a scarcer commodity than its corporate sponsors expected. In the crucial debate over collective bargaining, for example, "self-government of industry" looked more like a barroom brawl than a gathering of sagacious and disinterested industrial statesmen. Lacking the ability to compromise their own differences regarding Section 7-A, big-business leaders lost the ability to decisively influence labor relations and helped produce the political forces that made the Wagner Act both possible and, finally, necessary.

Nor was the debate over 7-A an isolated instance. The NRA cartelization effort generally—of which 7-A was but one component part—depended for its success upon organized business' ability to arrive at voluntary standards and to apply those standards throughout the industrial economy. Sophisticated corporate leaders like Gerard Swope recognized early that business was too diverse to accomplish such a task without federal assistance, or at least the threat of federal enforcement as a last resort. The fact that Washington's powers might well have to grow relative to those of private corporations did not alarm him. Swope believed it was only necessary for business leaders to remain cohesive enough to direct the growth of federal power along paths that would best serve the collective long-term interests of the corporations that they headed. Swope's proposals for a National Chamber of Commerce and Industry and National Economic Council were meant to be key steps in precisely this direction.[28]

Swope's logic, however, was not persuasive to the vast majority of his corporate peers. Even in the elite confines of the Business Council, Swope's ambitious approach toward the creation of permanent forms of NRA planning was not widely shared. CEOs like Alfred Sloan and Pierre du Pont simply could not accept any business-government partnership that required Washington to make substantial use of its powers of compulsion, most particularly in the strategic labor area. To the likes of Sloan and Du Pont, the NRA was to remain a kind of New Era relic in which government might request data from industry, state its recommendations to national trade associations and individual corporations, and bargain for their voluntary fulfillment. Given such a willingness to ignore the reality that pure voluntarism with no enforcement machinery simply could not deal with bottom-line issues of power and money in the unsettled political environment of the early New Deal, it is not surprising that the Sloans and Du Ponts had completely soured on New Deal "experiment" by the summer of 1934—or that the alienation of corporate leaders like these destroyed the NRA's effectiveness as it had earlier destroyed that of the National Labor Board. The eventual Supreme Court judgment in May of 1935 that the National Industrial Recovery Act was unconstitutional only drove the final nail into a coffin that had already been constructed by widespread corporate intransigence.[29]

The intransigence of the Sloans and Du Ponts of the corporate establishment was in large part a function of ignorance. Such men simply were not very well aware of how the federal government worked. The Business Council, for example, tended to ignore Congress' crucial role as a power center throughout the 1930's. Congressional leaders like Senator Wagner were very seldom invited to Council functions during this period.[30]

Instead of looking at the federal establishment broadly, business leaders generally preferred to concentrate their attention upon the executive branch, and most particularly upon the President, as *the* source of political initiative and power. Many of the CEOs who participated in the affairs of the Business Council during the period under discussion perceived themselves to be only slightly lesser potentates than the man whom they considered the CEO of the federal government, Franklin D. Roosevelt. As a result of such perceptions, these corporate leaders viewed public policy in essentially one-dimensional terms—as a very largely autonomous process of high-level interaction between the managers of the corporate establishment and the executive branch.

The analogy businessmen made between managing and governing, between private and public power, was fundamentally flawed. FDR was not a superior version of a corporate manager, but a practical politician trying to nudge political forces into the legislative and programmatic channels that would best guarantee his continued political survival. Where businessmen thought that Roosevelt ordered, he, in fact, brokered. Where they believed that he led, he more often followed, as the debate over Section 7-A nicely demonstrated.[31]

However inaccurate, businessmen's perceptions caused them to confuse cause and effect all too often. Most blamed FDR and his top aides for creating political forces (like industrial unionism) that they only, and necessarily, responded to. In complaining loudly about supposed conspiracies of Roosevelt or the much-overrated Brain Trust, businessmen were vainly trying to kill the messenger for bearing bad news. It did not often occur to the corporate mainstream that the New Deal was not the cause of change, but rather a result of changes in the wider American economic and political order—changes that could not have been successfully contained within the limits of the preexisting status quo. So while big businessmen grumbled, industrial workers, like farmers, the elderly, and those other groups able to achieve the necessary political visibility or clout, eventually forced the federal government to become the final guarantor of their collective welfare—much as businessmen compelled Washington to assist them with loans and investment capital from the multibillion-dollar RFC, Himalayan tariff rates, and an eventually unsuccessful program of nationwide cartelization.

Not all corporate leaders, of course, made the mistakes outlined above. Conservatives like Alfred Sloan might look upon trade unions as an adult form of juvenile delinquency and think of Franklin D.

Roosevelt as a closet communist, but the Walter Teagles, Gerard Swopes, Louis Kirsteins, Henry Dennisons, and W. Averell Harrimans knew better. New Deal politicians, such men realized, were trying to save capitalism, not bury it. Acting on this knowledge, this articulate minority of American capitalists managed to keep a definite and important corporate presence alive in Washington throughout the six reform years of the New Deal (1933–1938). This presence, discrete as it was, allowed American capitalism to bridge the transition from the era of welfare capitalism to the era of the welfare state.

Quiet Diplomacy: Social Security

The activities of Business Council members Gerard Swope, Walter Teagle, and Marion Folsom (Eastman Kodak) in connection with the formulation and passage of the Social Security Act of 1935, the centerpiece of New Deal social welfare legislation, provide excellent examples of the way in which articulate corporate leaders preserved a business presence in Washington and, thereby, achieved partial victories where business would otherwise have suffered thoroughgoing defeats.

Corporate involvement with the program of publicly guaranteed minimum-welfare standards for the masses that Americans came to know as Social Security began early. Corporations, like state governments and private foundations, were a major source of social welfare expertise in America's relatively decentralized political order. So when President Roosevelt appointed a Committee on Economic Security (CES) to draft comprehensive welfare-standards legislation in the summer of 1934, he told Edwin E. Witte, the staff director and moving force of the Committee, that an advisory council should be created to provide expert counsel and to help build political support for the eventual bill. The group, Roosevelt concluded, should be chaired by "a man like Gerard Swope or Owen D. Young." Witte had no objections, having worked closely with businessmen throughout his earlier career as a social welfare specialist in Wisconsin.[32]

Though Roosevelt was later prevailed upon by several Cabinet officers to change his mind and appoint a nonbusinessman to the chairman's post, corporate leaders were well represented in the CES hierarchy throughout the formative stages of the Social Security debate. Walter Teagle, for example, was selected for membership on the advisory panel "because," in Witte's words, "he was the chairman of the Unemployment Insurance Committee of the Business . . . Council. . . ."[33]

Teagle's selection was logical enough. Throughout the first stages of the CES' work, unemployment insurance was the most important single topic of discussion for corporate and noncorporate experts alike. The businessmen, who, like Teagle, represented firms that had long experience with designing and implementing voluntary unemployment-insurance schemes for their employees, argued for the creation of a public sector unemployment-insurance program modeled as closely as possible upon private sector programs. First, they argued for a plan financed by the joint contributions of employers and employees. This would, in the view of men like Gerard Swope, make workers jointly responsible with management for maintaining their social welfare standards. Secondly, Teagle and Swope argued, unemployment insurance should not be administered by the federal government nor the state governments. Instead, administration should be in the hands of national industrial trade associations. Once again, the logic behind the Swope Plan of 1931 emerged full-blown.

Third and most importantly, an American social welfare system, unlike its Western European counterparts, should not be wholly or partly financed by public funds. Instead, it should be "self-financing" and independent of the public treasury and governmental taxing power.

Gerard Swope had explained his opposition to government involvement in the financing of social welfare programs in testimony he had earlier given to a Senate committee:

> *Senator Glenn:* I presume that you have given considerable thought to the idea of Government contributions [to an unemployment insurance system] . . . have you not?
>
> *Mr. Swope:* Yes, sir. . . . I think that industry ought to take care of its [unemployment] difficulties and problems. You see, the moment government begins to help there is no economic restraint. You can vote money . . . [but] the moment the General Electric Company or any industrial organization . . . provides for these various [problems] it is reflected in costs. . . . And selling prices reflect costs; and therefore the people who use the product will ultimately pay for that [unemployment insurance] service; whereas, of course, if you vote the money by Government assistance your general public will pay for it through taxation, which is very general and very indefinite.[34]

Government, then, would oversupply welfare services unless it created welfare programs that were designed and run as closely to private sector programs as possible.

To further ensure that private sector principles would serve as the foundation for a public sector unemployment-insurance program, Swope, Teagle, Folsom, and other interested businessmen argued that the program should have provisions for what, in private sector insurance jargon, was called experience rating. This would allow companies with lower rates of layoffs to make lower payments into the unemployment insurance fund, and penalize higher-layoff companies with higher payments. The analogy to private sector practices was obvious. The lower the risk of ever needing the insurance, the lower the premium charged to the insured.[35]

As finally formulated, the unemployment insurance provisions of what became the Social Security Act of 1935 were not an unalloyed victory for the corporate advisers, but neither were they a defeat. Businessmen, in effect, had to split the difference. On the issue of contributions, employees were exempted while businessmen themselves were not. Corporations, then, had to pick up the tab. Nor were industrial trade associations made responsible for administering unemployment insurance funds. Instead, this responsibility devolved upon the states.

Public financing for unemployment insurance, however, was another matter entirely. Here, the businessmen's logic generally prevailed. States would draw up and administer their own plans, but state money would not be contributed to the insurance funds. Nor would the federal government have such financial power or responsibility. Unemployment insurance would, then, remain a "self-financing" system and as such presumably had built-in guarantees against overexpansion. The relative decentralization of the state-administered unemployment insurance system also did nothing to inhibit states from adopting any form of employer payment schedule that they desired. As things turned out, forty-one states had adopted "experience rating" systems by 1939. So here, too, the corporate argument proved more persuasive than not.[36]

As the corporate and noncorporate experts of the Committee on Economic Security hammered out compromises on the nuances of unemployment insurance, however, they were almost overtaken by events. A group with no interest in the subject at all entered the national political arena in force with a simple demand for money.

This group was the nation's elderly. Many of America's older citizens had been pushed into involuntary retirement by the Depression. Many more had lost what savings they had put aside for retirement in the rash of bank failures that had taken place in the desperate years between 1931 and 1933. Thousands upon thousands of these elderly citizens were utterly destitute, and dependent upon local charities that simply did not have the funds necessary to meet their needs.

Out of this misery among the nation's aged emerged the Townsend Movement. Led by Francis Townsend, a retired doctor from California, the elderly became a potent political force by 1934. Thousands of Townsend organizations and clubs began dotting the country. Their tens of thousands of members vociferously demanded that anyone over the age of sixty be paid a pension of two hundred dollars a month from the federal treasury on the single condition that they spend the entire sum within that month.

The Townsend Movement's program was strange as economics, but even so it posed clear political dangers for Roosevelt, the Democrats, and the experts on the Committee on Economic Security. The Townsendites viewed social welfare primarily as a matter of providing retirement pensions to the nation's elderly, and only secondarily as a matter for expert compromise on an unemployment insurance program.[37]

The experts soon got the message, and added retirement to unemployment as a focus of concern. More, they sought to provide the retired with a variation of what they had earlier agreed upon for the unemployed: a self-financing "old-age insurance" program.

This process of formulating legislation about, and gathering political support for, the retirement insurance elements of the Social Security Act was also a process in which corporate leaders like Gerard Swope, Walter Teagle, and Marion Folsom were intimately involved. By December, the CES experts had designed a program that owed much to the social welfare approaches of businessmen, as opposed to those of federal bureaucrats.

To assuage the passions of the Townsendites, the Social Security retirement program incorporated two untraditional features. First, it gave an unprecedented grant of administrative responsibility in the social welfare field to the federal government. Washington—not the states, localities, or private groups—would run the retirement program and participation in that program would be compulsory for the vast majority of citizens. Second, Washington was allowed to appropriate special monies for distribution to the financially pressed state and local governments to enable them to provide income and other support services to particularly needy elderly people, the blind, and single-parent families with dependent children.

Here the similarities with the Townsend program ended, and the similarities with the unemployment insurance program already worked out by the Committee on Economic Security's experts began. First, this was to be a self-financing program funded by joint contributions from workers and their employers. No federal funds were required. Washington would administer, but not finance—at least overtly. Secondly, under the provisions of the program, workers and their employers paid into a Washington-based retirement fund from which workers drew benefits after retirement. Only those with employment records, not everyone over the retirement age of sixty-five, received benefits. This ensured that America's social welfare system would continue to be connected with the private labor market. Third, an employee's Social Security retirement benefits depended on the level of wages that he had earned during his working lifetime. The more a worker earned, the more he and his employer contributed to the worker's individual Social Security account, and the more the worker would receive from that account during his retirement. The use of this benefit schedule, instead of one that paid the same retirement income to everyone, guaranteed that America's public welfare system would continue to accept the private sector's—and private industry's—judgments as to an individual's economic worth.

The CES program's most conservative feature was its financing plan. Social Security's retirement program would support itself without taking money from the general revenue. In other words, contributions were to flow into the Social Security coffers at a greater rate than benefits ebbed out. This feature facilitated the use of analogies drawn from the private sector to describe the expansion of the public sector. The operative metaphor, in fact, was the homely piggy bank. A worker dropped his Social Security retirement contributions into the bank during the course of his working lifetime. When the worker retired, the federal administrators responsible for the Social Security retirement fund broke the bank and gave the worker the benefits of his mandatory prudence.[38]

As might be imagined, the Committee on Economic Security's expert proposals satisfied the Townsendites not at all. They wanted lots of federal money, and they wanted it immediately. They did not want a system based upon private sector analogies with a small program of federal grants to the states and localities for the relief of distress. The Townsendites attacked the CES plan and sought to replace it with their own.

At this stage in the drama, businessmen entered the political arena to convince the politicians—notably some wavering officers of Roosevelt's own Cabinet—that the relatively conservative proposal that they had helped to write was the only way to go. Their efforts were very successful. As one highly placed staff adviser to the CES later put it:

> Fortunately, included in the [Advisory] Council [of the Committee on Economic Security] were Walter C. Teagle of the Standard Oil Company of New Jersey, Gerard Swope of General Electric, and Marion Folsom of Eastman Kodak and others well acquainted with industrial [retirement] pension plans. Their practical understanding of the need for contributory old age annuities on a broad, national basis carried great weight with those in authority. They enthusiastically approved our program. . . . The support of progressive industrial executives in December [of 1934] ensured that a national system of contributory old age insurance would be recommended to the President and the Congress. Even last minute concerns on the part of Secretary [of the Treasury Henry] Morgenthau and President Roosevelt on the financing of the system failed to reverse the momentum gained.[39]

Businessmen like Swope, Teagle, and Folsom did more than soothe the nerves of jittery Cabinet officers. They went on to use the Business Council as a key source of corporate support for the compromise proposals on social welfare legislation that they had been so largely responsible for creating. Early in May of 1935, for example, the Social Security bill was wending its way through Congress. The U.S. Chamber of Commerce was not pleased, and strongly attacked the legislation in a series of resolutions. Few elements of the New Deal legislative and administrative programs, in fact, were spared. All were evils that should be torn out of American society root and branch. On the very day that the Chamber adopted its resolutions, however, Gerard Swope led a twenty-man delegation of Business Council members to a well-publicized meeting with President Roosevelt at the White House and gave "qualified approval" to the Social Security legislation. The labors required to convince twenty big businessmen to publicly support anything that Roosevelt was doing in the month that Senator Wagner's National Labor Relations Act was in the final stages of being passed into law must truly have been enormous. For all that, there were corporate leaders ready to undertake them.[40]

Nor did Folsom, Swope, and Teagle's assistance stop there. Once the Social Security Act was passed in August of 1935, federal administrators were faced with the gigantic task of creating millions of retirement accounts for the individuals paying into the Social Security program. This job might appear to have been simple, but it was not. No such thing as a computer existed, and the program started out with only five hundred people to do the bookkeeping. When it is considered that federal officials had also somehow to identify and create accounts for the additional millions of already-retired or soon-to-retire Americans who were initially scheduled to start receiving Social Security retirement benefits in 1942, it is no great wonder that Washington looked around for assistance.

It found it in the person of Marion B. Folsom, who had only recently initiated a retirement pension program for the twenty thousand employees of the Eastman Kodak Company. Folsom, who was also then serving as the chairman of the Business Council's Social Security study group, used his corporate connections to route technical advice to government officials through the Council and to help create 202 regional Social Security centers throughout the nation. Interested Council members also used their good offices to help Social Security officials recruit the director of the Industrial Bureau of the Philadelphia Chamber of Commerce as the "czar of registration" for the Social Security program. In yet another way, interested private businessmen helped launch the American version of the welfare state.[41]

The businessmen knew the importance of what they had accomplished. Throughout the remainder of the Depression decade, the Business Council remained a recruitment center for corporate expertise in the social welfare field. Council members like Edward Stettinius, Marion Folsom, and Gerard Swope were called upon for assistance again as programmatic issues came up—or as extensions of Social Security coverage were proposed with sufficient political weight behind them to demand a federal response. Decisions arrived at during this continuing process were not always to the liking of all of the individual corporate leaders involved. Involved, however, they remained. And, in the course of this involvement, the Gerard Swopes of the corporate world did a good bit to mold the structure of the welfare state as Americans know it.

A letter that Gerard Swope wrote to FDR on May 25, 1937, then, can be understood as a subtle reminder of business assistance. But one day before, the Supreme Court of the United States had turned back legal efforts to destroy the Social Security Act by affirming the statute's constitutionality. Swope expressed himself as

> delighted to read the Supreme Court decisions covering ... unemployment insurance and contributory old-age pensions. . . . I congratulate you very heartily not only on the decisions but [on] your imagination and courage to blaze these new trails in the United States. It seems almost beyond belief to think that in three short years this great change has been accomplished. It is an outstanding record that I should think would satisfy even your ardent desires, and it is surely a record that the country will applaud today and appreciate for many, many years to come.[42]

Just to be sure that Roosevelt got the message, Swope announced in a nationwide radio address a year later that

> I believe wholeheartedly in the need for Social Security legislation, and am in particular accord with the section covering old-age benefits, which I think today stands as a great forward-looking and constructive achievement of this Administration.

GE's president sent a transcript of his address to the White House, and followed up with congratulatory telegrams later that same year. It did not, certainly, hurt to remind Roosevelt of favors tendered. Nor did Roosevelt fail to respond in the effusive style he usually reserved for politicians to whom he owed favors.[43]

Learning How to Cope

The domestic reform phase of the New Deal profoundly shocked the majority of the nation's big-business establishment, and placed most of it in visible and angry opposition to an activist state. The future, however, belonged to those corporate leaders who understood that the firms they headed could survive and prosper in an era of increased federal power and political responsibility. These businessmen realized that Washington was never again going to assume a minor part in their lives, and understood that participation in the give-and-take of national politics was an essential element of their future careers.[44]

By 1938, such politically aware and involved big businessmen were becoming very valuable indeed in Washington. Increasing war tremors in Europe and Asia alerted even the most liberal of politicians to the need for corporate assistance to meet the challenges involved in what would very likely turn out to be the nation's second experience of twentieth-century technological war. In the intricate administrative ballet which ensued from these fears of renewed world conflict, those business leaders who had not alienated themselves from Washington would come to exercise great influence as a matter of simple organizational necessity.

2

MOBILIZING THE ARSENAL OF DEMOCRACY, 1938–1943

Mending Fences

EARLY IN 1935, as the forces of reform were gathering strength, Chairman Owen D. Young of the General Electric Company gave an address entitled "Courage for the Future" to an audience of Boston business executives. After surveying the profound changes that were affecting American political and economic institutions, Young waxed philosophical. His listeners should remember, Young began, that the New Deal was not the first reform interlude the country had experienced. A century before, Tennessean Andrew Jackson had come to Washington to give the masses a "square deal," but his administration had eventually ended up being "more conservative than radical." The same might very well prove to be the case with President Roosevelt and the New Deal.[1]

A little more than three years after Young spoke, the logic of his remarks was very evident indeed. By the fall of 1938, the domestic reform phase of the New Deal had ended. The causes of this phenomenon were various. A misguided effort to balance the federal budget by choking off relief expenditures helped produce the severe "Roosevelt recession" of 1937–1938, which threw almost 3 million people out of work and undermined popular confidence in federal policymakers. White House political miscalculations, such as the abortive efforts to reorganize the Supreme Court in 1938 and to purge prominent conservatives from the Democratic party during the 1938 election, added credence to long-standing conservative charges that Roosevelt and his closest advisers were arrogant men out of touch with the popular will. Militant labor struggles, particularly the wave of over 450 sit-down strikes involving over four hundred thousand workers that rippled through the nation's industrial heartland during 1937, unsettled middle-class elements increasingly prone to believe that the organized labor movement was trying to move too far, too fast. Finally, Roosevelt's perceived status as a "lame duck" incumbent diminished his effectiveness as a power broker on Capitol Hill.

The 1938 election results mirrored the changing political mood. Though Roosevelt tried to improve liberal political fortunes by attacking big business, creating the Temporary National Economic Committee to investigate monopolistic skulduggery, and engaging in gloves-off bargaining such as that detailed in the Prologue of this book, his efforts were only partially successful. House Democrats ended up losing 20 percent of their total strength as the Republicans gained 81 seats. House GOP membership almost doubled to 40 percent of the total (164 seats). Midwestern and Northeastern liberal Democrats were all too prominent on the political casualty lists. In the Senate, the situation was somewhat better. There, the Republicans gained only eight of the thirty-two seats that they contested, and composed only 25 percent of the body's total membership. When Republican votes were added to those of disaffected conservative Democrats, however, it was clear that the Senate, too, was a place where proposals for additional liberal "experiments" would face very rough going indeed.

War scares further exacerbated liberal problems. The 1938 elections were held during the tense period following French and British agreement to carve up Czechoslovakia as a means of achieving "peace in our time" with fascist Germany and Italy. Vocal and articulate minorities of the electorate opposed to such appeasement of totalitarian designs agitated for a program of national military mobilization to forestall further aggression—by force if necessary. A broad range of public opinion was increasingly prone to sanction military-preparedness drives to enable the United States to successfully isolate itself and the Western Hemisphere from the contagion of war if conflict in Europe proved inevitable. Recently introduced techniques of public opinion polling provided eloquent evidence of the trends. By the end of 1937, "69 per cent believed that the United States should enlarge the army, 74 per cent approved a larger navy, and 80 per cent supported an enlarged air force." Following the

Czechoslovak crisis and the 1938 American congressional elections, "the already impressive majorities had grown to 82 per cent for a larger army, 86 per cent for a larger navy, and 90 per cent for a larger air force."[2]

Such overwhelming popular concern with mobilizing the country militarily presented national leaders with political advantages and political problems. On the one hand, Democratic politicians could institute a grand new spending program for military preparedness without suffering many of the slings and arrows that conservatives customarily reserved for federal fiscal policies that produced large amounts of red ink in the national budget. Roosevelt, in short, could run up the deficits necessary to prime the pump of national economic recovery by allowing the military services to place huge orders for aircraft, ships, and tanks. On the other hand, however, the Democrats had to do all they could to ensure that the goods the armed forces wanted were quickly and efficiently produced. This, in turn, meant that the nation's political leaders had to rebuild the bridges linking them with the nation's corporate establishment.

This necessary process of rapprochement between public and private power was made easier by the fact that key elements of America's big-business leadership were also interested in cooperation. The Business Council was the most important forum for such compromise-minded corporate managers, as it had been throughout the New Deal era.

Immediately following the 1938 elections, an important attempt to renew this rapprochement occurred. Late in December, Roosevelt summarily fired Daniel C. Roper as Secretary of Commerce and replaced him with presidential alter ego Harry L. Hopkins. Of all the men that Roosevelt could have selected for this Cabinet post, it seemed that Harry Hopkins was among those least likely to elicit substantial support from businessmen or business organizations. Hopkins' liberal credentials were impeccable. In his youth, he had once briefly registered as a socialist. He had also long been prominently identified with most ambitious efforts of the Roosevelt White House to move toward activism in areas like unemployment relief, emergency public-works jobs programs, and domestic social welfare legislation. To a great many members of the corporate world, appointing Harry Hopkins to Commerce was like deputizing the fox to guard the chickens. Acting upon such assumptions, business organizations including the National Association of Manufacturers and the

Chamber of Commerce moved heaven and earth to block Hopkins' appointment.[3]

W. Averell Harriman, however, had quite different ideas about Hopkins. For over two years, Harriman had been the chairman of the Business Council. During that time, he had accumulated a good deal of political savvy about how Washington worked, and about the ways in which big businessmen could best go about capitalizing on their political investments. By April of 1938, Harriman was advising Business Council members that they could no longer afford to keep confusing political cause with political effect, and that such errors only exacerbated businessmen's problems. As Harriman put it:

> We have assumed that the President and Congress would oppose public trends that we did not like. If they had done so, they would have sacrificed their political careers. They have been blamed by business for putting their careers ahead of public duty, and yet we would not advocate that a firm, in order to perform a patriotic service, should court bankruptcy by, for example, expanding its business in order to relieve unemployment when there is no prospect of the expansion yielding a profit.[4]

Through this political logic, Harriman convinced the Business Council to issue a public statement unanimously welcoming Harry Hopkins to his new Cabinet post as Secretary of Commerce. Congressional conservatives were thunderstruck, and bemused defenders of the free-enterprise faith circulated unfriendly rumors to the effect that the Business Council was being run by a bunch of "tame millionaires" who were hell-bent on helping the radical Hopkins subvert capitalism.[5]

W. Averell Harriman, of course, had quite different purposes in mind. His willingness to support Harry Hopkins was, in fact, a political strategy of no little subtlety and imagination. Franklin D. Roosevelt, be it recalled, was considered to be a lame-duck incumbent. No American President in history had ever defied the unwritten rule against seeking a third term of office. The question for political pundits to ponder, then, was how Roosevelt would go about arranging his political succession.

In the appointment of Hopkins, a goodly number of Washington insiders thought they had found an answer to this absorbing question. One Republican senator from Pennsylvania summed up this perceived wisdom when he observed that "I think that the President saw that the Department of Commerce had been a pretty good route to the Presidency [for Herbert Hoover] and he was training Harry." The fact that Hopkins, like Hoover, had not risen to the status of a presidential contender via elective political office added substance to the senator's shrewd analogy.[6]

Harriman's strategy, then, was to position the Business Council to undertake expanded political activity by giving important support to a man who was being prominently mentioned as Roosevelt's probable political successor. In addition, Harriman and his supporters believed, cultivating Hopkins would in the short run assure them of that rarest of political commodities, access—even if Hopkins, Roosevelt's closest political intimate, failed to win the 1940 presidential sweepstakes. Hopkins, if nothing else, was the best pipeline to the White House around.[7]

The significance of the Business Council's activity was not lost on Hopkins. He was no fuzzy-minded utopian dreamer, but a practical politician in search of allies. Within days of assuming his new post as Secretary of Commerce, newspapers like the *New York Times* prominently featured stories about Hopkins' efforts to increase the advisory stature of the Business Council and to lessen some of the frustrations involved in the political bargaining that one impatient Council member characterized as "a constant hurdle race over wastebaskets."[8]

For the moment, Harriman's strategy appeared to be working. Within a month, however, Hopkins was unexpectedly stricken with a series of illnesses that left him a dying man. After making an energetic start in his new Cabinet post, Hopkins became incapable of fulfilling his official duties—or of performing the unofficial ones necessary to build himself a political empire within the Department of Commerce. A reluctant Roosevelt refused to accept Hopkins' resignation for over a year, but even so Harriman and the Business Council were effectively denied the benefit of Hopkins' entree to the Oval Office. The Hopkins interlude clearly demonstrated, however, that Business Council eminences representing the leading powers of the nation's industrial establishment were willing to come to terms with an expanded federal government and the liberal Democrats who were running it.

Other evidences of this cooperative tendency in Business Council opinion and activity are not difficult to spot. Correspondence among Business Council leaders during the two years following the 1938 elections was littered with references to the need for big businessmen to explore "how management must change its strategies and structures to make sense of new environments in which top managers must function." Nor were more activist managerial initiatives lacking. As early as 1936, for example, Business Council members Henry Dennison, Ralph Flanders, Lincoln Filene, and Morris Leeds (Leeds and Northrup) began to draw up what they called a "constructive businessmen's recovery program." This was aimed at demonstrating that a segment of the nation's corporate leadership could articulate policy proposals relevant to a political environment in which the regulatory and guarantor responsibilities of the federal government had enlarged substantially. To assist them, Henry Dennison went headhunting for technical assistance, soon hiring a young academic economist from Harvard, John Kenneth Galbraith.[9]

With Galbraith's help, the four businessmen pieced together proposals for economic recovery which were published late in 1938 under the title *Toward Full Employment.* In the book, a cautious approach toward the new and unorthodox doctrines of Keynesian economics was made. The tax system should be used to increase consumption and decrease saving. Wealthier savers and businesses should be taxed more, while wage earners should be taxed less. Further, there was no immutable need for federal budgets to be balanced at all times. Instead, Washington should tax less and spend more when the economy was in a slump, and tax more and spend less during booms; using what later became known as countercyclical techniques, it could thus perk up the economy during depressions and damp down the economy during periods of rapidly growing prosperity. Deficits were necessary, then, to help accomplish economic recovery, but they need not be permanent. For, as government used its taxing and spending powers to moderate booms, it could run up revenue surpluses to retire the debts left over from earlier deficits. The federal government's budget could be balanced *over the course of the business cycle,* instead of being balanced each and every fiscal year. The support for short-term deficit financing expressed by the authors of *Toward Full Employment* provided another important indication that a segment of the nation's corporate leadership was seeking a rapprochement with federal power.[10]

Such indications were very attractive to incumbent politicians in the unsettled international climate following the 1938 elections, for 1939 was a year that began inauspiciously and speedily worsened. In

mid-March, Nazi Germany occupied those portions of Czechoslovakia not surrendered to it by the British and French six months
before. Two weeks later, a fascist regime backed by Germany and
Italy came to power in Spain after a bloody three-year civil war.
Early in April, Italian troops invaded and conquered Albania. By the
end of the month, Adolf Hitler was demanding that Poland make
territorial concessions to Germany. It was apparent that war was a
strong possibility.

Any lingering doubts about the imminence of war were removed
on August 23, 1939, when Nazi Germany and Soviet Russia signed
a ten-year nonaggression pact that cleared the way for Hitler to bring
his "new order" to Eastern Europe. A few days later, on September
1, Nazi armies moved, invading Poland along a wide front. Britain
and France thereupon declared war on Germany, which did nothing
to help Poland. On September 17, that unlucky country's fate was
sealed when Russian forces rolled into it from the east. By the end
of the month, the grisly process of Russo-German partition was
complete. Not content with cutting a deal with Hitler, Joseph Stalin
moved to further protect Russia from "imperialist" contagion. In
November, Soviet forces attacked Finland, and shortly afterward
gathered reluctant Lithuania, Latvia, and Estonia into the well-
armed bosom of Mother Russia.

In the midst of such runaway *Machtpolitik,* the Roosevelt administration made its first important efforts to mobilize America for
war. In the process, the pace of the reconciliation between big business and federal power was accelerated.

False Starts and True

Reconciliation, however, was neither immediate nor simple. It was
not a question of businessmen and bureaucrats liking each other, but
of their needing each other; and this process of determining needs in
common took time. Large numbers of business leaders continued to
equate Roosevelt with the devil and refused to cooperate, either
because they believed his experience of presidential power was fast
drawing to a close, or because they considered that, war or no war,
America's economic and strategic interests were not in imminent
risk. For all this entrepreneurial resistance, however, there were men
who understood that a powerful federal government had come to the

United States to stay and that they had to position themselves to cooperate with that power in the event that military emergency did come.

The first halting indication that a convergence of political and corporate interests was occurring appeared in the first week of August, 1939. As Nazi and Soviet leaders arranged the destruction of Poland, Franklin D. Roosevelt announced the creation of a War Resources Board (WRB) to oversee the government's fledgling defense effort. More to the point, he selected Edward Stettinius of U.S. Steel to chair the group, and gave him the responsibility of picking associates to help him. Stettinius promptly selected fellow CEOs Robert E. Wood of Sears, Roebuck; Walter Gifford of AT&T; John L. Pratt, a director of the General Motors Corporation; and Harold G. Moulton of the Brookings Institution, as well as MIT President Karl T. Compton. Shortly thereafter, investment banker John Hancock of Lehman Brothers was added to mollify Bernard Baruch, leader of America's World War I industrial mobilization drive.

The War Resources Board, however, was no quasi-regal gathering of industrial barons with wide-ranging mobilization powers. It was, instead, a trial balloon: a paper agency whose existence enabled Roosevelt to gauge important elements of the political weather. First, how interested were businessmen in cooperation and what sort of terms would they try to set for their assistance? Second, and more important, how tolerant would public opinion be of overt attempts to create a mobilization "partnership" between big business and the executive branch? In appointing Stettinius as chairman of the War Resources Board, Roosevelt signaled that the time had come to begin scouting the political territory, and that he had been listening to the conciliatory messages being routed to him through organizations like the Business Council. The ball was now in the businessmen's court.[11]

Once having picked up the ball, Stettinius began fumbling it. First, he failed to include representatives of organized labor or organized agriculture on the WRB. Instead, he selected four businessmen who had been prominently involved in industrial mobilization during the First World War and the abortive NRA interlude, and went on to leaven the mix with two academicians presumably representing "the public interest." The resulting Board reminded many skeptical New Dealers in and out of Congress of the corporate "self-regulatory" order that they had seen in operation during the first two years of Roosevelt's presidency, and they wanted nothing to do with it.

Stettinius himself did nothing to increase the WRB's credibility with liberals by making public remarks that suggested that some mystical abstraction called "the business community" could be counted upon to oversee efficient mobilization by itself.

Political reaction to such rhetorical excess was immediate. In the weeks following its creation, the War Resources Board became a lightning rod for criticism from both the left and the right. Liberals complained that big business was being given a monopoly over mobilization and that the White House was abdicating power to its corporate enemies. Liberals and conservatives alike made the rafters ring with charges that the WRB was a creature of the House of Morgan, the Du Pont family, or other, less clearly specified corporate cabals.[12]

Alerted by the blast of criticism, Roosevelt promptly backed away from the mobilization agency he had called into being. Early in September, only six weeks after creating it, Roosevelt cheerfully demolished the War Resources Board by announcing that the panel was merely a kind of temporary seminar to allow big businessmen to familiarize themselves with defense issues and that no real industrial war-mobilization effort was planned. By the end of the month, the WRB was dead.

The speedy demise of the War Resources Board demonstrated that the Roosevelt administration had no intention of risking very much of its political capital either to enable businessmen like Stettinius to educate themselves in the nuances of bureaucratic survival, or to undertake massive industrial mobilization for war. Given the political environment in which Roosevelt operated, such calculations made a good deal of sense. The fast-paced Nazi and Soviet conquests that occurred during the fall of 1939 and the winter of 1939–1940 produced widespread moral outrage and support for firming up the nation's hemispheric defenses. But fewer than one in ten Americans believed that the fate of Poland or Finland required an aggressive American response. Instead, there was an overwhelming popular desire to ensure that the United States remained isolated from the Old World's problems.[13]

Such determination was intensified by the unwillingness of either Britain or France to conduct an aggressive land or air war against Nazi Germany. As the Nazis and Soviets were busily rearranging the balance of power in Eastern Europe, the English and French forces maintained a purely defensive posture. This "Sitzkrieg" or "Phony War" stretched on, month after month, into the spring of 1940. To many Americans, it looked as though fascism might have satisfied its expansionist appetite. Throughout this period of deceptive calm, the White House made no move to engage in an ambitious effort at defense planning. America, like Britain and France, waited in a sort of enervating limbo. Meanwhile, Adolf Hitler picked his targets.

The targets were hit. April of 1940 marked the beginning of a harrowing series of military disasters in Western Europe. On April 9, Nazi armies launched surprise attacks on neutral Denmark and Norway. Copenhagen fell in twenty-four hours, Norway within three weeks. On May 10, neutral Holland, Belgium, and Luxembourg were invaded. The Netherlands surrendered within four days. Only two days later, German forces lanced through the Forest of Ardennes and blasted their way into the rear areas of the bewildered French Army. By May 28, Belgian forces capitulated. The very next day, British and French forces began a desperate retreat from the Continent at Dunkirk. Two weeks afterward, Italy entered the war on the German side. Eight days later, the broken French government surrendered and the collaborationist Vichy regime was set up in the regions of the country not already occupied by fascist forces. In the space of ten frightful weeks, Germany, with a late assist from Italy, had conquered Western Europe and imposed a Pax Germanica of awesome and deadly proportions. As German warplanes began streaming across the English Channel in hopes of knocking Britain speedily out of the war, Romanian, Bulgarian, Hungarian, Portuguese, Spanish, and other representatives hastily traveled to Berlin to ingratiate themselves with the leaders of the "Master Race."

The shocking events of the spring of 1940 forced businessmen and bureaucrats alike into new efforts at reconversion planning. Congress, alert to the increasingly strong public demands that Washington ensure an adequate hemispheric defense, began churning out a series of military appropriations bills. Authorization levels doubled from $2 billion to $4 billion as German armored units sliced through France. Within a year, no less than $40 billion had been appropriated, and further gargantuan appropriations were in the works.[14]

The debate, after the spring of 1940, was no longer whether to mobilize for defense. Everyone aside from diehard Roosevelt haters favored that. The problem was how America's mobilization was to be conducted. Trade journals like *Iron Age,* the *Wall Street Journal,* the *Commercial and Financial Chronicle,* and the *Magazine of Wall Street*—which had earlier waxed eloquent that war mobilization would provide golden opportunities for New Dealers to "do away with the profit system and the Constitution in one fell swoop"— muted their voices. Bitter-enders in the metal trades and the Chamber of Commerce continued to grumble that government controls of any type were destructive and that a return to pure and unadulterated laissez faire was essential. Even the National Association of Manufacturers, however, stopped protesting against a large defense program following the fall of France. As business opinion regrouped itself, big-business spokesmen moved to involve themselves more extensively in mobilization planning by intensive interaction with federal officials. Cooperation, however, was hardly automatic, and corporate and government power brokers had to work hard to resolve disagreements.[15]

On the issue of administrative control of the mobilization drive, for instance, compromise-minded corporate leaders such as those composing a majority on the Business Council maintained preferences for an NRA-style solution. One central agency headed by a mobilization czar should be created to transmit government's military requirements to industry. The czar of the mobilization should then work with industrial trade associations to meet these needs. To further ensure efficient cooperation between the public and private sectors, organized business should be exempt from the antitrust laws during the period of emergency. This had been the pattern mobilization had taken during World War I under "Czar" Bernard Baruch of the War Industries Board, which had been called into being by President Woodrow Wilson. It was also the administrative solution recommended to President Roosevelt by the short-lived War Resources Board.[16]

Franklin D. Roosevelt, however, was no Woodrow Wilson. He had tried the czar–trade association route to mobilization once during the NRA period and had found it lacking. If Roosevelt had anything to say about it, the federal government was going to do more than be an umpire in a game in which organized business set the rules. To underline his convictions, Roosevelt buried the never-publicized War Resources Board recommendations deep within his confidential files, and appointed the Secretaries of Agriculture, Commerce, Interior, Labor, Navy, and War to a Council of National Defense on May 28, 1940.

A new committee of Cabinet officers was only part of the story. Cabinet officers could not make tanks or prospect for iron ore. So the actual day-to-day work of mobilization was the province of a National Defense Advisory Commission (NDAC) set up to determine production priorities. Instead of a single czar, Roosevelt appointed the Cabinet committee as a kind of absentee (and inactive) board of directors of the defense effort, and placed operational responsibilities in the hands of the NDAC.

To further ensure that the NDAC would not develop czar-like attributes during the lengthy periods during which the Cabinet "directors" were not in session, Roosevelt went on to staff the Commission with a panel of experts with balkanized powers and responsibilities. Three businessmen (all Business Council members) were placed in charge of the industrial heart of the mobilization drive. William Knudsen of General Motors handled production and Edward Stettinius was in charge of materials and priorities, while transportation was the responsibility of Ralph Budd of the Burlington Railroad. Joining the businessmen on the NDAC, however, were four other people representing nonindustrial constituencies and interests. Sidney Hillman had responsibility for the labor area of the NDAC's work; Leon Henderson, formerly the research director of the Temporary National Economic Committee, handled price stabilization; AAA administrator Chester Davis dealt with agricultural issues; and academician Harriet Elliott was responsible for consumer protection.

The organizational chart of the National Defense Advisory Commission alone looked like a wiring diagram drawn by a mad electrician. But this lack of administrative orderliness missed the point. In setting up the NDAC in the way that he did, Roosevelt—not for the first time in his political career—was sending different messages to different political interest groups. By appointing half his Cabinet as a very largely *pro forma* Council of National Defense, Roosevelt reassured skeptical liberals and antitrusters that the executive branch, not corporate leaders, would maintain final administrative control over mobilization. By officially creating the NDAC as an advisory body, and by creating seven different expertise areas for his Commission, Roosevelt was allowing three business representatives to assume primary responsibility for increasing arms production while, at the same time, hedging these businessmen round with a majority of four other commissioners who were not businessmen. Everyone was being given—or at least promised—something.

Amid all of the resulting organizational complexity, two things were clear. First, Roosevelt was carefully positioning himself to steal his political opponents' thunder by bringing nationally known businessmen to Washington to assume responsibility for mobilizing the private sector for war. Second, this intricate administrative balancing act was part of Roosevelt's decision to make an unprecedented bid for a third term as President of the United States.

He took another step toward a third term on June 20, 1940. Only three weeks after creating a National Defense Advisory Commission that brought compromise-minded big-business leaders into the mobilization drive, Roosevelt named two leading Republican political personalities to his Cabinet. Henry I. Stimson, Herbert Hoover's Secretary of State, became Roosevelt's Secretary of War, and Frank Knox, the GOP's vice-presidential nominee in 1936, became Secretary of the Navy. In one stroke, two nationally known critics of the Roosevelt administration's dilatory mobilization efforts had been appointed to top defense posts. The significance of the Stimson and Knox appointments was obvious to political professionals. From here on, Roosevelt could and did present himself to his party and the electorate as the head of a bipartisan government of national unity which was energetically preparing the nation to defend its vital interests. In mid-July, Roosevelt was triumphantly renominated by the Democrats to be their presidential candidate.

The Willkie Phenomenon

Roosevelt's political finesse won him his party's nomination, but it did nothing to increase big-business support for a third-term candidacy. In fact, leading corporate spokesmen who had backed Roosevelt in 1932 and again in 1936 deserted the President in 1940 over the third-term issue. Prominent among the defectors were key members of the tiny minority of nationally known business executives who were of Jewish descent.

The political experience of General Electric's President Gerard Swope was an indicator of the phenomenon just described. In normal circumstances, Swope's approach to national politics was as cynical as that of a Roman emperor. Swope, in short, played for power, not ideology. By 1940, however, a number of personal circumstances had combined to make Swope fearful of the ideological implications of Roosevelt's effort to achieve an unprecedented third term in office.[17]

Central to this anxiety was Swope's Judaism. Though very few of his corporate peers were aware of it, Swope was the son of upper-class immigrant German Jews who had fully acculturated themselves within America's Gentile culture. Gerard Swope carried the acculturation process one step further by rising to the top of America's thoroughly Gentile, and overwhelmingly Protestant, big-business hierarchy. Despite the fact that Judaism was an almost invisible part of his corporate character, however, Swope greeted the triumph of anti-Semitic fascism in Germany with great concern. The fast-paced Nazi victories of 1939 and 1940 did nothing to lessen Swope's fears and, as the 1940 presidential election approached, Swope privately shared his growing concerns regarding possible political analogies between Adolf Hitler and Franklin D. Roosevelt with David Lilienthal, a prominent New Dealer who, like Swope himself, was of Jewish extraction. During their conversation—held on October 12, 1940—Swope told Lilienthal that

> I'm against the third term, you understand; I told the President so just a week or so before the [Democratic] convention; [I] told him I thought he ought to . . . decline a third term. "Gerard," he said, "you're always too dramatic. There is no danger in a third term so long as there are free elections." That's the [same defense FDR] used the other day in his Philadelphia speech. But there's nothing in that; Hitler had elections [in 1933] too.

In his private journal, Lilienthal, who disagreed with Swope's "third term phobia," nevertheless concluded that Swope's beliefs were those of an "honest, sincere man" as opposed to a "Roosevelt hater."[18]

Had Roosevelt been faced with an inept or ultraconservative Republican challenger in the 1940 election, it is possible that Swope's principled opposition to a third term would not have caused him to abandon Roosevelt. As it was, however, Swope and other corporate political activists like him had excellent reasons to prefer the competition, in the person of Wendell Willkie.

Of all those who have been major-party presidential candidates in this century, Wendell Willkie was one of the two most clearly part of the big-business establishment. (Corporate lawyer John W. Davis, the Democratic candidate in 1924, was the other.) In 1933, Willkie, a conservative Democratic lawyer, became the president of the mammoth Commonwealth and Southern utility corporation. Throughout the domestic reform phase of the New Deal, Willkie assumed a leading role in trying to stop liberal efforts to expand the powers of the Tennessee Valley Authority and to increase the scope of federal activity in energy and natural-resources development projects. During the course of his frequent visits to Washington, Willkie had many occasions to make use of the political entree of corporate leaders like Gerard Swope. Willkie, in fact, arrived at one of his most important compromises with Tennessee Valley Authority head David Lilienthal at a private meeting that their mutual friend Swope arranged for them at a Washington hotel early in 1939.[19]

Wendell Willkie, then, was a known quantity to big businessmen such as those who made up the leadership of the Business Council. Like them, Willkie understood that American corporations no longer could act as if Washington did not exist, and he realized that the chief executive officers of large corporations had to stay abreast of power relationships in the nation's capital in order to protect their firms' economic and political interests. Along with General Electric's Gerard Swope, the Union Pacific Railroad's W. Averell Harriman, and U.S. Steel's Edward Stettinius, Wendell Willkie was one of that small group of prominent capitalists who had managed to keep a big-business presence alive in Washington during the worst periods of tension between America's political and economic leaderships. Further, he was an articulate business internationalist who supported defense mobilization—presumably along more "cooperative" lines than any Franklin D. Roosevelt had yet essayed.

For these reasons, Willkie's candidacy was generally greeted with enthusiasm in "enlightened" entrepreneurial circles. GE's Chairman Owen Young, for example, referred to Willkie as one of the "forward-looking businessmen" that Young wanted to see in public office. Business Council Chairman Harriman also admired Willkie, and contributed heavily to his campaign. (No neophyte at politics, Harriman hedged his bet by also giving substantial sums to Roosevelt.) *Fortune* magazine boomed Willkie's presidential bid. Willkie even engaged the loyalty of hitherto reactionary businessmen like Alfred Sloan of General Motors. In August of 1940 for example, Sloan's right-hand man, GM Vice-President Donaldson Brown, wrote that Willkie gave "too much of a blanket approval to Social Security," but, for all that, promised more efficient and businesslike leadership than FDR had been able to provide. Furthermore, Brown made what was, for a General Motors executive, a remarkable admission about the economy. Responding to a friend's complaint that

Willkie was merely a turncoat Democrat who looked at free enterprise as "merely a method of organization and not a fundamental [i.e., unchallengeable and unchangeable] concept," Brown replied: "Isn't this [dynamic view of capitalism] actually a concept which we have to accept?" Even General Motors, it seemed, had come a long way from the heady days of the NRA and the National Labor Board, a period when it had not been unusual for big businessmen to excoriate Roosevelt for all manner of radical skulduggery.[20]

Despite all the support he received from big-business leaders, however, Wendell Willkie's presidential effort failed. Businessmen then had to make their peace with the continuing reality of Franklin D. Roosevelt's presidency.

That reality was not all that easy for businessmen to accept. Before the 1940 elections, corporate leaders could at least hope that Roosevelt would be unsuccessful in his efforts to sell himself as the experienced leader needed now, more than ever, to pilot the nation through troubled times. After November of 1940, however, it was clear that military mobilization would remain an issue and that "reform" was not going to magically disappear from the political lexicon of Washington.

Bargaining Begins in Earnest

Following Roosevelt's triumphant reelection, corporate-governmental bargaining regarding the shape and direction of the mobilization program began in earnest. From November of 1940 until the anxiety-filled weeks immediately after the Japanese attack on Pearl Harbor, big-business leaders engaged in complex bureaucratic infighting with the Democratic regime.

The business leaders' defense-related presence in Washington— like the specific bargains that they sought to strike with federal power —was motivated by fear. As corporate managers like William Knudsen and Edward Stettinius realized, FDR was more than capable of proceeding on his own in the event that business cooperation in the mobilization drive was not forthcoming. The results of the 1936 election and its aftermath had proved that to even the most skeptical of entrepreneurial observers. Understanding that a "strike of capital" against Roosevelt was a futile exercise which could only undermine their own already-weakened popular credibility and clout, Stettinius, Knudsen, and the Business Council members they recruited to assist them on the NDAC and its successor organizations tried to lead the mobilization drive in directions that would best protect corporate interests. In the process, they formulated four types of demands on their political opposite numbers—in essence, the price tag for big business cooperation with the prewar defense effort.

First, nothing about the defense program should forward "socialism." In particular, Washington should not use the cloak of mobilization to unilaterally construct or operate industrial facilities to produce goods that would in any important way compete with those being offered or developed by private firms.

Second, defense mobilization should take place in a gradual enough fashion that United States corporations could continue their production of civilian commodities at normal or near-normal peacetime levels as they geared up for military production.

Third, federal leaders should use their taxing powers to provide large-scale mobilization incentives for investors and producers in the private sector. In particular, Washington should avoid passing excess (or "windfall") profits taxes; should not seek legislation to limit the profit margins of companies active in defense production; should allow war contracts to be drawn up on a "cost-plus" basis; and should change the tax code to create "accelerated depreciation allowances" that would allow businessmen to write off the total cost of their defense-related investments in plant and equipment at a very fast rate.

Fourth, though Washington should use all the taxation incentives necessary to enable private capital and capitalists to finance (and profit from) the production of military hardware, the federal government should also step in as a financial guarantor of last resort to provide credit or credit guarantees in those especially risky or politically sensitive industrial areas where private capital refused to tread. Specifically, the Reconstruction Finance Corporation should underwrite the massive investments necessary to rapidly increase the production of strategic commodities.

The first guarantee that the business leaders demanded of Roosevelt may have appeared farfetched to outside observers, but it was not so to businessmen. "Socialism" was a smear corporate leaders had directed at the New Deal and its works for so long that a goodly number of them had almost come to believe it. Even Washington habitués like financier John Hancock and Edward Stettinius could exchange private correspondence as late as October of 1939 that contained worried speculations regarding the possible tendencies of liberal New Dealers to use defense planning "as a basis for pushing the idea of permanent industrial controls" and as a means of establishing new state-owned and -operated enterprises, particularly in the area of energy generation. As it happened, there were more than a few liberal Democrats and closet socialists scattered through the New Deal agencies in the war years who *did* wish to use the mobilization drive to develop radical programs. These men, however, were in no position to exercise any but the most tangential influence in Congress or the executive branch in the early years of the mobilization. Roosevelt, always the realist, did not hesitate to eschew socialism as an aim of his third-term administration. Had he chosen a more romantic or ideological alternative, Congress, which had successfully contained all of the President's earlier efforts to forward his pet power projects like the St. Lawrence Seaway and the Passamoquoddy tidal-power scheme, would have run right over Roosevelt. An antisocialist guarantee, then, was an extremely easy one for the Democratic party leadership to make.[21]

The second guarantee, however, proved more stress-inducing and complicated. Big-business leaders, in effect, wanted America's military mobilization during the period after the 1940 elections to proceed along the comparatively leisurely lines that had earlier been followed before and after America's long-delayed entry into the First World War. World War II, in this view of the matter, would likely be a repeat of World War I. America eventually might have to involve itself in the conflict, but it would have more than sufficient time to do so in a way that did not heighten corporate difficulties.

Here some history is in order. Throughout Woodrow Wilson's abortive great crusade, American corporations never fully mobilized themselves for war. Instead, production in many strategic industries was initially maintained at normal peacetime levels. Military requirements were then met in an interstitial or "added-on" fashion. By the time the United States declared war against Germany in April of 1917, a gradual shift to greater and greater military production was taking place. Industrialists, however, generally sought to organize the shift in ways that allowed them to cut into their civilian production and markets to the least possible extent. General Motors, Ford, and other American automobile companies, to take but one example, *never* stopped manufacturing civilian passenger vehicles at *any* point during the war. Instead, they reluctantly retooled only a part of their total productive apparatus to build the tanks and other complex machinery necessary for modern technological war. So gradual was this process in the nation's industrial economy that no American-built tanks, airplanes, or heavy-artillery pieces were successfully delivered to the fighting fronts during the eighteen months that the United States was an active combatant.[22]

Corporate reluctance to mobilize for war either quickly or completely during the 1917–1918 period had a strong economic logic. A similar logic applied—and even more strongly—in the depressed economic circumstances of 1940–1941. Throughout the 1930's, the vast majority of American corporations, large and small, had operated in more or less severely restricted markets, and had fought to maintain their market shares in a diminished economy. In addition, most major American corporations were not producing at anything even close to their full capacity in the 1940–1941 period. U.S. Steel, General Electric, and other giant firms possessed large reserves of idle plant and equipment, reserves whose very existence ate into their already relatively low profits.

Both of these characteristics of entrepreneurial life in Depression-era America led businessmen to be extremely leery of either alienating their established civilian customers by restricting their output of nonmilitary items, of making large investments to boost their overall productive capacity beyond the levels that might be profitable in a postmobilization civilian economy. As Bruce Catton puts it:

> A grim specter haunted [big businessmen's] minds in [the period from the outbreak of World War II in Europe until Pearl Harbor] . . . the specter of going back, some day, to ordinary peacetime pursuits and finding the nation [and, more particularly, themselves] equipped with more productive capacity than could profitably be employed. This specter was back of the resistance to the expansion of basic capacity, back of the resistance to a [full-mobilization] defense program . . . that would make such expansion unavoidable. The nation had just come through a decade in which men were painfully confused and irritated by the fact that the mere ability to produce more than was needed somehow seemed to mean that they had to get along with less than was needed. A too ardent defense program . . . which expanded production all along the line, with no concern whatever for the way it might have to be used after the war—was not to be embraced lightly.[23]

Facing such dangers, American businessmen refused to place their already existent civilian markets at risk or to expand their basic industrial capacity very materially. As 1940 stretched into 1941, federal policymakers sought to meet the resulting problems by making deals on the third and fourth elements of the corporate agenda: taxation and credit guarantees.

Taxation is an abstruse and involved area. Suffice it to say here that the two-year period preceding Pearl Harbor witnessed a carefully orchestrated effort on the part of the nation's business leadership to persuade federal leaders to structure the national tax system in a way that would allow business to retain as much of its mobilization-related profits as possible.

Corporate efforts to bend the tax codes to business purposes were made easier by the fact that the Roosevelt White House was fast running out of negotiating room. Public clamor for accelerated defense production made delays politically dangerous—even if these delays were occasioned by attempts to keep businessmen's hands as far away from the public purse as possible.

Recognizing that continued defense-production delays could only hurt them, Roosevelt and his top aides lent their assistance to businessmen and their conservative allies on Capitol Hill. Late in 1940, a series of tax bills was rushed through Congress that promised corporate cooperation with defense efforts would prove to be very profitable indeed. The White House helped frustrate the efforts of congressional liberals to pass an excess-profits bill that would tax back a large portion of the war-induced windfall profits accruing to corporations. An excess-profits bill finally became law, but it was shot full of so many special privileges and exemptions that it did very little to offend corporate sensibilities. Roosevelt also helped turn back another congressional effort to limit profit margins—especially in key industries including aviation and shipbuilding. Again, a law was eventually passed. The Roosevelt White House, however, effectively gutted the legislation by adding riders to the bill which gave mobilization officials administrative discretion to periodically "renegotiate" defense contracts in such a fashion that profit margins were calculated as a percentage of contract costs. These cost figures, in turn, were juggled so as to keep corporate returns high enough to avoid business criticism. A Business Council report noted several years later, "Business is extremely fortunate in the men who now direct the work of these [Renegotiation] Boards and control their policies." Cooperation with such men had allowed business to avoid "more drastic measures" aimed at "taking the profit out of war."[24]

Another key element in this business-government accommodation involved an accelerated depreciation provision incorporated into a tax bill passed by Congress in October of 1940. A depreciation allowance is what a firm pays to itself in order to have capital available to replace its existing productive assets as they depreciate in value—as they wear out or become technologically outmoded. The depreciation allowance may be deducted from the firm's taxable income, thus decreasing its taxes.

Under the terms of the tax bill, all businessmen who invested in defense facilities were allowed to depreciate them fully in only a very few years. Companies "could write off annually 20 per cent or more of the costs of the [defense] facilities . . . in contrast to the standard [nondefense] depreciation rates of 5 per cent for buildings and 10 per cent for equipment allowed by the Bureau of Internal Revenue." A firm, in short, could build an airplane plant for $10 million, stock it with an additional $10 million worth of equipment, and fully recover the costs in five years or less—instead of the normal twenty years for buildings and ten years for equipment. Businessmen who qualified for the accelerated depreciation program by building plants "primarily" concerned with defense production were issued certificates testifying to their eligibility for tax largesse.

Not all firms benefitted from tax reductions in such a wholesale fashion as that detailed above. Still, Washington issued over $5 billion worth of accelerated depreciation certificates during the war, and the program ended up costing the U.S. Treasury approximately $440 million in forgone revenues.[25]

Renegotiation and accelerated depreciation, then, instituted a cost-plus approach to war production. Businessmen were enticed into the defense market by special taxation incentives, and then kept in that market by periodic contract renegotiations which guaranteed the overwhelming majority of them against losses, no matter how unlucky, improvident, or inept they might be as entrepreneurs. When businessmen met cost problems that they had failed to anticipate, federal mobilization officials proved more than willing to revise their cost estimates upward to cover these additional costs and to guarantee profits. This process was hardly marketplace capitalism pure and simple. Businessmen and bureaucrats, however, were hardly anxious to insist upon theoretical niceties in a period of steadily worsening international emergency. As Secretary of War

Stimson put it in a memorable phrase: "If you are going to . . . go to war . . . in a capitalist country, you have to let business make money out of the process or business won't work." In 1940 and 1941, the Roosevelt administration did even more: it *guaranteed* that corporations would profit from mobilization.[26]

Washington, as it turned out, went even further. In addition to guaranteeing profits by means of the tax code and renegotiation, it used its guarantor-of-last-resort powers to provide credit for warplant construction and to actually build plants that private businessmen then used to produce certain "risky" commodities.

Here again, a brief note of explanation is in order. Accelerated depreciation and renegotiation were all very well as enticements for businessmen to enter the market to either produce types of goods for which there was a demonstrated peacetime civilian demand, or build plants that could easily be converted to such productive uses after the war emergency had passed. Such taxation and contracting incentives, however, were of relatively little use in persuading private corporations to build factories to produce items that could *not* be profitably marketed in normal peacetime conditions.

The entrepreneurial risk factor was particularly relevant to the production of crucial defense items such as airplanes and aviation parts, aluminum, magnesium, aviation fuel, and synthetic rubber. An automobile company, for example, could expand its productive capacity to build, say, armored cars, and plan on being able to convert that capacity to make civilian passenger automobiles or heavy trucks in peacetime—goods for which there was a traditional and comparatively well understood market demand. An aircraft-manufacturing company, however, was in a very different position. The airplanes that it manufactured were not "traditional" goods that enjoyed a broad, deep, or even long-standing market. They were, instead, luxury items with little or no demonstrated mass market potential.

To make the point clearer, two statistics are useful. In 1940, the entire American aircraft industry employed fewer people than the nation's candy and confectionary firms. That same year, United States aviation companies produced a total of just over three thousand combat and large transport aircraft—twenty-three hundred of these for foreign buyers. In May of 1940, however, as Nazi armies —and the Nazi Luftwaffe—advanced through Western Europe, President Roosevelt appeared before Congress to announce his desire to have air power become one of the centerpieces of America's defense effort. Roosevelt wanted, he said, "to see this nation geared up to the ability to turn out at least 50,000 planes a year."[27]

Presidential speeches like this were all very well. No aircraft manufacturer in his right mind, however, was going to increase his production capacity by a minimum of almost twenty times without massive government assistance.

Through the instrumentality of the Reconstruction Finance Corporation, such assistance was provided. Since its creation in 1932, the RFC had served as a last-ditch source of credit for banks, railroads, and other businesses that had been denied access to traditional private-sector capital markets. If, say, private banks thought an investment was too risky to make, or if the stock and bond markets were too skittish, the RFC would often enter the picture as a lender or financial guarantor of last resort.

Under the terms of legislation passed late in 1940, the Reconstruction Finance Corporation broadened the scope of its guarantor role. The RFC was allowed to increase its direct investments in particularly risky defense-related industries such as aircraft manufacturing, and it did so with a will. By 1945, as things turned out, the RFC accounted for one third of the $25 billion that was invested in American defense-production facilities.

The biggest part of the money that the RFC spent (approximately $7 billion of the $8.3 billion total) was not simply loaned to private firms. Instead, an RFC affiliate, the Defense Plant Corporation (DPC) was created in August of 1940 to hire corporations to build defense plants. Once built, the plants were leased to industry for the duration of the war. Lease fees were quite often nominal. Once the wartime emergency passed, DPC sold to industry those plants that industry wanted—often at bargain-basement prices. Other facilities —those that private industry did not want—were mothballed. So when all else failed, federal officials, in addition to guaranteeing profits and holding out the attraction of tax benefits, paid private businessmen to build plants, rented those same facilities to businessmen (often, indeed, the same businessmen) at very low rates, and then went on to sell the plants back to the private sector at moderate to very low prices. Here was "state capitalism" with a vengeance, using many of the devices that are seen as inventions of "Japan, Incorporated," by contemporary Americans.

The avalanche of profit and taxation guarantees, production subsidies, and credit guarantees made war capitalism a relatively risk-free proposition. American capitalists, who, like entrepreneurs everywhere, know a sure thing when they see one, responded marvelously. There was little reason to hold back when profit-and-loss worries, credit concerns, and other nagging uncertainties of everyday business operations were effectively removed from the picture. By the middle of 1941, American corporations were eagerly gearing up for defense. Planes, tanks, and ships began flowing in huge and ever-increasing numbers from the factories and workshops of the nation. Money just as regularly flowed from the public treasury to speed the process along. The mammoth federal public-works project called World War II had come to America with a vengeance. The RFC's Defense Plant Corporation alone was "responsible for adding more than 10 per cent to the nation's wartime productive capacity." An additional 40 percent, Gerald T. White estimates, was accounted for by federal accelerated-depreciation largesse. Half of the "production miracle" of a nation that came to pride itself, quite rightly, on being the Arsenal of Democracy, was made possible by simply taking most of the risk out of corporate life. Few businessmen lamented the situation.[28]

Pearl Harbor and Beyond

The Japanese attack on Pearl Harbor on December 7, 1941, relegated a good deal of the technical bargaining described here to the deep background of public concern. The attack, likewise, altered the tone of corporate response to mobilization. Businessmen's worries regarding the overexpansion of productive potential very largely ceased, and the nation's political, military, and industrial leaders got down to the more essential business of preserving the country's existence. The financial deals cut by the Roosevelt administration in 1940 and 1941, however, went a very long way toward ensuring that businessmen would profit from their patriotism.

It is not correct, however, to assume that business—or even big business—triumphed as a result of America's war mobilization. Mobilization, as we have seen, did increase the stature and influence of big businessmen in Washington policy and planning councils. This could hardly have been otherwise. Somebody, after all, had to build the complex weapons of modern war, and the nation's corporate establishment contained the single largest conglomeration of technical and managerial skills that America possessed. To have failed to include businessmen in the mobilization would have been to guarantee catastrophe.

For all this, the Roosevelt administration did not easily hand over power or authority to business leaders during the period of war emergency. Instead, it engaged in a struggle, full of complex bureaucratic infighting, aimed at containing the spread of corporate influence within government.

The process began in January of 1941, almost a year before Pearl Harbor. While he was handing out taxation, profit, and credit incentives wholesale, Roosevelt appeared to yield to long-standing big-business urgings for the appointment of a single all-powerful czar for war mobilization by abolishing the balkanized National Defense Advisory Commission and replacing it with an Office of Production Management (OPM) headed by William Knudsen of General Motors.

Appearances, as so often in Roosevelt's bureaucratic jugglings, were deceptive. "The creation of the Office of Production Management," journalist I. F. Stone shrewdly noted at the time,

> was one of those feats of sleight-of-hand of which Mr. Roosevelt is a master. No nursemaid could have distributed a box of candy among a crowd of squalling children more skillfully.
>
> Mr. Knudsen was made Director General of the Office of Production Management, an imposing title that seemed to make the General Motors man boss of defense. But Sidney Hillman was made his coequal in power, though with a title a shade less important, Associate Director General. The army and navy, which feared subordination to civilian authority, were given a voice in the OPM. Secretary of War Stimson and Secretary of the Navy Knox were made "members" of the Office of Production Management.
>
> This still left final power in the hands of the President. If Mr. Knudsen and Mr. Hillman . . . disagreed, the White House was the only court of appeal. No real change in power had taken place.[29]

To further limit OPM's power, Roosevelt went on to create a bevy of other bureaucratic fiefdoms around the OPM to deal with price-control, agricultural, labor, and consumer matters. The big businessmen in the OPM, Business Council members all—Knudsen, Stettinius, John D. Biggers (Libbey-Owens-Ford Glass), and Donald Nelson (Sears, Roebuck)—were, once again, ringed by representatives of opposing interest groups, as they had been during the NDAC period. Meanwhile, Roosevelt retained his dominant role as a mediator and broker.

Big-business leaders, however, maintained their hopes that FDR would, finally, centralize war production powers—and place most of them squarely in business' hands. William L. Batt, who took W. Averell Harriman's place as Business Council chairman, wrote to Edward Stettinius in May of 1940 that the Council "could form the nucleus for industrial cooperation and could be used as the principal instrumentality for drafting the services of important representatives of management" to direct the war mobilization drive.[30]

By August of 1941, the first step in this process again briefly appeared to have been taken when Business Council member Donald Nelson was appointed to head a short-lived Supply Priorities and Allocations Board (SPAB) created to resolve the growing number of squabbles between the military services and the OPM regarding which war production goals should have priority over others. Again, however, Roosevelt played the politics of fragmentation. Nelson's authority was undermined by another in a dizzying sequence of bureaucratic balkanizations. In all the confusion, the single term "priorities" stood out. Somebody, sometime would have to be given authority to negotiate the requirements of the armed services, the civilian economy, and our Allies-to-be.[31]

The time for decisive action arrived soon. Just over five months after the SPAB's birth, America's tremendous defeat at Pearl Harbor impelled the Roosevelt administration to undertake a further, and considerably more genuine, centralization of defense production authority. Late in January of 1942, the comic opera complexities of the OPM and the SPAB were abolished forever. In their place the War Production Board (WPB) was created. Like the SPAB before it, the WPB was headed by Donald Nelson. In his new post as War Production Board chairman, however, Nelson reported directly to the President and enjoyed a large measure of public notice and bureaucratic wallop. Japanese bombs had alerted everyone to the fact that somebody had to make the decisions necessary to institute an all-out mobilization for war, and Roosevelt had appointed Nelson to be that person. Roosevelt's choice, given the scope of the job the WPB had in front of it, was logical enough. Sears, Roebuck's nationwide production, allocation, and sales operations demanded the same sort of synthetic abilities to set priorities, set and oversee contracts, and set production and delivery schedules that Nelson had already demonstrated.[32]

With the appointment of Donald Nelson, a big businessman was back in the driver's seat regarding defense for the first time since the ill-fated War Resources Board headed by Edward Stettinius had self-destructed almost two and a half years before. Interested parties in Congress and the press greeted Nelson as the "mobilization czar" they had long been awaiting. Even so, the political fates were little kinder to Nelson than they had earlier been to Stettinius or the ill-used William Knudsen.

Nelson started out well enough. Gathering fellow Business Council leaders like William Batt (SKF Industries), Sidney J. Weinberg (Goldman, Sachs), and Charles Edward Wilson (Gerard Swope's successor at General Electric) around him, Nelson took steps that clearly illustrated his agency's power. In February of 1942, the interminable debate over full or partial mobilization in the auto industry was resolved by the issuance of an order banning the companies from building any more civilian passenger cars "for the duration" of the war. Directives regarding rubber tires and other strategic commodities were handed down. By June, the first nationally coordinated allocation of a broad range of raw materials began. By November of 1942, businessmen and bureaucrats on loan to the War Production Board instituted a Controlled Materials Plan, closely modeled upon distribution and forecasting procedures developed earlier by General Motors and other large corporations, to govern the apportioning of steel, aluminum, copper, and other crucial materials and components for a myriad of military uses.[33]

In the midst of such furious activity, however, Donald Nelson made a crucial mistake that sapped his ability to lead and eventually destroyed his claim to czarlike authority. Nelson's mistake was not rhetorical—as his predecessor Edward Stettinius' had been. Instead, it was organizational. Nelson failed to exercise effective administrative control over the mobilization efforts of the armed services—the U.S. Army and Navy.

When Donald Nelson assumed the chairmanship of the War Production Board, a business leader had finally, after years of piecemeal centralization and pseudo-centralization, been given power commensurate with his mobilization responsibilities. Nelson's supporters—among whom were numbered a good many of the activists on the Business Council—assumed that one of his first moves would be to inform the Army and Navy that they could no longer enter into contracts for any military items without his—Nelson's—consent. This is a basic tenet of executive authority. The leader must make sure that his followers or bureaucratic underlings report to him regularly and refer all proposed actions to him for a final decision. Had Nelson insisted upon primacy over military procurement decisions, his czar status would have been undeniable. Every time the generals or admirals wanted something, they would have had to obtain Nelson's and the War Production Board's agreement. No agreement—no guns, ships, or tanks.

Nelson, unfortunately, hesitated to assume this final authority—and responsibility—regarding military procurement. As his sympathetic biographer, Bruce Catton, summarizes:

> [Nelson hesitated] to make himself the man who signed the contracts and placed the initial orders with industry. [For he believed that the effect of this authority] would be to cut himself in on the making of purely military decisions, for which he had no stomach. The man who signs the contracts for military goods can be, in the long run, the man who determines that weapon A gets built ahead of weapon B, that weapon C does not get made at all, and that weapon D is more to be desired than weapon E. For better or for worse, Nelson voted to leave procurement in military hands and to exert control through coordination and policy-setting rather than through outright expropriation [of the military leadership's right to place final arms orders largely independently of the War Production Board].[34]

Nelson, in short, did not want to take a large share of the final responsibility for deciding which weapons got built and which did not. Given that the American military then looked as if it was in very sorry shape indeed, Nelson's decision to leave the much-maligned generals and admirals and the civilians in the War Department in charge—rather than humiliating them publicly by taking over—made a good deal of short-term public relations sense. It did not, however, make very much long-term administrative sense.

Nor did it take Nelson and his supporters long to realize this fact. The bureaucratic chickens that they had let out of the nest "came home to roost by flocks and droves and myriads" within months. The War Department and the Army and Navy chiefs, Catton continues,

> retaining the power to buy the munitions [they needed without getting prior War Production Board agreement] . . . promptly translated that power into an assertion, endlessly repeated, of [their] primary right to say how the munitions should be produced and how the civilian

economy should be operated; and there was no final way to deny that assertion because any agency [like the armed forces] that spends sixty-odd billions of dollars a year in the American market is going to have a good deal to say about how the market operates, whether it technically ought to have such a right or not. The Army bought enormous quantities of heavy goods . . . and because the Army [not the War Production Board] was actually placing the orders for these items, and negotiating with the manufacturers who were to produce them, and not merely notifying a civilian agency that it had to have them [and letting that agency, the War Production Board, do the actual ordering and negotiating], the Army was inevitably directly concerned with such matters as the ultimate supply of steel, the uses to which the steel was put, the way in which it was divided up, and the decisions that were made on other claims for part of the steel [e.g., allocation decisions within the defense market and between the civilian and military sectors of the economy].[35]

The division of authority that Donald Nelson all too readily agreed to at the start of his WPB chairmanship, then, effectively guaranteed that the mobilization activities of the War Production Board would involve "an endless series of head-on collisions" with the military services and their war production activities.[36]

As the collisions increased in number and severity throughout 1942, Donald Nelson and his business and bureaucratic coworkers in the War Production Board lost as many battles as they won. They also lost the backing of the White House. President Roosevelt, no stranger to bureaucratic infighting, wanted Nelson to formulate workable compromises with the armed-forces chiefs that would keep disagreements between the services and the War Production Board from undermining Roosevelt's political prospects. Nelson, however, could not comply with Roosevelt's desires. For in failing to assert clearly his primacy over the military services at the very start of his tenure as mobilization chief, Nelson had opened a Pandora's box that he could not close. Once they were allowed to set and fulfill war production priorities almost independently of the War Production Board, the generals and admirals discovered—as generals and admirals had often discovered before them—that they were short of everything, and required massive supplies of all strategic commodities to do even a minimal job of achieving their military goals.

As military demands for strategic materials and parts intensified, Donald Nelson's star as war mobilization czar steadily dimmed.

Roosevelt, whose Democrats faced stiff Republican challenges in the congressional elections of 1942, cast around for a means of repudiating Nelson without appearing to repudiate his own previous conduct of the mobilization effort. On October 3, 1942, a way was found. As so often before, Roosevelt downgraded Nelson—and protected himself—by creating another layer of bureaucracy. In this instance, Roosevelt appointed longtime political operator and former Democratic senator James F. Byrnes of South Carolina to occupy a newly created position as war mobilization chief. Byrnes, who operated directly out of the White House, was thereby made superior to Nelson and the War Production Board. The mobilization disagreements that Nelson had failed to umpire either quietly or successfully would, in future, be resolved by a "super-umpire" who had spent most of his adult life cutting political deals in the nation's capital. Nelson stayed on in Washington for another year, watching his authority constantly diminish in scope. From November of 1942 on, however, ultimate authority regarding war mobilization was once more in the hands of the politicians manning the Roosevelt White House. World War II, like the Great Depression, was not an emergency that businessmen dealt with according to their own lights. It was, instead, an exercise in organization and planning in which corporate leaders and their opposite numbers in government engaged in in an often symbiotic relationship. Learning the nuances of such a relationship, as Donald Nelson, William Knudsen, Edward Stettinius, and scores of other big businessmen like them learned in Washington during the war, took time.[37]

Experience Begins to Count

By the end of 1942, American big-business leaders had had just over three years of experience with big government in a period of wartime emergency. Military mobilization, for all its fits, starts, and frustrations, was a new experience for many members of the nation's big-business establishment, one notably and even refreshingly different from that of the Depression emergency that had preceded it. The Depression, for example, had induced or exacerbated disagreements, sometimes violent, concerning the relative powers and privileges which were or should be enjoyed by various organized interest groups within America's industrial society. The wartime emergency, however, deflected many, if not all, of these internal antagonisms onto a common set of external national enemies. Big businessmen, who had lost much in terms of popular status and political power during the Depression, regained a good deal of that status, and a lesser amount of that political power, during the war.[38]

The wartime emergency also had a second, even more important, effect. It ended the Great Depression. In so doing, the war, unlike the Depression before it, allowed business and government leaders to cooperate more effectively with each other than they had in the recent past. Cooperation between large corporations and the state became fundamentally a matter of dividing gains rather one than of apportioning losses. Whereas big-business and government leaders had often seen themselves as players in a zero-sum game during the Depression—a game in which one side's losses were the other side's gains—war produced a very different situation. In the new game, both sides could win, and often did. The federal government could grow in order to wage war. The private sector, for its part, could profit handsomely from the conflict. Big businessmen had good reason to be in Washington during the years analyzed here, and government leaders had equally good reason to want them there.

The growth of a big-business presence in the nation's capital, then, was a necessary element of the huge public works project known as World War II. The extent of this presence can be gauged by examining the makeup of a single Business Council meeting—one held November 14–16, 1941, on the eve of Pearl Harbor. The following thirteen Business Council members gave a symposium for their corporate peers on the nature of the mobilization drive:

William Batt	Business Council chairman and director of the Materials Division, PM; later one of Donald Nelson's assistants at WPB
John D. Biggers	Special minister to the United Kingdom for War Production and Supply
William Clayton	Deputy administrator, Federal Loan Agency; later Assistant Secretary of State and Undersecretary of State for Economic Affairs

William Knudsen	Director, OPM; later consultant to the Army and the WPM
Donald M. Nelson	Executive director, SPAB; later chairman, WPB
Philip D. Reed	Deputy director, Materials Division, OPM
Edward R. Stettinius, Jr.	Lend-Lease administrator; later Secretary of State
Sidney J. Weinberg	Bureau of Industrial Advisory Committees, OPM
Walter C. Teagle	Member, National Defense Mediation Board
George H. Mead	Alternate, National Defense Mediation Board
Rolland J. Hamilton	Alternate, National Defense Mediation Board
Roger D. Lapham	Member, National Defense Mediation Board
Vannevar Bush	Director, Office of Scientific Research and Development (the institutional midwife of the Manhattan Project)[39]

Men like these, almost invisible to the general public, were essential to American participation in the Second World War. Along with their partners in the federal bureaucracy, they made "Arsenal of Democracy" more than an empty phrase. During their wartime activity in Washington, business leaders like W. Averell Harriman and Edward Stettinius, joined by a new, younger set of men who rose to positions of executive power in a decade and a half of Depression and wartime emergency, adjusted to a vastly expanded federal government and positioned themselves to respond creatively to future challenges. As we shall see in the following chapter, their activities were crowned with a good deal of success.

3

BUSINESS POLITICIANS AND THE ACCEPTANCE OF AN ACTIVIST STATE

Reasons for Optimism

AMERICAN BIG BUSINESSMEN had cause for good cheer as the nation's war production drive moved into high gear in 1942 and 1943. Cost-plus contracting, RFC plant construction, and the accompanying elements of risk-free war capitalism poured a river of federal dollars into parched corporate treasuries. The status of businessmen began to rise again as Washington officials scurried about recruiting business experts to perform the thousands of specialized administrative and production tasks made necessary by the war. President Roosevelt's oft-repeated intention to restructure his administration along national unity lines increased the entree and influence of articulate leaders of large corporations in policy councils.

Large corporations and their leaders profited from war mobilization in another way. The military services, anxious to get military goods produced and delivered, used the broad discretionary powers given to them by civilians like Donald Nelson to place most of their orders with the nation's biggest industrial firms. This massive armed forces purchasing helped produce a profound change in the structure of America's economy. As one historian of the period observes:

> In 1940, when the defense program began, approximately 175,000 [small to medium-sized companies] were providing some 70 per cent of the manufacturing output of the United States, and one hundred [large] companies produced the remaining 30 per cent. By March, 1943, even though twice as much [output] was being produced, that

ratio had been reversed. The one hundred companies previously holding only 30 per cent now held 70 per cent of war and civilian contracts,
and were still gaining in proportion to the others. . . . The great bulk
of federal funds expended on new industrial construction had [also]
gone to the privileged one hundred companies.[1]

The spectacular profitability of war mobilization also served to
remind big-business leaders of the usefulness of institutions that enabled them to consult with the federal officials responsible for doling
out the dollars. Chief among these forums for discussion, influence
peddling, and mutual recruitment was the Business Council.

As full-scale war mobilization began in the aftermath of Pearl
Harbor, Business Council members appeared to be prone toward an
optimism that bordered on self-congratulation. As early as January
30, 1942, for example, Council minutes included the following paean
to the organization's existence:

We are proud of the fact that more than 35 of the men who have been
or are members of this small group have been called to serve their
Government in positions of great responsibility. The Nelsons, Harrimans, Batts, and Claytons and many others of similar serviceability
may be said in large part to owe their present positions of trust to their
post-graduate education at the Department of Commerce.[2]

It was as if the big businessmen of the Business Council believed
that Washington had finally become a place where they could operate simply and expeditiously once again—and where a profitable
patriotism would automatically ameliorate all of the wrenching political struggles of the preceding ten years.

If business leaders such as those who composed the elite membership of the Business Council supposed that war would solve their
problems for them, they soon learned otherwise. Two major political
issues continued to divide corporate and political leaders throughout
the war. The first of these was wartime labor policy, over which
serious frictions developed almost immediately. The second, longer-
term issue concerned the directions that postwar reconversion planning should take—planning aimed at avoiding a renewal of the
Depression once the Axis powers were defeated. Both issues bedeviled the corporate consciousness throughout the war, and both
forced the activists of the Business Council to continue their search
for new ways of adapting themselves to the uncomfortable realities
of federal power.

Cutting Deals: Wartime Labor Policy

War—like the Depression before it—induced no widespread change in corporate labor policies or concepts. Since the passage of the National Labor Relations Act of 1935, big-business leaders had, at best, maintained a surly silence about the extension of the legal and organizing rights of trade unions. The Business Council proved to be no exception to the rule. The organization continued to oppose legislation that favored AFL or CIO affiliates over company unions, supported efforts to have the labor act ruled unconstitutional by the courts, and engaged in an unavailing litany of complaints regarding the formulation and implementation of federal labor statutes.[3] Even when giant member-companies of the Business Council signed collective-bargaining agreements with trade unions (as U.S. Steel did with the CIO early in 1937), the contract only allowed for proportional representation as opposed to majority rule.[4] Only the merest handful of Council luminaries—most notably Gerard Swope—did anything substantial to try to ameliorate tensions between the AFL and CIO, and organized industry.[5]

Immediately after Pearl Harbor, however, the Roosevelt administration tried to improve this situation somewhat by capitalizing on the swell of patriotic outrage against the Japanese. On December 11, 1941, Roosevelt called a national Labor-Management Conference to reach agreement on basic labor policies to be applied for the duration of the war. A judicious use of public opinion, Roosevelt hoped, might impel corporate and trade union leaders to put aside many long-standing differences and cooperate to end strikes and lockouts during the wartime emergency. To help things along, Roosevelt asked William Batt, then chairman of the Business Council, to name all of the dozen employer representatives to the conference. Batt complied—selecting the majority of the delegates from among the group of men who were, or would shortly become, members of the Business Council. Council representatives included Cyrus Ching (U.S. Rubber), Charles Edward Wilson (General Electric), Paul Hoffman (Studebaker Motors), Reuben Robertson (Champion Fiber Company), W. Gibson Carey (Yale and Towne Manufacturing Company), and West Coast shipping tycoon Roger Lapham. To avoid alienating other national business organizations, however, the remainder of the employer group consisted of NAM activists like Charles R. Hook of Armco Steel (also a Business Council member), W. P. Witherow of the Blaw-Knox Company, and Robert M. Gaylord of Ingersoll Milling Machines.[6]

On December 17, 1941, Roosevelt's Labor-Management Conference convened in Washington. Facing the twelve employer delegates were six AFL representatives (including President William Green), six CIO members (including John L. Lewis), and two "public" moderators. In short order, the labor and management leaders agreed to forswear strikes and lockouts and to submit contract and other disputes to a soon-to-be-created National War Labor Board (NWLB) to be composed of four labor, four management, and four public members. Shortly thereafter, however, the meeting deadlocked.

At issue was the question of "union security." Trade union leaders wanted to make sure that the huge number of workers beginning to flood into defense plants would be required to join AFL or CIO unions in order to get the wage and other benefits that the unions had so recently won from management in many large corporations. Every worker that walked through the gates of a unionized plant, then, should be required to join a union as a condition of receiving permanent employment, and should further be required to remain in that union once he had joined it. This way, the labor leaders hoped, management could not weaken the unions' hold in plants where they had organized or won contracts, by dividing older workers from newer workers.

Such logic held little appeal for the management delegates. They were willing to agree not to discriminate against people who were already members of unions in return for a no-strike pledge. The National Labor Relations Act required such nondiscrimination, in any event. But they did not want to be put in a position where they were required to more or less automatically induct new workers into AFL or CIO unions as one of the conditions of hiring or retaining these workers in the first place.

Business representatives, unsurprisingly, preferred an "open-shop" alternative to the "closed-shop" proposal set forth by the unions. In an open shop, new workers could join a union if they wished to, but they would not be required to. Nor would a person who was a member of a union be prohibited from ending his association with that union at any time. The businessmen, then, wanted what they had always wanted, proportional representation. Most of them also hoped that the attractiveness and membership of AFL and CIO unions alike would decline, given time and the relatively affluent economic circumstances that the war had created.

John L. Lewis, however, would have none of it. Determined to use organized labor's bargaining power to the utmost, Lewis mocked employer statements regarding proportional representation and the open shop. "I have heard," he orated to the conference, "this open shop talk before. The open shop is a harlot with a wig and artificial legs, and her bones rattle. But how much will she produce?" The message was clear: employers had to do something substantial to reassure unions regarding the maintenance and expansion of their membership, or face strikes and slowdowns that would cost them heavily in terms of war-contract revenues.[7]

Complicating Lewis's and the other labor leaders' fears of employers intentions were their equally justified fears of each other. Open-shop conditions not only gave employers room to exercise their anti-union instincts, they also posed the threat of worsening the ongoing struggle between the crafts-dominated AFL and its industrial-union-oriented rival, the CIO.

Ever since the CIO's secession from the AFL five years before, the two labor federations had been fighting each other tooth and nail. A central element in this struggle involved jurisdictional disputes between AFL and CIO unions. AFL affiliates raided their CIO equivalents, and CIO unions did not hesitate to do the same. Unions in both national labor organizations often claimed to represent workers in the same industries or industrial specialties—and both branded their opponents as illegitimate or worse. The strikes and work stoppages which resulted from this war between the unions bedeviled the lives of even compromise-minded businessmen. The AFL, for instance, might stage a strike or other job action against a particular plant one day because its management had entered into negotiations with or otherwise recognized the existence of the CIO. The CIO, for its part, might strike the same plant the very next day if management responded to AFL pressure by either breaking off contact with the CIO or entering into negotiations with the AFL. All in all, businessmen were often placed in a classic no-win situation, with the confusion compounded by the clear willingness of many employers to play AFL and CIO unions off against each other in the hope of weakening both.[8]

AFL and CIO leaders at President Roosevelt's Labor-Management Conference, then, insisted upon union security—and opposed the open-shop sentiments of employers—partly to protect themselves from the raids of rival unions.[9]

Organized labor's demands for organizational and membership protection were more than the businessmen from the Business Council and the NAM could bear. Roosevelt, however, was in no mood to see the meeting that he had called into being end on a note of utter deadlock. So the President acted to save his own political stature by speedily ending the Labor-Management Conference once it became clear that union security was not an issue that could be easily or quickly resolved. The National War Labor Board that the conference members had helped to call into existence, Roosevelt promised, would work out the whole union-security matter later. Two more weeks passed before Roosevelt, on January 12, 1942, announced the makeup of the new agency. Of the four employer delegates initially selected for the twelve-man group, three (George H. Mead, Cyrus Ching, and Roger Lapham) were members of the Business Council.[10]

During the months that followed the creation of the National War Labor Board, its business members sought to reassure AFL and CIO unions regarding their organizational existence and membership rolls without accepting the demands enunciated by John L. Lewis. The Business Council did likewise. The Council, in fact, had been quietly addressing itself to the question for some time. Early in 1941, for example, it had provided three of the four employer delegates—and several alternate delegates—to the National Defense Mediation Board, which had had a short and unhappy life as a peacetime predecessor to the National War Labor Board.[11]

In the prewar deliberations, the Business Council had focused upon three elements of the union security question that were particularly unsettling to managerial instincts: the closed shop, the union shop, and "maintenance of membership." Under the terms of closed-shop contracts, workers that a firm hired had to be members of the union that a company had contracted with at the time of their hiring. In the case of union-shop contracts, a union's control over the labor force available to a firm was not so complete. Management might hire workers who were not members of the particular union that their firm had a collective-bargaining contract with. These same workers, however, would be required to join the union within a few months after their initial hiring if they wished to have permanent jobs. Otherwise, they would have to leave the employ of the company. Finally, under the terms of collective-bargaining agreements that contained maintenance-of-membership provisions, management agreed that any worker who was a member of a particular AFL or CIO union when the firm signed a contract with that union was required to remain in that same union during the entire period that the union's contract was in force. Closed-shop contracts, then, gave unions relatively complete control over the labor that management could *hire*. Union shops, on the other hand, determined which workers management could *permanently retain*. Maintenance-of-membership provisions restrained workers' ability to shift their union allegiance during the course of a contract, and also restrained managers from seeking to play competing unions off against one another—or to inveigle workers out of unions altogether.

Council concern about union demands for closed-shop, union-shop, or maintenance-of-membership protection was illustrated when a special report on such matters was presented to the group on October 9, 1941, by Charles Hook, the chairman of the Council's Industrial Relations Committee. After stating that organized business needed to do a better job of coordinating its positions on labor issues during a period of tightening labor markets, Hook assured Council members that their peers on the National Defense Mediation Board were opposed to union efforts to pressure federal officials to support closed-shop, union-shop, or maintenance-of-membership provisions. Only those companies that had voluntarily signed such agreements in the past, Hook continued, should be expected to agree to them at any future time.

Mobilization was drying up the reserves of unemployed labor available to certain industries, however, and strengthening the bargaining power of the larger AFL and CIO unions. So, Hook continued, big-business leaders should "give some consideration to collective bargaining on an industry-wide basis at least in some situations." Otherwise powerful unions might succeed in enforcing closed shops, union shops, or maintenance-of-membership agreements upon the weaker companies within an industry. Then the unions could turn around and try to use these gains as precedents in policy discussions with federal officials. These federal officials, in turn, might try to force such contract provisions upon the stronger companies.

Finally, Hook concluded, big businessmen had to become more sophisticated about presenting their side of the whole union security issue. It no longer accomplished anything for the managers of large firms to simply oppose union demands for the closed shop or maintenance of membership by arguing that such provisions violated the "freedom of employees." Instead of using such shopworn arguments, businessmen should reason differently—arguing, for example, that they needed all the capable workers they could get to maintain defense production and, therefore, opposed being forced to avoid hiring or to fire any worker who refused to join a union in plants where closed- or union-shop contracts came into effect. Thereby, the closed-shop issue could be used to put unions on the defensive.[12]

Following the creation of the National War Labor Board, the Business Council continued to keep its eye on the union security issue that it had earlier addressed. By March of 1942, it issued an official statement on the closed-shop, union-shop, and maintenance-of-membership questions. The statement, enunciated at a time when the NWLB was trying to formulate national policy on these two issues, provides a convenient summary of the labor relations goals that the compromise-minded leaders of the nation's big-business establishment tried to achieve during the period.

The Council report began by treating with the "closed shop and its many variations," terming this "one of the most emotional issues in labor relations" and "one which is threatening to cause more interruptions to production than any other single issue." During World War I, the Council continued, the federal government had decided that all prewar closed-shop arrangements should remain in force "but declined to order any extension of this principle though it gave assurances that the right of employees to bargain collectively [in other circumstances] would be protected."

The organized labor movement had, the report added, become a good deal more powerful than it had been during America's earlier war. "Under the National Labor Relations Act a closed shop has received a special [i.e., federally sanctioned and supported] legality when voluntarily arrived at, but it is generally conceded [i.e., by businessmen] that the requirement of union membership should not be forced by a Government agency."

Thus far, it appeared that the Council was simply telling New Deal politicians and the National War Labor Board to stay as far away from labor issues as was humanly possible. Appearances were deceptive. After a few more verbalisms, the Council's logic began moving in a quite different direction.

"It has, therefore, been suggested," the statement went on, "that the issue of compulsory union membership [including closed-shop, union-shop, and maintenance-of-membership provisions] be removed from the area of arbitration by the War Labor Board and be left to the parties themselves to work out." Anti-union business organizations including the National Association of Manufacturers, in other words, wanted Washington to do nothing at all about the question of union security, so that business could fight out its differences with organized labor in a normal peacetime fashion.

The Business Council, however, refused to give any support to such relatively conservative corporate proposals. "The effect of such a policy" of government nonintervention regarding the whole union security issue "would be to return this issue to the field of pressure tactics between union and management with all the implications on production efficiency that the emotionalism of this issue involves." Strikes and lockouts, in other words, would become widespread unless a government body like the NWLB arbitrated the issue successfully. "If the unions are told that they can expect nothing from the War Labor Board on their maintenance of membership problems, but are free to make the best deal they can with the employer, it is easy to imagine the friction which will be created. The question is complicated by the fact that two rival [union federations] are in the field each trying to build up and hold its membership."

The big-business membership of the Council, in short, was not about to jeopardize its wartime profits by risking a strike wave by AFL and CIO leaders seeking to achieve organizational security and additional memberships by simultaneously contending against anti-union employers and each other. Smaller businessmen such as steelmen and metal-trades entrepreneurs in the Midwest and South might be willing to risk a strike wave on the assumption that an impatient and increasingly conservative Congress would rescue them by passing legislation banning strikes, drafting strikers into the military, or otherwise suppressing an organized labor movement that they despised. Such anti-union business interests, however, were going to get no help at all from the Business Council despite the underlying sympathy of its members.

To make this point clear, the Business Council statement did more than simply state its desire for peaceful compromise under federal auspices. It proceeded to sketch out the sort of compromise that it wished the National War Labor Board to make. In the process, it entirely ignored the very real existence of anti-union employer organizations like the NAM.

First, the Business Council made the rather gratuitous statement that "with the statutory protection from employers which unions now enjoy, their problem of [organizational and membership] security relates more to inter-union activity than to hostile employers." Jurisdictional strikes, in other words, were the basic problem—as far as larger industrialists anxious to get on with the profitable business of war capitalism were concerned. "The first thing necessary therefore is to find some way of providing [for the] *status quo* as between unions." Some kind of maintenance-of-membership standards must, in other words, be enforced by the NWLB to stop inter-union raiding between the AFL and CIO.

Once having admitted the need for compromise on maintenance of membership, the Business Council proceeded to the other outstanding union-security issue: the closed shop. Here, too, the Council hoped to achieve compromise on the basis of the status quo.

"The next step," the report continued, "should be [for the National War Labor Board to make] a declaration of policy as to what position an employer must take on the question of requiring a man to belong to a union in order to secure or retain a job. . . . It seems obvious that some policy should be adopted under which maintenance of *status quo* with respect to closed shop provisions could be the compromise on which all could agree in the interest of winning the war."

In conclusion, the Council put forth its proposal for a wartime national labor-relations policy—a policy that "could be put into effect by suitable legislation or an executive order providing . . . for the duration of the war no employer shall seek to change any terms of an existing contract which have to do with maintenance of membership, check-off dues or other so-called closed shop provisions, nor shall any union seek to secure such contract provisions whcrc not already in existence."[13]

The Business Council, then, proposed a deal guaranteeing that the AFL and the CIO could keep everything they had already won if they would stop fighting each other over the allegiance of workers for the duration of the war. In exchange, the big businessmen would restrain anti-union businessmen from seeking to abolish such contractual gains as the unions had previously made at their expense. For the rest, however, organized labor should not press hard to achieve union security provisions like closed shops, union shops, or maintenance-of-membership agreements in industries or firms where they had not *already* succeeded in getting them written into their collective-bargaining contracts. Labor-management cooperation, then, would consist of big business supporting the gains that labor had made, so long as there was a halt to raids by one union upon another that led to tangled jurisdictional disputes that stopped production. Labor, for its part, was to freeze its demands for additional measures of union security for the rest of the war.

The unions, however, were interested in achieving more than big-business tolerance for the union security gains that they had already made. They wanted, at the very least, to achieve additional organizational and membership protection from corporations that had not conceded such to them before the United States got directly involved in the war. The comparative advantages the unions enjoyed in the tight labor markets spawned by the war only increased labor leaders' resolve to capitalize upon their opportunities.

Businessmen such as those on the Business Council and the National War Labor Board then faced a new problem. If the status quo was unacceptable, what additional compromise could be formulated that came as close as possible to freezing union-industry power relationships for the duration of the war?

The agreement that was eventually arrived at involved maintenance of membership. Under the terms of the compromise, unions generally gave up the right to try to force new closed shop contracts upon industry during wartime. In return, these unions were given guarantees that workers who voluntarily joined a particular AFL or CIO affiliate would be required to remain dues-paying members of that union or forfeit their jobs. So long as unions did not violate wartime no-strike agreements, they enjoyed federal assurances that they could keep all the workers that they attracted, for the duration of their wartime labor contracts. When, in addition, unions succeeded in winning collective-bargaining rights at previously unorganized plants during wartime, maintenance-of-membership provisions were forced upon management—even if they were not part of the specific contractual agreement that management had signed.[14]

The labor-management agreement just described was developed gradually and reluctantly by the big businessmen most directly concerned. The business (and Business Council) members of the NWLB, for example, initially did all they could to oppose the extension of maintenance-of-membership provisions, arguing for instance that such regulations violated the rights of individual workers who might wish to cease their association with unions. Shopworn arguments—Charles Hook's caveats to the contrary—died hard. Throughout the spring of 1942, the NWLB's business representatives waged a running battle to ensure that trade union strength would increase as little as possible during the wartime mobilization. But the labor and public members of the Board allied against them. By late summer of 1942, de facto understandings had been substantially worked out. The public and labor majority of the Board regularly awarded maintenance-of-membership guarantees to unions not engaged in strikes, worker intimidation, or other disruptive tactics. Management members, just as regularly, agitated for "escape clauses" in maintenance-of-membership provisions—even after it became abundantly clear that the vast majority of the workers who were allowed to vote on the matter in NWLB-supervised elections did not particularly value management's concern for their individual freedoms. Neither businessmen nor their opponents, however, made the slightest move to resign or otherwise abandon their cooperation with the National War Labor Board because of their continuing disagreements regarding the administrative nuances of the maintenance-of-membership issue. Those unreconstructed free-enterprisers who sought to equate the Board's support for membership maintenance with totalitarian dictatorship—Sewell Avery of Montgomery Ward among others—were ruthlessly squelched. The Business Council's Roger Lapham went so far as to call Avery's argumentation "a damn bunch of half truths," and another industry member charged Avery with having done "the greatest dis-service to industry and the private enterprise system of any concern in the United States." Avery could orate all he wanted; meanwhile, the big businessmen of the Council would make the best deal available to them under the circumstances.[15]

Uneasy though the compromises involved often were, the wartime collaboration symbolized by the existence of the National War Labor Board had decided advantages for both big businessmen and the organized labor movement. Organized labor—most especially the young and organizationally vulnerable CIO industrial unions—enjoyed the benefits of a federally guaranteed breathing space to consolidate their gains in the nation's mass production trades. Big businessmen, for their part, gained a relatively peaceful labor environment in which unions were unable to compete ruthlessly for a decidedly bigger slice of the employee and profits pie. De facto compromises on maintenance of membership, in addition, allowed the ranks of trade unions to grow by over 4 million from Pearl Harbor to V-J Day, as the nation's corporations—the larger ones in particular—waxed fat on military contracts.[16]

However, not all businessmen saw the light of compromise. Business interests active in the affairs of organizations such as the NAM and the U.S. Chamber of Commerce continued to equate collective bargaining with sin. Even big-business politicians such as those of the Business Council accepted the reality of aggressive trade unionism only grudgingly. Unions still struck the majority of Council members as antisocial cabals. Such men, however, were a good deal more willing than the heads of small or medium-sized firms to recognize that the good old days of the open shop, proportional representation, and company unionism were over for good. As early as May of 1944, for example, George Mead reported to the Business Council that organized business must, in the future, insist upon pressing federal leaders to adopt legislation requiring "some degree of statutory union responsibility." Businessmen should do this, moreover, "rather than hoping for some return to prewar conditions." Compromise and conciliation under federal auspices, then, were all very well during a period of risk-free war capitalism. But once the rivers of defense production dried up, it would be time for big-business leaders to seek to limit union power through the agency of the federal government in more ambitious ways.[17]

The same mixture of a short-term willingness to cut cooperative deals and a longer-term concern regarding the future implications of those deals was evident in Business Council leaders' attitudes toward federal attempts to influence the direction of America's industrial economy after the war. Planning for reconversion to peacetime circumstances provided, in fact, an opportunity for these business politicians to expand the scope of their political influence.

During the first year of the war, the question of what peace would mean to American businessmen was obscured by the more pressing matter of creating and supplying armies, navies, and air forces. By late 1942, however, the eventual defeat of all the Axis powers appeared increasingly certain, and corporate minds were increasingly concerned with the challenges of peace. An important means of channeling such concerns into action was a new organization that was created to allow big businessmen to affect the formulation and implementation of postwar public policy: the Committee for Economic Development (CED). In the creation of this agency, the leadership of the Business Council figured very prominently.

Planning for Peace: The Committee for Economic Development

Business leaders had cause for worry by the end of the first full year of war. The conflict was being won, but there were signs that liberals were seeking to follow through upon military victories abroad with political victories at home. War had turned liberal reform agendas into subsidiary concerns. Once peace returned, liberal forces would await only favorable opportunities to try to expand the scope of their power.

The question, then, was not whether reconversion would occur, but rather what type of economic and political order would result from the process. On the resolution of this crucial question, corporate and liberal leaders differed profoundly.

The scope of the difference was illustrated when the liberals fired the first shot in their campaign to advance postwar reform. The agent of the deed was a body called the National Resources Planning Board (NRPB), a small research arm of the Roosevelt White House that had been quietly issuing reports on matters such as flood control, federal-state cooperation, countercyclical spending, public works employment, and other matters for most of its short and unremarkable career. The Board's staff was composed of academicians—mainly economists—and was watched over by a panel of university administrators and three businessmen: Business Council veteran Henry Dennison, Beardsley Ruml of Macy's, and Frederick A. Delano, a retired railroad magnate who was FDR's uncle. Delano, additionally, chaired the little group.[18]

In February of 1943, the NRPB assumed a high political profile on the release of a report in which it outlined a proposal for a New Bill of Rights for postwar America. Washington, the report argued, had assumed unprecedented economic responsibilities during the Depression. Since depression might well occur again after peace came and federal military spending decreased drastically, the federal government should be prepared to further expand the scope of its guarantor role. To assist this process, the Board drew up an agenda which called upon Washington to guarantee "full employment for employables" and "a job for every man released from the armed forces and the war industries at the close of the war, with fair pay and working conditions." While they were at it, federal officials should also "guarantee and where necessary underwrite [in other words, finance] equal access to security, equal access to education for all, equal access to health and nutrition for all, and wholesome housing conditions for all."[19]

Conservatives greeted the National Resources Planning Board's clear call for an expanded federal reform agenda based upon peacetime full employment with a distinct lack of enthusiasm. Congressional right-wingers went further: only five months after issuing its report, the NRPB was forced to disband after Congress refused to vote it a budgetary appropriation and, for good measure, ordered all of the agency's research files transferred to the National Archives for permanent political burial.

However, President Roosevelt then proceeded to go out of his way to make rhetorical commitments to follow through upon the reform agenda that his defunct NRPB had laid out. As so often in FDR's career, ideological orientation was a function of immediate political interest. By the time NRPB enunciated its glowing visions, relations between Roosevelt and the left wing of the Democratic party had soured. Liberals had watched glumly as big businessmen streamed into Washington to manage the wartime mobilization. Worse, from Roosevelt's point of view, was the fact that the conservative English government of Prime Minister Winston Churchill was beginning to come forth with a series of semi-official reconversion proposals of its own. The much-discussed Beveridge report of 1942, for instance, advocated "full employment," national health insurance, and the expansion of existing social welfare programs in terms of both coverage and benefit levels. As such goals were also a part of Democratic liberals' own pending reform agenda, political grumbling commenced in earnest.[20]

To improve his standing in liberal circles—and to position himself for a fourth-term presidential campaign—Roosevelt shifted leftward once again. On January of 1944, he even went so far as to deliver a State of the Union message, to the same Congress that had killed the NRPB, calling upon the nation to accept an Economic Bill of Rights that would authorize Washington to provide the very employment, income, educational, welfare, and housing guarantees proposed earlier by the deceased NRPB. Clearly then, conservatives had a fight on their hands. Killing messengers like the National Resources Planning Board was not enough. They were going to have to formulate postwar reconversion agendas of their own, or face the strong possibility that liberal Democrats and their political supporters would win by default.[21]

Business politicians like those of the Business Council were not slow to react to the challenge. Such men had, in fact, been laying the foundations for a "positive business response" to reconversion for some time. Enunciation of the liberal reform agenda only accelerated this process.

The focal point for this big-business activism was the Committee for Economic Development. CED's roots stretched back even before Pearl Harbor, when two businessmen, Paul Hoffman of Studebaker and William Benton of the Benton and Bowles advertising agency, had begun to sound out a collection of University of Chicago administrators, business publicists, and corporate CEOs about the creation of a research organization and discussion forum that influential businessmen could use to clarify policy proposals and translate those proposals into political reality in Washington. Throughout the summer and fall of 1941, Benton and Hoffman—occasionally assisted by University of Chicago President Robert M. Hutchins—contacted people and drew up tentative lists of those they wanted to recruit for their proposed research and policy group. Such activity, however, produced little in terms of substantive organizational results.

For example, months were wasted in efforts to enlist a few labor representatives. Benton and Hoffman started out with a clear preference for "scholars" over "active union leaders." After consultations with the chairman of the National Labor Relations Board and others, however, the two businessmen reluctantly realized that only active and nationally known trade union leaders would provide the legitimacy and celebrity that they desired. Advisers then suggested Sidney Hillman of the Amalgamated Clothing Workers, David Dubinsky of the International Ladies Garment Workers, and George M. Harrison of the Brotherhood of Railway Clerks as possible candidates. None excited the businessmen—or university President Hutchins. Finally, in October of 1941, advertising executive Benton wrote auto maker Hoffman that "Bob [Hutchins] says the three names merely illustrate the validity of your feeling of union leaders in general." This feeling was hardly a positive one. It was as if the two corporate executives had considered inviting fire-breathing dragons to a garden party before recognizing the magnitude of their mistake.[22]

Benton and Hoffman were getting nowhere fast. So, three weeks before Pearl Harbor, Hoffman made use of his status as a vice-chairman of the Business Council to get his and Benton's proposal for a big-business research and policy group presented to a general Council meeting.[23]

Initiating the contact with the Business Council proved decisive. Even before Benton and Hoffman arrived with their proposal, influential Council members such as Marion Folsom had expressed concern that big-business leaders were not paying enough attention to the economic challenges that would follow the end of the mobilization-induced boom in output, employment, and income levels. The 1930's bust had cost corporate managers plenty in terms of status and political clout, and a postwar bust might have even worse effects upon capitalists—and capitalism—during the 1940's. Slowly but surely the Council had responded to Folsom's concerns, not least because it believed that liberal politicians would use reconversion to their exclusive advantage if businessmen themselves did nothing. As evidence of their determination to avoid any such outcome, Council members agreed to the creation of an Economic Policy Committee and appointed Folsom to head it. By the time Hoffman and Benton appeared on the scene, a Council delegation had already called upon Commerce Department officials to loudly protest the fact that "certain recent reports on postwar planning by the National Resources Planning Board" had "neglected business and industry."[24]

Benton and Hoffman's proposal, then, fell on receptive ears. America's abrupt entrance into the war on December 7, 1941, further firmed up corporate leaders' resolve to act. Equally important was the fact that Pearl Harbor persuaded Secretary of Commerce Jesse Jones the time was ripe for him to lend his considerable clout to the efforts of corporate leaders.

Ever since replacing Harry Hopkins at Commerce in August of 1940, Jones had been looking for ways to use his Cabinet status to increase the scope of business influence in Washington. In the wake of the Benton and Hoffman proposal, Jones worked to energize the Business Council to take action. By the end of January, 1942, Jones and newly elected Business Council Chairman R. R. Deupree of Procter and Gamble were already traveling to corporate watering holes spreading the gospel that (in Deupree's words): "The challenge which business will face when this war is over cannot be met by a laissez-faire philosophy or by uncontrolled supply and demand. Intelligent planning . . . and courage will be needed to carry us through the reconstruction period."[25]

Moving beyond speeches, Jones sponsored meetings in which Business Council leaders and Commerce Department officials worked out the concrete organizational details of the businessmen's postwar policy-and-planning effort. This process, begun in April of 1942, was completed by September.[26]

The organization that resulted from this intensive corporate-government cooperation was the Committee for Economic Development. Organizationally, CED was cleverly bifurcated to allow the big-business politicians of the Council to increase the scope of their influence without appearing to do so at the expense of competing business interests and groups.

At the top of the CED organizational hierarchy sat a board of trustees initially composed of twenty men. Of this number, fourteen had served or were serving as active members of the Business Council at the time of their appointment. Three of the remaining six trustees were tapped for the Council shortly after affiliating themselves with the CED. This overwhelming Council representation within the CED's highest governing body provided impressive confirmation of the fact that—in Jesse Jones' words—the members of the Business Council were "in fact, cosponsors of the movement" that had made CED possible in the first place.[27]

On the next rung of the organizational ladder stood the CED's chairman, Business Council Vice-Chairman Paul Hoffman. Under him was his close associate William Benton, CED's vice-chairman. These two men, in their turn, oversaw the operations of the two major operational components of the CED: a Research Division headed by Business Council activist Ralph Flanders, and a Field Development Division headed by Council member Marion Folsom.

Flanders' Research Division was the core of the prewar Benton-Hoffman proposal for a big-business research and policy group translated into concrete organizational reality. Joining Flanders in leadership roles within it was a handful of business leaders grouped into a Research Committee. This group functioned as a sort of general staff which set overall policy goals and agendas for the CED after consultations with various groups of academic advisers. Prominent among this small group of corporate Brain Trusters were Business

Council members William L. Batt, Chester Davis, Charles Edward Wilson, and Beardsley Ruml.[28]

Highly placed business leaders like these did not lack for organizational influence—or for money. An early CED memorandum made this abundantly clear when it announced that no less than half of the quarter-million dollars that Business Council member Clarence J. Francis of General Foods had raised to finance the CED's first year of operations was going to go to the Research Division. Flanders and his group, in turn, used the money to finance research in two major areas:

> First: Government and business policies growing out of the war itself—such as rationing, price controls, ownership and operation of [federally financed or built] war plants [after the war], et cetera— many of which will call for action and decision immediately on or shortly after the cessation of hostilities. . . .
>
> Second: The long-range policies of government and business which should constantly be kept in view during the postwar transition period and which, in a peacetime economy, contribute most to optimum and high productivity.[29]

CED's Research Division, then, was responsible for formulating postwar policy to allow business leaders to deal with both short-term and long-term political challenges to the established corporate order, well in advance of the return of peacetime conditions.

Research and policy agendas were one thing, but a need also existed to turn such agendas and proposals to practical account during wartime. Employers, in other words, had to start doing something now to ensure that high employment levels would be maintained after war plants closed, or face the danger that opposing political interest groups would deal with the problem in ways that businessmen disliked. This, in its turn, required that the big-business politicians of the Business Council and the CED find a way to mobilize wider corporate constituencies to help them carry out their reconversion effort. The heads of General Electric and Eastman Kodak, for example, might plan for their segments of the industrial economy all they wanted. Unless they could get active support for their ideas among the tens of thousands of businessmen heading small to medium-sized firms in other areas of the economy, however, their efforts might be very largely wasted. The grass roots of industrial America had to be mobilized, and the eventual instrument of that mobilization was the CED's Field Development Division.

If Ralph Flanders' Research Division was the staff element of the CED's structure, Marion Folsom's Field Development Division functioned as its line counterpart. Field Development's task was not to make policy, but to disseminate proposals through the heartland of industrial America and get them acted upon. Folsom's unit went about its work in a creative and sophisticated way. Most importantly, it did not attempt to function in a centralized or heavy-handed fashion. Nor was it composed—as the Research Division very largely was—of Business Council eminences. Instead of being the Business Council under another name, CED's Field Development unit served as an organizational bridge between the business politicians of the Council and competing business organizations, including the U.S. Chamber of Commerce and the National Association of Manufacturers.

Here again a little background is in order. When the precise organizational form of the CED was being decided upon, a minority of the corporate leaders that had been called together by the Business Council and Secretary of Commerce Jones argued that the CED should be a very centralized body. One disgruntled Kansas City banker, for example, wrote Jones and one of his chief assistants in June of 1942 that the only way for the nation's business leadership to plan effectively for reconversion would be to expand the Business Council "in such a way as to make it truly national in its makeup." The Council should then proceed to work closely with the federal government through the Commerce Department. It should, further, be *the* voice of business. For "the United States Chamber of Commerce and other national organizations of business" had, very probably, "become ineffective" and "should be thoroughly and drastically reorganized." The banker continued:

> It seems to me that it is only by such a cooperative movement [centralized under the organizational auspices of the Commerce Department and the Business Council] that we can hope to attain results and to be part of a workable postwar economy. The average business man [in the Chamber of Commerce, NAM, and other national business organizations], of course, will say that he is not interested in such an arrangement, and that what he is thinking of after the war is to get government out of business and so on, but the fact remains that the problem [of postwar reconversion] is so large and business and the individual have been and will be so regimented that it will be impossi-

ble to immediately take government out of business. If the managers of business can cooperate and work out plans and policies that will make the business machine function and provide employment and adequate profits, it seems to me that this . . . must be attained with the help and cooperation of the Government. The time is passed, I believe, when so-called business as a group can stand alone. There must be cooperation of a type we have never seen before in this country.[30]

This proposal to restructure the Business Council as a centralized agency that openly mediated between the federal government and the nation's business community—well as it reflected the private opinions and hopes of men like Ralph Flanders, Marion Folsom, Paul Hoffman, and other Business Council activists—ignored certain important political realities, and did not, as a result, persuade such men, or Secretary of Commerce Jones. Like the Kansas City banker, Jones and the Business Council leaders understood that the "average business man" had never accepted the reality or the legitimacy of enhanced federal power, and tended to give exceedingly short shrift to any corporate leader who appeared to be too willing to do so. As we have seen, the Business Council had suffered heavy criticism from business traditionalists when it tried to cooperate with federal leaders during the NRA period. For example, upholders of the free-enterprise faith howled when Business Council leaders tried to stave off federal "interference" in labor relations by collaborating with AFL leaders to establish the National Labor Board. Relations between the Business Council and other business organizations were strained further when well-known Council eminences like Gerard Swope and Marion Folsom worked together with Washington bureaucrats to design a Social Security program. Nor did the Business Council's apparent willingness to buy labor peace during wartime by compromises on union security issues please the NAM or the Chamber of Commerce one bit. As a result of such disagreements, the Business Council had a bad reputation in conservative business circles. Some particularly contrary entrepreneurs persisted in seeing the organization as a bunch of tame millionaires who had become accomplices to New Deal criminality. Any approach to reconversion planning based upon an expanded and strengthened Business Council, then, ran the risk of being seen as a "New Deal ploy," thus worsening tensions among national business organizations and diminishing corporate leaders' collective ability to accomplish anything.[31]

Political realities like these led Jesse Jones and Business Council leaders to make the CED officially independent of the federal government in general and the Department of Commerce in particular. CED thereby enjoyed a "private" status that the quasi-public Business Council did not. Such realities also caused Jones and his corporate coworkers to downplay the fact that CED leaders maintained close working relationships with Commerce officials and to avoid mentioning the obvious fact that the Research Division of the CED was merely a group of Business Council activists operating under another name.[32]

Even more importantly, however, the Business Council activists' desire to form cooperative alliances with the heads of small and medium-sized businesses so prominent in the affairs of the NAM, Chamber of Commerce, and other national business organizations prevented the CED's Field Development unit from being set up as a centralized action agency, as the Kansas City banker and others had initially proposed.[33]

Instead, Field Development confined itself to expediting, encouraging, and publicizing actions taken by other regional, state, and local business groups that had no direct institutional affiliation with the CED. The process worked as follows: first, the small Field Development office in Washington persuaded twelve men to serve as regional chairmen for the CED reconversion-planning drive. Most of these men were not connected with the Business Council. The regional chairmen, in turn, enlisted district or state representatives who spread the CED message by recruiting local business leaders to head reconversion-planning drives in most of the major industrial centers throughout the United States.

Each of the local planning bodies that the CED's Field Development group helped to call into existence functioned independently of the national CED organization. CED also created eleven "action committees" composed of national trade association officials to provide specialized advice in areas like sales, marketing, new technologies, transportation, advertising, and job retraining to local groups that requested it. No local planning agency, however, was required to act on such advice unless they found it persuasive. There was, therefore, no well-spelled-out "CED line" local groups were expected to follow.

CED's Field Development unit basically established a national network for promotion and propaganda that functioned on the twin principles of decentralization and voluntarism. If, for example, a group of businessmen in a local Chamber of Commerce, Kiwanis Club, Rotary organization, or NAM chapter attempted to shape the postwar economy in their particular market area, the CED's regional and national offices were more than happy to publicize their efforts, provide advice, and applaud heartily when problems were seriously addressed. Rather than creating a well-integrated national organization of its own, the CED simply tried to convince such managerial, trade, or professional groups as already existed to focus their attention on postwar economic problem solving. Once the process began, CED then sought to guide such groups' efforts in directions that the CED itself favored. CED's action arm, then, served as an auxiliary of already established local, state, and national business associations instead of seeking to compete with them for members, money, or other elements of organizational power. This strategy of indirection and influence worked well. By the end of the war, over two thousand autonomous CED-inspired or -assisted post-war planning groups were busily at work throughout the industrial heartland of the country. All were motivated by the same over-riding concern that the reconversion to peacetime economic conditions be made smooth and profitable enough so that a wrenching depression would not again threaten the existence of the market-place capitalist system.[34]

To further assure national business organizations of their benign and cooperative intentions, CED officials and Secretary of Commerce Jones were also careful to make a gentleman's agreement with the leaders of the NAM and the U.S. Chamber of Commerce as the CED was being formed. The CED, the understanding went, would cease to exist once the postwar reconversion had passed. To convince the skeptical, the Chamber of Commerce's wartime president, Seattle small businessman Eric Johnston, was shortly afterward appointed to the Research Committee of the CED. Almost simultaneously, Johnston was asked to become a member of the Business Council. The Johnston appointments symbolized Business Council leaders' willingness to cooperate with other influential national business groups. For before Johnston's selection, no president of either the Chamber of Commerce or the NAM had been an active member of the Business Council since both national business organizations had broken openly and bitterly with the New Deal in early 1934.[35]

Accepting the Activist State

The creation of the CED, then, was the centerpiece of a carefully thought out and shrewdly organized effort to expand the scope of Business Council activists' influence across all segments of the nation's corporate community during the period when corporate leaders faced the twin challenges of war and eventual peacetime reconversion. The CED allowed businessmen to enunciate "positive" responses that did not ignore the reality of expanded federal power.

Having set the stage so carefully, Council notables were able to score some impressive early successes. By November of 1943, for instance, CED Field Development Director Folsom was chosen to be the staff director of a Special Committee on Postwar Economic Policy and Planning created by Senate conservatives in the wake of their swift abolition of the luckless National Resources Planning Board. The CED's entree to congressional circles improved appreciably. As the network of the CED's organizational influence spread, its public statements began to receive wide coverage in the popular and business press.[36]

One statement, in particular, served to focus attention upon the new businessmen's organization and to gain for it valuable national credibility and a coherent image. In October of 1944, *Fortune* magazine carried the full text of the CED's "The Economics of a Free Society: A Declaration of American Economic Policy." Appearing over the signature of CED Vice-Chairman Benton, the essay spelled out just how far the compromise-minded corporate politicians of the Business Council and the CED were willing to go to resolve longstanding differences concerning the place of an expanded federal government in the postwar American economy.

After making all the usual pious comments about freedom, small business, and marketplace competition, the CED declaration got down to cases. Three points were made to assure federal leaders that realistic big businessmen were willing to recognize the "new role of government" in the key areas of collective bargaining, fiscal policy, and the provision of social welfare services—a role made necessary by the fact that the 1930's Depression had demonstrated that the self-regulating competitive market of Adam Smith and the neoclassical economic tradition was a thing of the past.

The CED started off by recognizing that a powerful organized-labor movement had come to the United States to stay. "To compensate for the weakness of their individual bargaining position," the CED intoned, "wage earners need the [federally guaranteed] right to combine into organizations for collective bargaining. . . . Provided that the power of these organizations is not permitted to stifle technological progress, or unduly to limit access to jobs, or in other ways to be abused, labor unions can serve the common good."

The message was simple. Big businessmen of the CED and Business Council stripe were going to do nothing to help their less-enlightened brethren in efforts to root out and destroy the AFL and CIO after the war. In return, the corporate leaders hoped that federal leaders would use their powers to control unions that might become too greedy about matters like the closed shop, extremely restrictive apprenticeship regulations, and refusal to accept automation.

Next the CED addressed the hoary issue of the federal government's role as final guarantor during periods of economic emergency. "Prolonged and severe depressions . . . cannot be accepted as natural or irremediable phenomena." Government did, indeed, have the responsibility for "establishing fiscal, monetary, and other policies" to "help prevent the fever of inflation and the paralysis of deflation and depression." The New Deal, in short, had not been a dream that would vanish with the dawn. Nor had it been the statist nightmare that unreconstructed conservatives like Herbert Hoover, Henry Ford, Pierre du Pont, and Alfred Sloan supposed.

To get the point across more clearly, CED included "expenditures for public works," "intelligent handling of the national debt," and "enlightened control over credit and money" in the list of "constructive policies" Washington should undertake. The public-works spending element of the statement was the clearest. It was all right for Washington to employ some people, some of the time, to do some things, and thereby act—occasionally—as an employer of last resort. Franklin D. Roosevelt, then, was not a communist dupe for letting jobless youths plant trees. In "intelligent handling of the national debt," CED leaders had coined a truly wondrous euphemism for federal willingness to run deficits during depressions as a means of boosting national employment, output, and income levels. "Enlightened control over credit and money" was an opaque phrase that could mean almost anything, though it clearly implied that the strengthened administration controls over the Federal Reserve System instituted during the domestic reform phase of the New Deal were not unacceptable to the CED's leadership. All the carefully hedged phrases added up to one thing: the business politicians of the CED did not expect Washington to disappear or revert to pre-Depression (or prewar) "normalcy" after peace came—any more than they expected trade unions to do so.

This latter point was made quite clearly in the third element of CED's statement—the one concerning social welfare services. "Through their federal government, [the American people] have wisely provided in the past, and should continue to provide in the future, a program of social security—unemployment insurance and old-age pensions" for those in need. The Social Security Act of 1935, then, was not in CED eyes a matter for further political argument. (Here we may recall that CED leader Marion Folsom was among the original drafters of the legislation.) Social Security, like trade unions and short-term federal deficit spending, was acceptable to the CED. Acceptance of such realities, the CED statement added, resulted "from the lessons of recent experience."[37]

The CED's widely publicized 1944 policy statement accepted *already existing* New Deal realities. It did not, however, propose any agenda for the further expansion of federal activity in any of the three areas just discussed. The point is crucial. While CED did not, on the one hand, give any support to conservative efforts to broadly roll back key elements of the New Deal, neither did it advocate any important elaboration of these same New Deal programs. CED business leaders basically sought to make the status quo into a medium of big business–government rapprochement in the postwar period.

CED, as things eventually turned out, succeeded better than its leaders may have expected. After peace returned to the United States in August of 1945, a combination of forces undermined liberals' abilities to carry through on their unmet reform agendas. Most important in this regard was the rise of postwar affluence. The freely predicted postwar depression that businessmen and others feared failed to materialize. Unemployment rolls swelled briefly as almost 12 million people returned to civilian life. The economy, however, proved more resilient—more capable of absorbing resources and redirecting them toward profitable peacetime purposes—than skeptics affected by almost fifteen straight years of unprecedented domestic and international emergency had supposed. While America boomed, popular concerns regarding future employment, income, and welfare security decreased—as did popular receptivity to ambitious reform drives.

Growing Cold War animosities between Russia and the United States also complicated domestic reform efforts. The alliance of convenience that proved victorious against the fascist powers never disposed the leaders of the United States or USSR to trust each other's wartime motives or postwar purposes. Within six months after V-J Day, heretofore obscure disagreements about the two nations' spheres of political authority, economic influence, or outright military control had become front-page public issues. As early as March of 1946, only 7 percent of the American people expressed approval for "the policy Russia is following in world affairs." Two months later, 58 percent agreed with the statement that "Russia is trying to build herself up to be the ruling power of the world." Within a year, three fourths of all Americans had come to the same conclusion.[38]

As concerns regarding Russian global intentions abroad grew, less and less political time or energy was left over for accomplishing substantial reforms at home. The Cold War, like the hot war that had preceded it, focused attention upon external threats—often at the expense of internal problems. In such an environment, security became more a matter of protecting the nation from a new set of foreign totalitarian enemies than a matter of dealing with joblessness, poverty, collective-bargaining procedures, or income maintenance.

In addition to affluence and the Cold War, postwar reformers were hindered by a sudden change in presidential leadership. Franklin D. Roosevelt's death in April of 1945 removed from the scene the wily political improviser with whom liberal forces had done much of their political business in Washington for over a dozen years. Replacing him was the less congenial Harry S. Truman—a graduate of the political machine of Kansas City, Missouri, who had gone to the U.S. Senate in 1934, gained national repute by investigating defense production delays during World War II, and been selected as FDR's vice-presidential running mate in 1944 as part of an effort to mollify the conservative wing of the Democratic party. Even with Truman's name on the electoral slate, Roosevelt had had an unusually difficult time winning reelection, gaining only 53.4 percent of the popular vote in the closest presidential race since 1916.

By the time Truman was thrust into the presidency, then, clear evidence existed that political support might be ebbing away from the Democrats—at least as far as the White House was concerned. Being nothing if not practical politicians, Truman and highly placed Democrats in Congress paused to see which way the political wind was blowing in the immediate postwar period. As they did so, articulate business politicians such as those directing the affairs of the CED and the Business Council moved to forge new cooperative relationships with federal leaders. These relationships were to rest on three main pillars. First, big-business leaders sought to reassure the Democrats of their intentions by refusing to join in right-wing business efforts to destroy major elements of the New Deal status quo at home. Second, they moved to ensure that the Democratic main- stream would not push for ambitious expansion of New Deal domestic reform initiatives. Third, the businessmen joined their efforts and skills to the movement to create a bipartisan foreign policy aimed at the containment of communism abroad.

4

CONTAINMENT AT HOME AND ABROAD, 1945–1953

Peace Breaks Out

As PEACE RETURNED to the United States in 1945, the corporate politicians of the Business Council were positioning themselves to stay abreast of political events. The formation of the Committee for Economic Development was a key element of this organizational and intellectual process. Whatever else happened, Council and CED activists wanted to make sure that influential big-business voices were heard loud and clear during reconversion.

The fact that Franklin D. Roosevelt died at an early point during this period proved beneficial to the business leaders. A political transition occurred during which the Democratic party—its congressional liberal wing in particular—was temporarily left leaderless. Harry S. Truman's reluctance to take ambitious policy initiatives, and his practical-politician's desire to avoid alienating important constituencies before knowing how much he might need such groups' assistance in the future, created a temporary power vacuum in Washington. Liberal and conservative forces alike tried to fill that vacuum in order to shift the balance of political power in their favor. Liberals, as had been the case so often before, acted first. If nothing else, they had been in Washington longer than most of their conservative counterparts—and so knew more about where the political ammunition was stored.

The business politicians, however, had also been in Washington for a long time—for almost fifteen years, in fact. This lengthy experience with the reality of expanded federal power had not turned all of the chief executive officers of the Business Council or the CED into savvy political operators. It had, however, made a significant number of these men much more knowledgeable about government than they had ever been before.

This new knowledge paid off; the business activists of the Business Council and the CED scored some notable successes in their efforts to mold political circumstances in their interest. This chapter will focus upon corporate politicians' efforts in three major policy areas: postwar social welfare legislation (the full-employment struggle of 1945–1946), postwar labor legislation (the passage of the Taft-Hartley Act of 1947), and postwar efforts to contain the spread of communist influence abroad by economic and military means (the Marshall Plan of 1947–1948 and the Korean War mobilization of 1950–1952).

The big-business activists succeeded for one essential reason: they were finally able to evolve realistic strategies that allowed them to utilize available political opportunities. The question, for such men, was not whether Washington would remain powerful. A decade of depression and several long years of world war had decided that question in the affirmative. The question, rather, concerned the uses to which expanded federal power would be put. Whose interests were to be forwarded—and at whose expense—by the inevitable exercise of federal might? Having made this critical shift in political perception, businessmen came to realize that they, too, could make use of Washington in new ways. In the process, the CEOs of the larger American corporations finally began the long process of coming of age politically.

Containing the New Deal at Home: The Fight Over Full Employment, 1945–1946

Full employment was the single most decisive social welfare policy issue of the immediate postwar period. Into this battle, New Deal liberals poured vast amounts of their remaining political leverage in hopes of achieving a breakthrough that would enable them to exploit the victories they had gained before war had put social welfare programs and proposals on the political sidelines for the duration.

Business leaders were prepared for the fight. Ever since the issuance of the Beveridge report in Britain and the destruction of the

National Resources Planning Board, Business Council and CED activists had been tracking the progress of their liberal opponents on the social welfare front. Marion Folsom, for example, told the Business Council as early as January of 1943 that it was "a good time for businessmen to interest themselves in this [social welfare] problem and to explore the prospects for new legislation." Folsom's logic proved persuasive enough for the Council to reconstitute a Social Security Committee that had been dormant for several years—and to appoint Folsom to head it.[1]

Ralph Flanders was another Council-CED activist who paid early and intense attention to postwar welfare proposals. Flanders was especially concerned about the full-employment ideas contained in both the Beveridge report, and in that of the short-lived National Resources Planning Board. After reading a published version of the Beveridge proposals early in 1945, Flanders wrote a letter to a CED staff assistant detailing some of his initial objections. "One of the axioms" in the report, Flanders observed, "is that the number of jobs looking for workers should be greater than the number of workers looking for jobs . . . [and that] then the worker is a free man. It is difficult to take any other position than that. It does [however] raise a parallel question. Should the business man have so much business he doesn't have to hunt for customers. I doubt it."[2]

While businessmen like Flanders were formulating questions and obtaining advice, the full-employment issue ceased to be merely theoretical in nature. In January of 1945, three prominent liberal senators—James E. Murray of Montana, Robert F. Wagner of New York, and Elbert Thomas of Utah—introduced a bill aimed at enshrining full employment in law. Under the terms of their proposal, Washington was to "assure the existence at all times of sufficient employment opportunities" for those seeking work. An annual National Production and Employment Budget was to be drawn up to help federal policymakers determine what level of investment was necessary to ensure full employment in that year. If the private sector generated this level of investment, well and good. If it did not, however, Washington would enter capital markets with loanable funds priced at rates aimed at attracting private firms, state governments, and local governments into the investment marketplace. All this was standard Depression-era RFC procedure—with a new Keynesian twist. In the event that full-employment levels of investment still were not achieved by federal loan intervention, the White

House, with the advice and consent of the Congress, would then proceed to invest money on its own account for public works and other federally financed projects. If all else failed, then, Washington would become not only a lender of last resort but an investor of last resort.[3]

The senators' full-employment proposal produced a swift conservative response. Prominent papers including the *Wall Street Journal,* the *Journal of Commerce,* and the *New York Times* expressed complete and utter opposition to the bill. National business organizations including the NAM and the Chamber of Commerce were not far behind. Full employment, such groups claimed, was a legislative Trojan horse that willful radicals were using to disguise their nefarious purposes. If passed, the full-employment bill would be another step along the slippery slope to "state socialism" and collectivist serfdom.[4]

While other business organizations blustered about subversive intentions, CED and Business Council leaders proceeded in a more sophisticated fashion. By the early summer of 1945, business politicians had begun intensive consultations to formulate a common position on the full-employment proposal and draw up a common strategy for weakening the bill.

One of the first concrete results of these meetings was a letter that was sent to Senator Wagner by Business Council and CED leader Ralph Flanders in mid-June of 1945. In the letter, Flanders went considerably beyond the free-enterprise rhetoric of the NAM and the Chamber of Commerce in an effort to sound out cooperative themes.

In his letter to Wagner, Flanders proposed compromise solutions to the full-employment problem. Starting on a positive note, Flanders stated his support for federal efforts to do more to provide jobs for people in need of them. He assured Wagner that he had recently come to accept the fact that the right to a job was a "legitimate right." Then the caveats began. The right to a job, Flanders continued, had duties attached: "The individual has no right to a job unless he is productive and self-reliant, and energetically seeks employment. To assign the right to individuals who do not possess these qualities is to subsidize idleness and social parasitism."

Nor could organized labor's or the federal government's duties be ignored Flanders went on. Unions should end "restrictive practices" that hindered full employment, and government should avoid policies that lowered business confidence and thus decreased businessmen's willingness to invest. If private investment lagged badly, Flanders warned, government-financed public works investment would provide no final solution to national employment problems. For Washington would find it impossible to guarantee work on an "enormous" scale (such, for example, as would have been required to achieve full employment during the Depression) "except by controls which approach the organization of a totalitarian government. . . . We have had such enormous Government employment during the war, but to provide the same volume [of employment] in peacetime, it would be necessary to continue the totalitarian features of wartime control." Government, then, should be very careful about initiating large public-works employment programs, and generally strive to keep the scope of such guarantees as restricted as possible.[5]

Flanders' letter to Wagner was motivated by many of the same concerns as those that were being expressed by Flanders' counterparts in the NAM and the Chamber of Commerce. Flanders, however, presented his concerns in a much more sophisticated fashion than these other business leaders. Instead of implying that congressional liberals like Wagner were parlor pinks or socialist dupes, Flanders carefully enunciated a "yes, but" position. He started off by agreeing with the essential validity of Wagner's concerns regarding full employment, and then calmly proposed amendments aimed at limiting the practical effects of Wagner's bill. The NAM, the Chamber of Commerce, and the business press might prefer vinegar, but Ralph Flanders and the businessmen around him were being careful to use honey.

As it happened, Flanders' letter to Senator Wagner was only the first in a long series of Business Council and CED efforts to amend the full-employment proposal. By early July of 1945, none other than the Dean of the Harvard Graduate School of Business Administration—Donald K. David—had been picked as the behind-the-scenes head of the Full Employment Committee of the Business Council. David's subsequent correspondence with CED Chairman Paul Hoffman, Business Council Chairman George M. Humphrey (M. A. Hanna Company), and others illustrated the process by which big-business activists went about the job of containing postwar liberal social-welfare initiatives.

On July 12, for example, David wrote to Humphrey: "I think that the planning aspects of the [full-employment] bill as it stands today are definitely bad. Furthermore, I think the mechanics are not workable. I believe [however, that] there is a splendid opportunity for government to *promote* a high level of employment. I think it is indeed a dangerous doctrine for the government to *insure.*"[6]

David's letter made important points and spelled out policy alternatives that guided all subsequent Business Council and CED efforts to modify the full-employment bill. Instead of guaranteeing anything, government should merely promote." Instead of talking about "full" employment, big-business politicians proposed, Washington should content itself with adjectives like "high," "abundant," or "fuller."

David's crucial differentiations were not lost on Business Council and CED activists. One week after David wrote to Humphrey, he received a worried letter from CED Chairman Hoffman. "I was in New York yesterday," Hoffman began, "and had a chance for a short visit with [CED member Beardsley] Ruml. I hope you can persuade him that there is a considerable difference between promoting and assuring [full employment]; a difference which at the moment he doesn't give much weight to."[7]

Hoffman needn't have worried. Ruml was, indeed, easy to persuade—if he needed any persuading at all. More to the point, it was also a comparatively easy task for leaders like Hoffman to convince the full membership of the Business Council and the CED to go along with David's proposed strategy to weaken the full-employment bill. By carefully enunciating a "yes, but" position on the proposed legislation, business leaders could operate in the very considerable gray area between the positions enunciated by Senate liberals and conservative business organizations. Slowly, Business Council and CED members were learning that those who stake out the earliest and best claims to the political middle ground in American politics are usually the ones who walk away with more than their share of the public-policy prizes. By August of 1945, for instance, Beardsley Ruml was telling congressional committees that all controversial terminology like "the right to work," "the assurance of employment," and even the phrase "full employment" itself should be removed from the bill so that "the greatest harmony may exist among all who believe that it is both appropriate and necessary that the federal government direct its full power toward the goal of full employment." Ruml's rationalization for the weakening of the bill that he was advocating was a masterpiece. "There is some doubt in my mind," he began, whether it is necessary or even desirable to define precisely what we mean by "full employment." It is a concept that will change from decade to decade as our ideas with respect to the relation between work and freedom change. A definition can hardly have any substantial practical consequence as to what is recommended or legislated under the bill. Why not leave the term "full employment," like "liberty" and "justice" to stand as a goal of democratic government, and to derive its specific content from the will of the people as expressed from time to time by their free institutions.[8]

Sophisticated political infighting like this meshed with the activities of conservative congressmen and senators who were engaged in a parallel effort to strangle the full-employment bill in its crib. Like the big businessmen, the congressmen realized that the safest way to attack the liberal legislation was to water down its conceptual underpinnings without appearing to do so publicly. Specifically, they tried to weaken those portions of the bill that held the "very statements of obligation and assurance which had originally caught the imaginations of liberal and labor supporters."[9]

The congressional process began quickly enough. As the full-employment bill moved through the Senate early in the fall of 1945, conservatives attached key amendments to the proposal that robbed it of much of its substantive effect. By the time the bill finally passed the Senate on September 28, 1945, by a huge margin, all unequivocal statements regarding the right of citizens to employment and the direct responsibility of the federal government to assure full employment had been removed. The arena of legislative action then shifted to the House of Representatives.

In the House, conservative business organizations, the NAM in the lead, moved in for what they hoped would be the kill. The CED and the Business Council, however, did nothing to ally themselves with the NAM's strident efforts to utterly destroy the legislation. Such a strategy, the Council and CED realized, was politically costly. Business leaders or organizations that opposed efforts to address the postwar employment issue too strongly were all too easily attacked by liberals as supporters of unemployment, renewed depression, and the like.

So while business organizations like the Chamber of Commerce of the State of New York ineptly played into the liberals' hands by issuing statements that, for example, supported the acceptance of an occasional depression as being part of "the price we pay for freedom," and as NAM spokesmen were assuring congressmen that "no greater discouragement for business" than the full-employment bill could be contrived by man or beast, the big businessmen and their congressional allies continued to press forward with their "yes, but" strategy.[10]

By October of 1945, such moderate pressure tactics began to roll into high gear. The Business Council, for one, met to ratify a report drawn up by its Full Employment Committee and to forward that report to the White House. The report, largely a compendium of previous CED policy statements, illustrated big businessmen's concerns that the teeth just taken out of the original Senate version of the full-employment bill should not be restored by either the House of Representatives or President Truman himself.

The Business Council's report on the full-employment issue followed the by now standard CED practice of starting off with a *pro forma* statement that federal concern with postwar full employment was both necessary and desirable. It then went on to try to placate congressional moderates by adding that a "reorganization of the congressional machinery and of the relationship of the Executive and the Legislative branches with regard to fundamental economic matters" was a good thing. Congress, it continued, should set up a permanent Joint Economic Committee (which it eventually did) to study such matters. The White House, for its part, should remain content with a temporary *ad hoc* commission to do its *studying* for it. (The President eventually got, over Council and CED opposition, a permanent research staff: the Council of Economic Advisers—CEA).

After demonstrating its clear support for studying things, the Council went on to add copious warnings against the federal government's trying to *do* anything. It expressed its "grave doubts" about the now defunct elements of the original full-employment bill, which had proposed the creation of annual National Production and Employment budgets aimed at allowing Washington to become an investor of last resort and, thereby, a guarantor of full employment. To ensure that the White House got the message, the Council continued that "we feel that too much reliance is still placed on the efficacy of residual compensatory spending as a remedy universally applicable at all times to our economic ills." The Council statement concluded that because what was left of the original full-employment bill did "not present a coordinated program of action," the bill was "dangerous in its implied promises." The fact that CED and Business Council leaders had been trying for months to ensure that no coordinated program of action would ever be passed was not, of course, mentioned.[11]

Logic like this, of course, was not persuasive to Senate liberals like Robert F. Wagner—and may not have affected the thinking of Harry S. Truman in any substantive way. It did, however, prove persuasive to St. Louis banker John W. Snyder, a Business Council member and longtime presidential intimate, who had been selected by his friend Truman to oversee the dismantling of the wartime mobilization program. Early in November of 1945, Snyder (a man whom Truman would shortly appoint to be his Secretary of the Treasury) offered testimony to the House committee pondering the full-employment bill. The results were distressing to liberals. Snyder came out in opposition to the fundamental principles that had caused men such as Wagner to draw their bill up in the first place—and took potshots at the usefulness of federal deficit spending during depressions into the bargain. Liberals sought to repair the damage Snyder had wrought, but Snyder's hostility to the principles of what remained of the legislation, a historian of the employment act has concluded, "was a major breach in the phalanx of Executive [branch] pressures" to get the bill passed in something remotely approximating its original form.[12]

With Snyder's defection from the White House ranks, the full-employment bill's days were numbered. In short order, the House committee voted down the amended Senate bill by an overwhelming margin. During the month that followed, House moderates and conservatives redrafted the full-employment bill into the Employment and Production Act of 1946, which eviscerated the original liberal proposal. During this revision process, the CED gladly joined with the Chamber of Commerce to provide important assistance in reworking the legislation.[13]

What finally emerged was a bill that proposed nothing more than that the federal government create some research machinery to evaluate the state of the economy. Federal officials could study all they wanted to, but they were not going to be given any additional authority to do anything that they were not already doing.[14]

Between November of 1945 and February of 1946, the few remaining fires of the full-employment fight sputtered out as House and Senate conferees resolved the minor details of a final bill based on the House version. At this point in the game, Business Council and CED spokesmen started to relax—but not all of them. A long-time Council staffer who had lived through all the battles of the Depression decade grumbled to Donald David as late as November that the wretched remnants of the bill still had the potential of becoming "the wolf of socialism attired in sheep's clothing," and that Truman's apparently lukewarm support of the bill was really part of a sincere presidential effort to placate "a substantial though subversive political element." David, however, knew better, and so informed the remaining skeptics within the Council. On the February day when a final legislative version of the gutted full-employment bill was agreed to, David wrote the aforementioned Business Council staff aide that the "pretty innocuous" bill would soon be agreed to by the White House. One week later, President Truman signed the Employment and Production Act of 1946 into law. The corporate politicians of the Business Council and the CED had won their first substantial victory in their campaign to halt the extension of postwar liberal reform initiatives.[15]

After placing its imprimatur on this innocuous piece of legislation, the Truman administration did nothing further to upset corporate sensibilities regarding the full-employment issue. Truman, in fact, waited six months before appointing anybody to chair the new Council of Economic Advisers—the economic research body created by the 1946 act. When Truman did move, he selected Edwin G. Nourse, a mild-mannered academic economist without left-wing contacts or convictions. Nourse, in his turn, went out of his way to state that the new advisory body that he headed had no animus at all against marketplace capitalism or business-government cooperation. Nourse's successor, Leon Keyserling, was similarly reassuring. Within the limits imposed by a neoclassical economic ideology, government would expedite the process by which businessmen maximized investment, production, employment, and income levels within society. Private corporations, not state authorities, would retain the primary responsibility for guaranteeing the good life to postwar industrial America. "Among the industrial democracies of the world," Daniel Patrick Moynihan later observed, the United States and Canada alone "had not instituted a post-war economic policy that gave the first priority to continued full employment. Accordingly, it became impossible to base other social policies on the presumption that all able-bodied persons in need of income would [be able to] obtain it first of all by working."[16]

The Battle Continues: Big Business, Postwar Labor Policy, and the Passage of the Taft-Hartley Act

By the time the battle over full employment was concluded early in 1946, the CED had become a noteworthy organizational fixture on the American corporate scene. Business Council activists who had created CED to help them bridge the transition from a wartime to a peacetime world might have been forgiven for concluding that the organization had served them well.

Council and CED activists went further than self-congratulation. They decided to turn the CED into a permanent organization aimed at providing big businessmen with long-term policy options and positions. This process generated more than a little friction. The CED, after all, had been created as purely a temporary organization, and a gentleman's agreement with the U.S. Chamber of Commerce and the NAM stated that the CED would cease to exist once the peacetime transition was past.

All such understandings aside, however, CED leaders used the occasion of their early victories in the full-employment fight to argue for a continuation of the organization. Following discreet (but possibly none too polite) bargaining with the Chamber of Commerce and the NAM, CED spokesmen essayed a compromise. All research activities of their organization would be continued. All efforts to mobilize wider business constituencies such as those that the CED's Field Development division had undertaken on a decentralized, community-by-community basis during the war, however, would be ended. Thereby, the CED could continue to provide enlightened conservative guidance to interested businessmen, at the price of ceasing the active grass roots organizing that placed it in competition with other national business associations. If the NAM or the Chamber of Commerce was interested, CED spokesmen continued, they might merge their organizations with the component parts of the CED's far-flung grass roots affiliates.

As events transpired, the CED leaders' abrogation of part of the wartime gentleman's agreement that had furthered cooperation with other business groups was quietly resolved. The efforts to interest the conservative NAM and Chamber of Commerce in keeping the possibly competing CED grass roots organization alive failed dismally, and the Field Development division was abolished. CED research, however, continued on without interruption. Big-business politicians were willing to travel part of the distance necessary to reassure smaller entrepreneurs that they were not trying to limit their influence or power. They were not, however, willing to utterly and completely abolish the private research organization they had created to enunciate moderate rather than extremely conservative solutions to the problem of increased federal power.[17]

Evidence of big businessmen's continuing desire to influence the formulation and implementation of federal policy in new ways was not hard to find in the immediate postwar period. As the struggle over full employment was ending, another round in the ongoing conflict regarding national labor-relations policy was beginning in earnest. The business politicians of the CED and the Business Council were not slow in giving it their full attention.

The postwar labor struggle owed much to organized labor's experience during the wartime mobilization. From 1941 to 1945, businessmen seized the opportunity provided by the war to equate continued labor militancy with a lack of patriotism. They sought, further, to use federal power to limit trade unions' ability to make significant organizational and membership gains in a period of tight labor markets. The businessmen's success, as we saw in the preceding chapter, was only partial. Business Council representatives on the War Labor Board, for example, had had to moderate their opposition to the inclusion of union security clauses in wartime labor contracts. In the realm of wartime wage policy, however, corporate efforts to blunt labor's ability to capitalize on its war-induced contractual advantages were considerably more successful.

During the early months of the Second World War, the War Labor Board struggled to define a generally acceptable position on wage issues. Wage control was clearly a key element in any effort to control wartime inflationary pressures, which could threaten national economic stability. The question, however, involved who would do the controlling—and who would be controlled. Acting in a largely *ad hoc* fashion, the War Labor Board initially proposed that wages be increased no faster than overall increases in the cost of living. Thereby, the Board hoped, workers could be protected from the effects of wartime inflation and, at the same time, restrained from forcing large wage demands upon industry—demands that would only worsen the inflationary situation faced by the entire country.

By September of 1942, however, the executive branch acted to firm up the Labor Board's resolve. With widespread congressional support, Roosevelt introduced and quickly passed into law the Economic Stabilization Act, which sought to keep wages, prices, and salaries from rising higher than the levels they had reached on September 15, 1942. Instead of allowing wartime wage rates to rise in tandem with wartime price levels, the White House and Congress were trying to freeze wages and prices by simply placing a cap on the upward movement of both.

Here the problems really began. In the months following the passage of the Economic Stabilization Act, prices edged higher. Black markets started to flourish, and some businessmen edged their way around price controls by diluting the quality of their goods. Labor leaders grumbled that price controls weren't working, and that wage rates should continue to rise in proportion to the continuing increase in the wartime cost of living. The immovable cap on wages, they continued, must be removed in order to keep workers from losing real purchasing power. The Roosevelt White House ignored the suggestion.[18]

Economic infighting soon commenced in earnest. The public and business members of the War Labor Board opposed efforts to remove the cap on wartime wage rates. Labor representatives on the Board responded by filing protest after protest. After these verbal attacks proved unavailing, trade union leaders looked for legal avenues around the rigid wage limitations. Fringe benefits soon became one of the preferred means of evading federal controls. Many unions bargained for—and often got—nonwage perquisites like paid vacations and company-financed medical plans. A considerably smaller number of the most powerful unions—notably the United Mine Workers—blasted holes through Washington's wage ceilings by threatening nationwide strikes that would tie up war production. John L. Lewis, in particular, became identified in the public mind with a domestic version of gunboat diplomacy. The grandiose threats emanating from the ostentatious Lewis proved unfortunate for organized labor as a whole, in that they provided ammunition for conservatives anxious to blame all mobilization problems upon the trade unions that many of them despised.[19]

The ultimate result of all this administrative brawling was that wartime wage restrictions were gradually but substantially weakened. The problem, from the unions' point of view, was that wage limitations were not watered down as thoroughly or quickly as the price limitations were. As a result, workers were relatively worse off than other occupational groups—notably businessmen and farmers.[20]

Conscious of the relative deprivation that their members had suffered during wartime, ambitious trade union leaders sought to force postwar wage scales up—particularly to compensate for the loss of lucrative overtime earnings as all-out war production ceased. In addition, many union spokesmen acted on the basis of their individual self-interest. Militancy on wage issues would, many assumed, guarantee their own organization's continued survival. Ongoing jurisdictional feuds between the AFL and the CIO had been put on the back burner by the maintenance-of-membership compromise worked out during the war. When peace returned, however, internecine labor factionalism once again became the order of the day throughout American industry. By the late summer of 1945, the nation was experiencing an intense postwar strike wave. During the last three months of that year, the total number of man-days of idleness caused by strikes was almost three times as large as the figure for the worst wartime year. In 1946, the situation was five times worse again: 116 million man-days of work were lost to strikes. Four and a half million workers downed tools—a larger number than in any previous year on record.[21]

In such an atmosphere of renewed labor militancy, relations between the Truman administration and union leaders steadily worsened. As early as August of 1945, a close associate of CIO President Philip Murray wrote one of Truman's top White House aides that "Murray feels keenly that the president is attempting to do the whole job of reconverting [to a peacetime economy] without so much as asking labor to kiss his royal ass, so far as taking part is concerned." The problem, the note continued, was that Truman had "turned the whole job over to the industrialists."[22]

Truman, for his part, was in no mood to take such attacks by labor leaders kindly. A few weeks after receiving Murray's complaints, Truman confided to his private diary that "like every 'new rich,' and person who comes into power suddenly, 'Labor' has gone off the beam. The job now is to bring them back." The new President's resolve was further firmed up by subsequent warnings from

Cabinet officers that the Democrats would fare badly in the upcoming 1946 congressional elections unless they did something to short-circuit labor unrest.[23]

In the midst of all this backstairs controversy within the Democratic party, congressional Republicans—in the person of Senator Arthur H. Vandenberg of Michigan—seized the initiative. On July 30, 1945, Vandenberg proposed that the Truman White House call a national labor-management conference to "lay the groundwork for peace with justice on the home front. . . . Responsible management," Vandenberg intoned, "knows that free collective bargaining is here to stay and that progressive law must continue to support it and that it must be wholeheartedly accepted." The thing for Truman to do was to select a group of business leaders, counterpoint them with a group of labor leaders, and lock them all in a room until they could come to workable compromises on ways of avoiding strikes.[24]

Truman cared nothing for Vandenberg's grandiloquent rhetoric. The Democratic President realized, however, that he was beginning to run out of political negotiating room. If the Democrats appeared to be doing nothing, Republicans like Vandenberg would cheerfully lay the political blame for postwar strikes on their opponents' backs —and keep it there as long as it took to weaken the new administration's tenuous mandate to provide further legislative aid and comfort to trade unions. In an effort to forestall such eventualities, Truman finally acted. Late in October of 1945, he called a National Labor-Management Conference together in Washington.

What resulted from Truman's initiative was an unwieldly assembly of old friends and old enemies. Eighteen management representatives—the vast majority of whom represented medium-sized firms powerful in the affairs of the National Association of Manufacturers and the U.S. Chamber of Commerce—were joined by an equal number of labor representatives from the AFL, the CIO, the United Mine Workers, and the railroad unions. These thirty-six men were charged with trying to work out unanimous agreements on collective-bargaining policy, jurisdictional disputes, strike prevention, wage increases, union security provisions, and a host of other, more technical issues. Government, as a distinct party in interest, was not represented at the conference—although three *pro forma* public "moderators" were appointed. By advertising the meeting as a purely private affair, Truman hoped to shift the burden of blame for continuing labor unrest from the public to the private sector.[25]

As it happened, the National Labor-Management Conference did nothing in particular and did it very well—perhaps a little too well for Truman's taste. A month of well-publicized meetings produced broad agreement on a handful of nebulous generalities. The major issues dividing business and trade union leaders were not substantially resolved. This fact was obscured, however, behind surface good cheer from management and labor leaders alike. Meanwhile, it was business as usual on the picket lines. Fearful that further benign inactivity in Washington would only redound to his political discredit, Truman stepped in to call a speedy end to the Conference a month after it had begun. To try to salvage something from the affair, Truman thereupon threatened that government would act on its own initiative to restore industrial peace. This threat, given the relative weakness of Truman's congressional mandate on domestic labor-relations issues, proved to be as insubstantial as the National Labor-Management Conference had been. Strikes continued to increase in number and severity in key industries including steel, automobile manufacturing, and coal. Within six months, Truman was reduced to the expedient of threatening to draft strikers into the military, in an effort to hammer out a settlement in the strategic railroad industry.[26]

Amid all of the wrangling regarding postwar labor policies, elements of continuity and change in American big businessmen's attitudes toward organized labor were present. As in the past, big-business leaders distrusted labor leaders profoundly and sought to limit the growth of their power wherever and whenever possible. But now big businessmen were unwilling to take the political risks involved in trying to smash unions by means of open-shop crusades, such as those that had been successfully undertaken in many industries immediately after World War I. Instead of hiring strikebreakers and fighting trade unions tooth and nail, the leaders of large corporations relied upon peaceful techniques. Managers sought to wait unions out by accepting long strikes. More importantly, they called upon the federal government to intervene in order to bring a halt to unsettled labor conditions—through legislation, if necessary. Big-business activists, on the basis of their experiences in wartime mobilization, were finally coming to understand that Washington was a tool that they, too, could use to further their interests.[27]

The process of entrepreneurial adjustment involved here, however, was hardly an easy one. Labor relations, like no other issue, generated intense suspicion and hesitancy in the minds of corporate managers. As a result, the postwar rapprochement between organized business and federal power was a gradual one, at best.

An early step along this road was taken by the corporate politicians of the Business Council in October of 1945. As part of their preparations for the National Labor-Management Conference, the chairman and vice-chairman of the Council's Labor Policy Committee (Charles Hook of Armco and H. W. Prentis of Armstrong Cork, both past presidents of the NAM) commissioned a report on desirable changes in labor legislation, which was approved by the full Council and taken to the subsequent Conference meeting. Though Hook and Prentis were the only two active Business Council members to attend the deliberations, their report served as a basis for other business groups' postwar labor-relations programs.

The Business Council's labor policy report started off by sounding familiar corporate themes. Union "coercion or intimidation" of employers should be prohibited and a "bona fide labor organization" for collective-bargaining purposes should consist of any organization of employees "where there is no demonstrated company domination." These two planks merely restated businessmen's long-standing hostility to violent picketing and to NLRB skepticism regarding the independence of firm-specific company unions unaffiliated with the AFL or the CIO.

The third plank of the Business Council report was, likewise, old material—with slightly new twists. Internal union financial and electoral processes should be opened up to federal inspection. Further, the Council recommended, unions should be required to meet "certain reasonable standards" of internal governance as a precondition for being covered under the terms of the National Labor Relations Act. These unions should, in addition, be required to register with some government agency and receive certificates of good standing for collective-bargaining purposes. Washington, in short, should license trade unions.

The Council report then proceeded to address the comparatively new issue of union security. Its views were not conciliatory. "Any provision," the report began, "which requires a person to become or remain a member of a labor organization or to pay dues, in order to get or hold a job . . . should be excluded from the scope of legally required [collective] bargaining." Closed shops (which required a worker to be a member of a union at the time he or she was hired) and union shops (which required workers to join a union after a certain period of time if they wished to continue their employment), then, should not be subjects about which employers were required to negotiate with trade unions. Here the Business Council plainly registered its discontent with the contractual advantages—mainly union-shop provisions—that strong unions had been able to achieve during the World War II mobilization.

Following this hard-line statement were several more aimed at ensuring management's right to bargain with unorganized minorities of workers free from union interference, and guaranteeing that supervisory workers like shop foremen would be ineligible for membership in trade unions. Unions, the Council statement went on, should also be prohibited from bargaining about matters that were exclusively managerial in nature. Under the rubric "exclusively managerial," the Council saw fit to include everything from the scheduling and subcontracting of work to work rules, discipline, job classification, rate setting, merit increases, the promotion and demotion of workers, and the administration of fringe-benefit programs. Unions, then, should concern themselves only with the most general questions involving the wages and hours of their members.[28]

As if all this weren't enough to chill the hearts of trade union leaders, the Business Council had further *desiderata* in mind. Its members wanted sympathetic strikes and secondary boycotts outlawed. Jurisdictional strikes should also be prohibited as "unfair labor practices." Though the Council expressed itself as being opposed to compulsory conciliation and arbitration of labor disputes, it did support such action when strikes affected any "industry or activity of vital importance which through strike or lockout poses serious hardships to the community." Such determinations of serious hardship, it continued, should be made by an "impartial administrative agency." Washington, then, should be able to ban strikes in conditions of peacetime national emergency, as it had earlier done in wartime.

Concluding its catalogue of what it termed "moderate," "constructive," and "dispassionate" proposals, the Council put itself on record in favor of recommendations that unions should be persecutable under the antitrust acts "when their actions are detrimental to the public interest," that labor organizations should be "prohibited by permanent law from making any contributions in connection with any political convention or primary or general elections," and that unions should be restricted from bargaining with employers on an industrywide basis. Powerful unions, in short, were to be forced to bargain in as balkanized a fashion as possible—whereas the same logic was not to apply to industrywide action by powerful employers.[29]

In the unsettled labor relations climate of the immediate postwar period, no tabulation of big-business proposals like the foregoing had the faintest chance of being seriously considered by trade union leaders. Catalogues of desired changes in labor law like the one that the Business Council had outlined, a disgruntled William Green of the AFL later remarked, proceeded "from the false assumption that the [trade union] lambs have grown so formidable that the welfare of the [employer] wolves is now in jeopardy." CIO spokesmen were no more conciliatory, seeing the Council's report as merely part of an employer effort to use federal power to chip away at many of the gains that organized labor had won during the preceding fifteen years. As a result of such negative perceptions, the Council position paper had no measurable impact upon the thinking of the labor delegates to the National Labor-Management Conference.[30]

Business Council spokesmen, however, came away from the National Labor-Management Conference considerably more satisfied with their influence upon the employer participants in the meetings. "One of the important results of the conference," delegate H. W. Prentis reported to a Council meeting in December of 1945, "was [the creation of] a united front on the part of management delegates." This united front, as expressed in unanimous statements adopted by employer representatives at the close of the Conference, echoed most of the ideas expressed in the Business Council position paper.[31]

This unity of NAM, U.S. Chamber of Commerce, and Business Council representatives was not an accident. It was the result of a convergence of corporate opinion on labor-relations policy issues in the immediate postwar period. Such convergence did not mean that the corporate conservatives active in the affairs of the NAM and the Chamber of Commerce saw eye to eye with the relatively pragmatic corporate politicians of the Business Council and the CED. Far from it. It meant, rather, that both right- and left-wing businessmen were shifting their political positions in order to capitalize on postwar opportunities. In the process, both groups ended up pursuing parallel courses toward different ends.

Corporate conservatives, for their part, concentrated upon

means. They strove to appear moderate by calling a halt to a decade of fruitless efforts to repeal the National Labor Relations Act of 1935 outright. Such grand reactionary gestures had satisfied the ideological desires of traditionalist employers who despised the whole concept of federally guaranteed collective-bargaining rights. They had done very little, however, to limit the growth of union power. In the months immediately following the end of the war, therefore, the leaders of many previously rabidly anti-union employer associations —particularly the NAM and the Chamber of Commerce—turned back efforts to push their organizations into another futile campaign to destroy New Deal labor legislation root and branch. Instead, they sought to gradually change national labor policy and weaken trade union power over a period of years. Rather than trying to kill trade unions outright, conservative business leaders decided upon a policy of slow legislative strangulation. Conservatives, then, changed their short-term tactics rather than altering their long-term strategy.[32]

Relatively liberal business leaders like those grouped in the Business Council and the CED, however, tended to be more sophisticated —or at least realistic—than their conservative opposite numbers. Right-wing businessmen generally assumed that the powerful unions that had grown up during fifteen years of economic and military emergency were hothouse plants—parvenu institutions that did not truly reflect the interests and opinions of large numbers of their members. As unrepresentative bodies, unions would gradually wither away as business-backed legislation was passed into law enabling workers to exercise their individual rights regarding their conditions of employment.

Corporate realists like Paul Hoffman, Charles Hook, and H. W. Prentis knew better than this. Powerful trade union movements, such men realized, were going to remain permanent fixtures on the American industrial scene. The question was not whether unions would be strong, but how they might be limited in the exercise of their powers. Realizing that the politics of gradualism would not decisively undermine union strength, pragmatic business activists concentrated their efforts on containing the expansion of the collective-bargaining rights claimed by the organized labor movement.

Ideological distinctions like the ones just discussed did not overly concern the leaders of the American labor movement. AFL and CIO luminaries did not place much value upon businessmen's public rhetoric. Nor did they normally spend a great amount of their time pondering the nuances of corporate leaders' world views. Instead, they watched what businessmen were doing.

When labor leaders examined businessmen's actions in the immediate postwar period, they observed that corporations—large, intermediate, and small—were mounting a coordinated effort to discipline the labor movement. Whether discipline was a prelude to outright attack was an unanswered question in many unionists' minds. So, rather than placing any trust in corporate policy statements, activist labor leaders became even more firmly persuaded that the best postwar defense was a good offense.

This aggressive strategy, however, backfired badly. Unions had looked comparatively good during a depression era in which businessmen were seen by many people as arrogant and uncaring fools whose imprudence had produced widespread social and economic catastrophe. Then, the union struggle for power was insistently advertised in David-and-Goliath terms. By the end of World War II, however, unions were no longer organizational poor relations. In the dozen years preceding 1945, total trade union membership had grown from 3 million to 15 million. Corporate Goliaths—given the relative affluence of postwar circumstances—also looked far less vicious than they had when the nation's chief problem had been the apportioning of scarcity instead of the managing of abundance. Labor leaders, however, remained wedded to 1930's rhetoric, and intensified their problems by resolutely ignoring the negative effects of the renewed civil war between the AFL and the CIO that erupted in the wake of the removal of wartime labor controls. Jurisdictional disputes alone cost unions much in terms of all-important popular support from those tens of millions of middle-class Americans who couldn't tell the difference between a shop steward and a steam shovel.

In a successful effort to capitalize upon growing public impatience and skepticism about the claims of powerful unions, big businessmen began to use their considerable talents to mount a public relations blitz aimed at recovering the political initiative regarding the resolution of labor problems that they had so emphatically lost during Franklin D. Roosevelt's presidency.

An essential element of this corporate strategy was the oft-repeated statement that pragmatic managers of large companies were no longer out to destroy unions. The hitherto reactionary Ford Motor Company was one of the pacesetters in this. As early as

January of 1946, Henry Ford II, newly appointed as chief executive officer of his grandfather's corporate domain, was going out of his way to make soothing comments. The corporation that he headed, Ford stated, had "no desire to 'break the unions,' to turn back the clock. . . . We do not want to destroy the unions. We want to strengthen their leadership by helping them assume the responsibilities they must assume if the public interest is to be served."

Efforts to "solve the human equation in mass production," Ford continued, required an "improved and increasingly responsible union leadership" that would allow union contracts to be "written and agreed upon with the same efficiency and good temper that marks the negotiation of a commercial contract between two companies."[33]

Ford's speech, entitled "The Challenge of Human Engineering," was characterized by the logic that had earlier motivated the abortive efforts of corporate liberals like Gerard Swope and Henry Dennison to work out compromises on national labor policy during the initial phases of Franklin D. Roosevelt's presidency. Instead of railing at unions for being illegitimate organizations whose existence was a result of foul plots hatched in Washington, Henry Ford II and a new generation of big-business leaders were coming to understand that unions were power structures that could be analyzed, influenced, and incorporated within management's ongoing administrative calculations. In the immediate postwar period, the "human engineering" approach enunciated by Ford characterized the labor relations policies of dozens of the nation's largest firms. Neither relatively liberal corporations such as General Electric nor conservative companies like General Motors mounted frontal assaults on unions. Instead, they upgraded their labor relations bureaucracies, improved internal corporate grievance procedures, sought to cultivate as moderate and enlightened an image as possible in terms of their public discourse, and waited out lengthy and expensive strikes. As unions attacked them, big businessmen temporarily allied themselves with their smaller and more conservative brethren to mount a campaign aimed at winning over the minds of the American public—and of its legislative representatives on Capitol Hill.[34]

In these efforts to influence the future direction of federal labor policy in their interest, the big-business activists of the Business Council and the CED—joined by the NAM and the Chamber of Commerce—were using the same kind of "yes, but" strategy that had worked so well during the crucial early stages of the struggle over postwar full-employment legislation. Instead of adopting a negative position, business leaders were advocating "*more* government intervention on behalf of the employer in order to balance what [they] considered excessive government support for trade unions."[35]

The businessmen's strategy paid off handsomely. Labor leaders fell into the trap of arguing against any change in labor law proposed by businessmen without putting forward a reform agenda of their own. Thereby, they lost their political leverage—in just the way, in fact, that businessmen had lost theirs in the 1930's. The Truman White House, likewise, was able to mount no effective opposition to corporate initiatives. Bedeviled by foreign policy problems and lacking any coherent strategy for dealing with postwar strikes, Truman, too, floundered—diverting himself from his mounting political problems by penning ferocious private attacks upon uncooperative labor leaders, in which he variously characterized them as traitors, communists, or cowardly demagogues who had luxuriated in home front luxury while brave men died on foreign battlefields protecting them.[36]

Truman's feral reactions had cause. By the middle of 1946, the new President was in a quintessentially ironic political situation. Truman was personally anxious to assume an activist stance and discipline particularly unruly union leaders by supporting legislation aimed at requiring cooling-off periods before strikes could occur and by making unions more legally liable for breach of contract. Presidential aides passed this information on to the Business Council's Labor Relations Committee, among others. When, however, Truman tried to pass legislation aimed at accomplishing these twin goals on Capitol Hill, congressional conservatives, with the widespread backing of all important national business groups, appended additional planks to the legislation banning jurisdictional strikes, outlawing secondary boycotts, and placing other legal limitations upon trade unions along the lines suggested by the management delegation at the National Labor-Management Conference of 1945. The Business Council enthusiastically lent its support to these efforts to weigh down Truman's initial proposals with a bevy of extras, and protested strongly when Truman eventually decided to veto the resulting bill in order to avoid the risk of alienating labor generally.[37]

Just after vetoing the bill mentioned above, Truman sought to decrease corporate pressure upon conservatives in Congress by leaving the White House to pay his first visit to a meeting of the Business Council held at a Washington hotel. Truman assured Council members in a brief address that he really had a lot in common with big-business leaders (whom he privately referred to as the "cartel boys"). Straining after an identity of interest that did not exist, the President remarked that when he had failed in the haberdashery business just after World War I, he made it a special point to pay back every cent of money he owed to the firm of one of the Business Council members then present in the room. Presidential financial rectitude like this was guaranteed to elicit applause from any entrepreneurial gathering. Truman's homey anecdotes, however, could hardly persuade businessmen not to capitalize upon their growing legislative opportunities. The symbolism of Truman's appearance before the Business Council was itself an eloquent testimony to the degree to which the nation's corporate leadership was recovering political initiative. In Franklin D. Roosevelt's time, Council delegations had traveled to the White House for meetings with the President. In Truman's presidency, the roles of host and guest began to be reversed.[38]

The results of the congressional elections in November of 1946 made the scope of corporate opportunity very evident indeed. Capitalizing upon widespread public impatience with the Truman administration's credibility problems on the domestic political scene, Republicans gained a total of fifty-five seats in the House and thirteen in the Senate. For the first time in sixteen years, Republicans had control over both chambers of the national legislature, and were able to outvote their opponents 245 to 188 in the lower and 51 to 45 in the upper house.

Following this impressive conservative political resurgence, employer campaigns to achieve legislative solutions to their labor relations problems began in earnest. Congress proved receptive to these initiatives. No less than seventeen separate bills to modify New Deal labor policy were swiftly introduced in the House of Representatives alone. Conservative initiatives benefitted from the weakness of labor union opposition. Union leaders, as their political situation worsened, continued to simply oppose, thereby isolating themselves with a negative and do-nothing political image.

Congressional conservatives took advantage of organized labor's political debility to ramrod an extremely tough labor-law reform bill through the House in March and April of 1947. The House version, whose passage was orchestrated by New Jersey Congressman Fred Hartley, was a "Christmas tree bill"—one that had something in it for everybody. All of the important planks in the Business Council's labor policy report of October, 1945, for example, were included in the legislation, as were other provisions aimed at abolishing the National Labor Relations Board, outlawing mass picketing, scourging communists from labor unions, making it easier for employers to prohibit unions from striking by means of court injunctions, placing a wide spectrum of internal union affairs under close judicial scrutiny, and threatening unions with a variety of legal punishments for violating the rights of individual employees who did not wish to join an AFL or CIO affiliate. Although NAM representatives assumed a relatively high political profile in the closed-door sessions during which the House bill was pieced together, corporate lawyers from a wide variety of other trade associations and individual firms were also intimately involved in the process.[39]

The locus of legislative action then shifted to the Senate, where somewhat more moderate (and considerably better organized) conservative forces under the leadership of Robert A. Taft of Ohio were in control. These Senate Republicans proceeded to excise some of the harshest elements of the House bill, including items that had earlier been placed upon the conservative reform agenda by the business representatives who had attended the National Labor-Management Conference eighteen months before. This process of legislative pruning proved agreeable to the House Republican leadership. For, as Congressman Hartley himself later explained, he and his House peers "deliberately put everything we could into the House bill so that we would have something to concede and still get an adequate bill in the end."[40]

Once in Senate hands, the conservative campaign became unstoppable. By June 5, 1947, the final version of the Taft-Hartley Act had passed both houses of Congress. Two weeks later, Truman vetoed the legislation. Three days after that, two-thirds majorities in both houses passed the first major revision of national labor relations policy in a dozen years into law over White House opposition.

Taft-Hartley was a sprawling, complex piece of legislation. The law prohibited some exercises of trade union power and sought to limit others but did not substantially address itself to other variations on collective-bargaining themes. Legislative prohibitions in the act included bans on the closed shop, jurisdictional strikes, and secondary boycotts. Employers were also freed from any legal requirement to bargain collectively with unions composed of foremen or other "managerial or supervisory" employees. Unions whose officers were unwilling to sign anticommunist loyalty oaths were denied federal protection of any sort. Unions were also required to give employers sixty days notice before seeking modifications in, or termination of, a contract, and could, in the event that a particular strike was deemed to affect adversely the national health and safety, be ordered by federal officials to return to work and accept federal mediation services during a mandatory cooling-off period of up to eighty days' duration. Rounding off the list of major proscriptions was a prohibition (none too successful, as it turned out) against individual unions' making contributions to the campaign of any candidate for elected federal office.

Limitations on union power contained in the Taft-Hartley Act included a clear recognition of employers' rights to file damage suits against unions for breach of contract or for efforts to intimidate employers or employees by violent means. Though union shops were not prohibited, two elements in the act sought to constrain their growth. First, the act allowed the various states to maintain such legislation banning union shops as they already had—or to pass new legislation if they wished. Taft-Hartley, then, permitted the union shop, but also allowed any state law prohibiting union shops to prevail over the federal act. This bit of legislative legerdemain elicited intense opposition from the AFL and CIO. Secondly, Taft-Hartley required that all union-shop contracts that AFL or CIO affiliates might win from reluctant corporations be agreed to by a majority of all workers in those plants. This particular wrinkle was placed in the act by conservative businessmen who continued to believe that workers would, if given the opportunity, oppose contracts that stripped them of their individual freedom by requiring them to join a union as a condition of their permanent employment at a particular factory. Plainly, a significant segment of right-wing opinion, exemplified by the NAM, had not quite lost hold of the delusion that powerful unions were really nothing more than unlucky wounds from which the nation might speedily recover. The fact that 94 percent of the almost 2 million workers who had the opportunity to cast ballots on union-shop contracts during the first year of the Taft-Hartley Act voted for such contracts demonstrated the foolishness of that belief.[41]

However, Taft-Hartley did not embody all the elements of the immediate postwar Business Council–NAM–Chamber of Commerce consensus. Employers did not, for example, get everything excluded from the realm of "legitimate collective bargaining" that they wanted excluded. Unions were effectively constrained from organizing lower-level managers like shop foremen, but the broader campaign to limit union bargaining to the realm of wages and hours alone by the passage of a legislative diktat proved unsuccessful. Neither were businessmen able to obtain a legislative ban on mass picketing. And they failed (by the slimmest of Senate margins) in their attempts to include a ban on multi-employer bargaining by trade unions in the Taft-Hartley Act. Employer efforts to amend the antitrust acts so that they could use them as one more legal club to discipline unions, likewise, got nowhere in Congress.

Taft-Hartley, then, was not an unalloyed corporate triumph. Still, business groups like the NAM and the Business Council had gotten quite enough for their immediate purposes. Labor had been handed a severe political defeat. This, more than any technical element of the legislation (about which most workers knew very little, in any event), served notice on trade unions that businessmen, too, could play the congressional labor relations game.[42]

Passage of the Taft-Hartley Act, then, marked the completion of the second stage of the process by which organized business recovered the political initiative in the immediate postwar period. Instead of continuing its frontal assault on the fundamentals of New Deal collective-bargaining policy, a broad alliance of corporate interest groups successfully backed legislation that trussed up labor unions in a dense web of legal restraints, restraints that limited unions' ability to extend the scope of their power at the expense of managerial prerogatives. Once it became clear that liberal forces were unable to marshal sufficient congressional support to repeal Taft-Hartley—even after unexpected Democratic victories in the 1948 elections—the alliance of convenience regarding labor relations policy between the relatively conservative NAM and Chamber of Commerce and the comparatively moderate Business Council and CED swiftly broke down. From this time forth, big-business-backed organizations like the latter made no effort to expand the scope of their victories. Having used Congress to deny the postwar industrial initiative to the AFL and the CIO, larger corporations and their leaders were generally content to live with a status quo in which powerful trade unions figured prominently. The Business Council, certainly, was well pleased with its work. "We submit," the Council intoned in a report on Taft-Hartley that it produced in January of 1949,

> that the act has in general been beneficial and has not had the adverse consequences alleged. Union membership has increased by 1,500,000 since 1946. Wage rates have risen sharply. While industrial disputes have not been eliminated there has been a worth while reduction in the number of man days lost to industrial disputes. Jurisdictional strikes have been practically eliminated. Union leadership has become more responsible. Individual liberties of the worker have been protected and the public has been less of a victim of industrial disputes.

Federal power, it appeared, had redeeming value, so long as the nonmarket social controls that Washington exercised were used to protect businessmen along lines that they themselves suggested.[43]

Containing Communism Abroad: From the Marshall Plan to the Korean War

As the fight over passage of the Taft-Hartley Act drew to a close, a new and different legislative struggle began. In this conflict, however, the focus of political concern shifted from the domestic to the international arena. The question of the hour was no longer full employment or labor law reform. It was, instead, how to maintain a permanent and powerful American presence in continental Europe and the lands adjacent to the eastern Mediterranean. The same big-business activists who had earlier directed their energies toward containing New Deal social welfare and collective-bargaining initiatives at home moved to ally themselves with the nation's political leadership in order to contain the spread of Russian power and communist ideology abroad. In the process, corproate policy organizations like the Business Council and the Committee for Economic Development became bridges over which influential corporate leaders streamed into government, there to staff or advise a network of administrative agencies established to forward cooperative relationships between big business and federal bureaucrats. In the foreign policy field as nowhere else, rapprochement between the nation's corporate and political leaderships became a matter of compelling concern in the immediate postwar period. A federal government that had become powerful over the concerted opposition of most businessmen remained powerful, in substantial part, in order to maintain American economic, military, and political interests in strategic parts of the globe.

Europe was the major concern of corporate and governmental policymakers alike. Five years of war had ravaged populations and destroyed social, political, and economic infrastructures throughout the region. Postwar droughts and severe winters added to the formidable problems of national reconstruction. In such severe circumstances, fears of a Russian ideological and military threat to Western Europe and the eastern Mediterranean littoral grew. A Soviet Union whose army had conquered and occupied Europe east of the Elbe was likely, the argument went, to try to capitalize upon economic hardship, destabilize fledgling parliamentary regimes wherever and whenever possible, and finally turn the entire European continent into a collection of Marxist-Leninist puppet states. By the middle of 1947, three fourths of the Americans polled in national public opinion surveys agreed with the idea that the USSR was trying to "build itself up to be the ruling power of the world" in an aggressive and expansionist fashion.[44]

The growing public concern regarding Russian leaders' postwar intentions presented the Truman administration with a long-sought opportunity to expand the scope of the American role as a guarantor of last resort far beyond the Western Hemisphere. The United States, already accustomed to ambitious interpretations of the Monroe Doctrine that placed the nation in the position of being a regional police power, would now proceed to become the policeman of the noncommunist world. By May of 1947, the White House had successfully convinced Congress to appropriate $400 million to shore up friendly Greek and Turkish regimes in order to contain the spread of Russian power in the eastern Mediterranean. An era of Pax Americana had begun.

Emergency aid to Greece and Turkey was only the beginning of the long and by now familiar "containment" story. On June 5, 1947, the very day that Congress sent the Taft-Hartley Act to President Truman, Secretary of State General George Catlett Marshall outlined an ambitious and unprecedented program of long-term American economic and industrial assistance for European economic recovery, in a commencement address at Harvard University.

Marshall's proposal for a multibillion-dollar program of grants and long-term loans to interested European nations sounded very grand and philanthropic, far too much so for a formidable set of practical politicians on Capitol Hill. Republicans grouped around Senator Robert A. Taft of Ohio, in particular, had a long history of suspicion about "entangling alliances" with European powers, and even greater fears that any program of large-scale economic assistance that a Democratic White House initiated would, almost inevitably, end up being put to nefarious radical purposes. American wealth, Taft proclaimed, should not be used to establish a "European TVA." With the untrustworthy Truman in charge, feckless Europeans would very likely use the taxpayers' money to finance a thoroughgoing socialization of the European industrial economy.

Where Taft feared creeping socialism, Joseph Stalin feared capitalist subversion; after some initial hesitation, Russia's dictator told Truman that he had no intention whatsoever of allowing the Soviet Union or its military protectorates in Eastern and Central Europe to participate in the proposed program. Such Russian opposition stilled some of the more virulent opposition to the fundamental ideas Secretary of State Marshall had outlined, but it did nothing to quiet Republican and conservative Democratic concern regarding the nuts-and-bolts political issues of how much money to spend, the hows and whys of spending it, and the creation of an administrative structure to oversee the whole process.[45]

Such continuing conservative opposition placed Truman and his top policy advisers in difficult political circumstances. On the one hand, they wanted to help finance European economic recovery as a means of preventing a political radicalization that they believed could only serve to expand Soviet power. On the other hand, a powerful conservative coalition in Congress was not going to vote the necessary funds to accomplish the Truman administration program unless it got guarantees that the money would not be misused. To resolve the resulting stalemate, the Truman White House turned to big-business leaders for support.

The businessmen were glad, even anxious, to oblige. The Business Council and the CED had been worried about the Russian threat for some time. Former Business Council Chairman W. Averell Harriman, in fact, became one of the leaders in the push to expedite government-industry collaboration to deal with this issue. Harriman, FDR's wartime ambassador to the Soviet Union, had returned from his post in early 1945 convinced that the state of Russian-American relations was perilous indeed, and advocated a stronger American response toward Russian territorial claims in Eastern Europe and elsewhere. By March of 1946, Harriman, accompanied by two high-level State Department officials from the Russian and Eastern European division, got the chance to express his concerns to a meeting of the Business Council. Joining the corporate CEOs in the audience was Henry Agard Wallace, FDR's Vice-President from 1940 to 1944, a man who was then serving a brief and unhappy term as Secretary of Commerce and would soon be sacked by Truman for his opposition to the postwar containment strategy.

Harriman, in Wallace's words, delivered

> a strictly anti-Russian speech. Harriman made it clear that he was in accord with Winston Churchill and that we should be tough with the Russians, even though by doing so we were running the risk of war. He said the communists in every country were only stooges for Stalin and that they were out to overthrow our form of government. . . . Harriman made the point, however, that he was sure Stalin did not want war, and that he was going to do everything he could to expand territorially without war. Harriman thinks we are in the same position relative to Russia in 1946 that we were relative to Germany in 1933; that the important thing to do is to stop Russia before she expands further.

In Henry Wallace's skeptical estimation, Harriman's logic was "mostly the old, old stuff of the kind we have heard for 25 years." "Old stuff" or not, however, Harriman's views were of a type that had gained a great deal of credence in official Washington. Harriman, after all, gave his address to the Business Council flanked by two of the State Department's resident Soviet experts. Moreover, Harriman paused to elicit confirmations of his views from both men at regular intervals during his speech. The symbolism of this sort of thing was clear: Harriman's views were those of the Truman White House. The corporate leaders of the Business Council, Wallace fearfully confided to a private diary, found the speech "very impressive and were in enthusiastic accord with Harriman." To illustrate his point, Wallace described the reaction of Business Council and CED leader Paul Hoffman:

> Hoffman of Studebaker got up after Harriman had completed and said that he thought the talk was perfectly marvellous; that it ought to be given in every town in the United States, and he asked Harriman why he didn't go on a speaking tour carrying the banner.
> [Harriman replied that communist sympathizers in the CIO

would attack him mercilessly.] There was considerable discussion then on how important it was to fight any organization that had any commies in it.

"Harriman and his kind," Wallace concluded in his diary, "if they have their way, will bring on a war which will result in the United States eventually becoming a dictatorship of the left or the right."[46]

Henry Wallace, however, was in no political position to do much more than complain about what he saw as a spectacularly flawed approach toward postwar U.S.-Soviet relations. His logic got nowhere with the membership of the Business Council. On September 19, 1946, four months after Harriman's hard-line address, Wallace found himself in opposition to the Business Council again. Near the opening of another Council meeting in Washington, Wallace was strenuously attacked by longtime Council activist S. Clay Williams of the Reynolds Tobacco Company, for having sent a letter to President Truman stating that a "good many businessmen" were getting nervous about the growing size of the federal debt. Therefore, Wallace had argued, the White House should give serious consideration to reducing the levels of arms spending—then running at $13 billion a year, a dozen times the amount spent during the period immediately preceding the onset of the Second World War. Williams, speaking for the Council as a whole, crisply informed Wallace that his budgetary concerns were not appreciated. According to Wallace:

[Williams said] the general public will infer my phrase "a good many businessmen" to refer to [the Business Council]. He said that they resented the idea that they wanted the national budget cut at the expense of our preparedness. As a matter of fact, it was very clear in listening to Williams talk that he believes strongly in arming to the hilt to fight Russia. They did not put it that bluntly [Wallace somewhat lamely conceded] but that was the only conclusion I could reach from their psychological state of mind. . . .

[After Wallace cooled corporate tempers by assuring Council members that he did not doubt their devotion to military preparedness] the businessmen seemed to feel happy because they let me know their willingness to be taxed heavily so as to be in a position to fight Russia if the need arose.

Following this confrontation, the Council meeting relapsed into *pro forma* politeness. Hands were shaken, and expressions of mutual regard freely offered. Private opinions, however, were another matter entirely. Williams, Wallace confided to his diary, had probably been prevailed upon to mobilize the Business Council against him by "some of the reactionary Southern politicos. . . . On the other hand," Wallace continued, "Clay [Williams] himself is probably a force behind a number of the reactionary Southern politicos." Wallace, it appears, knew that political daggers were being whetted.

Less than twenty-four hours after penning these opinions, Wallace was summarily fired from his Cabinet post by Harry S. Truman. His successor was W. Averell Harriman.[47]

As Henry Wallace was being not so subtly eased out of high-level Washington public policy councils, big-business politicians were being eased in. This process occurred in two stages. In the first, businessmen were recruited to help formulate the proposals for postwar foreign economic assistance that the Truman administration was trying to sell to Congress. In the second, these same businessmen were recruited to implement the policies that they had done so much to create.

By June of 1947, the first stage of this process was well advanced. Nine days after Secretary of State Marshall spoke at Harvard, Arthur H. Vandenberg, the Republican chairman of the Senate Foreign Relations Committee, floated a trial balloon on his own. Vandenberg proposed the creation of a "bipartisan advisory council" to draw up specific recommendations regarding the scope and direction of America's foreign aid effort. The White House was glad to oblige, particularly after Vandenberg told Truman that he would not join in the fight against Robert A. Taft's obstructionist tactics until Truman guaranteed that businessmen would be able to participate substantially in the formulation of the program.

On June 22, the process of recruiting corporate expertise was completed. Secretary of Commerce Harriman was appointed chairman of a President's Committee on Foreign Aid, which was to draft specific recommendations regarding the Marshall Plan. Among the nineteen members joining Harriman on the Committee were nine businessmen, of whom five (in addition to Harriman) were members of the Business Council. Five of the nine also belonged to the CED —including CED Chairman Paul Hoffman. The remaining ten members of this "Harriman Committee" included six college administrators (three of whom were members of the CED's Research Advisory Board), two trade union bureaucrats (one from the AFL and one

from the CIO), an out-of-work politician, and the president of the
Brookings Institution, an influential Washington think-tank. From
the beginning of the Committee's existence, the business representatives were the ones who set the agenda and tone for the group's
work.[48]

In a little over four months of effort, the businessmen and their
confreres hashed out the basics of what would become the Marshall
Plan. Central to their program was a proposal that Congress allocate
between $13 billion and $17 billion for Western European economic
relief over a four-year period. To administer the program, the Harriman Committee proposed the creation of an independent recovery
agency whose director would be able to operate free of White House
interference and ideology. Nor should this czar of the recovery effort
be overly constrained by questions concerning the political systems
of the countries to be aided. After considerable discussion, Hoffman
had succeeded in convincing the group to include a statement in its
final report to the effect that "while this committee firmly believes
in the American system of free enterprise, it does not believe that any
foreign aid program should be used as a means of requiring other
countries to adopt it." By including this key statement, big-business
pragmatists like Hoffman and Harriman sought to short-circuit the
efforts of conservative ideologues like Taft and Herbert Hoover to
require Europeans to forswear all forms of parliamentary socialism
as a precondition for receiving American help.

The Harriman Committee's final report affirmed that aiding
Europe was not, as Taft and Hoover alleged, a question of charity,
but rather one of intelligent self-interest and the survival of American influence in the world. If the United States did nothing to help
the Europeans surmount their war-induced difficulties, the report
warned, all of Europe, Scandinavia, North Africa, the eastern Mediterranean, and the Middle East might fall under Soviet control. Even
England might be pulled into the Russian orbit. Such a result would
be cataclysmic in terms of American geopolitical and economic interests. Such isolation from a Soviet-dominated Europe would cause
"sweeping limitation of our economic and political life" and threaten
"our very form of government" itself.[49]

The Harriman Committee's fearful predictions were not a peculiar or extreme phenomenon in the political environment then developing in Washington. The concerns of W. Averell Harriman and
Paul Hoffman were exactly like those felt by the political leadership

of the Truman administration itself. They also accurately mirrored the views of those articulate business politicians that had been active in Washington ever since the early days of the Second World War.

In the State Department, for example, Business Council member William L. Clayton, a Texas cotton broker then serving as Undersecretary of State for Economic Affairs, evidenced views identical to those contained in the Harriman report when he told a pro-foreign-aid audience in New York that

> the Marshall Plan is not a relief program; it is a recovery program for Western Europe. Hence our interests rather than our humanitarian instincts should be mainly considered. . . . [If the United States refused to provide economic assistance] the Iron Curtain would then move westward at least to the English Channel. Consider what this would mean to us in economic terms alone. A blackout of the European market would compel radical readjustments in our entire economic structure. . . . changes which could hardly be made under our democratic free enterprise system.[50]

The Harriman Committee's recommendations gave Truman a large part of the political backing required to firm up bipartisan support for his European economic recovery proposals on Capitol Hill. The willingness of nationally known corporate leaders like Harriman, Hoffman, Williams, and others to push for foreign aid as a necessary antidote to Soviet imperialism opened up avenues of access to conservative politicians that might otherwise have been closed to the Truman White House. Such businessmen's conservative credentials legitimized Truman's concerns and made Congress more receptive to the idea of financing them.[51]

Final passage of the legislation instituting the Marshall Plan was not, however, an easy or automatic process. The congressional battle began when Truman introduced his proposal in December of 1947 —and continued for almost four months. Conservative forces— among which former President Herbert Hoover and spokesmen for the National Association of Manufacturers figured prominently— made a raft of criticisms of what Truman was trying to do and the way in which he was trying to do it. The foreign aid program, its opponents alleged, was an overly ambitious and ill-conceived "planning" effort based upon the false assumption that government could interfere with natural economic forces and forcefeed a wide-ranging industrial recovery in Western Europe. The export of billions of dollars of investment capital would only undermine the health of the domestic economy, increase inflation and unemployment at home, and very possibly fuel efforts to further regiment free enterprise. Truman's proposal went too far in giving Europeans money and not far enough in ensuring that that money would not be spent in profligate or radical ways. If the weak-willed Democrats really wanted to contain the communist menace, the way to do it was to confront the Soviet Union directly with America's military might, instead of finessing the issue by giving money to untrustworthy European regimes already seduced by socialist ideology.[52]

Corporate leaders who had already assumed a high profile in the foreign aid fight, assisted by other entrepreneurial notables including Owen Young and Philip D. Reed (Young's successor as chairman of General Electric), were not slow to use their influence with key Republican and conservative Democratic legislators to secure the passage of the Marshall Plan over right-wing business and political opposition. Legislators were lobbied, testimony was given to House and Senate committees, and admiring messages were sent to assuage the egos of congressional power brokers. In the midst of all this activity, the Committee for Economic Development sought to expedite a compromise by issuing a report designed to allay conservative fears that the Marshall Plan would become a massive giveaway program administered by New Deal bleeding hearts. The agency that oversaw foreign aid, the CED proposed, should be headed by the czar that the Harriman Committee had proposed. This independent administrator should report regularly to Congress, and should not be a Cabinet officer or high-level Washington bureaucrat. His staff assistants, likewise, should be practical men. Indeed, foreign aid should be run by businessmen—or, as the CED report rather more delicately put it, by "able men who served their country during the war years in dealing with questions similar to those presented by the program of [economic and industrial] cooperation" being proposed. Further, another high-level executive should be appointed as a roving ambassador and hard-nosed negotiator-in-chief with European business and government leaders.[53]

Early in 1948 the legislative logjam finally started to break. A brutal Russian-engineered coup in Czechoslovakia late in February induced a sudden war scare and shocked many hitherto recalcitrant or skeptical politicians into dropping their opposition to an imperfect, but reassuringly nonmilitary approach aimed at doing something about the Soviet threat. On April 3, Congress passed the bill instituting the Marshall Plan by three-to-one majorities in both the Senate and the House.

Moderate Republican leaders like Senator Vandenberg had allied with Democrats to give Truman an important legislative victory. Such cooperation, however, had a price, as Truman soon learned. In a conversation with Vandenberg on the day the foreign aid bill was passed, Truman was told in no uncertain terms that he must appoint a well-known businessman to run the program along the lines laid down by the Harriman Committee, the CED, and Congress itself. Six days later, the White House announced the selection of Paul Hoffman to head the Economic Cooperation Administration (ECA) established to distribute American largesse.[54]

Hoffman's appointment pleased W. Averell Harriman, who had been urging his selection as foreign aid czar ever since the earliest meetings of the Harriman Committee. Hoffman then returned the favor by selecting Harriman to become the ECA's contact man in Europe. American foreign aid had taken on a distinctly corporate tone.[55]

After assuming the number one and number two posts in the ECA, Hoffman and Harriman proceeded to staff their agency with a wide variety of experts, both corporate and academic. Many of these men (e.g., William Batt) had demonstrated their administrative talents and leadership potential during their years of affiliation with the Business Council and the CED. Others were recruited from major law firms and banks. Comparatively few of the ECA's personnel, however, came from the ranks of the career bureaucracy of the federal government. The business political activists who had supported the movement to redirect federal power to more actively contain the expansion of Russian influence were, in the end, the same people picked to run the central organizational component of America's nonmilitary effort to seize and maintain the postwar initiative in Western Europe.[56]

Once in operation, the Marshall Plan pumped almost $13.5 billion of American money into European economies during the course of the ECA's four-year lifetime. Back in the United States, Paul Hoffman used a burgeoning network of political connections to keep congressional appropriations flowing steadily into ECA's coffers and beat off occasional efforts by the State Department and other power centers to assert bureaucratic control over the program. Meanwhile

W. Averell Harriman circulated through Europe easing minds and expediting the influx of thousands of businessmen and technical experts who assisted European firms, trade associations, cartels, and governments in the areas of reconstruction and productivity improvement. Cooperative American trade union leaders also were enrolled to seek to moderate the socialist or communist ideological proclivities of important unions in Italy, France, and elsewhere.[57]

By the time Hoffman and Harriman left the ECA in 1950 (Hoffman to assume the presidency of the Ford Foundation and Harriman to become a top White House aide to Truman), the Marshall Plan experiment had assisted an impressive economic recovery in Western Europe. For all the accomplishment, there were relatively few to cheer it. Political attention had by then shifted from the economic to the military sphere. The outbreak of war in Korea convinced the overwhelming majority of American policy planners and opinion molders that the most important type of foreign aid that the United States could provide to the noncommunist world was military. The deep chill in the Cold War created by the Korean conflict, however, produced no wrenching changes in the steady pattern of political convergence on the part of corporate and government leaders. War, as it had done before, muted conflicts that were internal to America's political system—and reaffirmed the dangers posed to businessman and bureaucrat alike by dangers external to that system. Cooperative relationships flourished accordingly.

Containment Triumphant: War and Emergency Mobilization Return to America

Cabell Phillips of the *New York Times* was a skeptical man. By early 1950 he had been on assignment in Washington long enough to become convinced that a good deal of Harry S. Truman's "give 'em hell" populism was absolute poppycock. To prove his point, Phillips wrote an article for the June 3, 1950, issue of *Collier's* magazine detailing how the Truman White House was going about the job of trying to improve its political standing with powerful business constituencies well in advance of the 1950 and 1952 elections. These efforts, Phillips contended, were "a concerted and carefully organized program to persuade businessmen that the free enterprise system and the Administration are sharing the same life raft on a turbulent wave of the future. Either they pull together toward the same shore . . . or they will both be gobbled up by the sharks of Communism thrashing the waters just astern."[58]

Truman, Phillips continued, was doing more than trying to gain political points by assuring corporate leaders of his devotion to anticommunism at home and abroad. Truman and his top political advisers were easing up on federal antitrust prosecutions, seeking to curry favor with small-business groups by promising them easier access to lucrative defense markets, and circulating around the country giving speeches to business audiences which promised that the era of confrontation between business and government was at an end. Truman's chief economist, Leon Keyserling, for example, was telling gatherings of corporate notables that old Depression-era quarrels regarding the redistribution of economic and political power were passé. In affluent postwar circumstances, reslicing the economic pie was nowhere near as important as enlarging its total size. Business and government, acting together, should bend their combined efforts toward maintaining steady economic and industrial expansion. In this way, investment, productivity, output, employment, and income levels in the society would all rise. Businessmen would make higher profits, workers and farmers would enjoy higher incomes, and government could use expanding tax revenues to finance social welfare programs for the benefit of those unfortunates at the bottom of the economic ladder. In Keyserling's roseate view, business-government cooperation promised a better life for everyone. Anticommunism and public-private collaboration to ensure fast-paced economic growth were, therefore, two sides of the same coin.[59]

Collier's editors were dubious. "Specialized enticements" for big and small businessmen were all very well. But was the Truman White House really serious about making peace—particularly with the big businessmen that Democratic politicians had been publicly excoriating for years? Were Truman's activities anything more than short-term political pump priming?[60]

The Collier's editorial queries became academic a bare three weeks after they were posed. On the morning of June 25, 1950, North Korean forces invaded South Korea, and political pump priming commenced in earnest. The Truman administration acted instantaneously to commit the American military to the struggle. Then it faced the problem of enrolling businessmen in the anticommunist cause.

Truman's task was made a good deal easier by the limited nature of the war in Korea. Fearful that North Korean bellicosity presaged communist military adventures elsewhere, Truman and his top aides downplayed the nation's Asian conflict rhetorically and otherwise. The "police action" in Korea would not, Truman insisted, require the full mobilization of the American economy. What was needed, instead, was partial or "creeping" mobilization—one that would allow America to fight a small war in Asia and, possibly, a big war somewhere else at a later time. Guns, then, would not be allowed to interfere with butter, at least in the short run.

Three weeks after the North Korean attack, Truman spelled out what he meant by limited mobilization when he asked Congress for the power to raise corporate and individual tax rates sharply, to allocate strategic raw materials in order to avoid defense production shortages, and to control credit markets as a means of restraining inflationary panic buying. Truman also requested standby authority to impose wage and price controls in the event that a broader war developed. Congress took seven weeks to make up its mind about Truman's proposals. Conservative opposition to signing a blank check regarding controls was especially intense. In the end, however, Truman got almost all that he wanted. But to ensure that he didn't get any pro-union ideas, Congress forbade Truman to control prices within any industry without, at the same time, controlling wages within that same industry. Further, Congress granted Truman emergency powers for only nine months, at the end of which they would be subject to a thorough legislative review. All of Truman's oft-reiterated statements that he was no wild-eyed New Deal reformer to the contrary, congressional conservatives remained deeply suspicious of his supposed proclivities toward radical "experiments."

Having received his emergency mandate, Truman began a careful and indeed reluctant mobilization. Truman, as one biographer remarked, "initiated controls with the dedication of a man who starts looking for a job Monday morning hoping he will not find one."[61]

Businessmen were a key element in Truman's search for a hedged mobilization policy. As early as July 26, 1950, three Business Council members, W. Averell Harriman, Secretary of the Treasury Snyder, and George Marshall (recently retired as Secretary of State and soon to be appointed Secretary of Defense), met with Council, CED, NAM, and U.S. Chamber of Commerce representatives to brief them on administration plans and try to arrange cooperative relationships.

Initially, Truman's moves elicited no particularly fearful response, and a Wage Stabilization Board and an Office of Price Administration were created to oversee a voluntaristic program of wage and price restraint. Meanwhile, within the Department of Commerce, a National Production Authority was established to allocate strategic commodities.

Business Council members were prominent in the affairs of all these bureaucracies. Council member Cyrus Ching chaired the Wage Stabilization Board, and all its industry members were selected by the Council at the request of Truman's Secretary of Commerce, Charles Sawyer. Leading the National Production Authority was William Henry Harrison of ITT, another Council member. Harrison, like Ching, worked with fellow Council members staffing second-echelon posts. At the Office of Price Administration, the Business Council presence was less visible at the top. Primary price authority resided in the hands of Michael DiSalle, a former mayor of Toledo, Ohio. DiSalle, however, worked closely with the Council. By January of 1951, he was assuring Council members that he was not going to be bound by relatively liberal World War II precedents regarding industrial oversight and control. DiSalle called upon the Business Council to help him recruit businessmen to regulate industries of which they were already a part—no less than nine division heads, thirty-one branch managers, and two hundred departmental heads within his burgeoning agency.

Given such widespread involvement in the nuts and bolts of the early mobilization drive, it is not surprising that Council members made few public statements attacking Truman. CED leaders including Marion Folsom made the occasional speech underlining big-business activists' opposition to all-out wage and price controls, and businessmen in general grumbled when Truman and congressional majorities overrode their objections and passed an excess-profits tax to help finance a pay-as-you-go war. Otherwise, life went on as usual, replete with additional reassurances from Cabinet officers at Business Council meetings regarding White House opposition to anything smacking of rationing, production prohibitions, or other nonmarket sins. Meanwhile, entrepreneurial spirits were lifted by a new round of wartime accelerated-depreciation allowances that eventually accounted for "nearly 90 per cent of the expansion in commercial-type facilities for war production during the Korean War" and by impressive Republican gains in both the House and the Senate in the 1950 congressional elections.[62]

The Communist Chinese, however, posed a more intractable problem. American and allied armies initially enjoyed great success in their efforts to destroy the North Korean Army and restore the prewar boundaries separating the communist and the noncommunist sections of the peninsula. By October of 1950, North Korean aggression had been successfully contained and the 38th-parallel border restored. Impressive as the victory was, it led to unfortunate suppositions and consequences. Not content with containment, America's military chief on the scene, General Douglas MacArthur, promised Truman a quick and decisive rollback of communist power through the military conquest of North Korea. Official Washington, buoyed by optimistic reports from the battlefront and a predictable desire for revenge, decided to gamble on MacArthur's intuition. American and allied forces crossed the 38th parallel and marched on the Yalu River—ignoring Chinese protests that this act would bring them into the war.

The results of the rollback strategy were disastrous. Late in November, Chinese troops entered Korea in force, beginning a campaign that eventually forced American-led forces almost back to the 38th parallel. Victory in a limited war had been followed by defeat in a more extended conflict. Back in Washington, the Truman administration faced a full-fledged national emergency. While containing efforts by MacArthur and his conservative political supporters to recoup losses by widening the war to include air and naval attacks upon China, Truman elected to begin a more ambitious mobilization of the economy. Business Council member Charles Edward Wilson of General Electric was appointed to head a new Office of Defense Mobilization that was to serve as the command post for stepped-up military production at home. Shortly afterward, Truman finally cashed his blank check regarding wage and price controls: voluntary guidelines were replaced by federally enforced restraints.

Truman's actions gave corporate leaders pause. Chamber of Commerce and NAM representatives opposed Truman's expanded controls from the outset. Partial mobilization to fight a limited war was a hard concept to grasp, so difficult that relatively conservative business spokesmen tended to see it as a stalking horse for socialism.[63]

While conservative entrepreneurs blustered, Business Council and CED activists were a good deal more accommodating. Privately they met with a White House delegation headed by economist Leon Keyserling on the eve of the announcement of the expanded controls program, to tell Keyserling and his boss that controls weren't needed and wouldn't work. Publicly, however, members of both groups enunciated "yes, but" positions. Once it became clear that congressional and executive branch support for controls made them inevitable, Council and CED members shifted with the political winds as more of their peers were recruited to staff the mobilization agencies in Washington. Charles Edward Wilson and longtime corporate politician Eric Johnston (whom Truman appointed to a high controls post) were only the most visible representatives of this increased acceptance of wartime collaboration. Such men, in turn, surrounded themselves with corporate experts recruited largely from Business Council and CED member-companies.[64]

Corporate assistance had a price. CED and Council activists sought to link their support for wage and price controls in an unprecedented period of partial military mobilization, to federal cooperation in the realm of taxation and spending policy. Truman could fight the wider war with greater powers of compulsion; in return, however, he should make a start at forswearing New Deal reform precedents regarding how Washington raised its revenues and what it spent those revenues for.

The Business Council spelled out its requirements in a confidential report that it prepared in February of 1951. Since the New Deal, Washington had been extravagant in its spending and too inclined to soak the rich when it taxed. "In the past several years," the Council report complained, "differences of opinion on government expenditures have revolved largely around the issue of the appropriateness of various degrees of socialized spending, with at least a popular presumption that upper-bracket private incomes could be diverted by taxation to cover all public expenditures." The military emergency in Korea, however, should now lead to "drastic curtailment" and "rigid economy" vis-à-vis nonmilitary spending. The federal government, then, must pare down its social-welfare guarantor responsibilities.

Spending reductions alone, however, were not enough, according to the Business Council. Korean reverses had ballooned military expenditures, threatening deficits of as much as $16 billion. Keynesian economic theory to the contrary, deficits were a bad thing. All-out wars might require them, but partial mobilizations for limited conflicts should be handled on a pay-as-you-go basis. Therefore, the Council report continued, taxes must be increased further to pay for the costs of the new war. But these increases should under no circumstances "be levied with some ulterior objective of social or political 'reform' in mind."[65]

Instead of taxing corporations and high-income individuals, then, Truman should persuade Congress to agree to increased sales and excise taxes, raise taxes on middle-income groups, and close tax loopholes that benefited groups other than private industry.[66]

Tax increases aimed at middle-income taxpayers would have an additional advantage, the Council averred: they would drain away purchasing power from consumers—dollars that would otherwise fuel a wartime inflation that mere wage and price controls could not long contain. Terming inflation "our most serious economic hazard," one that might "completely disrupt our social and economic system and our long-term ability to remain strong in the face of the ever-growing Communist threat," the Council showed that the anticommunist crusade could be used to provide legitimacy for the pocketbook concerns of any political or economic interest group clever enough to link its domestic demands with the ultimate success of the national purpose abroad.

On a less cataclysmic note, the Council moved on to make a homey analogy that summarized its view on the wartime controls program: "Price controls, in effect, merely tie down the lid of the tea kettle, and if persisted in long enough, the tea kettle will blow up. What we need to do is to reduce the heat under it. A fundamental attack on the underlying causes of inflation . . . to keep private spending in line with goods available for private consumption is as necessary with price controls as without them."[67]

Truman, then, could have his controls program and retain big-business activists' support—so long as he avoided raising corporate tax rates, cut back nondefense expenditures, balanced the budget, and made the middle class pay for the war. One month after the Council spoke its mind, the CED edged a little further toward the center. Seconding the Council's call for excise and personal income tax hikes, the CED went on to argue that further increases in corporate tax rates were also necessary. Though differences of opinion among "corporate statesmen" were evident, both the Business Council and the CED positions on wartime controls were couched in compromise-minded terms compared with those put forth by traditionalist business groups like the NAM. Where the Council and CED sought to make deals, the NAM howled for blood, calling upon

Truman to dismantle all wartime controls, put a retail sales tax on everything, and fight a rigidly free-enterprise war.

Truman tried to compromise with the big-business moderates. He had little choice but to do so. His devotion to balanced budgets and a pay-as-you-go approach to financing the war was as complete as any businessman's. What Truman could not do, however, was to persuade Congress to pass the spending cuts and tax increases that might have satisfied businessmen like Marion Folsom and Charles Edward Wilson. Congress, by 1951, was in no mood to allow Truman to accomplish much of anything. Red scares at home and abroad were in full bloom, and the logic of political discourse on Capitol Hill suffered accordingly. When Truman introduced a tax bill that sought to raise $10 billion of additional revenue by means of excise, personal income, and corporate tax hikes, the bill was shredded by both the left and the right. Liberals argued that it was a massive giveaway to rapacious businessmen. Corporate conservatives in the NAM countered that the bill had pinko characteristics. By the time that the badly battered bill finally emerged from Congress, it was a mixture of exemption-ridden increases in personal, corporate, and excise taxes (no sales tax elements were included) that raised only half of the revenue Truman—with the CED's endorsement—had said was necessary. Truman signed the bill into law, assuming correctly that it was the best he was likely to get out of a sour and disputatious legislative branch. Corporate politicians' enthusiasm for Truman's leadership waned accordingly—as did their willingness to cut deals with a President whose ability to muscle legislation through Congress was becoming vestigial.[68]

The unhappy fate of Truman's tax bill, then, was part of a much wider political problem: the frustration and the often mindless discontent spawned by the Korean War. What had started off as a successful effort to contain communism expanded into an effort to win an easy victory in a rollback campaign. Easy victory was a chimera—as Truman discovered to his cost. Once Red China entered the conflict, the United States was faced with a choice among undesirable alternatives. It could accept the reality of a military standoff and negotiate an end to the fighting. It could continue to fight a long-drawn-out war of attrition with China to demonstrate the strength of the national will. Or it could take the chance of widening the war to China, using nuclear weapons if necessary to regain the military initiative and, it was hoped, knock the Chinese out of the war without involving neighboring Russia in the conflict. Choices like these were not appealing to the political leadership of a nation used to winning total victories—or to a populace unaccustomed to political wars in which the nation's enemies did not directly threaten the United States or the Western Hemisphere. By looking for bargain-basement conquests in Asia, Truman had helped bog the nation down in an unpopular and little-understood conflict. As the war continued, it sapped his ability to lead and its frustrations spawned a generation of political extremists who equated anything they disliked with communism.[69]

From early 1951 until the end of his presidency, Truman fought a rearguard action, trying—often vainly—to salvage something from the disordered political environment that his stupendous error in Korea had helped to create. In such circumstances, business politicians slowly withdrew their support from the failing executive branch. Throughout 1951, Business Council and CED statements continued to support the necessity of wartime controls as an anticommunist and anti-inflationary tool. Some of this support had a good deal of the *pro forma* about it, particularly as inflationary fears cooled, prices stabilized, the war in Korea was not followed by communist offensives elsewhere in the world, and truce talks were finally begun at the tiny Korean hamlet of Panmunjom. In December, the CED announced the end of its support for Truman's controls program. Three months later, the Business Council followed. By April 8, 1952, Truman's maladroit and unsuccessful attempt to avoid a serious strike in the steel industry by seizing the mills had alienated almost every important element in the American business community—the Business Council and CED included. Eric Johnston, Charles Edward Wilson, and other businessmen started streaming out of Washington even faster than they had streamed in just over one year before. The partnership with the Truman administration had most definitely come to an end. The most that compromise-minded businessmen were willing to do was to suggest that Truman be granted temporary standby authority to reimpose wage and price controls in the event that inflationary forces in the economy kicked up once again. In the contrary political environment then prevailing in the United States, even such hesitant efforts at leaving options open got nowhere. Congressional conservatives closed in for the kill, reducing the Truman administration's wartime mobilization to an empty shell by the summer of 1952.[70]

Corporate political activists did not view the demise of controls with regret. Big businessmen had not lent their assistance to the Truman administration's efforts with any great expectation that they would enjoy the exercise. What businessmen were engaged in was a political damage-control operation. Understanding that the all-out ideological opposition to controls favored by corporate traditionalists might give the political advantage to liberal "planners" desirous of placing permanent nonmarket constraints upon the economy, the big-business moderates of the Business Council and the CED cautiously supported wartime stabilization efforts that were considerably less extensive than those applied during the Second World War. This "yes, but" stance allowed the Council and CED to stay in the political game, and helped persuade an anxious Truman to recruit administrative personnel from both organizations as a means of trying to forestall criticism from congressional conservatives.

During the Korean War mobilization, as so often before in the immediate postwar period, corporate politicians made necessary accommodations with federal power. Moreover, they learned—gradually and sometimes reluctantly—to make use of the continuing reality of Washington's might, bending it to their purposes where possible and containing its expansion in other areas—particularly where the external communist threat did not appear to be direct, immediate, and compelling. As the presidential race heated up in the middle of 1952, businessmen could pause to admire their success in blunting the sword of domestic reform unsheathed during the New Deal. Moreover, they could look forward to the long-awaited possibility of a Republican political resurgence—personified in the figure of Dwight David Eisenhower.

5

"NEW CAPITALISM" IN THE EISENHOWER ERA, 1953–1961

The Election of Eisenhower

At first glance, General Dwight David Eisenhower looked like an unlikely capitalist savior. For over thirty years before his retirement from the service, Eisenhower had been a federal bureaucrat—albeit one engaged in fighting wars, that most traditional and universally accepted of Washington's guarantor responsibilities.

Despite this career history, Eisenhower was a golden political property. His service as Allied commander in chief in Western Europe during the Second World War had made his name a household word. Moreover, the aging general was a public eminence who had not squandered his political capital in the grudge fights of the 1930's and 1940's. Eisenhower, in fact, had never even voted during his military career—believing that political partisanship would conflict with his position as an officer. It was no accident, then, that a badly knocked about Republican party was attracted to Eisenhower in its search for new political blood; nor that defeated presidential candidate Thomas E. Dewey told Eisenhower as early as July of 1949 that Ike had not "frittered away his assets by taking positive stands against national planning, etc., etc." Eisenhower, moderate Republicans like Dewey hoped, could enable them to hold onto control of the GOP in the upcoming 1952 presidential race.[1]

The war in Korea only increased Eisenhower's political attractiveness to Republican moderates. The Truman administration's bungled rollback of communist power in Korea was a political time bomb waiting to go off. Opposition to the way that the war was being fought assumed almost universal proportions. Conservatives, impatient with the nuances of containment, clamored for victory. If the United States was serious about winning, it must fight an all-out war —against one or both communist superpowers, if necessary. Rightwingers within the Republican party were particularly vehement on the subject of General MacArthur. By firing him, Truman had only illustrated his lack of intestinal fortitude in the face of a thought-to-be-monolithic communist conspiracy.

Liberals also disliked the way that the war was being fought blaming Truman for weakly acquiescing in MacArthur's mad schemes for rollback on the mainland of Asia—schemes that had brought Red China into the conflict and helped produce a bloody stalemate around the 38th parallel. America, in this view of the matter, must speedily extricate itself from the stalemate in order to bolster its other, more strategically important interests around the globe. Liberals and conservatives offered profoundly different prescriptions for the Korean malaise but, along with less ideological or iconoclastic moderates in both major parties, they agreed that the patient was sick and needed a new doctor—one uncontaminated by political association with the disease.

What better man for the job than a famous and victorious general who had not been even remotely associated with America's postwar military and political problems in Asia? It took no great political expertise to realize that Dwight David Eisenhower could become the political man of the hour, and that the party that succeeded in recruiting him as its presidential candidate might well win the race to the White House. From 1950 onward, Eisenhower was besieged by Republican power brokers anxious to push him into the presidential race.

These efforts were complicated by divisions within the party itself. Ever since the World War II mobilization had begun over a decade before, the conservative wing of the GOP, led by former President Hoover and Senator Taft, had chafed at efforts of Republican moderates to recover a part of the political initiative that they had so emphatically lost in the 1930's by selective collaboration with the Democrats. Taft and Hoover were particularly opposed to key elements of the bipartisan foreign policy of containment that had induced powerful elements of the nation's big-business elite to cooperate in postwar initiatives including the Marshall Plan and the North Atlantic Treaty Organization (NATO). Collective security

based upon binding military and economic commitments that expanded American power far beyond its prewar hemispheric boundaries was a concept that stuck in conservative Republicans' craws.
The instincts of Hoover, Taft, and their supporters were nothing if
not antistatist. They feared that vastly enhanced military responsibilities abroad would produce a garrison state at home. Federal
power might then bury American capitalism alive under an avalanche of "temporary" emergency mobilization controls that would
in time become permanent. Socialism would follow. Right-wingers
like these had no love for Eisenhower, a man whose career exemplified the extension of exactly those foreign military and economic
commitments that they had so long opposed.[2]

However, Eisenhower enjoyed plenty of support in another quarter. Business political activists like Paul Hoffman admired Ike for the
same reason Taft and Hoover suspected him. Eisenhower was committed to the collective security strategy that Hoffman, W. Averell
Harriman, and their friends in the Business Council and the CED
had helped to create and administer. It was no surprise, then, to find
Hoffman among the leading lights in the drive to draft Eisenhower.
Taft and Hoover's knee-jerk reactions to the contrary, molders of
corporate opinion life Hoffman realized that government was never
going to revert to the old norms. The fundamental question was who
would control the power that did exist in Washington. Even corporate reactionaries got a part of the Hoffman message: Eisenhower
could win, whereas old congressional soldier Robert A. Taft could
not. By October of 1951, even an unreconstructed big-business
rightist like Ernest T. Weir was telling Eisenhower that only he, not
Taft, could save the nation from socialism.[3]

Businessmen like Hoffman and Weir were ably assisted by members of the military. General Lucius D. Clay, who had known and
worked with Eisenhower for twenty years, strategically positioned
himself to serve as a bridge between Ike and the big-business community. Following his retirement from active service in 1950, Clay was
made chairman of the board of the Continental Can Company and
joined the Business Council—becoming one of the only two career
generals ever enrolled in the group. (The other was George Marshall.) Using the Business Council as a base, Clay helped to orchestrate a series of corporate CEO meetings with Eisenhower aimed at
getting him on the Republican presidential bandwagon.[4]

Eventually Eisenhower ran, overcoming the competing Republican candidacy of Robert A. Taft and devastating the Democrats. Eisenhower's victory was almost foreordained. On the eve of the 1952 elections, the Democrats were in the midst of a full-blown civil war, pitting a dwindling number of Truman loyalists against party insurgents anxious to replace Truman with almost anybody.

As things turned out, "anybody" was Adlai Stevenson, a moderately successful governor of Illinois. Stevenson's candidacy illustrated the difficulties that the Democrats were having in moving boldly in any direction. Stevenson was the most conservative nominee that the Democratic party had put forth in twenty-five years— a sort of 1950's version of Jimmy Carter. While working as a lawyer in Chicago in the 1930's and 1940's, Stevenson had opposed passage of the Wagner Act, opposed the federal minimum-wage guarantees in the Fair Labor Standards Act of 1938, and argued against national health insurance. On the eve of his nomination, Stevenson affirmed his opposition to public housing, federal aid to education, expanded federal efforts to protect black civil and political rights, and deficit spending. By no stretch of the imagination could Stevenson be called a New Deal liberal. Instead, Stevenson was a conservative lawyer who was committed to the United Nations, foreign military and economic aid, and collective security arrangements like NATO. He was, in addition, anxious to do something to control the increasingly expensive postwar nuclear arms race between the United States and the Soviet Union. The Democrats picked Stevenson in 1952 and again in 1956 for the same reasons they picked Jimmy Carter in 1976 and again in 1980. Their party was in a shambles and they needed a man—in both cases a governor—from "outside Washington" to buy themselves protection from the political fallout from unpopular "limited wars" on the Asian mainland.[5]

Stevenson's relative conservatism possessed another advantage: it mirrored a shift within the Democratic party itself. The high-profile foreign threat in Korea, like the earlier ones during the Second World War, sapped enthusiasm for ambitious domestic reform initiatives. Postwar strike waves had taken the bloom off the trade union rose. Democratic eminences including a scattering of prominent New Dealers began backing away from the antibusiness stances that many of them had taken during the Depression decade. As the 1952 election campaign got under way, none other than David Lilienthal, Roosevelt's erstwhile director of the "socialist" Tennessee Valley Authority, had a new book published entitled *Big Business: A New*

Era. Large corporations, it seemed, weren't so bad after all. Besides, other interest groups in American society (e.g., trade unions) also had a great deal of power. The course for liberals to take was to enunciate "pluralist" positions that opposed dominance by *any* one class or group. Lilienthal and many another New Deal liberal, then, came to accept a view of the world remarkably like Harry S. Truman's. They were willing to defend what existed in terms of New Deal social and labor legislation. They were not willing to continue efforts to expand the scope of reform initiatives in a comparatively unreceptive political environment. Liberals of the 1950's, as Leonard Silk has said, moved back toward a "cautious probusiness liberalism . . . stressing economy and efficiency."[6]

The Democrats' rightward shift, however evident at the time, did not save their party at the polls. Stevenson lost to Eisenhower by almost 6.5 million votes. The Republicans also captured control of the Senate and the House by slim majorities. For the first time in twenty years, the GOP was back in control of the federal government —with its candidate occupying 1600 Pennsylvania Avenue. Businessmen, like other conservatives, savored a sweet and long-deferred moment of triumph.

The Republican Administration: Picking the Team and Formulating the Agenda

Eisenhower was elected to the presidency enjoying an enviable if undeserved reputation as a political ingenue. Once the cheering stopped, however, it was time to start the rough-and-tumble process of picking a Cabinet and plotting the general outline of future political battles. Key elements of the task of Cabinet selection were delegated to two trusted intimates: Lucius D. Clay and campaign director Herbert Brownell. Now Clay's connections with the Business Council really began to pay dividends to the organization in terms of political access and clout.

As reporter Hobart Rowen has told the story, Clay and Sidney J. Weinberg, an investment banker who was friendly with Ike and who sat on so many corporate boards that another Ike intimate described him as "an ambulatory quorum of American business," attended a "work and play" meeting of the Business Council just after the 1952 elections at a Georgia island resort. Clay and Wein-

berg stopped in at the meeting, and then promptly flew off to nearby
Augusta, Georgia, where Eisenhower was playing golf and planning
his Cabinet selections. In Augusta Clay and Weinberg consulted
with the President-elect and returned to the Business Council meeting to do some recruiting.[7]

The results of all this activity profoundly affected the shape of
Eisenhower's Cabinet. Ike tapped three Business Council leaders for
his team. George M. Humphrey of the M. A. Hanna Company
became Secretary of the Treasury and Charles Erwin Wilson of
General Motors headed the Department of Defense, while Robert T.
Stevens of the J. P. Stevens Company became Secretary of the Army.
Business Council leaders thus occupied two of the three upper-
echelon Cabinet posts (State, Defense, and Treasury). None of these
three men were well known to the country at large, but each had
established a good reputation among his corporate peers in the Business Council. Unsurprisingly, the three dipped into the Council's
talent pool to recruit assistants to help them with their new jobs.
Secretary of the Treasury Humphrey, for example, selected longtime
Council and CED activist Marion Folsom to serve as his Undersecretary, and retained him in that post until Folsom became the second
Secretary of the new Cabinet-level Department of Health, Education, and Welfare in 1955. For the Eisenhower administration, then,
the Business Council became a "veritable gold mine of leading personnel."[8]

Once in office, the businessmen and other conservatives recruited
by and for Ike struggled to sort out the priorities of the new administration. Joseph Stalin's sudden death in March of 1953, only two
months after Eisenhower assumed office, destabilized the USSR's
governing hierarchy and eased the process of negotiating an end to
the nettlesome Korean War. To help ensure a rapid settlement,
Eisenhower broadly hinted to the Chinese that he would not hesitate
to use nuclear weapons. As peace finally came, the Republican administration, with vociferous support from business groups including
the Business Council, speedily dismantled the *ad hoc* system of
wartime economic controls instituted under Truman.[9]

With these immediate tasks on the way to being accomplished,
it was time for Eisenhower to take a longer look into the political
future. The new President believed firmly that the Republican party
had too many "old mossbacks" in it who simply opposed everything
and fell prey to wild rumors about internal radical plots to under-

mine the republic. Eisenhower hoped to serve as a catalyst for the creation of a "new Republicanism" that would do more to preserve free enterprise and, at the same time, deliver social welfare, defense, and other services to the populace more efficiently than the Democrats had ever done. To guarantee efficiency, Ike recruited articulate corporate politicians to man his administration.[10]

Eisenhower's hopes for a "progressive" conservative party were based upon important, if rarely articulated, premises. The federal government was there, was very big, and was going to remain big. Instead of trying to dismantle the government, it was the task of intelligent conservatives to enable the government to do its job in cooperation with private interest groups, utilizing as much private, as opposed to bureaucratic, advice as possible. Thereby, a federal government which had become big in large part as a reaction to the failures of private power would remain big in conjunction with powerful organized interest groups. Government would not, in such a view of the matter, be a grand "pooh-bah" acting unilaterally, but rather would act as an expediter, a coordinator, and where necessary an umpire. In Eisenhower's mind, Herbert Hoover's aging dream of self-policing occupational blocs was joined (if none too securely) to a recognition of the necessity of a powerful central authority as an agent of change in a hostile Cold War world.

In his first speech to the Business Council in March of 1953, the triumphant President spelled out how his administration would depend upon a great deal of private, as opposed to bureaucratic, advice. Ike opined that the success of the Business Council over the years had "given the lead" to "every department of Government," which would now create advisory agencies similar to the Council to help it in its work. These advisory bodies would keep government in touch with "the daily thinking of American professions, American business, and American labor . . . [and] furnish us a balance wheel." Within months, Eisenhower's Secretary of Commerce, Sinclair Weeks, was sponsoring the creation of literally hundreds of industrial advisory groups manned by dollar-a-year men recruited from industry and legitimized by the newly created Business and Defense Services Administration. For most of the remainder of Ike's presidency, cooperation between businessman and bureaucrat was the order of the day.[11]

For all of Eisenhower's upbeat assurances, it was not an easy job for big businessmen to follow through on the conservative regime's glowing visions of public-private collaboration. The foreign policy sphere alone presented the corporate leaders of the Business Council and the CED, inside and outside of government, with more than their share of headaches.

Foreign Policy: The Ironies of Power

The basic quandary in corporate leaders' minds concerned power. Conservatives—big businessmen included—distrusted power, particularly when it was centralized in Washington. For years, Business Council and CED activists had been fighting to contain the expansion of federal power in strategic domestic areas including social welfare and labor legislation. As the Cold War gathered steam, however, these same businessmen found themselves in the unaccustomed position of also advocating an increasingly large, expensive, and activist government to contain the spread of communism abroad by both military and nonmilitary means.

The ironies of this situation induced occasional panic in the minds of even those big businessmen whose exposure to Washington was of long and varied duration. In May of 1948, for example, Paul Hoffman gave vent to frustrations that were quite similar to the apprehensions of conservative Republicans like Robert A. Taft. In an off-the-cuff address to his peers on the Business Council, the newly appointed administrator of the Marshall Plan said that war with the USSR must be avoided and that the United States "could afford neither defeat nor victory [in such a shooting war], calling attention to the tremendous cost of rehabilitation which is our burden after victory in the last war. He said that the maintenance of a garrison state involved such high military expenditures as to require a managed economy and thus we must win the cold war."[12]

By the time Eisenhower arrived in Washington as President, however, it was becoming mercilessly clear to corporate leaders like Paul Hoffman that the containment effort known as the Cold War was never going to be "won" by anybody. The USSR was not going to wither away and die of some internal communist disease. Like the United States, it was going to continue building up its conventional and nuclear arms in order to achieve a balance of power—and terror—to protect its interests and forestall a general conflict.

Getting accustomed to realities like these took time. Secretary of the Treasury Humphrey was particularly exercised about the horrendous costs of Cold War military spending. When Ike won the election, Washington was shelling out just over $75 billion, about $40 billion of which went for defense. Two more years of this sort of thing, Humphrey later remarked, "would have meant Communism in America." Eisenhower, less hyperbolically, called such arms burdens "intolerable."[13]

Even so, the Republicans proved unable to cut the mammoth postwar defense budget in any substantial way during their entire tenure in power. Pare some items they did. But the accelerated development of expensive high-technology weapons systems including jet bombers, intercontinental ballistic missiles, hydrogen bombs, and nuclear submarines caused overall military expenditures to rise $4 billion a year higher at the end of Eisenhower's presidency than they had been at the beginning of it.[14]

Humphrey also enjoyed the distinction of being one of the earliest members of Eisenhower's Cabinet to appreciate the ironies of Cold War permanent military mobilization. After two months in office, Humphrey returned to his native Cleveland to ruefully confess to a business audience that reducing federal spending was not going to be as easy a task as he and his business friends had thought. "When you get right down to it," Humphrey admitted, "somewhere from 80 to 90 per cent of the budget has nothing to do with just firing employees, or reducing what you may think are wasteful expenditures, but has to do with our security."[15]

It took Eisenhower and Secretary of Defense Wilson a little longer to understand the nuances of Cold War spending as applied to themselves and the national pocketbook. As Eisenhower intimate Arthur Larson later related:

> One day in the middle of the winter [of an unspecified year— though apparently one after 1954] I was sitting with Eisenhower in his office when Secretary of Defense Charles Wilson came in to talk about his budget. The conversation soon turned into a one-way harangue by Eisenhower, whose sole theme was that Wilson had to stay within his budget at all costs. "Not one penny over, do you understand? Not under any circumstances!" "Yes, sir," was about all Wilson could manage, looking almost like a schoolboy getting a scolding. The session ended with the most solemn, sacred, immutable promise by Wilson that, whatever it took, the line would be held and the budget not exceeded.

A couple of months later I happened to be with Eisenhower when Wilson again appeared. To an incredulous Eisenhower, Wilson managed to blurt out his confession: he was already two billion dollars over his budget. I shall never forget the protracted moment of blank silence that followed, while two men stared speechless at each other, as if in the presence of some gigantic, unknowable, uncontrollable force of nature."[16]

This "force of nature" called the Cold War was unsettling in another way: it posed particular problems to the Eisenhower administration because, though Eisenhower knew what he wanted to do (contain communism), he was not always too clear about how he wanted to do it. In helping to formulate answers to such questions, the business politicians of the Business Council and the CED played important roles.

The most significant thing about Council and CED leaders like Paul Hoffman and W. Averell Harriman was that—unlike the Taft-Hoover wing of the Republican party—they did not perceive the communist threat primarily in domestic terms. Instead, they viewed communism as an international challenge, as *the* foreign policy problem of postwar American life. In December of 1953, for example, while traveling in Thailand, Paul Hoffman met former World War II spymaster and departing American Ambassador General William (Wild Bill) Donovan. Hoffman, according to David Lilienthal, told Donovan in no uncertain terms that he had some serious missionary work to do upon his return to the States: "Said Paul to Bill: 'One of the things that I hope you will find time to do while you are in the U.S. this time is to persuade the American people that the fight against Communism is outside the U.S.; that it isn't fighting Communism where the fight is going on to fire a 6th grade arithmetic teacher.' "[17]

Muzzling the Far Right: McCarthy

If there was one person who required no persuasion regarding Hoffman's contentions, that was his fellow CED and Business Council activist Ralph Flanders. Flanders, moreover, was in a splendid position to help gag the congressional reactionaries of isolationist bent who were scourging the nation of "radicals." Flanders was a United States senator—first elected from his native Vermont in 1946, reelected handsomely in 1952.

Another man who enjoyed the status of senator was Joseph R. McCarthy, the most prominent and unscrupulous of the red-baiting politicians building a career out of exorcising domestic communist devils. He was also the target that Flanders chose to attack.

However, Flanders had to proceed carefully. The bones of other, less adept politicians littered the floor around McCarthy's feet. One fellow senator in particular had tried and failed to depose McCarthy during McCarthy's earliest days of public prominence immediately after the outbreak of the Korean War. That was William Benton, with whom Flanders had been intimately associated in creating the CED. Benton, appointed to fill out the term of a retiring Democratic senator from Connecticut in 1950, had assaulted McCarthy's record in 1951, elicited no great support from his party, and been defeated for election in 1952 in a notably sanguinary campaign.

Flanders, on the other hand, was not a Democrat, and therefore could not be so easily smeared by McCarthy as being part of a long-standing liberal conspiracy to sell the country out to Moscow. Nor could Flanders be branded a supporter of the Truman administration's inept handling of the Korean conflict.

Shortly after an armistice was finally arrived at in Korea in July of 1953, Flanders began to capitalize on the reduced level of political tension in Washington and the country. In March of 1954, Flanders launched his first frontal attack on McCarthy. By summer, Flanders was loudly calling for McCarthy's censure by the Senate—a potent, if symbolic, punishment. Joining Flanders in this effort were fellow corporate political activists William Benton and Paul Hoffman—both of whom provided extensive financial assistance to a lobbying group, the National Committee for an Effective Congress, that had sprung up to ally itself with Flanders in his effort to depose McCarthy. Flanders, initially acting without the support of prominent Democrats or Republicans such as John F. Kennedy, Lyndon Baines Johnson, or Richard M. Nixon, slowly began to channel the forces opposing McCarthy into effective political directions.[18]

Joining Flanders in his crusade against McCarthy's excesses was the membership of the Business Council. For three years, Council members had thought comparatively little about McCarthy. Corporate internationalists like Hoffman, Benton, and Flanders might oppose McCarthy for focusing the anticommunist struggle on the domestic rather than the international arena. The general run of Council members, however, were content to operate on the assumption that there was very little that McCarthy could do to immediately affect them or their interests. A handful of present and former Council members publicly approved of McCarthy; another handful publicly opposed him. The rest—the vast majority—kept their mouths shut and their heads down.[19]

Then McCarthy made a mistake. Early in 1954, he began to investigate "subversion" in the United States Army.

The Army, at first glance, appears completely unrelated to the affairs of the Business Council—until it is recalled that a former chairman of the Council, Robert Stevens, was Army Secretary. In attacking the Army, McCarthy was inadvertently interfering with the affairs of an elite corporate power center.

By April of 1954, the fat was really in the fire. In a series of nationally televised hearings that lasted over two months, McCarthy tried to publicly flay Stevens alive for all manner of administrative sins, like allowing a dentist with communist affiliations to ply his trade on an Army base in New Jersey. As the carillon of illogical conspiracy charges pealed out across the land, Secretary Stevens was publicly humiliated over and over.[20]

Stevens' public crucifixion did not sit well with the membership of the Business Council. Bob Stevens, after all, was one of them. Moreover, he was a man of impeccable, even die-hard, conservative credentials. Council leaders, therefore, went out of their way to demonstrate their continued support for Stevens as his televised agony continued. On his way to a Council meeting held at a posh resort outside Washington in May, 1954, Stevens was escorted from the airport by a special delegation of Council eminences and applauded by the assembled corporate chiefs as he entered the hotel's lobby. Shortly afterward, Eisenhower administration officials in attendance at the gathering were subjected to a torrent of abuse for caving in to McCarthy's grandstanding media tactics. This blue-chip corporate opposition to McCarthy, added to that of the numerous political enemies that the senator had already made, firmed the determination of hitherto reluctant Republican leaders to do something about McCarthy. By December of 1954, the senator's days as a reactionary political superstar were over forever.[21]

Investing in the Future: Expanding Foreign Aid

In moving to help destroy Joseph McCarthy, men like Ralph Flanders, William Benton, and Paul Hoffman were not being altruistic.

Big-business internationalists opposed McCarthy because he was fighting the right enemy—communism—in the wrong place. Army dentists were vastly less important than North Korean, Chinese, or Russian divisions. Moreover, McCarthy's destructive media tactics threatened to unravel the bipartisan alliance of congressional Republicans and Democrats that maintained the whole structure of postwar military and economic alliances exemplified by NATO and the Marshall Plan. To save collective security, then, Benton, Hoffman, and Flanders helped cut McCarthy's legs out from under him.

These men's ideas were in harmony with those of President Eisenhower, a devoted adherent to the view that the United States could not survive as a continental Gibraltar in a nuclear era. More, Eisenhower was anxious to expand the scope of American influence into new regions of the world—particularly areas, such as the Middle East, from which the United States imported strategic commodities including oil. Ike, like many another leader whose political career was forged during the Second World War, believed that private enterprise and public authority, working together, now had the duty to export American capital, technology, skills, and management techniques in order to foster economic, social, and political stability in the noncommunist world.[22]

As usual, there were problems to be overcome in achieving Eisenhower's vision. Public support for foreign aid was a fragile thing, particularly where economic assistance was concerned. Large and powerful segments of the citizenry considered American aid transfers to foreign nations to be a colossal giveaway program without a shred of redeeming value.

Businessmen joined in the howls of execration that greeted the Eisenhower administration's efforts to obtain congressional backing for increased foreign aid funding. *Business Week, Barron's,* the *Nation's Business,* the *Wall Street Journal,* and other respected business mouthpieces clamored for "trade, not aid" and argued that government should not interfere with "natural economic forces." Small-business organizations including the NAM, Chamber of Commerce, and National Federation of Independent Business added their voices in opposition to foreign economic assistance, although their attitudes toward shipments of military supplies to allied regimes were a good deal less negative. Even big businessmen such as those occupying prominent positions in Eisenhower's Cabinet were not happy with the prospect of continuing foreign economic assistance on a permanent basis. In June of 1953, for example, newly appointed Treasury Secretary Humphrey (whose influence on foreign economic policy was great for the simple reason that Secretary of State John Foster Dulles was almost completely uninterested in the subject) told a reporter for *U.S. News and World Report* that "foreign economic aid is pretty well gone—well on its way out right now."[23]

Other big businessmen including Secretary of Defense Wilson and Inland Steel's Clarence B. Randall also expressed strong reservations regarding foreign economic assistance—the latter in the report of a commission on foreign economic policy that he chaired for Ike in 1953 and 1954. A Business Council committee that drafted policy recommendations related to the so-called Randall Commission's report wanted nonmilitary aid scaled down as soon as possible. According to the Council committee, Uncle Sam should give nothing away—except guns. Washington, the policy memorandum concluded, should prepare itself to "provide aid for military purposes in the form of grants rather than loans; and other economic aid as loans rather than grants, and then only when such loans cannot be made by private or international sources."[24]

One business organization, however, proved to be a distinct and important exception to the general rule of entrepreneurial opposition to foreign aid. That group was the Committee for Economic Development. Throughout the 1950's, CED spokesmen enunciated constant support for global assistance projects and the necessity for federal involvement in them. Thereby, CED once again served as a hinge upon which big-business opinion turned.

The process began even before Eisenhower's arrival in Washington. Early in 1951, a Truman-appointed advisory panel chaired by Nelson Rockefeller, a trustee of the CED, issued a report entitled "Partners in Progress" calling upon Americans to back expanded foreign aid.

One group that was quick to rally to the Rockefeller report's banner was the CED. In 1952, Meyer Kestnbaum of Hart Schaffner and Marx, chairman of CED's Research and Policy Committee, was telling congressmen that America had to do more than just ship artillery, tanks, and men abroad in order to guarantee global peace and promote American national interests. "The Marshall Plan," he told one committee, "was successful precisely because it recognized and emphasized the social and economic aspects of European security. . . . [Efforts to rearm United States allies abroad] must be regarded as supplementing, not replacing, the cooperative effort to build a productive, stable, and united Western Europe."[25]

Kestnbaum's testimony was a nice way of reminding the congressmen that poverty breeds bomb throwers. The organization of businessmen that he represented—whose members had done so much to design and administer the Marshall Plan in the first place —had no interest seeing foreign aid killed.

Nor did Eisenhower. Throughout his presidency, Ike expended a great deal of political capital in trying to cajole businessmen, Congress, the public, and members of his own administration to back expanded foreign aid programs.

Crises abroad assisted his efforts very materially indeed. What Congress and corporate boardrooms would not do out of goodwill, they would do out of fear. Between 1953 and the end of Ike's first term, there was plenty for Americans to feel fearful about. Hypothesized communist subversion of extreme right-wing governments in Guatemala, Iran, and Egypt—plus the beginning of Russian overtures of economic and technical assistance to the fast-growing crop of nonaligned nations in Asia and Africa—made conservatives of all kinds much more receptive to the idea of using American economic, as well as military, muscle to contain forces deemed radical or destabilizing.

By the end of Ike's first term, then, big-business opinion had begun to shift from opposing nonmilitary foreign aid per se to opposing federal expenditures considered "wasteful" or "socialistic." (The latter sobriquet was applied to federal monies granted to foreign nations that were used to build state-owned plants.)[26]

This process of corporate conversion, however, was not a smooth one. Early in Ike's second term, for example, Treasury Secretary Humphrey, in a burst of unfortunate eloquence at a press conference, stated his opinion that unless the Eisenhower administration could reduce military expenditures substantially, the country would "have a depression which will curl your hair."

Congressional opponents of foreign aid pounced on the opportunity to try to disembowel "giveaway" programs, existing and proposed. Eisenhower was forced to do a great deal of damage control work. To the hapless Humphrey, Ike privately complained that business leaders were unfortunately confused about foreign aid, and that others in the country must therefore be in a state of "utter bewilderment." To Congress, Eisenhower sent messages that both military *and* economic aid to foreign nations were "truly defense programs."[27]

Eventually, Russia's launching of the Sputnik I space satellite helped to put the fear of Moscow into Capitol Hill cloakrooms and silence a good deal of the dissent. In the meantime, however, Eisenhower sorely needed allies to aid him in his cause.

He found the allies in the Business Council. Early in 1957, Council Chairman Harold Boeschenstein (Owens Corning Fiberglass) was approached by White House representatives and asked to create an unofficial Business Council committee to pressure Congress to pass Eisenhower's foreign aid bill at the levels of funding he wanted. Boeschenstein was happy to oblige and, though the effort was only partially successful (the bill passed, but at reduced funding levels), it mobilized impressive corporate and academic support for Ike's foreign aid efforts.[28]

By the next session of Congress, Boeschenstein and the Business Council were really on the team—making a study at Ike's request of "Soviet economic penetration" of underdeveloped nations, and formulating proposals for increased public-private cooperation in foreign investment and trade based on the long-standing corporate conviction that business can do anything if government allows it enough tax breaks. All the while, the CED hammered away at the point that the United States couldn't afford to sit around with its fingers in its ears—and that federal funds were essential in aiding needy lands where poor but noncommunist peoples dwelt. "It is not realistic," CED policy statements argued, "to suppose [as defenders of the free enterprise faith like the *Wall Street Journal* and the Chamber of Commerce were doing] that private capital can provide all, or even provide most, of the funds that can be effectively used" to industrialize poor countries in strategic geopolitical areas. The primary needs of the underdeveloped countries were in "basic economic facilities—transportation, utilities, sanitation—areas unattractive to private foreign investment." Only after these elements of the economic infrastructure were developed would the private sector be able to pick up the ball and run with it.[29]

By the end of Eisenhower's presidency, the shift in big-business opinion evident in the activities of the CED and the Business Council was finally coming to have a good deal of practical political effect. Legislation was passed establishing federal agencies that could issue foreign borrowers loans at lower-than-market interest rates and

speed the flow of federal grant monies abroad. Still-reluctant entrepreneurs were reassured by the enunciation of "tying clauses" that
required foreign recipients of American largesse to spend the money
in whole or large part for the purchase of goods built by American
companies. The program of foreign economic aid begun under Truman had been broadened substantially by Eisenhower. Truman had
created a Marshall Plan for Western Europe. Eisenhower created
a Marshall Plan for the world. In both cases, the Presidents and
their legislative-branch allies enjoyed the backing of the CED and
(somewhat more reluctantly) the Business Council, in expanding
federal power out into the world to help contain the communist
menace. In supporting Ike's foreign aid effort—as in sustaining that
of Truman before him—big-business politicians had once again
learned that a large and activist government was a tool that they,
too, could use.[30]

Conservatives and Keynes

Eisenhower never actually belonged to the CED, but the organization played a key role in acclimating his administration as well as
businessmen and other conservatives to the very often frustrating
world of government finance. Throughout the 1950's, the CED was
a font of right-wing Keynesian notions that pushed and pulled a
segment of the Republican party toward a reluctant and *ad hoc*
accommodation with countercyclical economic policy.[31]

The problem, as far as CED activists were concerned, was that
Eisenhower and many of his top aides did not have *ideas* about
economics, they had instincts. Instincts that told them, in the late
Herman Krooss' words: "Tax reduction would spur saving and incentives which would spur investment, which would spur production, which would spur income, and everybody would be much better
off. Any sort of tax reduction would do."[32]

This traditionalist approach (later revivified in the "New" Right
economics of Jack Kemp, Arthur Laffer, and the Reagan administration) saw the economy as inherently expansionist and branded government as an evil force that all too often interfered with "natural"
economic forces. The job of conservatives, in this view of the matter,
was to shrink the size of government, including governmental tax
exactions and, by all means, federal expenditures as well. Otherwise

government would be in the economically dangerous position of spending more than it took in, thus running deficits.

Deficit spending inflamed American conservatives—then and since—like few other subjects. Right-wingers might agree to the necessity of deficits during war (total federal debt rose from $50 billion to $250 billion during the period from 1940 to 1945). In peacetime, however, the mainstream conservative view was that government should always live within its income.

Depressions posed problems for this pristine conservative vision. Economic downturns such as that which followed the stock market crash of 1929 lowered federal tax revenues because the corporate and personal incomes that Washington taxed fell precipitately. If federal officials then decreased expenditures and increased tax rates to make up for the fiscal shortfall (as Herbert Hoover had done) they ran the risk of worsening the downward spiral of aggregate output, employment, and income levels in society. Balanced budgets at all times could be dangerous—as the Republicans had discovered to their sorrow.

The articulate businessmen of the CED were among those in corporate America best able to understand that balanced federal budgets were not an absolute necessity at all times. Men like Ralph Flanders and his longtime friend Henry Dennison understood early on that Washington had a duty, in periods of severe economic slack, to increase expenditures and/or decrease taxes to prime the pump of economic recovery. It also had a duty to increase taxes and/or decrease expenditures to cool off boom periods of overexcited economic expansion that might fuel demand-pull inflationary forces in the national marketplace.

In short, Flanders and Dennison were cautious Keynesians, men who believed that there were no natural or inherent forces making for full-employment economic equilibrium in capitalist society—and that the federal government must therefore assume significant responsibility for achieving overall economic stability and growth.

This belief had come to such businessmen before Keynesianism was even an established "ism." In December of 1931, for example, Ralph Flanders wrote a letter to the dean of the Harvard Business School complaining that Herbert Hoover's traditionalist understanding of the federal government's economic role was producing an unmitigated disaster. "In particular," he said,

I feel that the Government must come to long-time budgeting instead of trying to balance the budget in a given fiscal year. The latter practice is pernicious.

In the course of a business cycle there is a time to tax and a time to relieve taxation. There is a time to borrow and a time to repay. There is a time to expand expenditures and a time to contract them. There is a time to expand currency and credit and a time to contract them. One of our most urgent lines of action will be to get this viewpoint understood and acted upon by the Congress and the Administration.[33]

Flanders' biblical turns of phrase, unfortunately, had little impact upon the academic eminence to whom they were addressed and none whatsoever upon the Hoover administration. Flanders and a hardy band of businessmen like him, however, kept right on arguing that government must aim to balance the budget *over the course of the business cycle.* When times were bad, it must spend more than it took in. When good times returned, the reverse could apply, and the debt run up during especially severe downturns could be retired.[34]

By 1947, this cautious Keynesianism, opposed to the existence of *permanent* federal deficits and extremely suspicious about aggressive short-term tinkering with taxation and expenditure levels, had become the motivating creed of the Committee for Economic Development. CED personnel, particularly the core of professional economists staffing the New York offices of the group, worked to convince key Republican and Democratic policymakers in Congress and the executive branch that Keynes' attitudes toward federal budgeting were a necessary weapon in any nation's economic arsenal.[35]

The CED's persuasiveness was sorely challenged by the fact that key Democratic and Republican political leaders were economic illiterates. Roosevelt and Truman certainly hadn't known much about Keynesian theory. Eisenhower, similarly, gave little thought to economics, Keynesian or otherwise. His considerable skills were directed mainly toward military and foreign policy. Meanwhile, Congress was led by a shifting group of senior senators and representatives, many conservatives from the South and West, who conceived of the national finances as household budgeting on an immense scale.

All this made the CED's job of popular political education a difficult exercise at best. Still, the CED's men, including Herbert Stein, the group's research director and the future chairman of the

Council of Economic Advisers under President Nixon, had certain advantages. Chief among these was the fact that Eisenhower's ignorance of economics was so profound that he possessed comparatively little built-in conceptual opposition to anything. When the Eisenhower administration arrived in Washington, therefore, businessmen and others sympathetic to the CED viewpoint worked to keep Ike from sliding into the traditionalist economic camp by default.[36]

CED-oriented people had their work cut out for them right from the start. In January of 1953, congressional conservatives proposed a huge across-the-board tax cut for individuals and business corporations. Theirs was the old logic that lower tax rates would generate a torrent of saving and investment, and as a result the economic pie would grow so fast that a smaller-percentage federal tax exaction would actually mean an equal or even larger number of federal dollars in the U.S. Treasury.

This everybody-wins-and-nobody-loses approach to taxation was not accepted by Eisenhower or the men immediately around him. Ike and his Cabinet wanted tax reduction eventually, but first they wanted to get federal expenditures under control. Once the federal budget decreased to "normal" proportions, it would be the time to talk about tax reduction. Over the occasionally hysterical opposition of Senator Taft and the partial resistance of the NAM and the Chamber of Commerce, Ike ordered the pruning of expenditures unrelated to the military.[37]

Things went well for a few months. But as the forced-fed military spending for the Korean conflict declined in the wake of the signing of an armistice at Panmunjom, a brief and shallow recession took place during which unemployment levels rose to 6 percent.

Republican administrations—Eisenhower's included—do not like recessions, for the simple reason that Democrats, however inept their own handling of the economy may have been, start comparing GOP incumbents to the hapless Herbert Hoover. Ike, who had no intention of becoming grist for the Democratic mill, sought to do something to perk up the economy.

Eisenhower did not, however, essay the standard Keynesian solution—to his eventual cost. Instead of raising expenditures, he cut them. Instead of cutting corporate and individual tax rates, he tinkered with "pro-investment" targeted tax cuts such as accelerated-depreciation allowances. The White House "studied" other alternatives, but the CED's Herbert Stein was absolutely correct when he later noted that neither the administration, Congress, nor the federal bureaucracy had any "effective policy for fiscal measures in a more serious recession."[38]

A part of the problem was that the businessmen who ran Eisenhower's administration were reluctant to drink very deeply of the Keynesian cup. "The Keynesian system," as John Kenneth Galbraith succinctly observed at the time,

> implied an important [change in the relation of the federal government and the industrial economy]. For a doctrine that excluded the government it substituted one that made the government indispensable. Keynes was sufficiently unpalatable when he made the depression and inflation not adventitious and war-induced misfortunes but normal occurrences. He went on to make government the indispensable partner of business. In failing to recognize the prestige that goes with power and decision making in American life, American liberals [and those businessmen who supported a conservative application of Keynesian technique] failed to recognize that, for some businessmen, the Keynesian remedy was at least as damaging as the depression it presumed to eliminate. Even though the businessman might profit in a narrow pecuniary sense from the new role of government there was no chance that his prestige would survive intact. Where, in economic life, people had previously looked upon business decisions as the ones that shaped their destiny, now they would have regard for government decisions as well, or instead. Those of an Assistant Secretary of the Treasury on interest rates were now of more importance than those of any banker. Those of a regional administrator of public works on investment attained a significance greater than those of a corporate president. To share the prestige of decision making is to lose prestige.[39]

An indication of how reluctant businessmen were to accept the diminution of their status in the face of the Keynesian prescription was provided by the CED itself. During the early years of Eisenhower's presidency the organization engaged in a sometimes excruciating effort to dress up Keynesian economic thinking in the manner best calculated to appeal to conservatives.

Initially, CED policy statements were pretty tame. The report of a committee on the "postdefense transition" confined itself to recommending that a "shelf" of public works projects be created so that public monies could be more quickly doled out in the event of a renewed depression. This proposal did not even offend the instincts of Herbert Hoover, who had backed such moves in the 1920's. For the rest, CED's committee confined itself to saying that the "automatic stabilizers" (e.g., unemployment insurance) built into the American economy during the 1930's should be the "first line of defense" for Washington policymakers.[40]

Simply leaving New Deal–era programs intact hardly constituted a countercyclical antidepression policy, and CED staffers like Herbert Stein knew it. In October of 1953, five months after the first CED study for Ike appeared, Stein prepared another report, whose purpose was to expand a bit on his organization's earlier and rather timorous effort. Depending primarily upon automatic stabilizers, Stein realized, was simply not enough. These stabilizers could mitigate the negative impact of economic declines, but they could not, in and of themselves, guarantee a rise in levels of consumption, investment, or employment. People might not starve, but the economy might not recover either. Economic stagnation could ensue.

Therefore, Stein continued, it was necessary to bite the bullet— to accept Keynesianism—but to do so in the way that would offend businessmen the least. Monetary policy was an important element in this prescription. If, however, monetary policy alone was not enough (and Stein did not believe that it was) then the federal government should use its taxation powers to strengthen the economy in emergency conditions.

Here some technical background is in order. Keynesian theory says that government should not be chary of running deficits in periods of economic sluggishness. There are, however, various ways to run a deficit. For example, a government may keep taxes or tax rates constant and increase its expenditures, thereby pumping money into the marketplace at the cost of running a deficit. This approach might require federal officials to, for instance, finance civilian public-works projects—an approach as uncongenial to conservatives in the 1950's as it had been in the 1930's. Stein, therefore, did not advocate any such procedures.

Instead, he argued, the federal government should plan on keeping expenditures more or less stable during an economic downturn, but should also cut taxes. A deficit would ensue from this course of action, too. But federal officials, instead of spending more money and starting more programs, would only be performing their normal run of duties. Moreover, the federal government would not need to increase in size and power during depressions or recessions. Instead, assisted by tax cuts, the private sector would retain clear primacy regarding the job of economic recovery.

Further, Stein continued, federal officials should cut taxes in specific ways—ways that left relatively little up to their (possibly liberal) discretion. For example, instead of targeting a tax cut on a particular industry, region, or sector of the economy, Washington should cut one kind of tax in one simple way. Personal income tax cuts alone were enough to do the job. As Stein himself put it: "It is probably best to concentrate on a horizontal cut in the personal income tax. The power of this instrument is so great that if the problem of management can be solved in its use there will probably be no need to look further."[41]

Here was an argument of unusual sophistication and political insight. In reasoning thus, Stein and other CED activists who believed as he did were trying to carve out a secure middle ground between the moss-backed traditionalists of the right and the gung-ho young liberal economists of the left. The traditionalists, for their part, were informed that government did have the final guarantor responsibility regarding the overall economy and might have to run a deficit in emergency conditions. Liberals, on the other hand, were told that a conservative tax-cut approach to Keynesian policy was the preferred solution, and that expenditure-increase strategies were not the way to go. In addition, the federal government should not be ambitious about choosing which taxes to cut and when to cut them. It should simply pick an income group in the society (conservatives, then and since, have selected the higher groups for special attention) and cut their taxes, thereby freeing up additional private-sector wealth for useful activities.

In seeking to bridge the gap between traditionalist and Keynesian in the way that he had, however, Herbert Stein and his supporters in the business community had outrun the majority of the big businessmen to whom his remarks were most particularly addressed. Stein's persuasiveness suffered on two counts. First, it didn't address the key status-and-power issue that Galbraith had identified. Second, Stein's arguments posed the possibility that, as a CED study had pointed out in 1947, "we shall oscillate between adherence to the annual [balanced] budget principle in prosperity and belief in compensatory spending in depression. This could only mean an endless ascent to higher and higher government spending [to pay the finance charges on the ever-increasing debt], both in prosperity and depression." Big-business leaders such as those on the CED and the Business Council certainly did not desire to encourage the use of any tool —like deficit spending—that the federal government could use to make itself bigger at their expense.[42]

Here we should recall that businessmen had been through twenty unsettling years of federal expansion. A government that had spent only about $4.5 billion in 1933 was spending $75 billion by Eisenhower's first year in office. Washington, which had employed 250,000 soldiers and 600,000 civilians in 1933, was paying 3.5 million troops and 2.5 million bureaucrats two decades later. A government that had taxed corporate incomes to the tune of $400 million in 1933 was taking $22 billion out of corporate pocketbooks in 1953.[43]

No corporate political activist was anxious for such gargantuan numbers to swell further. Certainly sophisticated businessmen realized that the era of minimal government was forever past. In foreign policy, such men devoutly desired the federal government to remain large, well armed, and vigilant. But these same business leaders also desired to limit the growth of federal power. Basically, businessmen wanted a breathing spell, a time to gauge potentialities and acclimate themselves to changed realities while enjoying the comforting spectacle of a thoroughly Republican administration occupying Washington once again.

It was a nice prospect while it lasted. But the recession of 1953–1954, which the Eisenhower administration had done very little to stop, cost the GOP its control over both houses of Congress. Eisenhower and his corporate supporters were now forced to deal with the Democrats again in a very serious way.

The situation did not improve for conservatives as the economy swung upward once again and a tide of affluence flowed through the land. Aggregate income swelled, and stable federal tax rates ended up capturing an ever larger number of dollars. As inflation was only moderate during the 1950's (at least by comparison with the double-digit figures that Americans later came to expect), the federal establishment had a greater and greater amount of real wealth—and came under pressure from a bloc of liberal congressmen who wished to force the administration to use it if they could.

This, for conservatives, was precisely the problem. Unless tax rates were lowered, the bulging federal pocketbook might be opened to finance new social welfare programs and accomplish other undesirable extensions of federal power. As Ike's failed budget-cutter,

Defense Secretary Wilson, put it, "I have a feeling that until we reduce the taxes, the government bureaus . . . are not going to reduce the expenditures." Wilson knew about the problem if anybody did.[44]

Therefore, the Eisenhower administration backed tax reduction toward the end of its first term. These efforts got nowhere because the taxes (on upper-income groups and corporations) that the Republicans wanted to lower were not those (on lower-income groups) that the Democratic majority wanted to cut. The result was a standoff that pleased nobody.[45]

By the end of Eisenhower's first term, then, things did not look so rosy to big-business leaders. They had access and involvement in the executive branch, but they shared power in Washington with the Democrats. And, as Galbraith pointed out, power shared is power decreased.

The 1956 elections did not improve businessmen's mood substantially. Ike won overwhelmingly against Adlai Stevenson. Republicans, however, were unable to regain control of Congress. Though conservative Southern Democrats chaired key House and Senate committees, Business Council members were of sober mien regarding the electoral "half victory." Members, Hobart Rowen reported, were worried that Eisenhower might be drifting away from his previous adherence to traditional economic concepts regarding fiscal policy and balanced budgets.[46]

Such corporate concern had cause. The longer Eisenhower stayed in Washington, the more convinced he became that traditional Republican thinking on economic matters would have to be revised somehow in a "progressive" direction. The problem was that Eisenhower really did not know where he wanted to go.

The search for a direction was neither easy nor especially successful. The presidential head of the Republican party might want to move, and a segment of the big-business community grouped within the CED and to a lesser extent the Business Council might want to help him move. The problem was that neither Eisenhower nor CED activists like Herbert Stein were very well connected with the body of the Republican party, that sprawling association of local, regional, and state political bodies that reached out into the heartland of the nation. Though Eisenhower was able, with considerable effort, to get his major foreign policy initiatives like collective security firmly accepted as party policy, little energy was left over to galvanize support for high-profile domestic policy redefinitions. As an academic commentator accurately noted at the time, *Fortune* and a handful of other business journals backed Eisenhower's search for a new economic direction at home, "and the Committee for Economic Development has made of itself a businessman's Fabian Society," but the combined impact of these groups' efforts "is confined, and while they are in a good way responsible intellectually for the conservative enlightenment of the Eisenhower Administration, they scarcely reach the provinces."[47]

The Eisenhower administration's response to the recession of 1957–1958 illustrates the problems Eisenhower faced. When the recession began, the CED, true to its earlier policy statements, lobbied for a large one-year cut in personal income tax rates. The CED's efforts ran straight into the sand. Pressured by party traditionalists, Eisenhower opposed tax cutting for fear it would increase the size of the federal deficit. As the economic downturn stretched on month after month, unemployment levels reached 7.6 percent—the worst since the Great Depression. In the midst of these threatening circumstances, the Business Council met in May of 1958. Although a minority of the membership argued for the CED's conservative Keynesian tax-cut position, a majority of the corporate executives present were against a tax cut solution. The Council's lack of support for Keynesianism was, in Herbert Stein's later estimation, a decisive element in the failure of CED efforts to decisively reorient Republican economic policy.[48]

It is ironic that large federal expenditure increases finally, if unintentionally, helped push the nation out of the recessionary trough. The occasion for the spending had very little to do with any form of Keynesian thinking, but a great deal to do with the impact of Cold War fears on the government. In October of 1957, as the severe "Eisenhower recession" was beginning, the USSR launched a small basketball-shaped sphere into orbit: Sputnik I, the first artificial satellite ever to circumnavigate man's earth.

The American reaction was immediate. Congress was flooded with proposals to increase federal education subsidies, establish an American space agency, build rockets, and increase military spending across the board. Eisenhower tried to short-circuit as many of the big-ticket legislative items as he could, but his freedom of maneuver was restricted. Most legislators on Capitol Hill, after all, had never opposed spending and deficits if they were for defense purposes. In the wake of the panic that followed the Soviet Union's space initiative, bills were passed boosting federal armaments substantially. By the 1952 fiscal year, the Eisenhower administration's budget was deeply in the red. The $12.5 billion deficit of that year set a peacetime record to that date and far outran anything the supposedly prodigal spenders of the preceding Democratic administrations had ever been able to accomplish except in all-out war. Though Eisenhower refused to admit it, an *ad hoc* sort of military Keynesianism had arrived unheralded in official Washington. In the process, what CED opinionmakers had always feared came to pass. In good times, traditionalist budget balancing was the order of the day. When recessions began, deficits were run in an accidental fashion, very often for military purposes. When good times returned, pressure for tax cuts kept federal tax collectors from accumulating budgetary surpluses. The end result of all this was that a conservative administration presided over a debt increase of $27 billion in its second term alone —a sum equivalent to half of total federal debt outstanding in 1940. Deficit spending had come to stay.[49]

The political results of the 1957–1958 recession weren't long in arriving. In the autumn, 1958, elections the GOP lost thirteen Senate and forty-seven House seats so that it was outnumbered almost two to one in both legislative chambers. The effects of this disaster at the polls seeped through the hierarchy of the Republican administration and firmed the resolve of a minority of presidential advisers (among whom were numbered White House economist Arthur F. Burns and Vice-President Nixon) to get the conservative Keynesian message accepted.

Unrest also affected the corporate eminences of the Business Council, who had completely misread the economic picture and forecast no recessionary problems ahead. At the May, 1958, Council meeting previously mentioned, the schism in big businessmen's economic thinking was clearly evident in two Council committee reports that were forwarded to the chairman of Ike's Council of Economic Advisers. A special "antirecession committee" came out for the long-standing CED proposal to cut personal income tax rates, and added a proposal to cut corporate tax rates as well. The Council's taxation committee, however, was full of bruised—and even surly— corporate egos. Its members attributed the recession to what they said were twenty-five years of "unwise tax policy which has operated to reduce and even to stifle incentives to save and risk money in new enterprises." This sort of nonsense—blaming all economic troubles on political cabals that had originated with Franklin D. Roosevelt's arrival in Washington in 1933—received short shrift from Eisenhower's economic advisers and from Business Council members including Langbourne M. Williams (Freeport Sulphur) as well. Still, the Business Council committee's reluctance to officially recognize even conservative forms of Keynesian realities continued. Throughout the remainder of the Eisenhower administration, Council economic statements kept right on sounding a familiar litany. Federal budgets must be balanced, nonmilitary expenditures had to be reduced, and federal debt must be decreased. Tax rates on business, of course, were too high. And, in general, congressional Democrats were the source of all the ills that the American economy was heir to.[50]

Business Council reluctance aside, conservative Keynesian ideas began acquiring more and more political cachet among Republican political leaders—for the simple reason that they blamed the awful results of the 1958 election on popular opposition to what appeared to be Eisenhower's do-nothing policy. Some action beyond merely tinkering with the money supply was increasingly seen as a requisite of future political survival for candidates representing a minority party that had to attract large numbers of normally Democratic or independent voters to win seats.

One candidate proved especially anxious to reorient Republican policy before it was too late—for him. As the nation worked itself out of the recessionary depths, GOP presidential candidate Richard M. Nixon and his ally Arthur Burns accelerated their efforts to get CED-sponsored ideas clearly understood and acted upon by Eisenhower and his Cabinet. In May of 1960, Nixon went so far as to carry the conservative Keynesian gospel to the Business Council itself, telling a full Council meeting that he would cut taxes in the event of another recession. These efforts, however, produced no short-run political payoff.[51]

This failure exacted a political price. After a brief upswing in 1959, economic indexes briefly dipped down again in the election year of 1960. The results, once again, were unfortunate for the Republican party. Candidate Nixon lost by a hair-thin margin to Democratic standard bearer John F. Kennedy. Given that a disappointed Nixon assigned a large portion of the blame for his defeat to the recession, the time was coming when businessmen were going to have to accept Keynes whether they wanted to or not.[52]

Containment and Change

As businessmen looked back over the Eisenhower era in 1960, there were reasons for both optimism and pessimism. On the one hand, conservatives had never been able to reassert firm control over national policies as they had hoped. On the other hand, an exceedingly popular general had usually been able to hold the line on the domestic policy front while, at the same time, expanding the scope of American military and economic power abroad in ways amenable to the business politicians of the Business Council and the CED. Men like these had won their breathing space, their time to think and formulate new policy equations for a new era of big government.

The results of all this entrepreneurial cogitation were predictably mixed. In the economic realm, the beginning of a transition from Hooverite traditionalism to conservative Keynesian ideas had taken place. The CED illustrated the process most vividly, but change had taken place within the Business Council as well. Republican losses in the 1954 and 1958 elections had reminded businessmen that their best opportunities to exercise political and economic influence occurred during periods of steady economic growth when national problems could be either drowned—or at least managed—by a flood of resources and wealth. To pontificate about natural economic laws and do nothing else when recessions arrived was, just as it had been in the 1930's, a sure formula for failure. In foreign policy, business leaders had, by the middle of Eisenhower's presidency, climbed firmly on the bandwagon of the bipartisan foreign policy of containment that CED and Business Council activists had helped launch a decade before.

The 1950's, all things considered, had been kind to businessmen in many ways. Continuous hot war and Cold War tensions throughout the period put a premium on corporate expertise even while they undermined popular and political receptivity to "radical" ideas. Postwar affluence accomplished a large part of the same result. By 1955, *Time* magazine could even select a big businessman—President Harlow Curtice of General Motors—as its Man of the Year, the first time that that had happened since the 1920's. As business political activists pondered the future on the eve of the 1960 elections, the political spectrum in America appeared to a good many to have shifted, perhaps permanently, to the right. Business Council members at their May, 1960, meeting, Hobart Rowen wrote, had had their quarrels with Washington in the past, but now appeared quietly optimistic about the future. "Most," he added, "see the differences between the two parties as steadily narrowing." When Democratic President-elect Kennedy arrived in Washington six months later, the truth of these Business Council assumptions would be tested in a very decisive fashion indeed.[53]

6

THE KENNEDY
ADMINISTRATION AND
BIG BUSINESS, 1961–1963

Starting off on the Wrong Foot

IT IS IRONIC THAT the first Kennedy man to trouble the Business Council was a businessman himself. Luther Hartwell Hodges, the new Democratic President's selection to be Secretary of Commerce, was not a radical person—or even an especially liberal one. Hodges had grown up poor in the South, assumed the then traditional loyalties to the conservative wing of the Democratic party, run textile mills for twenty-five years, and then retired at age fifty-two to devote a decade to administering the state of North Carolina from the governor's mansion in Raleigh. The only thing unusual about the man was that he had acquired a modest reputation for enlightenment —for a Southern governor—regarding the slowly emerging black civil rights movement.

However, Hodges had one unfortunate political characteristic: he was a self-made entrepreneur who harbored deep suspicions about big businessmen in general and the elite corporate membership of the Business Council in particular.[1]

Hodges' suspicions about the Council were aroused further just before the 1960 elections when *Harper's* magazine in its September issue ran the first exposé of the Council's membership and operations ever to appear in a national magazine or newspaper—"America's Most Powerful Private Club." Following his appointment as Commerce Secretary, Hodges met privately with the exposé's author, reporter Hobart Rowen of the *Washington Post.* During their conversation, Hodges told Rowen he simply did not believe that a big-business group like the Council should have the "special channel to government thinking" that its peculiar quasi-public status had given it for the three decades since its creation. Further, Hodges continued, it did not look good that the Council was then headed by one Ralph D. Cordiner. Cordiner, the chairman of the board of General Electric, had escaped by a hairbreadth from being implicated in a massive price-fixing scheme in the electrical industry that had sent a dozen lower-level corporate managers to jail for criminal violations of the Sherman Antitrust Act for the first time in United States history. Privileged discussions of federal policy with such a person as Cordiner, Hodges reasoned, was equivalent to electing a murderer county sheriff. Finally, Hodges' felt his political turf was infringed on by the fact that even though he was Commerce Secretary, he could not select the membership or determine the agendas of meetings of this body of corporate managers who were supposed to advise him—and through him the rest of official Washington. After mentioning his concerns to Kennedy and receiving what he thought was a presidential nod, Hodges tried to change the composition and operations of the Business Council.[2]

The reform proposals that Hodges put forward to Business Council leaders were less than revolutionary. The new Secretary of Commerce wanted to exert his authority over the Council by assuming the power to approve or disapprove of all corporate executives tapped for membership in the organization. Hodges also wanted the right to appoint some heads of small and medium-sized businesses to the group, to determine the agendas of all Council meetings, and to set the dates for all Council functions. In addition, all Council meetings were to be open to the press and were to be chaired by federal officials as well as corporate representatives. Finally, Hodges wanted Council Chairman Cordiner replaced immediately. Hodges, in effect, was sending the Business Council a simple message: hereafter he would be the top banana in the organization. Further, the Business Council would have to obey structural and procedural rules that governed other civilian advisory bodies in the nation's capital.[3]

Hodges' effort to take charge of his department's corporate advisory body fared badly from the start. Part of the problem was personal: the North Carolina textile magnate and former governor utterly failed to impress the CEOs of the Business Council. Typical was the later recollection of Thomas J. Watson, Jr., of IBM that "Mr. Hodges immediately reflected to any of us who met him an anti-big-business feeling." Hodges' problem, Watson sniffed, was that he was a corporate nobody who simply didn't know "many so-called big businessmen or even small businessmen of national repute."[4]

However put out by Hodges' lack of corporate status, Business Council members did make some lackluster efforts to explain their position and improve relations. Council memoranda meant for Hodges pointedly noted that "because of the desirability of securing outstanding industry and community leaders, it automatically evolves that most of the membership [of the Council] comes from the larger firms." The wife of a Council member tried a more personal approach to soothing Hodges. Attacking the "troublemaker" Hobart Rowen's piece in *Harper's*, the lady announced that the Business Council was no "club," but a dedicated, disinterested, bipartisan group, whose policy recommendations had all too often been placed on dusty shelves to molder unread under past administrations. The Council wanted to help Hodges, but acceptance into the "bosom" of the group would take time, so the new Commerce Secretary shouldn't be pushy, partisan, or stiff in his dealings with corporate leaders. Finally, he should always be careful to call his wife by her first name—and to call corporate leaders' wives by theirs—when attending functions put on by the organization, in order to appear suitably "friendly."[5]

Lectures on social etiquette and the like did not impress Hodges. In a series of meetings with Council leaders held between February and April of 1961, Hodges threatened to abolish the Business Council outright unless its members agreed to the changes that he had outlined.

Initially it appeared that Hodges' get-tough strategy was working. In March, Council head Cordiner quietly left his post, being replaced by Roger Blough of U.S. Steel. Blough, together with Sidney Weinberg, Leonard T. McCollum of the Continental Oil Company, and others, persuaded the majority of Council members to go along with Hodges' demands for the moment.[6]

The moment proved to be extremely brief. In May of 1961, the Council held one of its twice-yearly "work and play" meetings at the tony Homestead hotel in Virginia. Hodges flew down for the weekend of meetings. Not one other prominent Kennedy administration Cabinet officer or other notable accompanied him, however. To add insult to injury, Hodges insisted on picking up the tab for all of the personal expenses he ran up at the resort (previously, corporations had paid all of federal officials' travel, lodging, and entertainment bills).[7]

None of this symbolism regarding the Council's demotion from a unique to a normal government advisory body was lost on the corporate eminences assembled at the Homestead. As the several days of meetings progressed, a series of ever more abusive attacks was launched against Hodges and the Kennedy administration. George Humphrey, Eisenhower's Secretary of the Treasury, proved particularly eloquent on the subject of the new Secretary of Commerce's upstart and wrongheaded efforts to interfere with long-established Business Council procedures and traditions.

Forty-eight hours of this sort of thing were enough for Hodges, who returned to Washington even more determined to bring the Business Council to heel. Throughout May and June, Hodges reiterated his demands that the Council recognize his authority and make some symbolic moves at least to open its membership and meetings. To underline his points, Hodges threatened to turn over all minutes of Council meetings to Justice Department antitrust officials on the chance that examples of corporate skulduggery were contained therein.[8]

Early in July, the Business Council decided that it had had enough of Hodges and his pressures. On July 5, 1961, a high-ranking Council delegation met with Kennedy in the White House to tell him that the group was disaffiliating itself from the federal government. Council Chairman Blough laid a memorandum on the surprised President's desk informing him that the group intended to broaden its base and would operate as a purely private group in the future. Kennedy was pleasant, but said nothing of substance in reply. One Commerce Department official in attendance at the meeting, however, was considerably more forceful in expression. "Gentlemen," he said to Blough and the other corporate executives as they left Kennedy's office, "you have just murdered yourselves."[9]

Nothing, in fact, was further from the truth. Almost immediately after Blough's group walked out the door, the Kennedy White House initiated a process of reconciliation with the Business Council. Just two days after the Council's unusual secession from the executive branch, presidential press secretary Pierre Salinger told reporters that Kennedy had assured Council leaders that their new "private" status was a good idea and that "the various government agencies would be glad to have such a group available for consultation."[10]

Within the next few weeks, Kennedy and his top aides effectively cut the remaining ground out from under Hodges' feet by ordering other Cabinet officers to cooperate with the reorganized Business Council. Hodges' efforts to put together a new Business Advisory Council within his department were squelched. Presidential right-hand man McGeorge Bundy ignored Hodges' repeated requests to forbid federal officials to address Council functions unless they were opened to the press. A bitter Hodges later concluded, "I did not get Mr. Kennedy's backing because he took the position, very erroneously, that [the Business Council] was now a different organization, and, therefore, should have different treatment. This was not very good."[11]

The Business Council's speedy rehabilitation within official Washington was certainly not very good for Luther Hodges. In undercutting his Commerce Secretary at the very beginning of his administration, however, Kennedy was pursuing wider goals. As Hobart Rowen wrote at the time, Kennedy's about-face came because he feared that the Business Council–Commerce Department divorce might lend credence to the charge that the Democrats were antibusiness. Kennedy had enough difficulties without a whispering campaign aimed at him emanating from corporate boardrooms. Overseas problems in Berlin, Laos, and Vietnam—plus the administration's own reckless determination to close the nonexistent missile gap—had boosted federal armaments spending substantially and caused more red ink in the national budget. Kennedy also wanted big businessmen's assistance in improving America's balance-of-payments position by boosting exports and negotiating tariff reduction treaties with foreign nations. The summer of 1961, then, was not a time when Kennedy could afford to burn bridges to anybody, especially since the comic-opera Bay of Pigs invasion had only recently made the vigorous young President look like a supreme fool in foreign policy.[12]

To further reassure Business Council members of his administration's good intentions, Kennedy sent White House aides Ralph Dungan and Myer Feldman on a goodwill mission to corporate America. The two men kept in touch with Council affairs through Robert T. Stevens (of the Army-McCarthy hearings) and Roger Blough, arranged private meetings between Council delegations and Cabinet agencies, and expedited the creation of a handful of Council "liaison committees" that were supposed to participate in close advisory relationships with the Council of Economic Advisers, the Departments of Treasury, Commerce, Defense, and Labor, and the White House itself.[13]

If appearances were any indication, the Business Council had completely defeated Luther Hodges' brief challenge to its authority. Appearances, however, were deceptive. Most of the liaison committees Kennedy created were apparently *pro forma* propositions. Within the Council itself, doubts were expressed regarding the wisdom of the actions taken by Blough, Weinberg, and others. Longtime Council member W. Averell Harriman, for one, was greatly alienated by what he considered to be the maladroit actions of leaders like Blough. By severing its official relationship with the executive branch, Harriman later recalled, the Council lost a good part of its ability to affect policy debates on high-level issues. Granted, he went on, no advisory organization can easily gauge the extent to which it influences the resolution of any particular political problem. However, the Business Council had traded a relatively close relationship with the White House for nongovernmental status and connections with a collection of Cabinet agencies often furiously at odds with one another. The Council, Harriman concluded, became "a bunch of fat cats who sit around and tell each other how important they are, but who have no real power" in the wake of its secession.[14]

Harriman's criticisms—strenuous as they were—did not convince more than a minority of Business Council members. John W. Snyder (Truman's Treasury Secretary) agreed that disaffiliation was an "unfortunate mistake." J. Spencer Love of Burlington Industries was also skeptical that the Council's declaration of independence would improve corporate prospects. Generally, however, Council members basked in a series of meetings with Kennedy and other high administration officials throughout the late summer and early autumn of 1961. When the Business Council had one of its quarterly conferences in Washington in September of that year, an address by McGeorge Bundy summed up the Kennedy administration's view that

the whole notion of drawing a line between anything as large and varied as the business community of the United States, and anything as complex and multifarious in its machinery as the Government of the United States is foolishness. You know that it's foolishness—we know that it's foolishness. . . . The questions which come up day in and day out between thousands of men of affairs and hundreds of men in the varying departments simply do not yield to these easy slogans [like "probusiness" or "antibusiness"]. You know it and we know it. And it's a game we ought to stop. And it's a game which I assure you this Administration will not play unless it is forced on us. It is important that we give up the easy contests between the business interest and the wicked Administration which have been part of our folklore before.

Hours before Bundy spoke, a party for forty Council members was held in the White House, where Kennedy and a bevy of Cabinet officers—including Luther Hodges—socialized with corporate leaders and echoed Bundy's message of peace and good fellowship. "We're back in business!" exulted Sidney Weinberg. Other CEOs, less ecstatic than their opposite number at Goldman, Sachs, left the Council meetings with a wait-and-see attitude about the next act in the Kennedy drama. They did not have to wait long.[15]

Round Two: The Steel-Price-Hike Crisis of 1962

U.S. Steel Chairman Blough had one supremely unfortunate habit. He liked to walk into the White House with surprise memoranda for deposit on John F. Kennedy's desk. Blough had done just this when the Business Council disaffiliated itself from the Commerce Department in July of 1961. The Business Council's new chairman did it again in April of 1962. This time, Blough's strategy produced spectacular and unsettling results.

The problem that Blough's second memo addressed had been developing for some time. Ever since the 1930's, wage, price, and employment patterns in the nation's steel industry had been a matter of intense concern to Democratic and Republican administrations alike. Steel's problem was that it was a symbolic industry. As steel went, conventional political wisdom assumed, so went the rest of corporate America. Given that steel was deemed to be so important a bellwether of wider economic trends, federal officials did not hesitate to involve themselves in the two- or three-year contract cycle that determined wage and price levels in the industry. FDR's political hardball with U.S. Steel has been described in the Prologue.

Steelmen's prospects for ridding themselves of politicians' interference did not improve very much after the Republicans returned to power in Washington. The problem was that the nationwide steel contracts negotiated during the Eisenhower era both came on the eve of presidential elections. In 1956 and again late in 1959, high administration officials including Secretary of the Treasury Humphrey and Vice-President Nixon pressured steel negotiators to make wage, price, and work-rule concessions that were uncongenial to the managements of the companies involved. In the 1959 bargaining round in particular, steel executives, after lasting out a mammoth 116-day strike, went back to the bargaining table and signed a settlement pledging them to increase wages substantially without raising prices. Nixon's electoral plans probably had an important role in producing this outcome.[16]

Following the razor-thin Democratic victory in 1960, steelmakers started reassessing their position. Had Nixon won, recouping the profits they had forgone by not raising prices in 1959 and 1960 would have been a comparatively simple matter of cashing in on political favors rendered. John F. Kennedy, however, was another story. Kennedy had come to power determined, among other things, to do something about wage-price spirals in key industries including steel, automobile manufacturing, and construction. Washington, in short, was anxious to short-circuit the process whereby powerful unions forced higher and higher costs upon industry and equally powerful industrial combines then passed such increased costs on to the public in the form of ever higher prices.[17]

The technique that Kennedy's economic advisers devised to deal with cost-push inflationary problems in oligopolistic industries like steel and automobiles was the so-called wage and price guidepost. In simplest outline, the guideposts were an attempt to equate price and productivity levels. First, government economists calculated the average annual productivity increase in American manufacturing over the course of the post–World War II period, a figure initially set at 3.2 percent per year. Then the economists applied their guidepost approach, in the following way: if, for example, workers in an industry where productivity had been growing at the average 3.2 percent rate wanted a wage increase, they could obtain up to a 3.2-percent hike without their employer's having to raise prices to recoup the profits lost to increased production costs. In this situation, prices would remain stable and neither management nor labor would lose anything. If, on the other hand, the same workers unfortunately succeeded in breaching the guidepost figure of 3.2 percent and won, say, a 6 percent wage increase, their firm might increase its prices by 2.8 percent (6 percent minus the 3.2 percent productivity increase) and still end up no worse off, in terms of profit, than it had been previously. The guideposts on wages and prices, then, were federally sanctioned voluntary standards aimed at controlling the moderate inflationary trends of the 1960's by tying wage and price increases in American industries to overall productivity increases in those same industries.

One of the first industries in which the guideline technique was tried was steel. Early in 1962, as U.S. Steel and other large corporations sat down for contract talks with the United Steelworkers of America, Kennedy administration representatives were much in evidence. They pressured union and management delegations alike to do their bit to halt the wage-price spiral within their industry by accepting wage-price-guidelines principles in the negotiations. The steelworkers' union agreed. The steel manufacturers, for their part, made vague pronouncements about free enterprise. When asked—by Kennedy and others—whether they had definite plans to raise their prices independent of any guidelines agreement that might be worked out, however, the steel executives remained silent.

The Kennedy administration took this employer silence to mean consent, and by March of 1962 thought that it had worked out a noninflationary deal. The steelworkers' union (which had hitherto received hikes of as much as 8 percent) settled for a contract requiring wages and fringe benefits to rise only 2.5 percent. As this 2.5 percent increase was estimated by Kennedy's Council of Economic Advisers to be a little less than the overall productivity increase in the industry, Kennedy and his people assumed that the steel manufacturers would not have to raise their prices at all. No company contacted expressed any opposition to this idea, and the steelworkers' union had signed new contracts with all major steel companies by April 7.[18]

Then, on April 10, 1962, U.S. Steel's Blough dropped a bombshell. At an appointment at the White House, Blough handed Kennedy a memo which stated that his corporation would raise prices on its goods by 3.5 percent across the board, effective immediately. Within twenty-four hours, almost all the other major steel producers in the United States fell into line behind U.S. Steel. Blough, in defending his actions, retreated into legalisms. He had not definitely promised *not* to raise prices. And besides, U.S. Steel and other firms needed relief from *past* wage hikes that had not been adequately compensated for in terms of price increases.[19]

Roger Blough's logic did not impress the Kennedy White House at all. Kennedy, in fact, was furious. "My father always told me," he commented to staff aides, "that steel men were sons of bitches, but I never realized till now how right he was."[20]

From Kennedy's perspective, the need to stop the steelmen from reneging on their implicit agreement to abide by his administration's wage and price guidelines was direct, immediate, and compelling. If he accepted Blough's actions without a fight, his anti-inflation program would be smothered in its cradle. Organized labor would become politically alienated. Innumerable interest groups might get the idea that Kennedy was a paper tiger who would cave in to pressure if it was delivered with sufficient panache.

In the days immediately following Blough's peremptory surprise announcement, Kennedy used his considerable skills to deliver some surprises of his own. The mass media played a key role in the process. During a nationally televised press conference the day following the Blough visit, Kennedy reviled the steel industry. The "simultaneous and identical actions of United States Steel and other leading steel corporations," he affirmed,

> . . . constitute a wholly unjustifiable and irresponsible defiance of the public interest. In this serious hour in our Nation's history . . . the American people will find it hard, as I do, to accept a situation in which a tiny handful of steel executives, whose pursuit of private power and profit exceeds their sense of public responsibility, can show such utter contempt for the interests of 185 million Americans.[21]

Presidential excoriation like this—plus threats from Secretary of Defense Robert S. McNamara that he would buy steel from firms that had not raised their prices whenever possible—produced a storm of conservative and corporate criticism of the Democratic administration and all its works. Kennedy's rhetoric had struck a very raw nerve. Within hours of his televised press conference, a misquote started circulating around Wall Street and other bastions of corporate America to the effect that Kennedy had damned *all* businessmen with a dubious paternity. Before long, a Business Council eminence like Sidney Weinberg could be seen walking down the street sporting an "SOB" (son of a bitch) pin in his well-tailored lapel.[22]

Corporate esteem for the Kennedy administration was not increased by the fact that his use of the presidential pulpit to jawbone a rollback of steel prices proved very effective indeed. By April 13, three second-tier steelmakers—Inland, Armco, and Kaiser—had refused to ape the U.S. Steel–led price increases. Fearful of losing market share to their smaller but more cost-efficient brethren, Blough and the other steel company CEOs reduced their prices as suddenly as they had raised them.[23]

Kennedy's victory was complete, and the corporate hysteria that followed it was almost universal. The day that U.S. Steel and other major producers announced their price decreases, William E. Robinson, a Business Council member who had just retired as president of the Coca-Cola Company, wrote a tense letter to his old friend Dwight David Eisenhower. The bases that Robinson touched nicely illustrated the ugly memories that Kennedy's actions had reawakened in the corporate psyche. "Dear General Ike," Robinson began, "Here we go again, back down that road to the babel of dissension, friction, acrimony, and class warfare that brought us close to ruin in the thirties and renewed itself in the latter part of the Truman regime. . . . What now about our free enterprise system . . . when [Kennedy] denies the right of a business to price its goods?" Robinson continued that Kennedy was taking "a quick sly opportunity to strike a blow for the planned economy that is unmistakably the prime objective of the administration. How the [Walter] Hellers, the [John Kenneth] Galbraiths, and the [Arthur] Schlesingers must have jumped for joy." He warned that "instantaneous retaliatory persecution" might well become a tool with which JFK could bludgeon big business to do his bidding.[24]

For all of the hypertensive imaginings of Robinson and other big businessmen like him, however, the fact remained that Kennedy had actually *done* very little to business. No substantive moves were made in the White House, for example, to use the antitrust weapon against offending companies, to clamp mandatory wage-price controls on the steel industry, or to kill an accelerated depreciation bill of special usefulness and profit to capital-intensive industries including steel. Instead, Kennedy men, with an occasional ill-tempered and inept assist from the President's brother Robert, tried personal persuasion and media diplomacy.[25]

It was Kennedy's media diplomacy that unsettled big businessmen the most. In using the powerful medium of television to question the validity of the steel companies' actions, the photogenic President was striking at these corporations' ideological legitimacy. Kennedy, in short, was using his office in exactly the way that Theodore Roosevelt had used it: as a "bully pulpit" from which to charge business men and others with not playing by the economic rules. Steel, Kennedy strongly implied, could not have it both ways. It would not do to welcome aggressive federal intervention in the collective-bargaining process and then turn around and argue that Washington should have no say at all in management's pricing decisions. Verbal smokescreens about "free markets" and free enterprise were all very well, but actually Adam Smith's neoclassical economic world had been dead, as far as the steel industry was concerned, for well over half a century. Roger Blough himself inadvertently spoke to this point when he tried to defend U.S. Steel's price hike in a news conference on April 12, 1962, by telling a bemused reporter for *Time* magazine that his corporation had to *raise* its prices because lower-cost foreign imports were making deeper and deeper inroads into the domestic American steel market.[26]

America's big-business establishment did not take kindly to Kennedy's pointing out the obvious fact that neoclassical economic theory had very little relevance to the day-to-day operations of the steel industry, or, by extension, even vaster reaches of the nation's industrial economy. In the wake of the steel companies' surrender on the price issue, a chorus of corporate chairmen and presidents echoed the thoughts of Coca-Cola's Robinson. Kennedy, such men alleged, was reopening all the old wounds of the Depression era. "Business confidence," the businessmen and their numerous journalistic supporters continued, needed to be speedily restored. Kennedy, presumably, had not only undermined popular faith in big business, but also big businessmen's faith in themselves.

The Kennedy White House initially resisted the oft-reiterated suggestion that it minister to bruised corporate egos. In its view, Roger Blough and the steelmen who had supported him deserved all they got—and more besides. Superficial pleasantries were exchanged with Blough and others, and administration officials continued their regular attendance at Business Council meetings to gauge corporate opinion and exchange ideas. But no ambitious efforts at rapprochement were attempted.[27]

Six weeks after the steel crisis, however, a serious shock wave hit the stock market. On May 28, 1962, a short-lived selling spree began that resulted in the greatest one-day loss in the market's history up to that time. Twenty-one billion dollars in paper value disappeared in five and a half short hours. Throughout the subsequent summer, corporate economists freely (and incorrectly) predicted a severe recession. The Business Council's committee for liaison with the Council of Economic Advisers added its voice to the general entrepreneurial outcry. Kennedy, the refrain went, had very largely caused the economic spasm and must do something to repair the damage.[28]

The object of all this corporate concern—John F. Kennedy—was not particularly adept at dealing with businessmen or business ideology. Businessmen, Kennedy admitted to close advisers and reporters alike, confused him. He did not know what made them tick, or how to go about the job of reassuring them on the home front while he implemented his administration's grand designs abroad.[29]

If Kennedy was confused, his chief White House counselor, Theodore Sorensen, was not. In June of 1962, Sorensen addressed a lengthy memo to the President outlining a short-term course of action for the new Democratic administration to take.

The problem, as Sorensen and others in the presidential entourage saw it, was that the price of any genuine big-business political support for Kennedy was too high. Some corporate opposition to the administration was "emotional, illogical, political and inevitable." That corporate opposition was of such a scale (and so multifaceted and industry-specific) that no Democratic administration had a prayer of ending it without junking almost its entire political and economic program. Even the ongoing Democratic effort to get corporate backing for a tax break to help underwrite new investment might well run into trouble from "those businessmen who prefer their subsidies to be more obscure, more traditional, and more ample." The thing to do, Sorensen continued, was to replace Secretary of Commerce Hodges, because big businessmen found him uncongenial. Kennedy should also instruct his Cabinet officers to increase their outreach to corporate leaders, and arrange a series of informal dinner meetings with prominent businessmen, "not organizational spokesmen," in the White House. "Any steps," Sorensen concluded, "taken for the primary purpose of pleasing the business community should be largely psychological, not substantive."[30]

Sorensen's logic held considerable sway within the administration—so much that he was able to orchestrate a broad executive branch effort to reassure big businessmen throughout the five months preceding the 1962 elections. Textile magnate Robert Stevens, for example, was assured by White House aide Myer Feldman at a Business Council meeting in June that a Textile Industry Advisory Committee would be formed within the Commerce Department to deal with the problem of low-priced Oriental imports. Other big-business leaders received similar pledges that their special interests would be looked after. The Business Council responded, somewhat naïvely, with grandiose discussions in its meetings of "government-business cooperation." When the congressional elections in November of 1962 produced no significant loss of Democratic legislative clout on Capitol Hill, however, Sorensen's effort to placate corporate leaders in a psychological, as opposed to substantive, fashion was scaled back. Hereafter, Sorensen told an Assistant Secretary of Commerce on November 9, "individual and spontaneous" efforts should take precedence.[31]

Making Friends: Conservative Keynesianism Arrives at Last

While the complicated game of corporate psychological encouragement was being played out under the eye of Theodore Sorensen, the Kennedy administration was initiating another, considerably more important, effort to enroll corporate support for its policies. By the summer of 1962, a clear consensus existed within the Kennedy administration that conservative Keynesian economic growth policies could serve as a foundation for an alliance of mutual convenience between organized business and the federal government.

The Kennedy administration's path to conservative Keynesianism had been halting and gradual. A good number of Kennedy men had arrived in Washington partial to Keynesian techniques that offended conservative instincts. These men—prominent among whom was economist John Kenneth Galbraith—advocated an *expenditure-increase* approach to pump priming aimed at fostering faster rates of economic growth. In this view of the matter, government should greatly increase its spending during periods of economic slack, and target the money on the people and places in society that needed that money the most. During the first year of Kennedy's presidency, the ideas of Galbraith and others like him held sway. The new President and his top aides announced their determination to end the flabby economic performance that had characterized the final three years of the Eisenhower era by initiating a grand series of spending programs in areas including defense, foreign aid, urban renewal, manpower training, federal aid to education, economic assistance to depressed areas, and medical care for the aged and indigent. This extra spending over and above federal tax receipts would increase the size of the national debt, but it would also, they affirmed, boost the economy out of a situation where unemployment hovered around 7 percent of the labor force.[32]

Congress, however, was having none of Galbraith's view of the world. Capitol Hill majorities gladly voted several additional billions for the military, but wanted little to do with the other spending items on the Kennedy agenda.

Military spending increases were helpful in priming the economic pump. Alone, however, they were not enough to do the job that Kennedy's economic advisers thought had to be done. So, having lost most of the battles on the spending front, administration strategists shifted their attention to the taxation side of fiscal politics.

Here, too, the Kennedy administration's experience was not an altogether happy one. During 1961 and 1962, the White House fought to get a four-part tax reduction and reform measure passed by Congress. The administration's bill aimed at providing tax relief (in the form of accelerated depreciation allowances and tax credits) for worthy entrepreneurial activity like new investment in plants and capital goods that created jobs. This tax relief, in turn, was to be paid for by higher taxes on the dividend and interest income accruing to higher-income individuals—and by taxing the income that American corporations earned abroad but did not repatriate to the United States.

Congressional majorities soon taught Kennedy's men some lessons about the realpolitik of tax policy on Capitol Hill. First, Congress passed the corporate tax cuts that the administration had asked for after adding some sweeteners of its own. Then Congress eviscerated the reform elements of the bill with the enthusiastic consent of business groups of all types. What had started out as a self-financing mix of tax cuts and reformist tax increases ended up as a $2.5 billion hole in the federal pocketbook.[33]

By the spring of 1962, policymakers in the Council of Economic Advisers and elsewhere in the Kennedy administration were beginning to get the message. First, congressmen liked to vote for tax cuts, the nearer to elections the better. Second, congressional majorities in both houses were opposed to large federal spending increases outside of the defense area. Third, most congressmen and senators were not very knowledgeable about economics and had little or no interest in learning about the nuances of Keynesian—or any other—theory.

Conscious of these political realities, Kennedy's Council of Economic Advisers began to fashion a fiscal program that would encourage faster economic growth without offending conservative instincts. Walter Heller and others wrapped up Keynesian economic techniques in the rhetoric favored by the economic traditionalists of the Hoover era. Tax rates, they argued, were too high to guarantee the growth rates required to boost the economy up toward full employment. Government was not leaving enough dollars in the private sector to be used for purposes of consumption and investment. What was needed was a large and permanent tax cut to benefit both individual and corporate taxpayers. These taxpayers, if left with more money than usual in their pockets, would go out and spend it to purchase goods and services, to finance research-and-development projects, and to buy new capital stock. The additional consumption made possible by a tax cut—and the additional production that would be unleashed in order to meet this increased consumption demand—would produce higher levels of investment, output, employment, and income in society, and thus accelerate the pace of the nation's economic growth.[34]

Once they had formulated their strategy, the CEA economists had to sell the package to the President. Kennedy, who had issued a ringing call in his inaugural for Americans to bear any burden (including tax increases) needed to carry out the nation's global strategy, initially proved reluctant. Lacking any grounding in economics, and advised by close aides like Theodore Sorensen whose skepticism about Keynesian doctrines was profound, Kennedy took refuge in homey analogies—telling CEA personnel at various points during the first eighteen months of his presidency that congressional conservatives would "piss all over" a big tax cut proposal, or that the White House would be "kicked in the balls by the opposition" if it did as the CEA economists were advising.[35]

During the summer of 1962, however, the President thoroughly reconsidered his opinions on Keynesianism. The negative fallout from the steel-price-hike imbroglio and the minipanic on the stock exchange led Kennedy to move toward open advocacy of a tax cut as a means of repairing his relationship with the business community.

Having made the decision, Kennedy proceeded to act upon it with characteristic vigor. In early June, 1962, as White House aide Sorensen was beginning his missionary work aimed at lifting the spirits of corporate CEOs, Kennedy traveled to New Haven to deliver his first explicitly Keynesian address to an academic audience at Yale University. In the speech Kennedy, prompted by his CEA advisers, was careful to avoid the expenditure-increase side of the Keynesian coin; instead he confined himself to outlining the virtues of a tax cut. Immediately following the conclusion of his address, Kennedy flew back to Washington to attend a meeting with Blough, Watson, and other Business Council members to do what he could to get their support behind the administration's conservative Keynesian tax-cut plan.[36]

Kennedy's job was not as easy as it might have looked. Businessmen, like other conservatives, generally love tax reductions, but corporate leaders also had long-standing concerns about federal spending—and about reserving as much as possible of any tax cut for themselves.

These concerns were spelled out in a memorandum that Council of Economic Advisers Chairman Heller sent Kennedy on July 14, 1962, detailing the results of a just concluded meeting with the liaison committee from the Business Council. Council representatives, it appeared, were willing to make a deal with Kennedy—if he could meet their price.

The Council group—Roger Blough, John Cowles of Cowles Publications, Donald David (formerly of Harvard and now at the Ford Foundation), Joseph B. Hall of Kroger Stores, and Charles G. Mortimer of General Foods—started off on a tough note: business confidence was way down, the recently passed accelerated-depreciation tax break was a "dud," the administration was not doing enough— Defense Secretary McNamara of the Ford Motor Company excepted —to decrease waste, and federal expenditures were rising too fast.

Having gotten all this off their chests, the Council members began to discuss the question at hand, namely tax cuts. Cuts were fine if they were made permanent rather than temporary (and they were). Decreases in upper-income personal tax rates had the highest priority. Closely following them in importance was a cut in the corporate income tax rate from 52 to 47 percent (47 percent was the figure eventually accepted). Cuts for lower-income individuals were not a legitimate priority, though they were a "politically necessary evil" if

Kennedy was to sell his package to Democratic liberals on Capitol Hill.

The White House, however, should be very careful not to adopt AFL-CIO–backed proposals to skew the tax cuts toward lower-income individuals. Any tax cuts the administration proposed should be large (Council members suggested a range of $6 billion to $9 billion while Kennedy's men preferred—and eventually got—a little over $10 billion). These cuts, moreover, "*must* be accompanied by a commitment to effect savings in government expenditures." Kennedy should drop his support for Medicare, federal aid to education, and other programs that would require additional spending. In return, federal deficits and increases in the national debt that resulted from the tax cut would not meet doctrinaire business opposition.

Walter Heller listened politely to this catalogue of corporate *desiderata,* carefully noted for Kennedy that the big-business delegation was no longer traumatized—as Eisenhower's corporate-dominated Cabinet had been—by deficits and deficit financing, and concluded that the Business Council representatives were trying to play a strong political hand. They had taken, he concluded, "by far the most conservative stance they have taken with us" since their secession from the Commerce Department in the middle of 1961.[37]

The Business Council group's message was hardly congenial to the White House. The message that the group delivered, however, came to have a powerful influence upon the way in which the Democratic administration's tax cut proposal was drawn up, legitimized, and eventually passed into law. Big businessmen clearly wanted Kennedy to act like a conservative Republican, and act like one he did, dressing his Keynesian program in every scrap of conservative clothing available.

After wrenching foreign policy problems including the Cuban missile crisis had been dealt with, the process of brokering the tax cut into being began in earnest. By early December of 1962, Kennedy was assuring a business audience at the Economic Club of New York that corporations and upper-income individuals would receive "favorable treatment" in his tax bill. Kennedy also promised his appreciative corporate audience that he would make reductions in nonmilitary spending, and went on to argue that the short-term deficits his tax program would cause were merely a down payment on future budgetary surpluses that would be used to retire a part of the federal debt. Touching every conservative base, Kennedy, in the opinion of a disappointed John Kenneth Galbraith, had delivered the "most Republican speech since McKinley."[38]

On the same day that Kennedy spoke in New York, the previously quiet CED declared its support of the administration's proposals. The CED argued very much as the Business Council's CEA liaison committee had done five months earlier. Corporate and upper-income tax reductions were the primary requirement. Lower-income cuts were an unfortunate political necessity. Restraint in federal spending was necessary. Increased federal deficits were something that businessmen could live with.[39]

CED supporters of the presidential tax cut program jumped on what was quickly becoming a very crowded corporate bandwagon. By the time that Congress started immersing itself in the details of determining precisely who would get what in the tax reduction game in January of 1963, the Kennedy White House strategy of presenting its Keynesian program in as conservative a guise as possible had really started to pay off in terms of business support.

Congress, however, was not to be rushed, and spent a year putting its constructions on Kennedy's initiative. The results of all this legislative cogitation and deal making were not unattractive to businessmen. As originally proposed, the Kennedy administration's bill allowed for $8 billion of personal tax relief and $2 billion of corporate tax cuts. The bill also included a *pro forma* package of $7 billion in tax reforms (i.e., increases) on real-estate tax shelters, oil depletion allowances, special tax credits for stock dividends, and other financial boons enjoyed by those wealthy enough to hide their assets behind special privileges contained in the tax codes. Congressional conservatives of both parties cooperated, over negligible White House opposition, in cutting the heart out of the tax reform elements of Kennedy's bill. They then tilted the billions of dollars of individual tax reductions toward wealthier taxpayers. Finally, Congress, with Kennedy's approval, voted to phase in all cuts over a three-year period so that the federal deficit would not be larger in any single year than the $12.5 billion record set by the Eisenhower administration during the 1959 fiscal year.[40]

Big-business political activists were not sitting idly by while all of this legislative activity was going on. Business Council members Henry Ford II and Stuart T. Saunders (Penn Central Railroad) took the lead in the creation of the administration-backed Business Committee for Tax Reduction in 1963, which eventually enrolled almost three thousand corporate heads in an influential panindustrial alliance to agitate for tax reduction. The group also, and with no opposition to speak of from the White House, argued energetically against any substantive effort at tax reform.[41]

The Ford-Saunders committee provided important elements of corporate legitimacy for the Kennedy tax cut plan during its entire passage through Congress. The group proved especially helpful in defeating efforts by conservative Republicans and Southern Democrats to force large-scale spending reductions on the Kennedy administration as a *precondition* for a tax cut. While Eisenhower was leading a charge of right-wingers who termed a tax cut without big expenditure cuts a species of insanity, Saunders and Ford went before congressional committees to argue that while spending cuts in the future were a good idea, they were not necessary as preconditions or as an immediate matter of practical economics. Now, Ford and Saunders told the congressmen, it was mainly necessary to get a tax cut passed—and for the Democrats not to spend any *more* money than they were already spending. Saunders, Ford, and like-minded big businessmen also cooperated with administration efforts to eliminate the opposition to the tax cut that remained within the membership of the Business Council. By October of 1963, this process was said by the *New York Times* to be well under way as Secretary of the Treasury C. Douglas Dillon, a Council member himself, issued a dire (and probably intentionally overdrawn) warning that there would be a severe recession and subsequent left-wing agitation in Washington unless a tax cut bill was quickly passed by Congress.[42]

From there on, it was all over except for the shouting as far as the tax cut bill was concerned. Conservative Keynesianism had arrived in the United States to stay. Kennedy had instituted no grand campaign to educate the electorate in the subtleties of federal fiscal policy or of Keynesian countercyclical techniques. Instead, concerned that an out-in-the-open Keynesian program would anger congressional conservatives and jeopardize others of his administration's far-flung political objectives, Kennedy defended Keynes' economics with right-wing rhetoric. He backed a tax-cutting, as opposed to expenditure-increase, approach to antirecessionary policy in order to enroll support from influential segments of the nation's big-business community including the leadership of both the Business Council and the CED. Reflecting on the whole tax-cutting experience fifteen years later, economist John Kenneth Galbraith summarized his liberal discontents:

> The tax cut was certainly more pragmatic in the sense that it produced more Establishment applause. I opposed it and favored the increased expenditures because the latter could be directed at the people and places that needed them most. The tax cut, by its nature, is confined to the more affluent part of the community: social expenditures go to those who need them most.
>
> But I had another fear, unlike some of my concerns manifestly justified by the results. I thought that if we ever started encouraging the economy with tax cuts, it would sooner or later become an uncontrollably popular measure with conservatives. And tax cuts would be urged as a way of getting public expenditures down.[43]

In the days of Reaganomics and the tax cut of 1981–1984, Galbraith's statement proved to be a prescient one indeed.

Expanding Relationships

By the time of Kennedy's tragic assassination in Dallas in November of 1963, the administration that he headed had had its ups and downs in its dealings with big businessmen. The steel-price-hike struggle and the stock market break in the middle of 1962, however, marked a watershed of sorts. Following these events, Kennedy and his men worked assiduously to repair their relationships with businessmen in order to try to buy themselves negotiating room to achieve the wider political purposes and policies of their administration. Kennedy did not *become* a conservative, but he acted like a conservative whenever possible, and publicly put conservative constructions on what he and his advisers hoped was legislation that would serve liberal ends. The tax cut of 1963–1964 was the key element in this process of rapprochement, but it was not all of it. Kennedy headhunters fanned out across the land looking for cooperative businessmen to do advisory and recruitment work. The Business Council's Thomas J. Watson, Jr., for example, selected the staff of the Agency for International Development, a centerpiece of the Kennedy administration's foreign policy effort aimed at the developing nations of Africa, Asia, Latin America, and the Middle East. Watson, as he later recalled, "used the Business Council almost entirely to do the job."[44]

IBM's Watson was also a moving force in organizing the White House Conference on National Economic Issues, which met in the immediate wake of the steel-price-hike squabble, and which served Kennedy as a platform from which to address the big-business leadership of the nation. After introductory remarks thanking the Business Council and the CED for helping him study problems like overseas tax havens and gold outflows, Kennedy enunciated a technocratic view of American politics that was intended to assure businessmen that the great reform struggles of the New Deal era were forever past, and that a new, sophisticated, disinterested, and informed liberalism had arrived to replace it. "The point I wish to make is this," Kennedy began,

> the problems facing us are all extremely difficult, they require the most sophisticated solutions, they are extremely different from the great national movements of the past—with the possible exception of medical care [Medicare], which is the only issue that arouses powerful feelings among the general public.
>
> We still have issues which arouse powerful feelings among specific groups—but, among the general public, issues of the type found in the Thirties, or in Wilson's or Theodore Roosevelt's administration, are now rare. The complexities of life today generate sophisticated technical questions which affect our economy and on which we ought to work in the closest concert.[45]

To demonstrate what he meant, Kennedy upgraded the importance and number of the administration representatives at Business Council meetings. He himself regularly attended the quarterly meetings of a high-level Labor-Management Advisory Group created by Secretary of Labor Arthur Goldberg to bring AFL-CIO and big-business leaders into closer—and, it was hoped, more cooperative—touch with one another. Business Council members Roger Blough, Thomas J. Watson, Jr., Henry Ford II, J. Spencer Love, John Franklin (United States Lines), and Richard Reynolds (Reynolds Aluminum)—joined by Elliot Bell, editor and publisher of *Business Week*—made up the management delegation to the Group. Remembering earlier Business Council opposition, Kennedy's economic advisers also retired plans to experiment with an American version of the taxation incentives and disincentives approach to increasing overall levels of economic and industrial growth developed in postwar France and known by the sobriquet of indicative planning. Galbraith and a handful of liberal economists and news commentators were dismayed by the result, but Kennedy had more important irons in the fire.[46]

The President also remembered the usefulness of the human touch in politics. Historian William L. O'Neill has remarked, "Businessmen, like other people, need love, and the less loveable they are the more they need it." The instantaneous notoriety given to the rumor that Kennedy had said that all businessmen were sons of bitches during the steel crisis demonstrated that corporate chief executives simply did not feel appreciated or respected by Kennedy, and so Kennedy started doing what he could to reverse this perception of himself and his administration.[47]

In mid-December of 1962, for example, Kennedy invited sixty active members of the Business Council to the White House for an off-the-record meeting. After the businessmen had been ushered into the East Room, Kennedy was introduced to the assembly by Roger Blough. The symbolism of the two former adversaries in the steel struggle standing cheek by jowl over cocktails was surely lost on no one.

Once the introductions were out of the way, Kennedy briefed the businessmen on the current problems of his administration. The Cuban missile crisis was not over yet, the President began. The verbal promise that he had made to the Soviets not to invade Castro's island again was surrounded by "many conditions and circumstances." Kennedy "left the impression," Robinson of Coca-Cola wrote former President Eisenhower, "that he intended nothing permanent on that score." "We are not," Kennedy himself concluded "out of the woods on the Cuban matter."

To further demonstrate his concern over Latin America, Kennedy lamented political and economic deterioration in Brazil, Argentina, Chile, and Guatemala before moving on to lambaste the French and British governments for what he considered to be their lackluster support for American efforts to contain communism in Laos. The British and French, Kennedy continued, were not even pulling their weight in NATO.

Shifting to the domestic scene, Kennedy assured the Business Council delegation that he was working conscientiously to reduce expenditures. Agricultural price supports, he added, were "monstrous," but it was politically impossible for him to reduce them. The problem was that farmers wanted price supports, but were unwilling to restrict production. The result was that more and more agricultural staples ended up in federal hands. Overall, the economy appeared to be in good shape, but Kennedy added (trying to sell his tax cut plan) he couldn't promise a thing for 1963. After a few additional minutes of informal discussion, the meeting closed with Kennedy expressing his hope that big business and the White House could work together for the national good.[48]

An off-the-record meeting like the one that Kennedy had engaged in with the membership of the Business Council provided businessmen with few if any state secrets and not much more information than most of them could have uncovered by a close reading of their daily newspaper. Information, however, was the least important thing that was being transmitted at a meeting such as the one described. Instead, Kennedy and the corporate leaders were engaged in a ritual observance. The President of the United States was taking time out from his killing schedule to chat politely and informally with a group of people whose opinions and actions mattered to him, and which were important to the nation as well. The fact that the meeting was held in the White House and that Roger Blough, so recently corporate public enemy number one, introduced Kennedy to his big-business peers made the symbolism perfect: Kennedy valued big business and big businessmen.

Of such symbolism and ritual many presidencies are made. The meeting with Kennedy, William Robinson wrote to Ike, encouraged him. Kennedy appeared to have been frank, less arrogant, and less full of "blind confidence" than in his earlier dealings with businessmen. Kennedy, Robinson concluded, might well be moving to "the middle of the road." If so, Kennedy was going to be a hard man to beat in the 1964 elections.[49]

As events turned out, an assassin's bullet made Robinson's suppositions academic within eleven months. Kennedy's successor as President, however, was a man who had a profound understanding of the human element in American politics and an equally profound commitment to using it, and much else besides, to rework the nation's political order in his own image. In this task of rebuilding American power at home and abroad, President Johnson looked for —and received—a great deal of support from the men sitting atop the commanding heights of the nation's big-business establishment. To his story we must now turn.

7

THE JOHNSON
TREATMENT, 1963–1969

Political Entrepreneurship

LYNDON BAINES JOHNSON well understood the symbolic uses of politics, presidential and otherwise. Therefore, the new chief executive of the United States entertained the Business Council at the White House only twelve days after John F. Kennedy's death. First the eighty-nine big businessmen attending heard a presidential address that complimented the past work of the Business Council and called upon its members to "assault the persistent problems of our generation and to help me put an end to them. .... We have," Johnson assured the businessmen, "much work to do together." Kennedy's still-unpassed tax cut and civil rights bills, Johnson added, were right at the top of this agenda.

Johnson then invited the business leaders into the Cabinet Room to engage in a one-hour "exchange of thoughts" with the Secretaries of the Treasury, Commerce, Agriculture, Defense, and Labor. It was doubtless a tight fit. By that point in time, however, it is doubtful that too many of the CEOs present were worrying about spatial considerations. Just to make sure the corporate leaders got the message, Johnson had White House cameramen photograph him with each of his business guests individually. Autographed prints were then promptly dispatched to each CEO's office. Like any good politician, LBJ understood that stroking of the sort he was then engaged in is twice as effective if quickly followed up by expressions of enduring regard.

To further ensure that the businessmen knew his mind, LBJ

invited the entire Business Council delegation back to the White House early in January of 1964 to have dinner. Johnson took the opportunity to brief his guests regarding the contents of his upcoming State of the Union message to Congress.

Presidential attentiveness like this is apt to leave even the most grizzled veteran of corporate or governmental administrative warfare a bit star-struck. And so it was with some members of the Business Council. "It's the first time in our history," one executive exulted as he exited from the State Dining Room, "that we've been invited to dine at the White House—it didn't even happen under Ike!"[1]

Gestures such as off-the-record briefings and dinners at the White House were only the start of a coordinated effort by the new Democratic President and his staff to enroll as many national interest groups as possible in a grand consensus aimed at creating a "Great Society" at home and abroad. Johnson had a dream. He wanted to become a revivified Franklin D. Roosevelt: a sharp political operator making use of every skill at his command to oversee the passage into law of a generation of social welfare legislation in the space of a single presidency. Johnson thought that he could accomplish a great deal of this task by working with a majority of the nation's biggest businessmen rather than against them. His political idol Roosevelt had had a difficult time cutting deals with businessmen because he had been forced, during most of his presidency, to operate in constricted Depression circumstances where the final resolution of political issues often boiled down to a struggle over who would have to accept economic losses. Johnson, however, enjoyed the comparative political advantage of being catapulted into the Oval Office early in a period of accelerating economic advance, during which the relevant political questions generally concerned the happier prospect of apportioning economic gains.

LBJ's tools for achieving the big business–government partnership that he desired were excellent. First, Johnson's attitude toward businessmen was genuinely friendly and respectful. A self-made man himself, Johnson liked tough, determined, take-charge managerial types, particularly those who would speak frankly in private and salt their conversations with witty or biting off-color expressions. Johnson's personal approach contrasted sharply with that of JFK, who had never really been able to shake off corporate perceptions that he was an arrogant rich kid from Harvard who had never met a payroll and would never care to learn.

Johnson's legislative skills were also vastly superior to those of his predecessor. LBJ's Good Ole Boy style of artful persuasion paid rich dividends in a Congress dominated by a generally conservative, Southern Democratic old guard who had seen many Presidents come and go as they accumulated the seniority required to chair key committees on Capitol Hill. Johnson's own Southern credentials, added to his seven years of service as Senate majority leader in the 1950's, helped him pursue what he knew to be the vitally important goal of remaining on permanently good relations with all kinds of congressmen and senators. No one would ever accuse Johnson of appearing to be—as author Norman Mailer characterized Kennedy —"a young professor whose manner was adequate for the classroom, but whose mind was off in some intricacy of the Ph.D. thesis he was writing." Instead, LBJ was a man, quite simply, to whom the almost infinite nuances of American politics were the very stuff of life.[2]

Johnson had the skills to make the deals. To work with big businessmen, however, Johnson first had to decide which ones were most worthy of his attention. It did not take him and his staff long to focus largely upon the Business Council. A businessman who served in high Commerce Department posts through most of Johnson's presidency and became the NAM's president later recalled, "I think surely that President Johnson, when he thought of labor he thought of George Meany; when he thought of business he thought of the Business Council. He would think of, when reminded, that the NAM and the Chamber [of Commerce] and a few other national organizations were there." When asked to list corporate executives who he thought were particularly high on Johnson's list, the same official listed W. B. (Bev) Murphy (Campbell's Soup), Albert Nickerson (Mobil Oil), Frederick Kappel (AT&T) and Sidney Weinberg. Murphy, Nickerson, and Kappel were all Business Council chairmen at various times during LBJ's presidency, and Weinberg, as we have seen in previous chapters, had been a participant in Council activities for twenty years.[3]

LBJ's choice of the Business Council and its leaders was an obvious enough one to make. Johnson wanted to speedily connect with a representative group of corporate leaders with national reputations and influence, men whose investment and other decisions were crucial in determining the rate and direction of American economic progress. He also wanted liaisons with big businessmen who were socialized to Washington's political folkways and accustomed to cooperating with federal officials in quiet efforts to resolve particularly vexing economic and industrial questions. Given such requirements, the Business Council was the best game in town. Its members had, with varying degrees of success or failure, been trying to play the power game in the nation's capital for thirty years. Therefore, the Johnson administration tried to avail itself of this reservoir of talent and political influence.[4]

The process of wooing the Business Council began almost immediately. Nor was the effort limited to expertly stage-managed White House events designed to massage entrepreneurial egos. At the previously discussed dinner meeting with the Business Council that took place in January of 1964, President Johnson told his blue-chip audience that he was going to cut future federal spending far below the levels projected by the Kennedy administration. One by one, Johnson's Cabinet officers rose to tell the corporate leaders where the cuts would fall in defense, agriculture, and atomic energy spending . . . and where lesser amounts of additional spending would be targeted in the social welfare area.[5]

The businessmen loved it. To understand why, we must backtrack for a moment. In Chapter Six, we saw how Kennedy's tax cut proposal faced rough going in Congress because of conservative fears that large tax cuts, without large spending cuts, would increase federal deficits and have other malevolent economic consequences. Even big businessmen who were especially supportive of tax cutting, men like Henry Ford II and the Penn Central's Saunders, had argued that federal spending certainly should not rise beyond the level already reached of approximately $100 billion per year, in the wake of a tax cut. Kennedy had promised businessmen that he would indeed roll back expenditures. He had, however, been vague as to how he intended to accomplish this. Businessmen, even those who understood and supported the Kennedy administration's conservative Keynesian strategy, might have been forgiven a certain skepticism concerning Kennedy's ability to get any substantial expenditure cut from a Congress with which he had never been on the best terms.

Johnson, however, was another politician entirely. At the January, 1964, dinner meeting, LBJ spelled out exactly what he intended to do about budget cutting, and further promised big businessmen that he would use his considerable skills to persuade Congress to go along. Total federal spending, Johnson affirmed, would be held at about $98 billion during the 1965 fiscal year.

Not surprisingly, the assembled corporate leaders generally responded favorably to Johnson's pledges to cut spending. "Business Council members who were privileged to attend the dinner meeting last night," John T. Connor of Merck and Company telegraphed the White House on January 8, 1964,

> were most enthusiastic about your approach to the important national and international problems that you discussed. Your mixture of dedicated concern for the nation's welfare and the welfare of human beings, coupled with your realistic appraisal of federal government fiscal responsibilities seemed just about right to me and many others with whom I talked. In spite of the difficulties ahead you will certainly receive strong support for your program in the business community.[6]

A minority of Business Council members remained to be convinced. Investment banker Weinberg, for example, cynically commented that during his experience in Washington, federal budgets had had a way of starting small and then growing to the extent that they required supplementary appropriations over the course of the fiscal year. Paul S. Gerot of Pillsbury Mills grumbled about the tendency toward growing social welfare spending. Defense contractor James Ling of Ling-Temco-Vought proved reluctant to accept the logic of cuts in military spending. Overall, however, the Council members' response to Johnson's spending initiatives was summed up by Wall Street lawyer Hardwick Stires: "That man made a lot of friends."[7]

Having made the friends, Johnson was equally careful to cultivate them. Among his earliest efforts to reassure businessmen about his intentions was a campaign against "waste and inefficiency" in federal agencies. The Council of Economic Advisers was directed to formulate plans to pare away thousands of jobs throughout the executive branch. Secretary of Defense McNamara, meanwhile, chopped a billion dollars out of the Pentagon's budget by closing a collection of obsolete military posts, airfields, and shipyards. Johnson temporarily recruited his old friend Robert B. Anderson, an investment banker who had served as Eisenhower's second Treasury Secretary, to coordinate the crucial early stages of the budget-cutting process. Johnson himself—in a move that liberal intellectuals lampooned but businessmen appreciated—brought the White House visibly into the waste-reduction picture by ordering the servants at 1600 Pennsylvania Avenue to economize on electric bills by shutting off unnecessary lighting whenever possible.[8]

Throughout the remainder of Kennedy's unfinished presidential term, Johnson's stock rose steadily among big-business leaders. Administration officials including Sargent Shriver, the head of LBJ's antipoverty program, and David Bell, LBJ's foreign aid chief, visited Business Council meetings bearing a message of cooperation. Bell asked Council members to help the Johnson White House "persuade Congress that tax benefits should be given to businesses investing in underdeveloped countries." Shriver, for his part, detailed administration plans to allocate $300 million for job training aimed at the hard-core unemployed. Would big business, Shriver asked, kick in the $30 million in matching funds that communities would be required to provide in order to participate in the vocational education program? The actual work of the program, Shriver continued, would be subcontracted out to private firms wherever possible, businessmen would get tax deductions on any matching funds they put up, and the whole Johnson "War on Poverty" would demonstrate that big business and government were not at loggerheads in the United States.[9]

Johnson's tactics worked well. By May of 1964, Business Council members were reported to be expressing "almost unqualified confidence in President Johnson and in the prospects for continued business expansion." By October, Secretary of the Treasury Dillon, having attended another Council meeting, informed Johnson that the atmosphere at the gathering was "far more friendly than any I have seen in recent years." The "Bourbons of business," as CEA Chairman Heller called them, were quite content. John Snyder, Truman's Secretary of the Treasury and a Council member himself, told White House aides that the Johnson administration was pushing all of the right buttons and was in "exceptional shape" as far as Council leaders were concerned. None of this led the new President to relax his efforts. LBJ held regular meetings with the White House liaison committee from the Business Council throughout the year. As CBS President Frank Stanton was among the members of this group, the meetings cannot have hurt him with the media. While all this was going on, corporate executives' occasional concern regarding perennial problems like antitrust prosecution was moderated by high-level suggestions from presidential intimates including Abe Fortas that such matters could be handled to businessmen's satisfaction through "sensible administration" of existing laws.[10]

The Goldwater Phenomenon

While Johnson and his men promised new worlds of cooperation and profit to big-business leaders, the right wing of the Republican party offered them the old-time religion in the person of Barry M. Goldwater. The conservative senator from Arizona and the hundreds of thousands of political activists across the country who made his candidacy possible expressed the underlying frustration of the Herbert Hoover–Robert A. Taft wing of the GOP. For twenty years and more, these conservatives had been alienated and distressed by the growth of federal power, remained skeptical of collective security, foreign economic aid, and other key elements of the Truman-Eisenhower bipartisan consensus on Cold War anticommunist strategy, and retained their desire to win the global struggle against Marxism-Leninism by somehow rolling back the frontiers of what they saw as a monolithic Soviet empire.

Finally, in Goldwater's presidential bid, the Republican right thought that it had a chance. Bypassing established party channels, the Goldwater partisans repeated precisely what the Willkie forces had done in 1940: they mounted a grass roots campaign that swept their candidate on to victory at the Republican convention over the opposition of the majority of party professionals.

While the Goldwater bandwagon rolled through the conservative heartland of the United States, Republican party elder statesmen were faced with a choice. Predictably, they divided in their assessments. Former President Hoover knew precisely where he stood, telling his old friend Clarence J. Francis of General Foods at the very start of the presidential sweepstakes in mid-1962 that Goldwater was his preference because he "doesn't mince words about being a conservatist" and because his was the candidacy that hewed closest to conservative (i.e., pre–New Deal) principles as Hoover understood them.[11]

Eisenhower, for his part, was not so sure. To Ike, the conservative problem remained what it had always been throughout his presidency. The Republicans had remained a minority party ever since the Depression. GOP candidates had to attract millions of Democrats or independent voters to get themselves elected in the first place. Once elected, conservative leaders had to face a Congress where the Republican party lacked anything approaching a majority position in either house. Republican Presidents, therefore, had to be capable of putting together and maintaining bipartisan coalitions with Democrats if they wished to govern effectively. The Republican right, Eisenhower believed, could neither win in the first place nor build congressional majorities even if an election miracle did take place.

So deeply did Eisenhower believe in the necessity of a bipartisan strategy for the Republican party that his first preference for a presidential candidate in 1964 was Southern Democratic banker and Business Council member Robert Anderson, who had served Ike as Treasury Secretary after George Humphrey unexpectedly had to leave Washington for private reasons in 1957. Anderson, as Eisenhower well realized, had skills considerably greater than those of a Cabinet-level administrator. Throughout Eisenhower's second term, in fact, the Republican President had used Anderson as a confidential contact man with two powerful fellow Texans who knew Anderson well, and who also held the balance of power on Capitol Hill: Speaker of the House Sam Rayburn and Senate Majority Leader Lyndon Baines Johnson. On a regular—sometimes daily—basis Anderson, Rayburn, and Johnson had met privately to make deals, exchange information, and sound out policy and legislative options. If any conservative in the country could deal with a Democratic-controlled Capitol Hill, Eisenhower believed, Robert Anderson was the man. Anderson, however, refused the invitation to run. So did fellow Business Council member Lucius Clay and Ike's brother Milton Eisenhower, then president of Johns Hopkins University.[12]

Eisenhower's lack of success in picking a Republican presidential alternative to Goldwater was part of a wider pattern of confusion within the GOP and the big-business circles that gave it so much of its financial and political muscle. Four men tried to stem the Goldwater tide by contesting the nomination. New York Governor Nelson A. Rockefeller had excellent corporate and political connections. A difficult divorce and remarriage on the eve of the GOP convention, however, made him too outré for the conservative mainstream. Michigan Governor George Romney, a former president of American Motors, also had widespread contacts, but generated no great corporate or popular enthusiasm. Former Massachusetts Senator Henry Cabot Lodge and Pennsylvania Governor William Scranton —both of whom entered the Republican primaries comparatively late—energized substantial support late in the presidential nominating process, but not enough to win the initiative from the Goldwater forces.[13]

Amid all the confusion in GOP circles, only one thing was comparatively clear: Goldwater enjoyed little support among big businessmen. Companies whose CEOs were willing to stand up and be counted in alliance with the Republican right included Armstrong Cork, Eli Lilly, Quaker Oats, Cluett Peabody, and a variety of steel and steel-related companies. Opposing Goldwater, however, were most of the longtime activists of the Business Council, men who had no interest in Goldwater's utopian dreams of an American capitalism that never was, and were equally uninterested in digging up scores of political and economic issues that had been laid to rest in a lengthy process of corporate-governmental accommodation over the course of the preceding thirty years.

The fact that big business opposed Goldwater was made clear in September of 1964 when a well-publicized meeting at the White House produced the National Independent Committee for President Johnson and Senator Humphrey, whose leadership announced their intention of enlisting business support for the Democrats in the upcoming elections. The group's initial membership (which eventually ballooned to three thousand chief executive officers) read like an honor roll of big-business political activists. Heading the list were Business Council members Henry Ford II, Robert Anderson, and Marion Folsom. Joining them were fellow Council stalwarts Henry Fowler, John Connor, Sidney Weinberg, Ralph Lazarus (Federated Department Stores), and Paul C. Cabot, a Boston investment banker. Other prominent businessmen included Thomas S. Lamont (Morgan Guaranty Trust), John L. Loeb (Loeb, Rhoades and Company), Raymond Rubicam (Young and Rubicam), Sol Linowitz (Xerox), Kenneth S. Adams (Phillips Petroleum), and Cass Canfield (Harper and Row). This aggregation, impressive as it was, considerably understated the extent to which CEOs of larger corporations were abandoning their traditional loyalties to the Republican party to back Johnson in 1964, for many corporate leaders would not allow the Democrats to make public use of their names during the campaign. *New York Times* stories in August, 1964, went so far as to estimate that 60 percent of the Business Council's members intended to vote for the Johnson-Humphrey ticket.[14]

Later calculations of corporate campaign contributions told the same story of massive corporate disaffection from the GOP. In 1956, Business Council members gave almost $300,000 to Ike as compared with a minuscule $4,000 to Adlai Stevenson. In 1960, the story was almost the same. Kennedy got $35,000 compared to Nixon's $250,000. In the 1964 election, however, this pattern shifted dramatically. Johnson received a reported $140,000 for his campaign, while Goldwater had to make do with only about $90,000. As liberal commentator David T. Bazelon observed at the time, the underlying meaning of all this corporate cash and political support for Johnson was that "a startlingly significant vanguard of the corporate barons" had begun a "serious institutional and political approach to Washington—at least for the time being."[15]

By October of 1964, the corporate shift to LBJ became a stampede as Goldwater toured the nation giving off-the-cuff speeches to the effect that Social Security might be made voluntary and that American military commanders abroad might be given authority to launch nuclear weapons on their own initiative. C. Douglas Dillon and Henry Fowler performed yeoman service for LBJ in recruiting backers from big, medium-sized, and small businesses in New York and elsewhere across the nation. Once recruited, these businessmen were funneled into Washington for a series of dinner meetings at which President Johnson addressed hundreds of executives at a crack. Johnson gave them the same treatment he had earlier given the Business Council, lauding McNamara's cuts at the Pentagon and promising that his Great Society social welfare programs would be possible "without great increases in Federal spending." Cutbacks in obsolete programs and "applying the same careful efficiency to government as a prudent businessman or householder applies to his own affairs" would do the trick. Calvin Coolidge couldn't have said it better. Meanwhile, White House photographers snapped additional reams of pictures—which were mailed to the businessmen with the appropriate presidential expressions of affection.[16]

Against this torrent of corporate political opposition, Goldwater and his backers proved relatively powerless. Charges were made that only defense contractors protecting their relations with incumbent Democrats were backing LBJ. When this strategy didn't work, Goldwater tried mudslinging, calling Johnson's vice-presidential running mate, Hubert Humphrey, a "semisocialist." This strategy, too, produced little in the way of meaningful results, for big businessmen could not envision the affable Humphrey leading a charge to nationalize General Motors and IBM. Even the hitherto stalwart support for Republican presidential contenders among American newspapers dropped catastrophically. (Newspapers, it is often forgotten, are businesses too.) Of the nation's top metropolitan dailies, only three —the *Chicago Tribune, Cincinnati Enquirer,* and *Los Angeles Times* —eventually decided to back Goldwater. Even *Life* and the *Saturday Evening Post* backed LBJ. It didn't take a philosopher to realize that Goldwater's candidacy was a dead duck. When the votes were counted in November, the Republicans went down to the worst presidential defeat in American history, winning only 27 million of the 70 million votes cast. Thirty seats in the House of Representatives that the Republicans could ill afford to lose also disappeared in the electoral maelstrom.

Reflecting on Goldwater's defeat a short time later, Marion Folsom discussed its effect upon big businessmen like himself. "I was talking with [John Kenneth] Galbraith not long ago," Folsom began.

> He finds that whether they came out for [Johnson] or not, the big business people were in back of Johnson, and that the people supporting Goldwater were generally small businessmen in small communities or small companies. I think that's probably true. They're pretty conservative. The people in the large companies have to keep up with the times . . . [while the small businessman] doesn't see the picture as a whole. He sees only a small part of it.

Folsom's interviewer then asked him if he thought that big businessmen had come to realize that the days when they could blame everything that they didn't like on government had passed. Folsom responded optimistically,

> Of course there are different types of business people, but I've found a great majority—like the people on CED and in the Business Council —to be pretty realistic. They might not like some of these things, but they adjust to it and they don't kick. And then they eventually come around to thinking: "Well, maybe we were wrong. Maybe this is the right way of doing things." That's one reason I think most of them are so impressed with President Johnson. He seems to have the right attitude toward business, and he gets things done.[17]

Expanding Upon Opportunity

Johnson certainly did get things done. In the wake of the overwhelming defeat of the Republican right wing's effort to reopen national

debate on a range of compromises on matters as various as Social
Security and nuclear arms control, Johnson's White House only
strove harder to achieve its vision of a grand national political coalition incorporating almost every major interest group in the country.

The first thing that Johnson did after winning election in his own
right was to reshape the executive branch. The Cabinet was the most
visible object of this political attention, and Johnson made sure to
send clear messages to corporate America as he changed personnel.
The very first to go was luckless Luther Hodges, whom Johnson (in
a move unusual for him) summarily sacked. Hodges had to fight to
get Johnson to delay announcing his enforced departure until after
he could rush over to the Commerce Department to announce his
"resignation" to his staff.

Johnson's replacement at Commerce was Connor of Merck and
Company, the executive who had sent LBJ the complimentary tele-
gram just after the new President's second meeting with the Business
Council. Johnson's message to Connor and his fellow Council members was clear: where Kennedy had recruited a business nonentity
who was suspicious of big businessmen and got the Business Council
into the headlines, Johnson was running an administration devoted
to cooperative purposes, and had appointed a leading Business Council member to Commerce to prove it.

Johnson's selection for Secretary of the Treasury was equally
reassuring to the corporate elite. The retiring C. Douglas Dillon was
replaced by Henry Fowler, who had helped LBJ recruit corporate
support in the 1974 campaign. Fowler, a Washington lawyer and
former Korean War mobilization official, was the Business Council's
legal counsel—a post he had held for ten years. Finally, Johnson fired
Attorney General Robert F. Kennedy, a man whom very few corporate executives liked.[18]

Big businessmen were even more appreciative of the policies that
followed hard upon the Cabinet changes. The Kennedy-initiated tax
cut was lauded by the Penn Central's Saunders at Business Council
meetings even before the election. After it, Johnson kept other, less
enthusiastic businessmen on board by holding meetings with prominent Business Council and CED members at the White House. With
Cabinet officers including Secretary of Defense McNamara in attendance, Johnson soothed the businessmen's fears that his administration's brand of conservative Keynesianism would produce
inflation or other economic ills. At one meeting on December 19,

1964, the President faced IBM's Watson, David Rockefeller of the Chase Manhattan Bank, AT&T's Kappel, Frazar B. Wilde, an insurance executive who was also serving as chairman of the CED, Frederick Donner of General Motors, Murphy of Campbell's Soup, David Cook of the American Electric Power Company, and the head of Merrill Lynch. Johnson's effort to sell his tax-cutting approach toward accelerating economic growth had some effect on Watson, Rockefeller, and Kappel. The latter two, however, announced vague desires for more spending cuts to go along with the tax cuts. Murphy and the president of Merrill Lynch agreed. Space exploration, most of the businessmen eventually said, was to be cut—a suggestion McNamara promptly squelched by announcing that the United States could not afford to be second to anybody in the race for the moon and what lay beyond. The CED's chairman made skeptical and confusing comments indicating that he was an extremely reluctant convert to the conservative Keynesian views of the research economists of his own organization. Donner opposed "experiments" on principle, admitting that he'd learned his economics forty years before. Cook, an old political friend of LBJ, gave his view that accelerated depreciation allowances for businessmen were a far better way to increase investment levels than were the across-the-board cuts the administration had actually passed.[19]

Johnson, plainly, could not afford to take business support for granted. These corporate leaders were with him on the tax cut, but their devotion to Keynesianism was hesitant and fragile. Pre-Keynesian folkways like Donner's forty-year-old economics might reassert themselves in the event of trouble.

To help ensure cooperation, Johnson asked the Business Council members at the meeting to go back to the Council with the word that the White House badly needed help in finding and recruiting able businessmen for jobs on various regulatory commissions and in Cabinet departments. The Council was receptive, and White House aide Jack Valenti was soon telling the President that the lists of possible appointees being provided by the organization included "VERY ABLE men." Meanwhile, Johnson kept sending signals to the Council. In May of 1965, for instance, he announced that federal excise taxes on telephone calls and automobile sales would be quickly reduced. On another occasion, he told the Business Council that the 1960's were going to be a "turning point in time" as far as business-government cooperation was concerned.[20]

By July of 1965, LBJ, with Henry Fowler's enthusiastic assistance, had rejuvenated the Business Council's liaison committee with the Treasury Department—a connection that had apparently languished under Kennedy. From here on, Council delegations met with Treasury officials every three months. In Washington, where access is half the political game and information is quite often the other half, Johnson's action was noticed. Even some of the more battle-scarred corporate veterans of the political wars were impressed. Fowler, after announcing the new liaison arrangements at a Business Council meeting, wrote LBJ that conservative Eisenhower intimate George Humphrey had told Fowler's wife that "every night he prayed for the health and welfare of the President of the United States." Humphrey apparently knew how to lay it on thick as well as Johnson did. Blough of U.S. Steel, who was also won over, later said that Johnson understood business problems better than any President he'd known—including Eisenhower.[21]

The administration and businessmen had achieved an apparent harmony. Newly appointed Attorney General Nicholas Katzenbach assured the Business Council's membership that more vigorous antitrust prosecutions were not planned, nor was a campaign against the wave of mergers between larger American companies that was then commencing in earnest. By May of 1965, an anonymous Council member interviewed by a reporter for *Newsweek* characterized business-government relations like this: "What the hell, business is making money. We've solved every damn problem except unemployment. We've got a President who listens to us, and one of our own men is Secretary of Commerce. It's no wonder you see people smiling."[22]

The smiles reflected the fact that the American economy was entering its fifty-fifth straight month of economic expansion without a recession. This five-and-a-half-year period of steady growth set a record. The American economy had never performed so well in peacetime since the start of the Great Depression, and more good economic news was to come. Economic growth rates during Johnson's incumbency were also higher than anything his Republican predecessors had enjoyed. Real GNP increases, which averaged only 2.5 percent a year in the Republican 1950's, more than doubled to 5.3 percent during the Democratic 1960's. This large-scale economic expansion—plus the effects of Great Society social welfare spending—produced significant improvements in the living standards of lower- and middle-income Americans. When Kennedy had first come to

Washington with Johnson as his Vice-President, two out of every five black families and one out of every six white families in the nation had incomes of three thousand dollars a year or less. By the time LBJ's Great Society programs were fully under way in 1967, these figures were down to one in three and one in eight families respectively.

Capitalizing upon the political opportunities inherent in the economic boom—and upon the almost mythic status that the martyred Kennedy assumed in the consciousness of the American electorate —Johnson achieved his lifelong dream of becoming another Roosevelt in terms of domestic social welfare legislation. Using every trick and stratagem at his command, LBJ and his men won passage of a series of reformist programs and laws in areas including medical care for the aged and poor, vocational training, federal aid to education, environmental improvement, urban mass transit, child care, pollution control, racial equality, voting rights, consumer protection, and poverty abatement. Merely listing some of the Johnson administration's scores of legislative accomplishments can only hint at the incredible success that LBJ enjoyed in working with amenable majorities in both houses of Congress to implement most of the liberal Democratic legislative agenda that had been waiting in the wings ever since the end of the domestic reform phase of the New Deal a quarter century before. Lyndon Baines Johnson had cause for a very great deal of pride and satisfaction in his presidential work.[23]

And yet, at the very summit of his political success at home, Johnson made the decision that doomed his presidency. In March of 1965, following fifteen years of incremental escalation of the Vietnam conflict on the part of both Republican and Democratic administrations, LBJ committed American troops to their second limited war on the Asian mainland.

At first, the Americanization of the Vietnamese civil war did little to undermine the grand alliance that the Johnson White House had created with big business and big businessmen. The businessmen, like most other Americans, thought that winning the antiguerrilla struggle in Vietnam was merely a matter of sending in American boys who would promptly crush the insurgents and turn control of the country over to pliant South Vietnamese political leaders. At Business Council meetings and in off-the-record conferences with the President and the officers of his Cabinet, Council members repeated that the organization was "100% solid" in its support for the war.[24]

Gradually, however, war brought problems in its wake. Victory did not come, American combat forces grew to gargantuan proportions, and billions of federal dollars flowed into the Indochinese theater of operations.

Within a year after Johnson committed the nation to war, the economic fallout from the conflict was creating the first cracks in the big business–government accord that the tax cut, the economic boom, and expert Presidential massaging had made possible. Though a wartime production boom kept unemployment levels falling, the inflation rate, steady at about 1.5 percent a year since the Democrats had regained control of the presidency, suddenly increased to a level of just over 2 percent a year.

Johnson's White House acted swiftly to try to repair the damage that inflation was causing in the boardrooms of corporate America. By March of 1966, the order had gone out to the Council of Economic Advisers and other bureaucrats to start assuring businessmen that "the nightmares and excesses of excess profits taxes and direct wage and price controls are not in the Administration's thinking." As far as LBJ and his top economic policy advisers were concerned, Vietnam was not going to become another Korea in terms of managing the economy on the home front.[25]

Rather than seeking to persuade Congress to pass wartime controls legislation, as Truman had done, Johnson put his hopes in moral suasion. A key element of the strategy was a continuation of the efforts that the Kennedy administration had initiated to encourage businessmen—particularly the CEOs of huge firms operating in oligopolistic markets—to obey the informal wage-price guidelines that Council of Economic Advisers economists had worked out. In particular, Johnson asked business and labor leaders alike to tie price and wage increases to overall rates of productivity growth within their industries and thus help maintain price stability. The strategy (which required both management and labor to agree that the existing division of the economic pie was sufficient, that income redistribution was unnecessary, and that gouging was undesirable) was not notably successful in a period during which inflationary concerns lowered the level of industrial discourse and decision making. Businessmen in low-growth industries including steel and powerful labor leaders in decentralized industries like construction gave *pro forma* public backing to the guidelines. Then they tried to push up prices for their labor or their products up as fast as they could. Steelmen, for instance, let the Johnson administration persuade the steelworkers' union to accept a 3.2 percent wage increase during the 1965–1966 bargaining round. The union accepted on the understanding that the companies could absorb all the increased costs without raising prices because automation had made workers' labor approximately 3.2 percent more efficient. The companies then tried a repeat of 1962 with a Machiavellian twist. Instead of making well-publicized across-the-board price hikes as U.S. Steel and its corporate allies had earlier done, the companies tried to slide up the prices on a varied mix of their diversified product lines in a gradual, seemingly uncoordinated fashion. The strategy did not deceive Johnson, and he used jawboning, thinly veiled antitrust threats, and other types of political hardball to delay the price increases.

Relief, however, was only temporary. Secretary of Commerce Connor refused outright to try to enforce the guidelines against his corporate friends. Secretary of Labor Goldberg proved equally reluctant to carry uncongenial news to his personal and departmental constituency at the AFL-CIO. The result was that more and more of Johnson's precious political capital was diverted from his high-priority effort to legislate the Great Society into being while fighting the Vietnam War. White House aides like Joseph Califano worked to preserve the program of voluntary price restraint, but it became more and more galling to well-placed labor and industry groups that wanted to use their power to maximize their own profits and incomes.

By the middle of 1966, labor and corporate lobbyists bearing demands for special privileges and treatment were swarming over the administration like flies on a dying animal. Top Kennedy aide Sorensen was recruited by General Motors to relay its corporate message to the upper echelons of the Johnson policymaking hierarchy. U.S. Steel hired recently retired Council of Economic Advisers member Otto Eckstein. Labor union leaders reminded White House staffers of who had voted for whom in 1964.

In the end, the combined pressure from unions, management, and hired political personalities was too much for the Johnson White House. The Kennedy-era guidelines, which though strained had remained generally intact until August of 1966, were effectively abandoned after that date. Verbal warfare then broke out in the private sector. Labor leaders denounced management for war profiteering. Management responded by blaming organized labor for all price increases. Both sides loudly emphasized their loyalty to marketplace capitalism, their ideological abhorrence for federal interference with collective bargaining and pricing, and their regret about the upward creeping inflation rate. "Somewhere, sometime," LBJ's chairman of the Council of Economic Advisers, Gardner C. Ackley, was finally led to lament, "we will have to find a way to convince the unions that they cannot continually push wage costs up, and to convince business that profit margins cannot continually rise." That somewhere and sometime never, unfortunately, arrived—then or since.[26]

While the Johnson administration was conducting its unsuccessful counterattacks against powerful unions and corporations on the wage-price front, the President was again using his personal charisma with the Business Council to try to negotiate anti-inflationary compromises attractive to big business. In March of 1966, Johnson invited a large delegation of Council members to another dinner at the White House. Over the course of five and a half hours, Johnson used all of his considerable talents to persuade the corporate leaders present to decrease their planned capital spending by 10 percent the next year to reduce inflationary pressures. Businessmen listened politely as Johnson asked them to forgo profits in a booming market as a matter of patriotism and enlightened self-interest, promised to do what they could, and went back to their home offices. There they received repeated follow-up calls and letters from presidential assistant Califano. Only 45 of the 150 businessmen who attended LBJ's dinner eventually committed themselves on paper to cutting back on their firms' investment plans. The other 105 maintained an eloquent silence. Patriotism and enlightened self-interest, plainly, were not going to do the job.[27]

The main problem that LBJ was having, by the middle of 1966, was this: big businessmen were willing to back him and his all-important Great Society social welfare programs, *if* these programs could be paid for without increasing the overall size of the federal budget much beyond the $100 billion limit that the Kennedy administration had reached. The fast-growing costs of what would eventually turn out to become a $150 billion bungled military adventure in Indochina, however, made such spending limitations impossible for Johnson to stay within. Johnson, who had hoped to cut waste in the Pentagon budget and use the billions saved to pay for aid to the poor and desperate, ended up a captive of military and political advisers who had other ideas. "Throwing money at problems" (though not the kind of problems the New Right now thinks caused every ill that Washington is heir to) subsequently commenced in earnest. By 1966, only a year after Johnson had promised the Business Council to hold spending just under $100 billion, his administration was spending $134 billion—$57 billion of which was going to the military. By 1967, the numbers had risen to $160 billion and $70 billion respectively. Meanwhile, social welfare expenditures for health care, housing, education, income support, and so on, by virtue of congressional sweeteners and other assists, rose by over $35 billion during the last five years of the 1960's.[28]

Big businessmen did not like budgetary arithmetic like this at all, and they let Johnson know it. Johnson couldn't ask the nation in general or its corporate taxpayers in particular to pay for more guns and more butter at the same time. Financing a war and a series of grand new social welfare programs was too much. Swelling the number or coverage of Great Society programs, then, should be delayed until the war was over and military spending reduced.

Roger Blough summarized the arguments as they developed at the time within the Business Council's ranks. Although "one or two" of the corporate leaders in the organization felt that Great Society spending and program coverage should not be curtailed, they were a distinct minority. The mainstream within the membership was very decidedly of the opinion (correct, as it turned out) that the country was heading for "a very serious demand-pull type of inflation and also a cost-push type of inflation" unless some hard choices were made between guns and butter. "Our friend Lyndon," Blough continued,

> was quite unwilling to see this. How could he win the 1966 election [for congressional Democrats] if he started to constrain welfare programs in order to conduct the Vietnam engagement. And how could he, once we got in to the Vietnam engagement, say, "Well, you can have enough money for 10,000 to 50,000 men, but you can't go over that because we don't have the money in the country to support that"! The difficulty was a cumulative difficulty on both sides. As one new welfare program came along, it would be supplemented by another. As one degree of engagement in Vietnam came along, it would be supplemented by another.[29]

Blough's analysis struck to the very heart of Johnson's dilemma. Unwilling to call for retreat in his War on Poverty at home or his war against Asian communists abroad, Johnson was spending too much federal money, increasing the size of the federal deficit, and losing carefully nurtured big-business political support. By October of 1966, the *New York Times* announced in a front-page story that the Business Council's membership was "for the first time since Lyndon Johnson became President . . . unhappy with the way things are going in Washington and the country." For the first time since coming to 1600 Pennsylvania Avenue, the wily Johnson was caught between a rock and a hard place. In trying to extricate himself, LBJ would, with extreme reluctance, take actions that further undermined his alliance with the nation's big-business establishment.[30]

The Beginning of the End: The Struggle Over the Tax Surcharge

Until the closing months of 1966, as we have seen, Johnson was doing extremely well. Even an article in the prestigious *Harvard Business Review* written during this period credited LBJ's "highly unique personal and administrative style" with producing "what may turn out to be the most remarkable ideological transformation of the century." Business leaders, the *Review*'s analyst continued, had "finally and with unexpected suddenness actively embraced the idea of the interventionist state." Big businessmen were evidencing "a remarkably tolerant and friendly attitude toward the complex congeries of national fiscal, monetary, and social welfare programs inaugurated during Mr. Johnson's first three years as President."[31]

Only one year later, the same author, again writing in the *Harvard Business Review,* somberly addressed the question of "Why Business Always Loses" and stated his belief that "history will show that business's current association with the Great Society has been largely episodic. It is an incident in time, not an element of a trend." Plainly, something very wrenching had happened to the system of cooperative relationships that Johnson and his administration had established with the nation's big-business leadership.[32]

The turning point was, very largely, the debate over tax and spending policy that occurred within the Johnson administration from the fall of 1966 to the summer of 1968. By early 1966, Johnson's economic advisers were telling him in no uncertain terms that expanding Vietnam War spending was going to play hob with the American economy unless he did something. His advisers asked the President to use monetary policy to tighten up credit and raise interest rates. Secondly, they tried to persuade Johnson to go to

Congress and ask for a temporary tax increase to pay for the increased costs of the war. Johnson agreed to the first of his advisers' suggestions, and directed the Treasury Department to cooperate with the Federal Reserve Board to rein in credit markets. Tax increases were another matter entirely, however. In this area of fiscal policy, he deferred taking any action.

The President hesitated on the tax front for good political reasons. Johnson knew that he could, if he so chose, wrap himself up in the flag and call for an outright war tax. To do so, however, would run the risk of reopening the Vietnam issue in Congress. This was not, from Johnson's perspective, a very good idea. As the months went on, casualties increased, and victory proved elusive, the Congress that had signed a blank check for the executive branch to fight the war was becoming increasingly restive and polarized. On the left, a minority of congressmen and senators were coming to believe that the war was a moral disaster that would sap the internal cohesion of the nation and infect America's global leadership with a disease from which it might not soon recover. In the middle and on the right of the political spectrum—in Congress as in the country generally—was a considerably larger group of people who were coming to believe not that the war was wrong, but that the Johnson administration was trying to fight it in an incorrect or self-defeating way. This latter group, then, was not opposed to the ends of the Johnson policy in Vietnam, but rather to the means the administration was using to achieve them. Though opinion on how to conduct the war varied a good deal, one visible conservative element within both the Republican and the Democratic parties argued that LBJ was a fool if he thought that he could fight a limited war. The thing to do, then, was to start fighting an all-out war against North Vietnam—a war that would, among other things, require the call up of National Guard and Army Reserve units on the home front.

But Johnson had no stomach for any such debate among hawks, doves, and fence-sitters in Congress or the country. Johnson feared that any call for a 1966 war tax would also give congressional conservatives all the political ammunition they needed to cut back on Great Society welfare programs as a patriotic belt-tightening measure. As a young congressman in Washington in the late 1930's and early 1940's, Johnson had seen right-wingers accomplish exactly that at the expense of liberal New Dealers. He had no desire to see the same thing happen to himself.

Further, Johnson's political instincts told him that Congress wasn't going to pass a tax increase anyway, no matter what he did or didn't do. In 1966, the United States was—officially—at peace. The Vietnam conflict was beginning to enter people's living rooms for a few minutes on television every night, but it had not become a clear and immediate part of Americans' day-to-day economic lives. Congress, Johnson concluded, would therefore be unlikely to take the political risks attendant upon raising taxes during what was popularly perceived to be peacetime. Congress, in fact, hadn't passed a tax increase in peacetime since 1937–1938, when FDR had induced a recession in his misguided effort to balance the federal budget. Moreover, 1966 was a congressional election year and legislators, Johnson reasoned, do not like to go before the voters just after levying higher taxes upon them.[33]

For all these reasons, then, Johnson decided against backing a tax increase. This element of his economic logic was very much to the liking of most big-business leaders in the country. Johnson, in fact, had polled the 150-man membership of the Business Council delegation at the previously described White House dinner in March of 1966 to ask how many of them were in favor of a tax increase. Not one hand in the room went up.

Some business leaders, however, were beginning to have second thoughts about taxes a few months later. In October, all the business (and Business Council) members on the Labor-Management Advisory Group that Kennedy had brought into being called for tax increases *and spending reductions* in a statement issued jointly with their AFL-CIO opposite numbers. The statement (coming as it did from those corporate chiefs with the closest relationship to LBJ and the Democratic party) suggested that no Great Society spending be touched, but that space, highway, agriculture, and river and harbor expenditures all be curbed. Meanwhile, Occidental Petroleum's Armand Hammer and a group of New York bankers, tired of the effects of the "tight money" policies maintained by the Treasury and the Federal Reserve Board, asked LBJ for a tax increase. By the end of the month, several anonymous members of the Business Council interviewed by *New York Times* reporters at one of the organization's regular meetings were said to think that tax increases would be all right *if* federal spending could be reduced at the same time. A tax hike and no spending cuts, the businessmen continued, would probably just mean more money for Great Society welfare programs —something the country didn't need just then.[34]

The majority of the members of the Business Council's committee for liaison with Johnson's Council of Economic Advisers, however, were not in agreement with the idea that tax increases and spending cuts were required. Spending cuts were desirable but tax hikes were unnecessary. After pondering the tax issue in December of 1966, the group, by a vote of 4 to 3, decided that tax increases not only were not required but dangerous. Treasury and Federal Reserve monetary policies, the CEOs apparently believed, had produced enough of a crunch in the money markets to cause a sharp slowdown in the economy that would commence early in 1967. The five-year program of investment tax credits that Kennedy had passed in his presidency was also coming to a close, the businessmen said, and this, too, would tend to slow down the rate of economic expansion. A tax increase, they concluded, would be counterproductive in that it would probably lead to a recession.[35]

Chairman Ackley of the Council of Economic Advisers took these Business Council opinions under advisement. One month later, as President Johnson was about to meet with a Business Council delegation, Ackley presented the economic options as he saw them. LBJ, he said, could:

a. Do nothing. Tell the country that the economy doesn't need a tax increase, and that the deficit isn't important. This is what most economists advise.

b. Try to balance the budget by a massive tax increase. This would almost surely produce a recession and an even bigger deficit than without it.

c. Combine a moderate tax increase [Ackley suggested a one-year, 6 percent tax "surcharge" on both individuals and corporations] with measures to stimulate the economy.[36]

The third alternative was the one that Ackley favored and the one that Johnson selected. Now Johnson had to sell the package to the country—starting with a Congress that might be more receptive to tax hikes now that the 1966 elections were past.

Selling a tax increase in the political climate prevailing in the United States during 1967 proved neither easy nor pleasant. Between the time that Johnson first decided in favor of a tax surcharge in January and the time that Congress was presented with an actual bill to increase taxes in July, the country entered a period in which, as

Ackley stated, its "social statistics" were "a mess." Racial frictions in larger metropolitan areas boiled over in a "long hot summer" that saw smoke from burning and looted neighborhoods blanket Capitol Hill itself. In cities like Detroit, scores died and hundreds were injured in widespread looting and pillage. Sensing Johnson's growing political problems, old adversary Robert Kennedy, impatient to assume the presidential mantle that he thought rightfully his, was positioning himself to try to defeat Johnson's renomination bid. Public opinion polls taken early in the year showed overwhelming opposition to tax increases; a whopping 65 percent of those questioned opposed the idea, while only 25 percent favored it. Finally, inflation was kicking up to a 3.5 percent annual rate as swelling military expenditures were made to maintain America's half-million-man army in Southeast Asia.[37]

Congress proved to have no interest in passing a tax increase. In 1967, Johnson finally faced the nightmare that he had avoided in 1966. So while conservative leaders including House Republican leader Gerald R. Ford pounced on Johnson's tax-increase proposal and argued that the Democrats could solve inflationary problems by simply cutting their wild welfare spending, Johnson went looking for powerful allies in his tax fight. As so often before, the road led to the Business Council.

What key White House advisers heard from the Business Council was not encouraging. In May of 1967, CEA Chairman Ackley reported to LBJ that Council corporations' opinion on a tax increase had hardened considerably. Now the previously divided CEA liaison committee was unanimously opposed to hiking taxes. Not only that, but Council meetings were full of worries regarding "the rising trend of Federal expenditures." There were no emotional attacks on "reckless spending" like the ones that Ford was making. "Rather, the attitude seemed one of resignation toward the inevitable public pressures for larger budgets." Ackley ended by trying to assure Johnson that he personally was still popular with Council members, and that they were all backing him on the war. But unrest over his domestic policies was evident too. Johnson, it appeared, would have to make some deals to bring the Business Council's member corporations into the struggle for a tax increase.[38]

Grim though the prospect was, Johnson knew what he had to do. For two years, the Business Council's membership had refrained from openly attacking any key element of the Great Society programs that LBJ had brought into being. However, the Council had been sending Johnson a steady stream of messages that federal spending had to be cut. It was not the programs that mattered to the Council; it was the money required to pay for them. To get corporate support for his tax increase, then, Johnson would have to pare billions of dollars from the federal budget. Having painted himself into a corner on Vietnam, LBJ couldn't touch military spending. He had, in fact, already done all that he could do to keep it from rising through the roof, and even so expenditures for the war exceeded estimates by over $5 billion in 1967 alone. This left only the Great Society. Nowhere else could Johnson find the billions in spending reductions that he needed to assuage the big businessmen and to get their backing for his campaign to raise taxes to tame inflation.

The process commenced on August 10, 1967, when the President met with a top-echelon corporate delegation in a two-hour off-the-record meeting at the White House. Present were C. Douglas Dillon; Henry Ford II; Secretary of the Treasury Fowler; Thomas S. Gates of Morgan Guaranty Trust; Werner Gullander, president of the NAM; Kappel of AT&T; Murphy of Campbell's Soup; Nickerson of Mobil; Rudolph A. Peterson of the Bank of America; Rockefeller of Chase Manhattan; Saunders of the Penn Central Railroad; Allen Shivers, president of the U.S. Chamber of Commerce; Alexander Trowbridge, Connor's successor as Commerce Department chief; J. Harris Ward of Commonwealth Edison; Sidney Weinberg; CED President Wilde; and Walter Wriston of Citibank.

Johnson started the meeting off on a somber note. The economic news was bad. Spending for Vietnam and other purposes had exceeded estimates by $8.5 billion, federal tax receipts were falling below expectations, and the administration was heading for what looked like a record-breaking $30 billion deficit. "We could," Johnson continued, "try to borrow all of that. We could tax it all. We don't think either would be wise." Borrowing that much money on the credit markets would cause interest rates to skyrocket and disturb the economy further. Trying to obtain the extra $30 billion from increased taxes would probably induce a severe recession.

The federal government could, Johnson continued, cut spending to help deal with the deficit problem. The difficulty here, however, was that of the $61 billion in nondefense expenditures that the administration projected making, all but $12 billion was "uncontrollable." Almost $50 billion in outlays could not be cut back unless

Congress amended the legislation mandating that certain payments be made to certain groups in society (e.g., Medicare and Medicard). Even eliminating all of the federal government's controllable nondefense spending of $12 billion would not eradicate the deficit.

What, then, did the White House plan to do? "The best way, we think," Johnson said, "is to cut 25 per cent from appropriations. . . . Just as we cut 25 per cent [or $7.5 billion] from appropriations, we hope to tax 25 per cent [or $7.5 billion], and then borrow 50 per cent [or $15 billion]." The tax-increase elements of the package would require that corporate and individual tax rates be raised 10 percent, instead of the previously advocated 6 percent.

The initiative in the discussion then shifted to the businessmen. Kappel said that Johnson probably had no alternative but to do what he was proposing. An unidentified corporate chief opined that spending reductions were a "terribly important element" to garner support for a tax increase. Johnson replied that he understood that, and blamed Congress for what he claimed was its unwillingness to let him impound or defer expenditures. Shivers then said he thought Johnson's proposals "realistic," but added the caveat that Congress would be unlikely to make the full $7.5 billion in cuts that Johnson wanted.

Gates picked up the spending-reduction point again. "The people," Gates affirmed (actually giving the view of big businessmen like himself), would buy a war tax, but they wanted expenditures pared back. Again, Johnson agreed that he would cut spending and chop away at congressional appropriations bills if necessary.

Treasury Secretary Fowler commented that the group had to move fast. "I have no doubt that every member [of Congress] is getting a reaction from the average tax payer [against a tax increase]. Unless we can mobilize the business leadership, we have a real problem. The men who know how business and finance operate must get the message over that the alternative of borrowing influences a risk to the economic balance of this country for years to come. The principal problem now is how to get this opinion [in favor of a tax increase] over. It's not a question of raising taxes, it's the lady or the tiger"—a grim but necessary decision.

Fowler tried to inject a positive note. The economy, he said, was probably on an upswing. The big businessmen present took Fowler's thought with a grain of salt, several stating that things did not look good as far as they were concerned. In the midst of this discussion,

President Johnson chimed in that he had doubts himself. "I've got a gut Johnson City feeling," LBJ concluded: "I'm scared."

Promptly counterpointing the President's expression of fear, Fowler reiterated his suggestion that "the business and financial interests . . . be marshalled quickly." Johnson suggested that the businessmen form a group taking the position that a reasonable course would be to have Washington compensate for 25 percent of the deficit through taxes, deal with another 25 percent by reducing expenditures, and account for 50 percent by borrowing. Johnson then called for a show of hands to demonstrate how many corporate leaders present in the room would back him. All the hands obediently rose, though several businessmen expressed the complaint that the proposed tax surcharge was too high.

Then, to help ensure that Johnson had gotten the point of the deal, Shivers returned once more to the spending reductions the businessmen wanted. Johnson, he said, had to come out strong for cutting expenditures from the very first. The implication was that *pro forma* political behavior would not be appreciated. Johnson repeated that he'd gotten the message.

The discussion then briefly shifted to the nuts and bolts of putting together a big businessmen's tax group, and the meeting closed. As the corporate leaders filed out of the White House, the White House Press Office issued to reporters copies of an utterly phony speech that Johnson was supposed to have just delivered to the businessmen regarding the laudable American economic advances of recent years.[39]

After they left their meeting with the President, the members of the big-business delegation (eleven Business Council stalwarts and the heads of the CED, NAM, and Chamber of Commerce) created a new version of the Henry Ford II–Stuart Saunders businessmen's tax committee of the Kennedy era. The only difference was that the new group Ford and Saunders headed was lobbying for a tax *increase* this time. By September, several hundred big businessmen had signed the group's first public statement in favor of the surcharge. Before Saunders and Ford were finished, they had brought approximately five hundred CEOs under their banner. All the tax statements emanating from the new Ford-Saunders group emphasized that multibillion-dollar spending cuts must accompany the tax increase, and that the increase should only be temporary.[40]

In the months that followed, administration figures regularly advised LBJ to keep reaffirming his devotion to spending reductions to the Business Council in order to prevent corporate disaffection from his administration from increasing. Johnson did what he could, but he was having a hard time making the cuts that business demanded as the price of its political support. Vietnam spending continued to rise, and Johnson initially proposed only $2 billion in nondefense spending reductions to Congress. Ultimately Johnson hesitated to cut the Great Society programs he'd labored so hard to build.

This hesitation—plus Johnson's inability to get Vietnam spending under control—cost the President heavily with Business Council members, most of whom had probably heard the story about the $7.5 billion in cuts that LBJ had repeatedly committed himself to making at the White House in August. By October, Council members were beginning to think they might have been had. "Almost to a man," the *New York Times* reported, "Business Council members strongly criticized the President in their private conversation for not proposing the spending reductions that key Congressmen say are a prerequisite to Congressional consideration of a 10 per cent tax surcharge."[41]

Two of the key congressmen that the Business Council members were referring to were conservative Southern Democrat Wilbur Mills and equally conservative Republican Gerald R. Ford. Mills, chairman of the House Ways and Means Committee, and Ford, House minority leader, both wanted to use Johnson's tax hike bill, in conjunction with the Johnson administration's inability to keep its military budget down, to force basic changes in the way that the federal government was operating in the social welfare field. "We have to focus," Mills stated in a speech he delivered in October of 1967, "on *what* the Government is to do as well as on how much it is to spend." Mills, then, wanted to have a new legislative debate regarding what Great Society social programs were really necessary and which ones weren't. Mills, of course, didn't put it so directly: political survivors in Washington never do. Congress, Mills orated, had to reassert its authority over "the recent sharp rise in Federal outlays and the proliferation of Federal government activity . . . [if] we want to pause in this headlong rush toward ever greater government."[42]

Johnson's entrapment in the ever more costly Vietnam War made him easy prey to such tactics. Refusing to disengage in Vietnam left Johnson no choice but to cut heavily in nondefense areas even while he fought to keep the likes of Mills and Ford from forcing him to cut too deeply and thus destroy key elements of his beloved Great Society. Johnson, struggling to retain some sort of legislative initiative, sweetened the pot by agreeing to $4 billion in nondefense spending cuts. This move, however, failed to satisfy congressional conservatives and brought down ferocious liberal wrath on Johnson's head. Why, liberals asked, should Johnson cut any social welfare spending at all—especially spending for programs he had created?

Here was the stuff of political tragedy. Mired in Vietnam, harried by congressional conservatives, and losing support from big businessmen because of his failure to cut spending, Johnson's acclaimed legislative magic touch was dying before his eyes. White House staffers close to Johnson mirrored the mood of decay and frustration that began to permeate the administration as 1967 drew to a close. "I am afraid that the reason so many businessmen and bankers are supporting you on the surtax," White House aide Harry McPherson wrote Joseph Califano late in October, "is so that they will feel free to increase prices and interest rates after you lose the surtax fight. You won't be in any position to put the screws on them as you did on the steel, copper, and aluminum people [in 1965 and 1966 during the wage-price guidelines program]. They will have fought the good fight, and it will be Congress' fault, not theirs, when the next round of inflation comes. This makes sense, but I don't know what to suggest doing about it."[43]

As 1968 began, White House personnel had even greater cause for gloom. The delays caused by Wilbur Mills and others had pushed the decision date regarding the tax increase into an election year, which further inhibited congressmen's ability to act. The widespread popular consternation that greeted the Tet offensive launched by North Vietnamese and Vietcong forces during the last week in January only made a war tax harder to sell to a legislative branch increasingly sure that the war was being conducted so badly that something drastic had to be done. War spending continued its rise as American commanders fought—successfully as it turned out—to regain the military initiative from their overconfident enemies. Johnson's political popularity, however, did not recover. In February, as Tet raged, former Governor George C. Wallace of Alabama, an overt racist, announced that he would run for the presidency on a third-party ticket, which eventually garnered him almost 10 million votes. In

March, public opinion polls showed for the first time that half of the American people believed the Vietnam War to be a "mistake." By the end of the month, a tired and desperate Johnson announced that he would not run for renomination for the presidency. Four days later, the Reverend Martin Luther King was assassinated by white racists in Memphis. The Negro rioting that followed King's murder was soon complemented by antiwar disturbances that closed Columbia University and other major institutions of higher education. Even as a start was made at coping with these crises of public order and Vietnam peace negotiations finally began in Paris, Robert Kennedy was assassinated in Los Angeles. Johnson's presidency, so nobly and successfully begun, was fast declining into horrible and ironic political turmoil.

Through it all, Johnson kept trying. In May, as his tax-increase bill lay languishing in Congress, the lame-duck President made his last effort to elicit corporate credibility regarding spending reductions. At a meeting of the Business Council, Johnson lauded the organization for the help that its members had given him with tax and other issues in the past, and told the business leaders that their help had never been more necessary to him than it was now. The White House, he said, had cut nondefense spending by $4 billion. It could do no more without harming the social welfare programs so dear to Johnson's heart. Congressional conservatives (who by this time had formulated a compromise position demanding that Johnson cut welfare spending by an additional $2 billion, making a $6 billion total, in order to get their go-ahead on a tax increase) were wrong in their objections and would, if successful, sow seeds of despair and frustration among poor Americans. Would the corporate leaders help? Johnson, after shaking hands with all of the 130 men in the room, returned to the White House to await their answer.[44]

He did not have to wait long. Within five days, a large group of Business Council members telegraphed Johnson that he must accept the $6 billion in spending reductions that Congress was demanding "even though the reductions exceed what you consider to be a wise level."[45]

Johnson's plea had failed, and he had no real choice but to comply with Business Council wishes. He still needed the Council's members, after all, to pressure congressional conservatives to back the tax increases that would bring the record-breaking budget deficit under some semblance of control. Congressional conservatives were saying that they would back a tax hike after Johnson made the spending reductions. But House Republican leader Ford had been saying for months that *only* spending cuts were required. Getting the tax increase passed, then, was going to be as much a matter of applied political muscle as one of quiet deal making. To apply the pressure, the big businessmen were essential.

Johnson was well aware that he had promised the businessmen repeatedly he would cut $7.5 billion as the price for his tax increase. If he didn't go along with Council demands for a somewhat lesser cut of $6 billion, the Council leaders with whom he had made his deal could turn around and back conservative efforts to dismantle the Great Society wholesale by the simple expedient of denying various programs funds. In the middle of 1968, Johnson did not need any more enemies, particulary ones as formidable as the membership of the Business Council.

So Johnson surrendered at last, in hopes that the Business Council could rescue his tax increase. That the group proceeded to do. By early June, Treasury Secretary Fowler was telling Johnson that no less than sixty CEOs and Washington lobbyists of some of the largest companies in the nation were meeting with him to map out the final stages of the campaign to get the tax surcharge bill passed. The big businessmen, Fowler added, intended to go about their work in the manner best calculated to successfully pressure, and if necessary bludgeon, reluctant congressmen into line. "The assignments," wrote Fowler, "will be made to the company representatives who are either headquartered or who have important plant operations in the District of the individual House member." Politics, as has often been said, is not exactly a demure business.[46]

Finally, on June 28, 1968, the job was done. The Johnson administration's tax surcharge achieved final congressional passage. The yearlong process had not left a good taste in anybody's mouth. Congress finally gave Johnson what he wanted but, by the time he got it, Vietnam War spending had risen so high that the remaining federal deficit, even after the tax increase and the $6 billion in spending reductions, was $10 billion higher than the $15 billion that Johnson had estimated to the big-business delegation in August of 1967. Further, big businessmen had been alienated by Johnson's shilly-shallying on expenditure reductions. They had finally forced Johnson to accept the $6 billion figure that Congress had compromised on, but remained displeased that the originally promised $7.5

billion figure was not reached. In addition, inflation, which had stood at 3.5 percent in 1967, was approaching a 5 percent annual rate during the early months of 1968. To top it all off, businessmen had to contend with temporarily higher taxes as a hoped-for antidote to this inflation. Altogether, it was not a confidence-inspiring economic picture.

The Democrats Fade Away

Throughout the twilight of his power, Johnson did what he could to restore the wrenched and torn grand consensus with which he had begun his presidency. IBM's Watson and others continued to assist Johnson in his successful efforts to defend tariff reduction initiatives that were begun during Kennedy's tenure. With the cooperation of Henry Ford II, John D. Harper (Alcoa), and J. Paul Austin (Coca-Cola), Johnson launched the National Alliance of Businessmen (NAB), an industrial association whose aim was to provide jobs and occupational training for the hard-core urban unemployed. This mixed public-private effort to expand upon a portion of the Great Society without recourse to the federal budget proved moderately successful at providing entry-level jobs so long as the economy's course remained headed generally upward. Even here, however, the contagion of Vietnam was felt. Leo C. Beebe, the Ford Motor Company executive dispatched to Washington by Henry Ford II to become the NAB's first administrator, described Johnson as being distracted by the ongoing Asian war. "The President really didn't have the answer. You could see that it was the most exasperating thing in his life. He was like a caged animal, I thought, just prowling back and forth incessantly thinking about this problem of Viet Nam. He was totally obsessed."[47]

As Johnson prowled back and forth seeking answers that did not come, big-business support gradually melted away from the Democrats. Businessmen were careful to avoid open breaks with Johnson —who remained personally popular in corporate circles despite all of his political misfortune. Corporate leaders, however, had comparatively little desire to involve themselves with the President's party, which was locked, by this time, in a full-fledged civil war over Vietnam. Business Council members, for instance, remained steadfast in their support for the war throughout Johnson's term in office, and so gave no support to dovish Senator Eugene McCarthy. Robert Kennedy fared little better. IBM's Watson backed him, but most other big businessmen, remembering Kennedy's tangential role in the steel-price-hike imbroglio in 1962, steered corporate donations toward Hubert Humphrey in order to undermine Kennedy. Following Kennedy's assassination, however, corporate interest in Humphrey started to wane. A campaign organization called Businessmen for Humphrey, however, did contain a list of letterhead celebrities of some corporate stature. Included among Humphrey's financial backers were four from the Business Council (Henry Ford II, Watson, Connor, and C. Peter McColough of Xerox) and other prominent businessmen including G. William Miller of Textron, James Ling of Ling-Temco-Vought, and Edgar F. Kaiser of Kaiser Industries. Just to be on the safe side, however, companies like Ford, LTV, and Textron contributed heavily to the Republican party as well.[48]

So far as the corporate mainstream was concerned, eight years of Democratic Presidents were enough. Big businessmen were tired of the Democrats' idealistic missions at home and abroad and of the Johnson administration's flailing effort to restore credibility to the wreckage of its Vietnam policy. Given the choice between a great society and an orderly one, the businessmen opted for order, and thought of the Republican party and Richard M. Nixon as the best ways to achieve this goal.

White House economic adviser Arthur Okun noted the decisive shift away from the Democrats as the election of November, 1968, approached. In October, he attended a Business Council gathering and reported back to Johnson that "the mood at the Business Council meetings was disappointing. I felt as though I had wandered into a Republican convention. With a handful of exceptions, most of the business leaders are licking their chops at the prospect of conservative economic management for the nation. They are especially excited about big spending and inflation."

What businessmen wanted, Okun continued, was a hard-eyed conservative type ruthless and capable enough to apply standard high-interest-rate and decreased-spending remedies that would squeeze inflation out of the economy by increasing unemployment— to as much as 5.5 percent of the labor force if necessary. Council leaders, Okun concluded, were also worried that the tough program of restraint they wanted to see instituted might prove politically unfeasible without the election of a conservative Congress willing to back up the determination that the corporate leaders did not doubt Nixon possessed.[49]

The political hopes and concerns of the Council's members proved justified in November, when Nixon, finally victorious in his lifelong race for the presidency, proved unable to attract sufficient votes to Senate and House candidates to allow the GOP to enjoy majority status in either chamber of the national legislature. The next four years, it appeared to many, might well be filled with brawling between the White House and Capitol Hill.

Johnson knew all this as well as anyone, and so, in December of 1968, sought to use his oratorical skills to convince big businessmen —and through them the incoming Republican administration—that a relapse into traditional economic solutions to the nation's problems would not work.

On December 4, Johnson went before the Business Council for the last time. After the traditional expressions of high regard for his "partners" in the group, the Democratic President reminded the corporate elite that the conservative Keynesianism of his administration had paid rich dividends in terms that businessmen should appreciate. "When I first entered public life," Johnson began,

> America was torn between two opposing economic theories: the "trickle-down" theory and the "sock-it-to-'em" theory [that advocated heavy taxation of corporate profits and income redistribution from the rich to the poor].
>
> But in this administration, we set out to do something new—to use a "New Economics."
>
> We decided to bake a bigger pie each year; a pie with more and bigger slices, including some for a direct attack on our neglected social problems.

"Economic growth," Johnson went on, "has been the most powerful social weapon in our hands." Yes, this growth had recently suffered from the blemish of inflation. Nixon, however, must be careful about demanding a "sudden slowdown in prices and wage costs," which would produce a recession. Trying to eradicate inflation too fast "won't give us instant price stability, but it would give instant misery throughout our economy." Forswearing old solutions and the economics of Herbert Hoover, Nixon, like Johnson before him, should strive for an "enlightened partnership" between big businessmen and federal policymakers that would transcend the shibboleths of the past and make economic growth—Kennedy's "rising tide which lifts all boats"—into a secure foundation for continued private-public cooperation and advance.[50]

As Johnson left the podium, the Business Council members gave him a round of applause. Now their task was to wait and see what the new Republican administration had in store.

8

NIXON'S THE ONE(?), 1969–1973

An Opportunity, Not a Mandate

WHEN RICHARD M. NIXON took office, millions of the nation's citizens trusted neither him nor the party that he led. This was a major—indeed insurmountable—obstacle for the new conservative President. Nixon, it should be remembered, barely managed to win the 1968 election at all, receiving only three hundred thousand more votes than Hubert Humphrey in a three-way race that brought 71.5 million people to the polls.

A large part of Nixon and the GOP's electoral problem stemmed from two historical events: the recessions that had occurred during the final years of the Eisenhower era and Barry Goldwater's presidential bid in 1964. The Eisenhower recessions did great political damage to both Nixon and the Republican party. GOP candidates ran very badly in the 1958 elections. Republicans continued to control one third of all Senate seats, but lost almost fifty seats in the House. The 1960 elections enabled the GOP to recoup a fraction of these congressional losses, but Nixon lost his initial bid for the White House by a razor-thin margin—thereby beginning to establish an image as a political loser. In 1964, things were worse yet, as the Goldwater catastrophe took with it several score Republicans in the House and gave the Democrats firmer control of Capitol Hill than at any time since the domestic reform phase of the New Deal. Johnson, enjoying a priceless political opportunity, was presented with the secure Democratic majorities that he needed to pass the Great Society programs over unavailing conservative opposition. These liberal successes, in turn, only added to the Republican party's growing reputation for failure.

The Republicans' troubles had important consequences. When the Democrats began to experience political calamities of their own as a result of Vietnam and a growth in racial conflict at home, the Republicans were so far behind in the electoral competition that they could not easily capitalize upon events to rebuild themselves into the majority party—a status that they had not enjoyed for half a century.

Here we might recall a few statistics. Between 1964 and 1968, those casting their ballots for the Democratic nominee for President fell from just over 60 percent to just over 40 percent of the electorate. No fewer than one in every five voters switched his party preference as a result of widespread discontent with the Johnson administration's perceived inability to bring "law and order" to either the nation's major metropolitan areas or the jungles of South Vietnam. Percentage losses almost identical to these had afflicted the Republican party in the depressionary trough that separated the 1928 and 1932 elections and ended a decade of conservative dominance in Washington. No such stunning political change, however, was produced by the 1968 elections. The massive disaffection from the Democrats did not lead to an equally massive swing over to Nixon and the Republicans. Instead, just over 10 million conservative but normally Democratic voters backed Wallace. In Congress, the story was only marginally better. The GOP gained a healthy seven seats in the Senate, but won only five additional places in the House of Representatives. After the dust had settled, the Democrats still held onto a fifty-vote majority in the House and a fourteen-vote preponderance in the Senate.[1]

Nixon, then, had reasons to moderate his joy after the election-night euphoria had passed. He had squeaked into office in a three-way race that pitted him against the Democrats and the Democrats against themselves. For the first time in just over a century, a new President assumed office without his party being in control of at least one of the two houses of Congress. Nixon had been denied the mandate that Johnson received in 1964, and had to content himself with an opportunity to influence events.

Nixon was not slow to take up the challenge. Like many others who have taken up residence at 1600 Pennsylvania Avenue, Nixon intended to become a great and well-remembered President. Further, he believed that foreign affairs was the arena in which such greatness would be achieved.

One important corollary of Nixon's desire to be a foreign policy President was that he had little desire to involve himself in the fine details of domestic politics as LBJ had done. Instead Nixon—like Kennedy—wanted to ignore such realities unless they directly affected his administration's global strategy. This, in turn, meant that Nixon had to recruit trusted associates to oversee domestic affairs for him.

The problem was that Nixon was not an especially trusting man. "I won the 1968 election as an insider," he later recalled, "but with an outsider's prejudices." In particular, Nixon the outsider distrusted what he termed the "iron triangle" of lobbyists, congressmen, House and Senate committee staffers, and longtime federal bureaucrats that had become established in Washington during the many long years of Democratic congressional dominance, and had formed cooperative networks that survived the comings and goings of many Presidents—notably Eisenhower. This triangle, Nixon assumed, provided a built-in constituency in favor of an ever bigger federal government.

Closely associated with the iron triangle in Nixon's mind was the "Eastern Establishment," a varied (and often ill-defined) collection of corporate CEOs, New York and Boston financiers, media executives, and prominent academics and intellectuals from Ivy League schools. This elite and well-connected group, Nixon suspected, had been exercising an undue, and generally liberal, influence on national policy—especially foreign policy—throughout the entire post–Second World War period. Establishment figures like Dean Acheson (Truman's Secretary of State) and Alger Hiss (a key Acheson aide whom Nixon had successfully prosecuted for perjury and possible espionage at the start of his congressional career), Nixon believed, simply lacked sufficient toughness, courage, and will to take on the leaner and hungrier leaders of the communist bloc.

To reverse this weak-kneed liberal and Establishment trend, Nixon gave out orders to recruit as many Cabinet and sub-Cabinet officers as possible from universities, financial institutions, and corporations located outside of New York, Boston, Philadelphia, and other Northeastern cities. Hard-nosed conservatives from the Midwest, West, and South, the new President hoped, would help him purge the federal bureaucracy of Democratic appointees who might "sabotage us from within or . . . sit back on their well-paid asses and wait for the next election to bring back their old bosses." Nixon's anti-Establishment rhetoric had the additional—and hardly unintended—result of assuring the Taft-Hoover-Goldwater wing of the GOP that Nixon was no "liberal" like Nelson Rockefeller or even Dwight David Eisenhower.[2]

As things turned out, Nixon's rhetoric was only partially followed up by action. In the realm of economic-policy making, for example, the White House recruited a collection of moderate to conservative Republicans, many from Midwestern universities and banks. For Treasury Secretary, Nixon selected Chicagoan David Kennedy, CEO of the Continental Illinois Bank, a Business Council member who had cut his teeth in Washington chairing a Treasury Department advisory committee that drew up a set of technical recommendations regarding ways to refashion budgetary procedure midway through Johnson's presidency. One of Kennedy's vice-presidents at Continental Illinois, Robert Mayo, became the White House's first budget director. The chairmanship of the President's Council of Economic Advisers went to Professor Paul W. McCracken of the University of Michigan, a conservative Keynesian economist. Joining McCracken on the three-man CEA was Herbert Stein, another conservative Keynesian who had been the chief economist of the Committee for Economic Development for almost twenty years. At the Commerce Department, Nixon installed Maurice Stans, a native Midwesterner with degrees from conservative Northwestern University, who had worked for Eisenhower as White House budget director, had raised copious amounts of campaign money for Nixon, and possessed useful contacts in New York financial circles. The new Secretary of Labor was George Shultz, formerly dean of the University of Chicago's Graduate School of Business and a follower of libertarian economist Milton Friedman.[3]

Getting Started

Nixon and his new economic team quickly discovered that they had their work cut out for them. In fiscal 1968, as we saw in Chapter Seven, the budget deficit that LBJ had hoped to keep at $15 billion swelled to just over $25 billion, breaking the post–World War II record of $12.5 billion set under Eisenhower. Inflation, meanwhile, was approaching a 5 percent rate, and the moderate but steady increases in real purchasing power that millions of American workers had become accustomed to during the affluent 1960's were fast coming to an end. Although a war-assisted boom continued as Nixon assumed office, inflation and deficit spending were problems that the Nixon administration had to face.[4]

Among the standard conservative remedies for dealing with existing economic problems, two were particularly recommended to the new Republican administration. A wide spectrum of conservative spokesmen, including big businessmen, called upon Nixon to use monetary policy with greater stringency than the Democrats had ever done to tighten up credit and thereby ease demand-pull inflationary pressures. Nixon's men moved ahead enthusiastically on this front, initially winning praise from those academic economists and others of the libertarian right who have long believed that monetary policy can, if correctly applied, accomplish everything—thus obviating the need for any kind of "big government" action outside of the defense area.

While the monetarists applauded, however, other conservatives were calling upon Nixon to act on another long-standing conservative desire: cutting federal spending. Expenditure reductions were favored under Nixon for the same reason as during Eisenhower's tenure—and for the same reason that had led Business Council members to force such reductions upon Johnson as part of the price for the tax surcharge in 1968. Less spending might allow a gradual return to balanced budgets, an end to deficit financing, and a cap on the steadily increasing national debt. Former President Eisenhower himself, even though his record of spending control had not been outstanding, advised his former Vice-President to rein in expenditures even if it meant being a one-term President. Eisenhower's chief economic adviser, Arthur Burns (whom Nixon would shortly appoint to head the Federal Reserve Board), also called for large-scale spending reductions as a necessary part of an overall inflation cure. Nixon, however, had no desire to be a one-term President, and even less to face the storm of criticism that would have followed any effort to make quick and deep cuts in either military or social welfare spending. He had, after all, seen what a comparatively modest version of such an effort cost Johnson in 1967 and 1968. Nixon, therefore, contented himself with delivering jeremiads against runaway Great Society spending that had, he affirmed, created naught but discontent and discord. No substantial moves, however, were made to cut federal spending. About $4 billion was pared from Johnson's last budget, but Nixon did not attempt any further reductions.[5]

Here a caveat is in order. Sophisticated conservatives realized that it was not necessary to cut federal spending in *absolute* terms. Overall population and other growth in society would, in this economically literate view of the matter, require *additional* expenditures to enable government to provide the *same* level and variety of services to ever greater numbers of individuals, families, households, and business corporations. What Nixon must do was to cut the *rate of growth* of federal spending in order to ensure that the federal government—and the "public sector" more generally—was not growing relative to (i.e., faster than) the private sector. Throughout the entire Nixon presidency, however, even intelligent conservatives' hopes went unfulfilled, while the unenlightened were appalled. Nixon not only never succeeded in cutting federal spending in absolute terms (none of his closest advisers ever prompted him to take such a self-defeating step), but in fact presided over a federal budgetary expansion that outdid anything his two Democratic predecessors had accomplished during their tenure.

This expansion was especially objectionable to most conservatives on two counts. Spending was controlled by the Democratic Congress in ways that the right did not like, and was uncontrolled in ways that they equally disliked. Federal military expenditures, for example, stayed more or less constant at about $80 billion a year throughout Nixon's term of office. Inflation, however, cut the purchasing power of that constant number of dollars in a significant enough fashion to lead to conservative complaints. During the same period, federal nondefense spending swelled from $185 billion to $270 billion a year. Nixon's final budget, for fiscal 1974, requested almost 60 percent more for social welfare programs than Johnson's last budget had in constant (i.e., inflation-adjusted) dollars. Total national debt, during the same six years, grew from $367 billion to $544 billion, an increase of $100 billion more than during all of the eight years that Kennedy and Johnson occupied the White House.[6]

Nixon's failure to cut the growth of spending or the growth of the national debt often was blamed on the activities of wild-eyed Democrats trying to buy votes with social welfare programs. Big-spender Democrats there were. They alone, however, were not sufficient to explain the developments detailed above. Nixon was simply unwilling to expend vast amounts of his political capital to throttle back spending. He would, as we shall see, also assist in increasing it where he thought that it would serve his electoral purposes.

Nixon's reticence on spending reductions gradually began to nettle conservatives, including big businessmen. As a result of the fact that spending did not decrease, taxes did not decrease either. Nixon, listening to the repeated advice of his economic team, reluctantly agreed to extend the 10 percent income-tax surcharge that LBJ had finally bludgeoned the Congress into accepting with big businessmen's help. The businessmen had wanted the tax hike to be temporary. With Nixon's extension in 1969, however, the temporary was beginning to assume the status of the permanent. Moreover, the Nixon administration made no effort to extend the 7 percent investment tax credit that the Kennedy White House had sold to Capitol Hill, even after it ran out at the end of fiscal 1968. This temporary tax cut was one that big businessmen had hoped would become permanent. At the end of Nixon's first year in office, then, federal spending was up, the national debt was up, taxes were up and edging higher due to the expiration of certain incentive programs, and inflation was higher than it had been in almost twenty years. Meanwhile, Federal Reserve Board and Treasury Department monetary-policy makers were fighting inflation unaided.

Monetary policy alone did not prove very successful in combating inflation. Monetarist Milton Friedman told top Nixon advisers that choking off money supply growth and a consequent increase in interest rates would begin to turn the tide within six months. Nixon's men in the Treasury and Federal Reserve Board cooperated fully, but nothing happened. Inflation as measured by the Consumer Price Index ran at 5.8 percent in the first year of the new Republican regime. In 1970, the figure increased to 6 percent. Meanwhile interest rates rose to levels not seen in the United States since the Civil War, industrial production declined, and unemployment rose from 3.5 to 5 percent. After a decade of boom, the American economy was finally stuck in another recession.[7]

None of this economic news was congenial to businessmen. Conservative Washington political commentators Rowland Evans and Robert Novak even claimed to detect a "startlingly rapid turn of sentiment against Richard Nixon in the business community" during the first five months of his administration.[8]

The almost immediate shift in corporate perspective that Evans and Novak said occurred did not, in fact, take place. A huge and varied group like "the business community" does not change its opinion on anything overnight. New York bankers certainly used available channels to complain about interest rate stringencies that fell first and hardest upon them. Other segments of the business world, however, took longer to start distancing themselves from the Nixon administration's economic policy. Throughout 1969 and on into the early months of 1970, for example, Business Council members gave Nixon their loyal, if increasingly skeptical, backing. Even Nixon's decision not to seek extension of Kennedy's investment-tax-credit program elicited no complaints. Instead, Council members tended to argue either that tax increases were a necessary if inconvenient part of the anti-inflation fight, or that the Democratic-controlled Congress would have ended the tax credit no matter what Nixon might have desired. Council members lauded Nixon's decision to appoint Arthur Burns to the Federal Reserve Board late in 1969. To further improve relations, Nixon made sure that a cross section of high administration officials including CIA Director Richard Helms briefed Council meetings regularly. Nixon himself also came before the Council to assure corporate leaders personally that no move would be made by the White House to revive the system of wage-price guidelines that had expired midway through Johnson's term of office.[9]

Even the Republican administration's own growing political troubles in Vietnam excited only the slightest ripple of concern among the Business Council's membership. Late in April of 1970, Nixon, as part of his strategy of phased withdrawal of American ground forces, "Vietnamization," and a stepped-up air war, launched United States and South Vietnamese forces in an invasion of neutral Cambodia. As American troops looked for arms caches and enemy formations, a shock wave of protest spread out across five hundred American college and university campuses. Subsequent shootings such as those that left four dead at Ohio's Kent State University symbolized the fact that the war abroad threatened to come home in a big and bloody way.

When the Business Council held one of its regular meetings in May, 1970, John Connor, LBJ's Secretary of Commerce and later chairman of the board of Allied Chemical, sought to convince his corporate peers that Nixon's widening of the war was fraught with disastrous political consequences. LBJ, he told Business Council members in a speech, had failed to fight a massive Asian war and also guarantee a healthy and expanding economy at home. Nixon's efforts would prove no more successful. The invasion of Cambodia, Connor continued, would only produce further dissension among the young, blacks, antiwar intellectuals, and other groups. As Connor spoke, a broad antiwar coalition was in the process of planning the final stages of a gigantic march on Washington that would bring between a quarter and a half million people to the nation's capital.

Business Council members, however, were not sympathetic to Connor's concerns. Allied Chemical's chairman had been expected to deliver an address on the probable economic consequences of the gradual American pullout from Indochina, but instead launched the most spirited attack any big businessman had yet dared to make against Nixon's conduct of the war itself. *New York Times* reporters who conducted interviews with anonymous Council members subsequent to Connor's speech concluded that his critical views were shared by only a small minority of his fellow entrepreneurs.[10]

Later in the summer of 1970, however, a sequence of economic events occurred that caused many big-business leaders to take a markedly more critical stance toward the Nixon administration. In June the multibillion-dollar Penn Central Railroad went bankrupt. This, the largest corporate failure in American history, shook the stock markets and fueled growing concerns that the United States might be headed into another 1930's-style depression. A few months later, Lockheed Aircraft was only saved from insolvency by a last-minute infusion of federal loan guarantees totaling almost $2 billion.

As business worries grew, Nixon finally started backing away from a strictly monetarist approach to dealing with inflation. Burns of the Federal Reserve Board was no libertarian ideologue like Milton Friedman. Instead, Burns reassured businessmen at a series of blue-ribbon White House dinners that he would assist in lowering interest rates, which then hung just below 10 percent, in order to help improve the long-term investment climate.[11]

Burns' assurances came at a good time. By October, the leading edge of corporate opinion within the Business Council was speedily moving toward an important reevaluation of the major cause of America's inflationary problem.

From Nixon's assumption of the presidency until late in the summer of 1970, corporate and governmental attention had focused on the demand-pull elements of inflation. Too many dollars were chasing too few goods as a result of large military demands added to those generated by a vigorous civilian economy. By mid-1970, however, these conditions had changed substantially. The civilian economy was in the midst of a recession, unemployment was approaching the 5 million mark, and the Nixon administration was halving the number of American soldiers committed to the war. Inflation, however, not only failed to moderate, but actually edged higher.

These stubborn conditions, since nicknamed stagflation, lowered the credibility of both conservative and liberal economists. They also increasingly impelled business leaders and conservative politicians to look away from the demand-pull and toward the cost-push elements of the inflationary problem. Powerful unions, the conservative argument went, had gotten hooked on big wage increases during the 1960's. When economic growth slowed and inflation accelerated late in the decade, unions persisted in their drive for pay boosts far in excess of any productivity increases workers may have achieved in their industry. Labor excesses were particularly severe in giant trades like construction, where powerful AFL unions faced a congeries of small and generally ill-organized construction companies and local contractors' associations. Corporations, "forced" to pass along added labor costs to the consumer because they preferred not to accept lower profits, operated within an economy characterized by steadily rising price levels. Business Council leaders told Nixon in a strongly worded statement delivered to the White House in October of 1970 that the federal government had to do something to restrain these excessive wage settlements. Only thus could the problem of inflation be truly solved.[12]

Corporate resolve to make the reluctant Nixon act tough on cost-push inflation only heightened in succeeding months. Nixon began to make public complaints against corporations that passed on higher labor costs in the form of higher prices. In January of 1971, for instance, Nixon, speaking from his San Clemente, California, estate, blasted the steel companies for boosting structural-steel prices by a whopping 12 percent only a few days after he had succeeded in convincing Congress to give them and other capital-intensive firms the benefit of accelerated-depreciation tax breaks worth about $4 billion a year. The companies, perhaps following a prearranged strategy, thereupon rolled their increases back to 7 percent. However, even a 7 percent increase in the middle of a recession where demand for steel was relatively low would have appalled Adam Smith. Nixon's use of jawboning in a manner similar to that practiced by Presidents Kennedy and Johnson reminded businessmen that Nixon might in fact blame *them* for inflation unless they were careful. Secretary of the Treasury Kennedy, after all, was circulating to Business Council meetings and elsewhere telling businessmen that *they* should be the ones to hold down excessive wage increases by simply accepting the rash of costly strikes that angry unions might choose to mount against their companies. Businessmen, for their part, preferred that the federal government, in the person of a Republican President, be responsible for the risks involved in bringing powerful trade unions to heel.[13]

The Nixon administration, as things turned out, had little choice but to do as the businessmen were proposing. A month after the Business Council had expressed its displeasure with the lack of strong federal action on wage restraint, the midterm elections of November, 1970, went badly for the GOP. The Republicans picked up two seats in the Senate, but lost twelve seats in the House. The party remained as far as ever from the legislative control that it craved, and the Democrats remained in an exceptionally good position to stonewall Nixon administration initiatives—particularly those relating to the domestic political scene. To win reelection in 1972, Nixon would have to do something dramatic to resolve the recession and inflation problems that had dominated the first two years of his presidency.

The Move Toward Controls

Concrete political considerations like these were on the agenda when Nixon called a meeting of his political high command four days after the 1970 elections. The problem, Nixon aides John Mitchell, H. R. Haldeman, John Ehrlichman, Robert Finch, Donald Rumsfeld, Bryce Harlow, and others concluded, was that the White House had not yet succeeded in taking charge. Inflation and unemployment remained the worst economic problems, but a growing balance-of-payments deficit and warnings from nervous European central bankers of an imminent run on the overvalued dollar exacerbated the situation. The Nixon administration's foreign policy initiatives were not immediately visible to the electorate. The Vietnam disengagement was proceeding, but the fact that Americans were still dying in combat precluded any reduction in the level of hawk-versus-dove confrontation. Senate Democrats were trying to cut back the military and financial authority of the White House to continue the war and were forcing Nixon to expend a great deal of political capital to kill such initiatives in the more prowar House. Two of Nixon's nominees to fill vacant Supreme Court seats had failed to win Senate approval, and the centerpiece of the Republican administration's social-welfare reform package, the Family Assistance Plan, lay dying in Congress. "What the people needed," Finch argued at the meeting, "was any action, bold action, positive action to show that the government was actively leading—controlling events."[14]

Nixon acted vigorously on Finch's advice. In mid-December, David Kennedy was replaced as Treasury Secretary by John Connally of Texas, a longtime LBJ protégé who, like many other Southern Democrats, had soured on his party as a result of the internal quarrel over Vietnam. Connally, Nixon hoped, was just the sort of tough and well-connected political operator who could knock heads together and get things done in the economic realm while Nixon confined his attention to foreign policy. Nixon believed that Connally's Democratic credentials could also buy essential bipartisan political support for administration economic policies on Capitol Hill.[15]

Connally's assignment had its daunting aspects. By January of 1971, public disenchantment with Republican economic policy was rife. Public opinion polls showed 68 to 73 percent disapproval ratings, while only one member of the electorate in four perceived Nixon as doing a good job. Workers, meanwhile, were voting with their feet. Throughout the early months of 1971, powerful unions went out on strike or bargained to win huge wage increases. Despite high unemployment rates and a generally slack economy, many were successful. Railroad workers, for instance, won a 42 percent pay increase over forty-two months, while steelworkers won 30 percent over three years. Pondering such facts, a chastened Arthur Burns was led to announce that "the rules of economics are not working quite the way they used to." Wage and price controls, Burns publicly concluded for the first time, had become an unfortunate economic necessity. Although well-placed economic policy advisers including George Shultz continued to believe that nothing was wrong that a stronger dose of Adam Smith's economics as interpreted by Milton

Friedman wouldn't cure, a perceptible slide toward controls occurred among second-echelon officials in the Treasury and the White House budget office. While debate raged within his administration, the President, never a devoted student of economics, was struggling through the summer to stop the *New York Times* from issuing the Pentagon Papers and creating the "plumbers" unit within the White House staff to plug the leaks plaguing his administration's behind-the-scenes foreign policy efforts. Burglary and "dirty tricks" became the order of the day as Nixon decided to crush his liberal enemies before they crushed him.[16]

In the end, ironically, it was these same liberal enemies who handed the Nixon White House the tools that it needed to turn domestic economic problems to its political advantage at last. On the eve of the 1970 midterm elections, the Democratic Congress passed legislation giving Nixon the right for a limited time to freeze wages, prices, rents, and salaries and to impose a system of outright wage and price controls on the economy. Democrats hoped that when Nixon refused to impose controls that would outrage many business and labor leaders as well as conservative politicians, he would appear to be shirking responsibility for managing the economy. To ensure that Nixon would not kill the bill, House Democrats attached it as a rider to a military mobilization bill that Nixon could not veto without destroying most of his legal authority to carry on the Vietnam War. Congressional Republicans opposed the Democrats' initiative, calling it an "election-year squeezeplay" and "devious Democratic demagoguery." GOP leaders complained the Democrats were signing a blank check so that they could criticize Nixon for not cashing it. In fact, the Democrats were giving him a broad grant of emergency war powers over the civilian economy such as no President since Truman had enjoyed. Nixon, for his part, was angry at being mousetrapped, but signed the bill in August of 1970. As he signed, Nixon grumbled futilely that the Democrats simply didn't have the courage to pass wage-and-price-control legislation themselves, and that he was not going to do the job for them.[17]

As Nixon grumbled, Democrats only criticized him for not using his broad grant of legislative authority to clamp controls on the economy. During the first six months of 1971, at least half a dozen Democratic senators seemed to be running for the 1972 presidential nomination and needed ammunition. Moreover, Edmund S. Muskie, Henry M. Jackson, Birch Bayh, Fred Harris, George McGovern, and Ted Kennedy did not want to give Nixon the opportunity to remind voters that the Vietnam War was as much their war as it was his. Focusing on bread-and-butter issues like inflation and unemployment might distract millions of voters from the Democrats' record of loyal legislative support for the conflict.[18]

None of this escaped Secretary of the Treasury Connally, a man to whom power politics was almost second nature. As the Democrats moved in for what they hoped would be the kill, Connally pressed Nixon to outflank them by using the discretionary controls authority that Congress had given him. Nixon, facing an increasingly intractable mix of high interest rates, inflationary wage settlements, increased joblessness, unsettled stock markets, and international monetary problems that threatened to divert him from his diplomatic designs abroad, finally complied. By July of 1971, secret efforts to draw up a controls program were made under Connally's overall direction. While Connally orchestrated economic policy, Nixon set off a shock wave in foreign policy when he announced on July 15 that he would become the first American President to visit mainland China for a summit meeting with that nation's communist leaders. Former red-baiter Nixon was beginning to look moderate and statesmanlike as the first public steps toward "detente" were taken.[19]

Nixon's next surprise was even more discomfiting for the Democrats. On August 15, 1971, a month after breaking the news about the China summit, the White House moved on controls. While Congressmen were engaged in home-state political work and other activities during summer recess, President Nixon went before the nation to announce the dramatic first phase of his administration's "new economic policy."

The single most conspicuous component of the Nixon administration program was a ninety-day across-the-board freeze on wages, prices, rents, and stock dividends, aimed at shocking producers and consumers out of any tendency to assume that inflation was inevitable. Complementing the freeze was a temporary 10 percent increase in taxes on all foreign imports, a 10 percent cut in foreign economic-aid payments, and a federal hiring and salary freeze. Nixon also called upon Congress to cut $5 billion in federal spending, and to pass two tax bills favorable to corporations, one an accelerated depreciation statute, the other a 10 percent investment tax credit to be given to all business firms purchasing American-built machinery. (Congress eventually complied with most of Nixon's request, cutting taxes by $26 billion over three years.) The American dollar was also taken irreversibly off the intergovernmental gold standard. Finally, Nixon announced that a Cost of Living Council overseen by Treasury Secretary Connally would be formed to "work with leaders of labor and business to set up the proper mechanism for achieving price and wage stability after the 90-day freeze is over."[20]

Political infighting then commenced in earnest. The outmaneuvered congressional Democrats sputtered and fumed to little immediate purpose. Labor leaders were similarly outraged. On August 18, 1971, for example, United Automobile Workers (UAW) President Leonard Woodcock, speaking to a convention in Boston, blasted Nixon's program as blatantly discriminatory, threatened that his union would "wage war" if the White House wanted war, and grimly noted that "Nixon's hand wielded the dagger, but the dagger was put there by leading Democrats in Congress." Reaction from academic economists was mixed and generally incomprehensible to the majority of the nation's citizenry, which was overwhelmingly supportive of the most easily understood element of the controls strategy, the freeze on wages, prices, dividends, and rents. Bankers and business economists had little enthusiasm for Nixon's policy, largely because many were frightened about the long-term effects of ending the dollar's convertability into gold. The stock markets, however, staged record one-day rallies in the wake of Nixon's controls speech, and industrialists and trade association executives cautiously applauded the administration's program.[21]

Most of the applause or complaint emanating from business and labor leaders was as calculated as it was sincere. Corporate and union heads alike understood that the real struggle regarding the Nixon administration's controls program involved the formulation and implementation of wage and price policy regarding the period that would follow the ninety-day freeze. Throughout late August and September of 1971, business and labor leaders told John Connally and others at the White House what they wanted Phase Two of the controls program to look like in concrete institutional and administrative terms.

Administrative Hardball: The Controls Program at Work

The fundamental issue dividing businessmen and trade union leaders in regard to the Nixon-era controls program was concerned with the locus of administrative power within that program. As debate over the design and operations of Phase Two progressed, organized-labor and organized-industry spokesmen enunciated sharply different approaches aimed at guaranteeing their respective economic and political interests.

Organized-labor leaders, for their part, wanted controls authority to be separated as far as possible from the White House and the Republican President who occupied it. The controls, AFL-CIO President George Meany and others argued, should be administered by an independent board composed of members of big labor, big business, and "the public" in equal numbers. This board would set its own rules and regulations and make wage and price decisions on a case-by-case basis. Having set standards, the board, not Congress, the judiciary, or the rest of the executive branch, would be responsible for enforcing them.[22]

Business leaders, on the other hand, wanted nothing to do with an independent wage-price board. As we have seen, corporate activists such as those composing the Business Council were frustrated by the power of unions and anxious to use federal power—especially presidential power—to roll back union wage gains across a broad front. Businessmen therefore opposed direct labor participation in setting wage and price standards and pushed for a controls program run directly by the White House. Big businessmen, including the heads of General Motors, General Electric, U.S. Steel, and Texaco, affirmed that government had a duty to assume the risks of wage bargaining with organized labor for them. In return, these Business Council members said, they were willing to accept "some form" of price control. By mid-September, big businessmen, joined by the heads of the NAM, U.S. Chamber of Commerce, and National Federation of Independent Business, took the message to the White House itself in a two-hour conference with President Nixon. "It is not totally clear," the *New York Times* rather too ingenuously reported after the meeting, "whether the business group thought that the private sector [i.e., themselves] should have a veto power over the decisions made by the Government board. But sources said that the consensus of the group was that business and other groups should restrict themselves to offering suggestions and making recommendations, leaving ultimate wage-price decisions in the Government's [i.e., the White House's] hands." Businessmen naturally believed that a Republican White House would choose to act on their own suggestions, rather than labor's.[23]

However, businessmen's preference for a purely governmental control structure (the head of the Chamber of Commerce went so far as to say that Treasury Secretary Connally should be appointed wage-price czar and rule "with the [rest of] the public sector playing no role") was not shared by organized labor, whose leaders refused outright to cooperate with Nixon unless they were given important input in the controls process. To get the point across, George Meany dropped hints that his labor federation's almost ironclad support for the Vietnam War might have to be reconsidered unless Nixon cooperated.[24]

As finally announced early in October of 1971, then, the Nixon controls organization was an institutional compromise—a bureaucratic animal with four heads. At the center was the White House's Cost of Living Council, which John Connally had midwifed into being. The Council's job was to coordinate the activities of three other groups, all with supposedly lesser powers.

The first of these groups was a Pay Board composed of fifteen members, five each from organized labor, business, and "the public." The public members were mostly academic economists with long Washington experience. Labor was represented by AFL-CIO President Meany and the heads of the largest four unions in the country: the UAW, the Steelworkers, the Machinists, and the Teamsters. The business delegation consisted of a California entrepreneur who had recently left a job as Undersecretary of Commerce, a Chicago publisher, a General Electric vice-president for employee relations, and two Business Council members, Leonard McCollum of Continental Oil and Benjamin Biaggini of the Bank of America. These men's job was to set and administer wage-control policy.[25]

Next, there was a Price Commission composed of fifteen "public" members, which was to set overall price standards and hear appeals.

Finally, there was a Dividends and Interest Rate Commission chaired by Federal Reserve Board Chairman Burns, which was to restrict credit and to limit stock dividends during the second phase of the controls program.[26]

Of the four bodies, the last had by far the easiest job. It took comparatively little of Arthur Burns' considerable persuasive power to cajole bankers into tightening up on their loans and hiking interest rates. Bankers, after all, generally abhor inflation. Nor was it difficult to convince corporate chieftains to retain earnings as opposed to paying them out to stockholders.

The Pay Board, however, was another matter entirely. The reason for the existence of the Board was simply to gain organized labor's cooperation with the controls program. The tripartite structure of the body—which labor leaders had demanded and businessmen had just as strongly opposed—demonstrated this fact. To further soothe labor leaders, Nixon, after receiving threats from Meany, assured the AFL-CIO's president that the supposedly superior Cost of Living Council would not have the power to veto decisions the Pay Board arrived at. Meany and the union leaders, then, had a good deal of the independence and distance from White House authority that they desired. This was disturbing to economists like Walter Heller and Eliot Janeway. Heller simply expressed concern, while Janeway tartly observed that business leaders had allowed organized labor to walk away with the Nixon controls program and were acting "like tame White House geldings."[27]

All equine canards aside, the Pay Board was a short-term victory of sorts for organized labor. However, union leaders had to face many problems once the process of Pay Board policymaking actually began.

The first of these problems was that Nixon's wage and price controllers included fringe benefits within their definition of wages. This was not to labor leaders' liking. Previous controls programs— the one during World War II, for example—had waffled on the subject of fringes, and often excluded them from effective control. This, in turn, gave powerful unions a chance to cheat. A union, for example, could pledge allegiance to federal wage standards, and then obtain substantive nonwage extras for its members like paid vacations, medical and dental insurance programs, extra coffee breaks, and other benefits that didn't show up in the weekly pay packet. Throughout the life of the controls program, labor leaders waged an undying, although none too successful, struggle to get fringe benefits excluded from consideration as wages.[28]

The second problem, from organized labor's point of view, was that Phase Two of the controls program threatened to wipe out many of the contract gains that particularly powerful unions had won shortly before the freeze went into effect in August of 1971. The steelworkers' union, for example, had gained a gradually phased in 10-percent-a-year wage increase for three successive years, only weeks preceding the freeze. Its leaders, and the leaders of other unions in similar positions, wanted to fully recoup the wage increases that the freeze had delayed. Public and industry representatives on the Pay Board, however, banded together to argue against allowing unions to make up what they had lost during the freeze. Instead the Board majority, though consistently and loudly opposed by the labor members, affirmed the necessity of a maximum of 5.5 percent for pay hikes in any one year during Phase Two. Meanwhile the Price Commission, assuming an average economywide labor-productivity rise of about 3 percent annually, tried to constrain businessmen to limit their price increases to a maximum of 2.5 percent per year.

Organized labor's complaints regarding what was termed the retroactive-pay issue were continuous and strident for obvious reasons: an unbending annual 5.5 percent wage guideline cost the members of powerful unions a great deal of money and threatened their leaders with possible loss of their elected union positions. Nor were union leaders' complaints stilled when congressional Democrats soon succeeded, over White House opposition, in adding to a bill renewing Nixon's wage-price controls authority for another year an amendment stating that all wage increases contracted for previous to the freeze and controls program must be paid "if they are not inconsistent with the guidelines." Secretary of the Treasury Connally told one congressional committee that such pandering to special interests would very likely turn the wage and price controls effort into a ridiculous exercise in futility.[29]

While all of this was occurring, a third issue further unsettled Pay Board members' efforts to achieve a workable compromise. Congress, when it stated that Nixon controllers should think seriously about allowing retroactive pay increases, also suggested that wage increases counterbalanced by increases in productivity be granted even if they exceeded the 5.5 percent wage guidelines that the Board had announced. In other words, if a union operated in an industry where labor productivity (measured, for example, by unit labor cost) had increased 20 percent during a given contract period, its members could legitimately claim and receive a wage increase of 20 percent without adding to inflationary pressures at all—and an increase of up to 25.5 percent without exceeding the wage guidelines that the Board was trying to apply to the economy.

Labor leaders strongly supported the idea of incorporating case-by-case productivity-increase considerations into the wage picture. Otherwise, they believed, management would have a green light to unfairly discriminate against laborers in certain industries by using the flat 5.5 percent guideline to deny them increases that their higher productivity entitled them to.

Initially, the business and public members on the Pay Board hemmed and hawed regarding the productivity issue. When a union insisted on it, workers in that union were granted productivity increases that exceeded the guidelines. Some of the productivity increases were real; others were imagined in order to excuse breaches in the guidelines by labor unions (like the United Mine Workers and the Railroad Switchmen) that wanted nothing to do with Nixon's controls. By November of 1971, however, the Price Commission, sensing trouble on the productivity issue at the Pay Board, moved to close this loophole by tightening up its enforcement on the price side of the wage-price equation. Companies in industries that had granted wage increases that the Price Commission economists deemed too large were restrained from passing along all of their increased labor costs in higher prices. A profit squeeze on some companies, particularly those in the coal industry, quickly resulted. Businessmen generally were rattled by the possibility that "a disparity between Pay Board laxity and Price Commission toughness" on the productivity issue would hurt them badly.[30]

This growing corporate concern led the corporate and public members of the Pay Board to toughen their stance on productivity. In March of 1972, almost six months after it had begun its work, the Board faced a decision regarding the wage claims of the often contentious West Coast longshoremen. Large-scale automation and containerization on the docks had boosted longshoremen's productivity throughout the preceding decade and lowered unit labor costs in the industry by 20 percent at a time when they were rising an average of 30 percent elsewhere in the economy. The longshoremen's union, therefore, asked for—and got—a 20 percent wage increase in a contract it signed with West Coast shippers.

The Pay Board then considered whether or not to allow the longshoremen their contracted-for increase. Over the united protests of the union representatives, the public and corporate members of the Board opposed the contract and ordered the union to accept a 15 percent wage increase. The Board's decision incensed George Meany and other AFL-CIO leaders. As Meany argued that the Board was stealing money from workers' pay packets, an employer member of the body explained to a reporter for *Business Week* that he and the other public and management representatives had "walked around" the productivity issue. "We cannot," the business-man continued, "base a national wage policy on the productivity of any one industry. We must base it on the national productivity averages"—in other words the economywide productivity-increase figure of about 3 percent annually that White House economists had been using ever since the dawn of the Kennedy and Johnson guide-posts efforts.[31]

Employer logic like this did not impress Meany or other trade union heavyweights. They thought that managers would try to rob labor by using the wage guidelines inflexibly, and the decision on the longshoremen confirmed them in their belief. The labor leaders on the Pay Board, we should understand, headed blue-collar unions in the automated and capital-intensive mass production trades, where labor productivity had risen relatively sharply since the end of the Second World War. Meany and men like him had no use for econo-mywide averages dreamed up by academic economists that lumped together their employee clienteles with a polyglot collection of other workers, many of whom labored in service areas like teaching where productivity per worker hadn't risen appreciably in a hundred years. The decision on the longshoremen then, proved to be the final straw. Meany and two other union leaders quit the Pay Board, never to return. The heads of the UAW and the Teamsters did not leave, but nonetheless the Board was speedily reorganized as a seven-man all-public body with no big-business or labor membership, and the skeptical were assured by the White House that nothing was wrong. By March of 1972, however, more problems were developing on the wage front.[32]

As businessmen battled labor leaders on the Pay Board, the second arm of the Nixon administration's controls bureaucracy, the Price Commission, was having troubles of its own, which only ex-acerbated the labor-management tensions within its sister agency.

The fundamental problem the Price Commission faced was that it had a terribly difficult job to do and wanted to do it without offending businessmen. C. Jackson Grayson, the business school dean who chaired the Commission, had fitful desires to take a strong public stand against firms that were attempting to evade or ignore the price controls program. The Nixon Cabinet officers who made up the majority of the Cost of Living Council, however, often suc-ceeded in convincing Grayson and others in the Price Commission to adopt a "run silent, run deep" strategy. The result was that such high-profile jawboning as the Commission undertook was of an occasional and inconsistent nature. One day a firm in a particular industry might be singled out for strong public condemnation. The next day, a competitor might get a soft knock on the back door and be told to stop an identical or very similar pricing practice. Businessmen of all types were predictably distressed by the Price Commission's lack of any systematic compliance strategy. No systematizing was possible in the mood of the time. For, at base, the conservatives on Nixon's Cost of Living Council and Price Commission could never truly decide whether or not they wanted to make full use of the controls powers that they had. Expecting Cost of Living Council members like Secretary of Agriculture Earl Butz and newly appointed White House budget director Caspar Weinberger to get ambitious about "Galbraithian" controls was about as vain a hope as could ever be imagined. As a historian of the Republican party has stated in another context, the controls program was an exercise in futility, because "the regulation of business in any economic milieu by administrators devoted to liberating business [from the "heavy hand of government"] makes for an ambivalent policy at best and no policy at all unless abuses are widely publicized."[33]

A Policy Falls Apart

Abuses there were, however reticent the Republicans were about publicly reporting them. A fundamental problem with all forms of wage and price control is that the difficulties of controlling prices exceed even those consequent to controlling wages. Firms can, for instance, adulterate the quality or change the size of their goods in an effort to slide around limitations that they do not like. In January of 1972, shoppers making their way down the aisles of East Coast supermarkets were treated to a spectacle put on by the makers of a popular cat food. A six-and-a-half-ounce can of the product, which had previously sold for seventeen cents, had just been replaced with a new and improved six-ounce can that sold for the same price. The weight reduction was equivalent to a 7.5 percent price increase, far in excess of the 2.5 percent hikes that Nixon controls officials were trying to persuade businessmen to accept. Consumers grumbled accordingly.[34]

Additional grumbling commenced as consumers were hit with

price increases on commodities and services specifically exempted from the Nixon controls program. Agricultural and processed food prices (as per our cat food example) remained outside the controls program for almost eight months. During that same period, shoppers in many major metropolitan areas were hit with increases of 10 percent and more in their food bills. Other exemptions regarding utility rates, medical care, and energy sources including petroleum also sapped popular faith in some high-visibility elements of the price control campaign that took a big bite out of people's paychecks.[35]

As the Price Commission struggled on, trying to close loopholes, restrict exemptions, and deal with all manner of creative accounting on the price front, their efforts faced a constant drumbeat of criticism, some informed and some not, from congressional Democrats and a constant undertone of business concern that the Nixon White House might sell the economy out to the unions. There was a presidential election in 1972, after all, and critics of a hundred different descriptions picked away at the edges of the Republican controls program with a grim intensity. Nixon, meanwhile, put very little of his presidential prestige on the line in the ongoing wage and price wars at home. Instead Nixon strongly avoided becoming personally identified with the controls program at all, confining as much of his attention as possible to foreign affairs in general and the Vietnam War in particular.[36]

During the spring of 1972, however, Nixon returned to the domestic economic arena just long enough to assist in a process of election-year economic-policy making that further undermined the ability of his inflation fighters to do anything more than temporarily halt the upward march of wages and prices. With the assistance of key economic-policy makers in the Treasury Department and the Federal Reserve Board, Nixon put out the word, as one high-level Republican later remembered, "that 1972, by God, was going to be a good year." Rapid economic growth and decreasing unemployment on the eve of an election, Nixon's instincts told him, would be very good news for incumbent politicians—a view confirmed by studies of recent elections commissioned within the White House budget office.

To accomplish the political triumph that boom times would bring, the Federal Reserve, under Arthur Burns' direction, increased the money supply by a whopping 10 percent as Election Day approached. Simultaneously, Nixon aides at Treasury increased federal spending during 1972 by 11 percent. "Every effort was made," Secretary of Defense Melvin Laird later recalled, "to create an economic boom for the 1972 election. The Defense Department, for example, bought a two-year supply of toilet paper. We ordered enough trucks to meet our expected needs for the next several years. . . ." (One hopes that the trucks were useful in hauling all the extra toilet paper to warehouses.) Not content with this, Nixon permitted congressional Democrats to pass a 20 percent increase in Social Security benefits on the eve of the election, and then went on to try and claim as much of the credit for the result as he possibly could. What Professor Edward R. Tufte of Princeton has called the "political business cycle" had commenced in earnest.[37]

The combined effect of all this economic stimulation was eminently predictable. By the last quarter of 1972, the American economy was growing at an incredible 11.5 percent annual rate and demand-pull inflationary forces were kicking up again in earnest. Nixon's cynical election-year economics did not please the Business Council, whose members and corporate economists unsuccessfully warned the White House about the dangers of too much fiscal and monetary stimulus in February and May. Nixon's determination to spur a boom, however, had an ironic effect upon the equally boom-minded Democrats: it removed the last prop from under the still feud-ridden Democratic party's presidential hopes. In November, with economic indicators for the short run appearing very positive indeed, Nixon smothered luckless and maladroit George McGovern at the polls, garnering an impressive 61 percent of the total votes cast. Once again, however, Nixon's personal political success did not translate into a wider victory for the political party that he headed. Republicans did gain 12 seats in the House (for a total of 192 of 435), but they lost 2 of their 44 seats in the Senate.[38]

For all that 1972 was 1968 all over again, Nixon still had cause for celebration as 1973 began. Administration economic spokesmen continued to attend Business Council meetings promising, as they had throughout the election campaign, that federal spending and deficits would be reduced from the very beginning of Nixon's newly won second term. Nixon, after all, could not run for reelection again, and so now it could be guaranteed he would take the right sort of conservative action without fear or favor.

As his Cabinet officers assured the big businessmen of their rediscovered devotion to all sorts of deep economic principles, Nixon provided some reassurance of his own. On January 11, 1973, Nixon went on nationwide television and radio to make a surprise announcement: Phase Two of the wage and price controls program, the Republican President assured his listeners, was at an end. Hereafter, Nixon continued, price and wage restraints were to be voluntary, "self-administered" by management and labor leaders in the private sector with only the loosest and most occasional federal oversight. Business organizations like the Business Council, the NAM, and the U.S. Chamber of Commerce approved of the news. They had been getting increasingly irritated about controls for months after it became clear that the Nixon White House was not going to stick its neck so far out as to subdue all especially belligerent unions for them. Liberal Democrats, meanwhile, sulked in their tents, positive that decontrol and a return to "free market conditions" was occurring too soon.[39]

In the months that followed Nixon's decontrol and the start of what he termed Phase Three, the truth of liberal predictions was fully borne out. By June of 1973, prices were increasing so fast that Nixon was forced to belatedly clamp a second wage and price freeze on the economy before formulating a short-lived Phase Four of "inflation monitoring" that few took seriously. By the third quarter of 1973, the inflation rate was hitting 7.5 percent. Three months later, after the OPEC embargo of oil shipments to the United States had commenced, the rate almost touched 10 percent. Labor was being crunched by skyrocketing prices. While AFL-CIO leaders' tempers frayed, Business Council meetings resounded with brave words to the effect that federal spending restraint, deficit reduction, and tight money policies remained the best way to fight inflation. As businessmen pulled the cloak of traditional conservative economic orthodoxy ever tighter about themselves, inflation, unemployment, federal spending, and the federal deficit all rose in grim conjunction like the four horsemen of a Republican apocalypse.[40]

As the first year of his second term in office progressed, however, the economy, bad as it was, proved to be one of the least of Nixon's political problems. The Watergate burglary of June, 1972, and the resulting cover-up of this and other dirty tricks perpetrated with White House connivance had begun to poison the Nixon presidency. On January 11, 1973, the same day that Nixon ended his administration's effort to do anything substantial about controlling wages and prices, the Democratic majority in the Senate picked North Carolina's Sam Ervin to head a special investigation into Republican campaign espionage. As the last American combat units left South Vietnam in the spring of 1973, Nixon found himself fighting for his political life. By May, concern as to the political fallout from Watergate had permeated the membership of the Business Council itself. Executives reported that their confidence in Nixon was "shaken," but went on to add that they also felt that "the Administration would ride out the storm and confidence in it would begin to rise."[41]

Smart corporate leaders, however, had long since ceased depending overly much on Nixon or his White House. As early as March of 1972, while AFL-CIO chieftains prepared to make their ill-tempered exit from the Pay Board, disgruntled big-business and Business Council activists were looking around for some way to recoup what they perceived to be their sadly flagging political fortunes. These corporate leaders' efforts to position themselves to respond more effectively to the increasingly disorganized political and economic circumstances of the 1970's resulted in the creation of an extremely important lobbying organization that came to play a key role in increasing big businessmen's political wallop in Washington during subsequent years: the Business Roundtable.

9

GERALD FORD, JIMMY CARTER, AND THE ASCENDANCY OF THE BUSINESS ROUNDTABLE, 1973–1980

The Birth of the Business Roundtable

JOHN CONNALLY WAS a savvy operator whom businessmen related to as well as or better than they had related to Connally's longtime political mentor, Lyndon Baines Johnson. Connally was also a politician who knew when it was time to leave Washington. In the spring of 1972, with his hopes of becoming Nixon's vice-presidential running mate in the upcoming elections fading, angry AFL-CIO leaders resigning from the Pay Board, and Nixon ordering federal economic policymakers to produce boom times or else, John Connally stepped down as Secretary of the Treasury.[1]

Shortly before Connally left Washington, he held a significant discussion with two Business Council members, Frederick Borch of General Electric and John D. Harper of Alcoa. Borch and Harper, like Connally himself, were concerned at the direction that politics was taking in Washington and anxious to get some high-level political guidance on what to do about their anxiety. Connally laid it on the line to his corporate visitors. Businessmen had to improve in political sophistication and techniques in Washington or else face political impotence. At about the same time as they met with Connally, Borch and Harper heard Federal Reserve Board Chairman Burns reiterate the view that the leaders of the nation's largest companies were simply not well enough organized to advance their collective political and economic interest in Washington.[2]

Following their conversations with Connally and Burns, Borch and Harper called together a meeting of about a dozen corporate

CEOs and their chief Washington representatives in March of 1973. Christening itself the March Group, the little body started its existence as a tiny but strategically placed association of action-oriented corporate executives anxious to learn more about the power game in Washington and interested in ventilating their views through private contacts with politicians and trade association executives.[3]

Businessmen had gotten rattled and had established organizations before, of course. But the CEOs of the March Group, later described by a participant in the organization's formation as the "action-oriented members of the Business Council," were more than usually serious about organizing themselves to undertake ongoing political activity. One of the first things that March Group organizers did to underline the intensity of their commitment was to make a rule that CEOs and their top corporate lobbyists, and they alone, could attend meetings. Underlings and stand-ins would not be allowed. No longer, so far as March Group activists were concerned, were CEOs of giant companies going to maintain only a *pro forma* presence in Washington or remain only episodically involved in the development of political and legislative issues that were of great concern to their corporations and big business generally. Instead, corporate chiefs were going to train themselves to arrive on the scene early and propose consistently, to take stands on important economic issues well in advance of those issues' reaching the legislative stage in Congress, and to improve big businessmen's image in the nation's capital. To help ensure success, March Group organizers also insisted that member CEOs make themselves available to personally perform lobbying activity on Capitol Hill and in the executive branch. Taking a page out of Johnson's political book, CEOs from individual companies were also strongly advised to target their congressional activity on senators and representatives from districts in which their firms had significant investments.[4]

Corporate assertiveness training like this was very much to the liking of Bryce Harlow, a man whose political skills were sharpened in the 1950's when he was Eisenhower's chief lobbyist and contact man on Capitol Hill. Harlow, a participant in the events described here, went on to become Procter and Gamble's chief Washington representative and policy adviser when the Democrats returned to the White House. He and other Washington lobbyists and corporate representatives like him had long been frustrated by CEOs' unwillingness to get more heavily and continuously involved in Washington. Harlow, in fact, had tried to push Business Council leaders to reorganize the Council as a high-profile corporate lobbying group during the steel-price-hike flap in 1962. What big businessmen needed, Harlow argued, was an organization that spent less time exchanging pleasantries with the President and more time learning how to throw its weight around effectively on Capitol Hill. Preferred access to segments of the executive branch—when Presidents chose to allow it—was all right as far as it went, but business leaders were too often caught in the position of responding to White House requests rather than formulating independent agendas of their own. The Business Council, Harlow sought to convince Henry Ford II, Sidney Weinberg, and others, should become a "Business Action Council" even if it meant sacrificing some of the friendly advisory and recruitment possibilities that the low-profile traditions of the Council made possible. Business Council leaders, however, were not persuaded by Harlow's logic, and opted for rapprochement along traditional Council lines.[5]

A decade later the activist arguments of Bryce Harlow and corporate policy advisers like him finally began to take hold in a big way. The previously discussed political and economic troubles of the Johnson and Nixon presidencies were important factors in accomplishing this shift in corporate mood. There was also, however, a new kind of challenge facing America's corporate leaders as the March Group began its work.

This challenge resulted from the regulatory revolution that occurred in the United States during the years from 1965 until 1972. In a little over seven years, a wave of environmental, workplace and product safety, antidiscrimination, consumer rights, truth-in-packaging, employee health, and energy-use statutes were passed into law as a result of the combined pressures of environmental activists and "public interest law" professionals, exemplified by Ralph Nader and his Nader's Raiders. Nader was bad enough, particularly after he sued mammoth General Motors for harrassing him in connection with his early work on automobile safety and forced GM's President James M. Roche to come out with a widely noted public apology. Equally galling was the fact that the explosion of scientific evidence regarding the harmful effects of various chemical substances forced highly variable and hard-to-predict costs upon industry. Worst of all, however, was the network of functional regulations and regulatory agencies that all the new laws brought into existence.

Here a brief historical sketch is perhaps useful. Previous to the 1960's, most federal regulation of business was of an *industry-specific* variety. The Interstate Commerce Commission set transportation charges and routes for railroads and, later, long-distance trucking lines. The Federal Communications Commission regulated radio and television. The Federal Aviation Administration looked after the commercial airlines. The Bureau of Mines, an arm of the Interior Department, concerned itself with the health and safety of coal and hard-rock miners and workplaces. And so on throughout the rest of the federal bureaucracy. A few regulatory bodies existed in Washington with mandates to oversee all of industry. The Securities and Exchange Commission and the Federal Trade Commission come to mind. The regulatory norm, however, was decidedly industry-specific in nature.

Industry-specific regulation of the traditional type, moreover, meant that firms and trade associations within given industries faced their own separate and peculiar sets of regulatory problems. Businessmen generally might complain about federal "meddling" in their corporations' affairs, but each businessman usually meant something very different when using the term. Given such divergent regulatory realities, corporate leaders had relatively few occasions to form ongoing antiregulation alliances that crossed industrial lines. Federal regulation of collective bargaining during and after the New Deal was one of the very few galvanizing issues that clearly and immediately affected the operations of a large number of businesses and produced a panindustrial alliance aimed—unsuccessfully as it turned out—at rolling back the tide. With the Wagner Act of 1935 as a decided exception, then, companies in different industries generally contented themselves with firm- or industry-specific action aimed at solving their regulatory problems by capturing administrative control over the particular boards, agencies, or commissions that were responsible for enforcing varied regulations upon them.[6]

The functional regulation undertaken in Washington in the 1960's and early 1970's, however, posed problems that could not be addressed by using established "capture" techniques. As Murray Weidenbaum, the economist whom Ronald Reagan later picked to head his Council of Economic Advisers, was among the first to point out, functionally oriented regulatory agencies are not amenable to domination by any one industry, trade association, or firm, however large. The reason is simplicity itself. The Environmental Protection

Agency, Occupational Safety and Health Administration, and Equal Employment Opportunity Commission—to name but three of the agencies recently created in Washington—were not established to regulate a particular industry. Instead they were set up to regulate *a segment of the operations of all industries.* The fact, then, that the new regulatory bodies have panindustrial mandates "makes it impractical for any single industry to dominate these regulatory activities in the manner of the traditional [industry-specific] model." Just as clearly, however, the creation of functional regulations affecting the environmental, quality control, workplace safety, hiring, and energy-use activities of almost all businesses also made CEOs in widely separated industries much more aware of business' common regulatory problems and considerably more interested in evolving collective means to resolve them.[7]

Big-business concern regarding the impact of the burgeoning number of functional regulations is easy to demonstrate. In May of 1966, Business Council Chairman Murphy blithely assured fellow Council members that Ralph Nader's activities were "of the same order as the hula hoop—a fad. Six months from now we'll probably be on another kick." By May of 1967, however, the mood at Council gatherings had begun to darken substantially. Charles Mortimer, the just-retired head of the General Foods Corporation, called upon big businessmen to form a united front in the battle against Nader and "consumerism." The latter, Mortimer claimed, was a dishonest attempt by agitators to provide people with protections "that they do not need." LBJ's White House aides who were in attendance at the meeting were assured by other Council members that Mortimer's views were "extreme," but discontent in corporate circles grew as more and more new regulations spewed out of Congress. By 1969, Secretary of Commerce Stans was excoriating Nader before Council gatherings and telling businessmen to start regulating themselves in order to make further legislation unnecessary. One year later, however, Nixon's special White House adviser on consumer affairs, Virginia Knauer, briefed Council members on the uncomfortable realities of "consumerism," and the chairman of the board of the Whirlpool Corporation said it was his considered judgment that the "consumer movement" and the functional regulations flowing from it were both here to stay. The opinion hardly pleased the assembled eminences of the Business Council. By May of 1971, however, none other than the CEOs of both Du Pont and General Motors had informed the Council that the Nader phenomenon and what flowed from it had acquired such widespread influence that continued frontal assaults against consumer-protection, environmental, and other new regulatory activity by businessmen would only be counterproductive. This unwelcome fact of corporate life in the 1970's caused widespread concern among Business Council members, as among businessmen generally.[8]

By the time the March Group was organized, therefore, its members, like all businessmen, were exceedingly nervous about regulatory issues. Indeed, as political scientist David Vogel has forcefully argued, corporate response to the regulatory movement of the 1960's and 1970's was essentially analogous to businessmen's reaction to the organized labor movement during the 1930's and 1940's. In both cases, businessmen perceived the threat facing them in panindustrial terms. This, in turn, led to widespread mobilization—class action, if one prefers—aimed at beating back the opposition. Functional regulation as undertaken during the Johnson and Nixon presidencies cemented big-business activists together and added a distinct sense of urgency to their mission. Moreover, these fears, added to the appalling political bedlam that was appearing in Washington as the Nixon presidency shuddered and began to die, impelled March Group leaders like Borch and Harper to seek to broaden the base of their fledgling organization by reaching out to a broader corporate clientele.[9]

Two of the key organizational elements in this broadening process turned out to be two recently formed business lobbies: the Construction Users Anti-Inflation Roundtable (CUAR) and the Labor Law Study Committee (LLSC). Both had been established in the wake of a surge in construction-industry labor costs that helped to topple the anti-inflationary wage-and-price-guideposts program of the Johnson administration. Shortly after the beginning of Nixon's first term, CUAR and LLSC representatives cooperated with White House efforts to moderate building-trade unions' wage demands by threatening permanent presidential suspension of a piece of special interest legislation called the Bavis-Bacon Act. Having firmed Nixon's resolve to force the unions back to the bargaining table, the CUAR and the LLSC merged in the fall of 1972 and renamed themselves the Business Roundtable.[10]

Here we must stop and consider a complicating factor. The CUAR and the LLSC were loose alliances of large firms and local and regional contractors' associations with one overarching interest: the weakening of well-entrenched craft unions. Their work was carried on, for the most part, by corporate lawyers and vice-presidents for labor relations—and by a shifting group of contractors' association representatives. Member corporations in both groups included General Electric, Ford, U.S. Steel, and Alcoa—all of whose CEOs were prime movers in the affairs of the March Group.

This considerable membership overlap proved significant. After the CUAR and the LLSC merged into the Business Roundtable, the activist CEOs of the March Group began involving themselves more and more deeply in the affairs of the new organization. The fact that recently retired U.S. Steel Chairman Blough was the first man to head the Roundtable spurred this process of participation. Blough had, after all, worked with March Group leaders like Borch and Harper for years, when all were serving on the Business Council.

In the year and a half after its creation, therefore, the Business Roundtable changed from a second-echelon and single-interest group into something very different. March Group activists telescoped themselves and their organization into the Roundtable. Rumors as to the political infighting and interest conflicts that arose from this process are murky and diverse indeed. What is apparent, however, is that the Roundtable's single-interest fixation on unions and their potential for causing cost-push inflation was superseded by a considerably broader mix of corporate public-policy concerns in areas including antitrust, regulatory reduction, and tax reduction. This organizational evolution was not sudden and immediate, but gradual. The influence of March Group CEOs apparently spread out over the Business Roundtable like an oil slick expanding across the surface of a calm midsummer pond. By 1974, Alcoa's Harper took over as the Business Roundtable's new president. As the process of institutional interpenetration continued, more and more CEOs of larger American corporations sent emissaries to Roundtable functions to scout out the territory. Many CEOs thereafter elected to join the new organization, and by early 1974 approximately one hundred top managers, most active in the Business Council as well, had enrolled. Simultaneously, the corporate lawyers and labor relations specialists who had previously carried the ball for their corporations within the Roundtable stepped back into supporting roles, and the construction industry representatives who had occupied a prominent place in the affairs of the CUAR and LLSC were gradually eased out of the highest echelons of the evolving successor organization. The CEOs of the March Group had, it appeared, merged with the members of the Roundtable—those from smaller firms, at least—in the way that a hungry diner merges with a piece of bread.[11]

Once the process of reorganization was well under way, the big-business political activists of the Business Roundtable faced the dilemmas of action. Not surprisingly, figuring out precisely what to do and how to go about doing it wasn't simple. From the March Group, the Roundtable had adopted the key notion that the direct and continuing involvement of CEOs in the group's policy planning and political action was essential. Apportioning responsibilities among these CEOs, however, took time—as did establishing the organizational and personal infrastructure within which these busy executives would operate. There is, therefore, no evidence that the Business Roundtable was either a perfected or an especially effective corporate lobbying institution during its earliest years.[12]

The Business Roundtable was struggling to learn the ropes of the power game during a period in which the political environment in Washington approximated that of a Central American banana republic undergoing a series of coups. In 1973 and 1974, nobody seemed to know what was going to happen next on the banks of the Potomac. The events of the latter half of 1973 in particular emerged as a kind of grim slapstick. During May and June, former White House aides John Dean and Jeb Stuart Magruder turned state's evidence in the Watergate case. On July 16, Nixon admitted that he had secretly bombed neutral Cambodia for two years without congressional authority. In a second stunning event occurring on the same day, another former Nixon aide told Watergate Committee members that Nixon had been secretly taping all of his White House conversations and telephone calls since 1971. Legislators fumed, and a struggle over custody of the elusive tape recordings promptly commenced. In October, Spiro Agnew resigned as Vice-President after being convicted of income tax evasion. Ten days later, Nixon sacked Watergate Special Prosecutor Archibald Cox and his own Attorney General in the "Saturday Night Massacre." Desperate moves to staunch the political hemorrhage that was destroying his administration began to defeat themselves. By November, Nixon's public approval rating had fallen to a miserable 27 percent, while a GOP senator anonymously remarked to columnist Elizabeth Drew that "everyone is sort of at the head-shaking stage. . . . It's got to the ridicule stage." By the end of the year, a public opinion poll commissioned by Congress showed that the American public "had more confidence in garbage collectors than—in declining order—the police, the press, the church, business, Congress or the White House."[13]

Like the dying beast that it was, the Nixon White House struggled on for eight more months before succumbing to its self-inflicted wounds. Not content with destroying himself, Nixon, by repeatedly and loudly linking his fate to that of the office he occupied, succeeded in inflicting a good part of the damage he had wrought on the presidency itself. On September 8, 1974, Gerald R. Ford, the first President in American history who had been elected to neither the presidency nor the vice-presidency, tore away much of the remaining respect in which the presidency as an institution was then held by giving Richard M. Nixon a "full and complete" pardon for all crimes he committed "or may have committed" while President. Twenty-seven months of wrenching constitutional and political crisis had at last come to a close.

Congress, like the executive branch, would never be the same again. Watergate helped unleash pent-up desires for democratization of congressional administrative, oversight, seniority, and procedural customs and regulations. The resulting legislative-reorganization acts of the early 1970's broke down party discipline and age-old congressional control mechanisms that had previously been the property of a handful of the most senior legislative barons on Capitol Hill. The unsettled political environment of these same years produced a notable increase in the rate of turnover among House and Senate officeholders. Junior senators and representatives about whom corporate executives knew little found new avenues of advancement open to them, and grabbed choice committee assignments that allowed them to exercise more political leverage than their seniors ever would have allowed in more normal times. Altogether, the early 1970's was a period during which the established political wisdom of official Washington did not count for much.[14]

Economic wisdom fared no better. By December of 1974, Ford was passing out "WIN" (whip inflation now) buttons in a fruitless effort to stem an accelerating inflation rate complemented by an increasing unemployment rate. In an unprecedented nationally televised address given at a Business Council meeting, Ford caught the spirit of the time well when he quipped that while being introduced at a business conference recently the moderator had said: "The greatness of America is that anyone can grow up to be president of an auto company, president of an airline, president of a utility, or President of the United States." Then he took a long pause and added: "That's just one of the chances you have to take!"[15]

Rolling Into Action

Shortly after Ford made his joke to the assembled members of the Business Council, the Council's sister organization the Business Roundtable started to flex its muscles. Two years of hard organizational work had finally made the Roundtable ready to give as good as it got in the Washington jungle.

The Business Roundtable was designed to be a disciplined political fighting machine, with a tight hierarchy of administrative control made up of a small Executive (or Planning) Committee, a larger Policy Committee, and a small group of task forces given primary responsibility for the day-to-day research and lobbying efforts of the organization.

At the top of the Roundtable hierarchy was—and remains—the Executive (or Planning) Committee. It is composed of the Roundtable's chairman (initially John D. Harper of Alcoa and later Du Pont's Irving Shapiro, GE's Reginald Jones, GM's Thomas Murphy, and Exxon's Clifton C. Garvin in a regular two-year sequence) and joining him are three vice-chairmen (currently Theodore Brophy of General Telephone and Electronics, James Evans of Union Pacific, and Walter Wriston of Citicorp). As chairmen retire, they enjoy emeritus membership in the group. Vice-chairmen, however, do not. Joining this small collection of corporate CEOs are a shifting group of men who chair Roundtable task forces.

This executive group functions quietly—so quietly that few people outside of the Roundtable know of its existence. It determines the agendas for all Roundtable meetings and has the right of first approval on proposed position papers, policy initiatives, legislative priorities, and all other important matters that come up for organizational consideration. The Executive Committee, in short, sets the Roundtable's lobbying agenda—an agenda that it tries to keep as short and pithy as possible, normally restricting it to between six and eight "priority issues" during the course of any two-year period.

Executive Committee recommendations are then passed down to the forty-five-member Policy Committee. This group meets once every other month, usually for a full day at a time. Normally, only member CEOs and high-level Washington lobbyists attend these meetings. Absenteeism is low. Acting on the advice of the Executive Committee—whose recommendations it seldom rejects but sometimes modifies—the Policy Committee ratifies the short list of important legislative issues that the Roundtable is to tackle; appoints the chairmen of all Roundtable task forces; reviews task force activities on a regular basis; and puts its imprimatur on all reports, recommendations, and other statements made in the Roundtable's name. Policy Committee members—like Roundtable chairmen and vice-chairmen—are publicly affiliated with the Roundtable. The names of the other members, however, are not publicized.

Such reticence has decided advantages: it cuts down on the number of nuisance requests from politicians or other business groups for Roundtable assistance on issues that the organization's leadership has no desire to tackle. It also obscures the extent to which the Roundtable is composed of and acts in the interests of the larger American corporations.

There is a good deal to obscure. Between 1974 and 1979, for example, the membership of the Business Roundtable grew from approximately 100 to 192 members. These 192 members, all CEOs, headed the industrial, financial, and commercial institutions dominating the American economy. They include:

—The 10 largest corporations in the 1980 *"Fortune* 500" list— Exxon, General Motors, Mobil, Ford, Texaco, Standard Oil of California, Gulf, IBM, General Electric, and Standard Oil (Indiana).

—From the *Fortune* list, 21 of the top 25, 40 of the top 50, 70 of the top 100, 113 of the top 200, and 131 of the top 500.

—The sixty-one members not on the *Fortune* list include the nation's four largest public utilities, three of the largest commercial banks (Citibank, Bank of America, and Morgan Guaranty Trust), and two of the largest life insurance companies (Prudential and Metropolitan Life).

—Also among the remaining sixty-one, the largest retailer (Sears, Roebuck), five of the largest transportation companies (Eastern Airlines, United, Union Pacific, TWA, and Southern Pacific), and a scattering of giant privately held companies like the Bechtel Corporation.

Taken together, then, the Executive and Policy committees of the Business Roundtable function as a council of elders within an organization whose power is not diluted by the presence of any small or medium-sized businesses and whose leaders are acutely conscious of the dangers of single-interest industrial pressure groups arising within the organization's elite corporate membership.

Roundtable elders exercise close control. They do not, however, assume the major responsibility for mounting lobbying campaigns. This task is delegated to the group of task forces. While the number of task forces existent at any given time has changed, and task forces have not proved to be equally active or effective, the actions of these Roundtable bodies were and are at the root of the organization's political power and influence in Washington.

The major areas of task force responsibility include: antitrust, regulatory reform, taxation, inflation policy, consumer interests, corporate constituencies, economic organization, energy, the environment, international trade, national planning and employment, social welfare legislation, and labor relations policy.

Roundtable task forces with responsibility for particular legislative areas like the ones listed above appoint "lead companies" to orchestrate action regarding legislation of special concern. The lead company is often, though not always, headed by the CEO who chairs the task force concerned. Roundtable personnel are guided by this CEO and assistants recruited from his corporation or borrowed from the staffs of other Roundtable member companies. To assure good coordination among task forces, a small and tightly run Washington lobbying office, headed since 1974 by longtime corporate lawyer and political adviser John Post, also plays a key supporting role. Typically, lead companies and task forces enter the legislative process early, propose their ideas consistently, enunciate moderate as opposed to extreme conservative remedies for the matter at hand, and provide pertinent supporting data and bill-drafting assistance to congressmen, congressional staffers, or heads of Cabinet departments and regulatory agencies who request it. If serious political problems develop, Roundtable CEOs are called to Washington to lobby on Capitol Hill, at the White House, or within various departments and agencies.

With all these organizational points understood, one can see that Bryce Harlow's old dream of creating a "Business Action Council" was finally accomplished by the builders of the Business Roundtable in a very impressive fashion indeed.[16]

From Ford to Carter

Once such a powerful corporate lobbying tool had been created, it did not take long for Washington insiders to realize that big business had dramatically increased its collective political strength.

Among the first evidence of decisive Roundtable activity was the defeat in 1975 of a bill that would have allowed state attorney generals to file class-action suits on behalf of citizens of their states to collect antitrust damages from corporations. In short order, two other efforts at strengthening antitrust laws were bottled up and killed in congressional committees. Meanwhile President Ford was apparently prevailed upon, at Roundtable urging, to announce his forthright opposition to the creation of a Consumer Protection Agency, a key item on Ralph Nader's legislative agenda. Other gains the Roundtable may have won are more debatable. It is not arguable, however, that hundreds of strategically placed politicians and journalists in Washington, their antennae long attuned to power, started paying very serious attention to the Business Roundtable.[17]

As America entered the Bicentennial election year of 1976, *Business Week* and other trade publications began noticing the Roundtable as well, particularly after it started becoming all too clear that Ford's White House was incapable of restoring very much credibility to the economic policy or to the Republican party generally. If the Republicans couldn't protect business (and in 1976 they couldn't even protect themselves), then it was apparent that business was going to have to learn how to do a better job of protecting itself— by playing for power, not ideology, and by working with Democratic Presidents and Congresses if it came to that.

The Democratic party, as events transpired, traveled a political course that only helped politically active big businessmen like those of the Business Roundtable to protect almost every interest they had. The left and left-center elements of the party tore themselves and each other to ribbons in an internecine race for the presidential nomination. By failing to unite at any time around a single candidate, the Ted Kennedys, Jerry Browns, George McGoverns, Frank Churches, Fred Harrises, Morris Udalls, and Henry M. Jacksons of the political world left the field wide open on the right of the party political spectrum. There James Earl Carter, Jr., a man without any national political reputation at all, proceeded to carve out just enough of a base of political support in a grueling series of caucuses and primaries to get himself selected as the Democratic nominee.

Once nominated, Carter capitalized on the Ford administration's less than sterling economic performance and on the still-simmering resentment over the Nixon pardon. Carter hammered away on what the Republicans had done wrong. Nixon had undermined popular faith in political leadership. Inflation was running at 10 percent a year. Unemployment was rising to almost 9 percent of the labor force. The federal budget was $45 billion in the red in fiscal 1975, and the fiscal 1976 picture looked even worse (the $66 billion deficit of the latter year would eventually set a postwar record that still remains to be broken). Carter was not, however, all that clear as to what he was going to do differently. The budget, he affirmed, would be balanced as the rate of growth of federal spending was gradually brought under control. The functional regulations of the late 1960's and early 1970's would be maintained, candidate Carter promised, but they would be modified to make them more cost effective. Marketplace arrangements would also become the order of the day in heavily regulated industries such as those in the transportation sector.[18]

The 1976 election, however, was not a battle waged primarily upon economic grounds. Ford avoided talking about the economy whenever possible. Things would get better, he affirmed, if the Democratic Congress stopped spending money and if conservatives like himself remained at 1600 Pennsylvania Avenue. Carter, for his part, claimed a Democratic President working together with a Democratic Congress could do the same job better. For the rest, Ford orated about the nuances of foreign policy and Carter promised a rebirth of trust, love, and human understanding—a spiritual renewal that would cleanse American political life of the stains of Vietnam and Watergate and make the government "as good as the people." When the voters finally spoke in November, they demonstrated little enthusiasm for either candidate. Carter won a slight edge of 50.1 percent in the popular vote, but ran behind almost all of the Democratic congressmen and senators who won election in that same year. Election Day readers of the *New York Times,* if their minds tired of the ponderous political speculation on the Op-Ed page, might have read a snippet of a story on page 16 that detailed how no less than five thousand people had rioted in a high-unemployment area of

Detroit after jamming into the personnel office at a Cadillac plant in search of jobs that didn't exist. Governing America was certainly not going to get any easier.[19]

Carter in Office

Jimmy Carter came to Washington with great hopes and a Democratic Congress that could help him achieve them. Carter was also, as it turned out, as determined as Johnson had ever been to govern in cooperation with big-business leaders rather than in opposition to them. Though lacking any secure big-business connections outside of a relationship with J. Paul Austin of the Georgia-based Coca-Cola Company, Carter sought to consult with a broad range of highly placed corporate chief executive officers early in his administration. In particular, Carter sought out prominent Business Council and Business Roundtable leaders including Shapiro of Du Pont, Jones of General Electric, Murphy of General Motors, and John DeButts of AT&T. Throughout the first year of his presidency, Carter and his top aides actively courted such big-business spokesmen, while at the same time being careful to check in with spokesmen from more traditional panindustrial organizations like the U.S. Chamber of Commerce and the NAM. Chief White House domestic affairs adviser Stuart Eizenstat briefed Roundtable leaders regularly. A Roundtable delegation trekked to Capitol Hill for an unprecedented meeting with the House of Representatives Democratic Steering and Policy Committee and House Speaker Tip O'Neill. Roundtable members including the heads of Du Pont, Exxon, Mobil, GM, GE, Chase Manhattan Bank, Bechtel, FMC Corporation, and Federated Department Stores cooperated with White House requests to work out and pass compromise legislation aimed at assuring Jewish groups that the Carter administration knew how to resolve the vexing and politically explosive issue of what to do about restraining American corporations from obeying the economic boycott that hard-line Moslem states in the Middle East were trying to enforce against Israel. Important corporate assistance was also provided for Carter's campaign to pass a new Panama Canal treaty in the Senate and to reform the upper levels of the Washington bureaucracy by amending the Civil Service Act. Relations between the Carter White House and businessmen looked so friendly that liberal Democrats who had never particularly loved Carter now worried that he was selling their party down the river. Hubert Humphrey, for one, felt so strongly about the subject that he used the occasion of his final visit to the White House in November of 1977 to issue a public warning to Carter that wooing big businessmen or any other kind of businessmen was a terrible mistake. Four months later, Humphrey was dead of cancer.[20]

The appearances of a thoroughgoing alliance between big-business leaders and the Carter White House were, however, deceptive. Carter was a conservative Democrat deeply committed to what one disgruntled Democratic senator very early termed "a set of beliefs on economics, fiscal and monetary policy based on the old small-town chamber of commerce virtues that are going to get him in trouble with liberals." Carter was not, however, able to negotiate anything like a complete or ongoing political armistice with organized-business power blocs like the Business Roundtable and the Business Council. Carter, in fact, lost most of his political credibility with business leaders more quickly than any of his predecessors save John F. Kennedy.[21]

Carter's political problems were threefold. First, he faced the strongest and best-organized corporate opposition any President had had to contend with since the domestic reform phase of the New Deal. Second, Carter had to contend with a Congress that had splintered into a diverse collection of mavericks and independents to whom party loyalty and legislative discipline were all too often irrelevant. Third, Carter had to chart a complicated political course between the hammer of special interest groups and the anvil of a disputatious Congress, without a very secure base of support in any segment of the Democratic electoral coalition outside of the South.

The challenge that Carter faced would have tried the skills of even a Johnson to the hilt. Carter, however, had little of Johnson's one-on-one persuasive power and almost none of Johnson's sense of legislative timing, ability to massage congressional egos and opinions, or skill at delegating the administrative details of government to loyal subordinates. Carter, if the external evidence of his administration is any indication, conceived of himself as being the top administrator in the federal government, a view that sapped his ability to become an effective popular leader and regularly led him to swamp himself in the technical details of programs, bills, and regulations to little profit or purpose.[22]

Still, Carter tried and tried hard. Carter began his presidency by offering businessmen corporate income tax cuts, federal spending controls, deficit reduction, and selective deregulation. Meanwhile liberals were asked to remain content with human rights, welfare reform, labor law reform, stricter environmental and consumer protection, and efforts to strengthen federal sanctions against employment discrimination that particularly affected blacks and women. The key point in understanding this policy mix is that the things that Carter offered liberals did not, by and large, cost very much money. Whenever pressure groups on the left of the Democratic party sought Carter's strong support for expensive legislative items like the Humphrey-Hawkins full-employment bill (a revivification of the original Full Employment Act of 1946) or the national health insurance bill backed by Ted Kennedy, the Carter White House gave such initiatives only *pro forma* support and did nothing substantive to stop conservative Democrats and Republicans from shredding the proposals. Whatever else Carter wanted, big new spending programs were not on the list. Instead of creating, Carter (as in his failed welfare-reform package) tried to reorganize what existed and to make it more efficient. Equally true to his fiscally conservative principles, Carter vetoed expensive new military weapons systems like the neutron bomb and the B-1 bomber and energetically, if none too successfully, sought to convince the unreceptive Soviet leadership to undertake a 50 percent cutback in atomic-weapons spending together with the United States, in order to get both nations' economies out from under the incredible financial burdens of the Cold War.

Carter gave it everything he had, but by the spring of 1978 his effort to wend a middle way between corporate and liberal political-power brokers was fading fast. Liberals, angered by still-rising inflation and unemployment rates, demanded that Carter spend more money and that he announce a mandatory wage-price freeze followed by a period of economic controls. Businessmen, equally anxious about the economic picture, argued against controls. While arguing, they also used their growing political clout in Congress to try to throttle key elements of the liberal regulatory agenda.

These corporate power plays paid off handsomely. During the spring and summer of 1978, both substantive and symbolic bills on the businessmen's hit list went down to defeat. The first, aimed at coordinating all existent consumer-protection programs into a single Consumer Protection Agency that would be given Cabinet rank, had been a priority issue with Ralph Nader for over five years. When the consumer constituency that he had labored to construct was recognized and protected by a Cabinet agency of its own, Nader reasoned, the consumer movement and the functional regulatory revolution that it had accomplished would have achieved a permanently guaranteed presence in Washington, one that businessmen couldn't gradually strangle. The Business Roundtable, Chamber of Commerce, NAM, and many other business lobbying groups, however, also understood the logic of Nader's arguments, and all participated fully in the successful effort of an umbrella organization known as the Consumer Issues Working Group to kill the Consumer Protection Agency bill.[23]

While Nader and other consumer activists were losing their battle, a broad alliance of AFL-CIO union leaders was faring no better. Once again, the Business Roundtable helped orchestrate a broad and firm corporate opposition to regulatory reform—in this instance a labor-law reform bill that would have strengthened the enforcement, access, and oversight provisions of the National Labor Relations Act in order to make it easier for unions to organize workers in the open-shop heartland of the industrializing American South. In May of 1978, the *Wall Street Journal* reported in a front-page story that Business Roundtable member companies were even providing free trips to Washington in corporate jets to small businessmen from states whose senators and representatives were still undecided on how they would vote. "I can't remember when we last experienced a lobby effort like this," one thunderstruck senatorial aide remarked. "I don't think they missed a single possible opponent of the bill in our state." By mid-June, the grass roots political mobilization that Roundtable personnel had helped engineer had frightened Congress sufficiently to send the labor-law reform bill down to a sound defeat. Organized-labor leaders cried foul, while prominent big-business leaders including Irving Shapiro, Thomas Murphy, and Reginald Jones made soothing statements that nothing ill had been intended. No political analyst, however, believed that majority opinion in any business organization—most especially the Business Roundtable— was not delighted with the fact that organized labor had been handed a big political setback.[24]

If any doubt remained that big-business political activists had vastly improved their political sophistication and strength in Washington, that doubt was removed in October of 1978 when the Carter administration belatedly embarked upon its own version of an anti-inflation economic controls program.

Carter approached economic controls with all the enthusiasm of a condemned man mounting the guillotine. Controls were anathema to Carter and to his top economic advisers as well. Carter was so reluctant to even appear to be sanctioning the idea of controls that he dithered about supporting a proposal that the Business Roundtable floated in February of 1977 to create a tripartite labor-management-public committee to discuss anti-inflation strategy. Finally, Roundtable leader Reginald Jones and George Meany proceeded on their own. In April of 1977, they announced their intention to use the Labor-Management Group, established under Kennedy and later re-established as a "private" group late in Nixon's presidency, to monitor the success or failure of Carter's anti-inflation efforts and to try to reach policy compromises. Business and labor representatives alike may have hoped that Carter would bring the government on board at a later date, but Carter administration officials were careful to distance themselves from the group.

A top-level organization like the Labor-Management Group did not like being ignored. Its members, after all, included the CEOs of General Motors, General Electric, U.S. Steel, Mobil, Du Pont, Jewel Foods, and the Bechtel Corporation—all Business Council and Business Roundtable activists—plus the heads of the teamsters', steelworkers', auto workers', seamen's, plumbers', and clothing workers' unions. The Carter White House, however, refused to give the Group any suggestions as to what it wanted, and apparently operated on the assumption that trade union and big-business leaders would be able to work out some all-encompassing "social contract" that would enable the private sector to restrain the wage-price spiral for the greater good of all, without involving the federal government in any substantive way.[25]

The struggle over the labor-law reform bill in early 1978, however, destroyed whatever illusions the Carter administration may have had regarding big-business and labor leaders' collective ability to come to any significant agreements. As the summer of 1978 stretched on into the fall, it became clear that inflation was increasing again and that powerful unions were intent upon protecting their members by bargaining for wage increases of as much as 10 percent per year. Nor were businessmen going to carry the ball for Carter. The Business Roundtable, for example, issued a report on the underlying causes of inflation in the summer of 1978, which listed all the standard conservative explanations for inflation: unions were too greedy, federal monetary policy was too lax, Washington was spending too much, and government regulations were adding to the costs of doing business. The idea that business might be playing some part in inflation was not even mentioned.[26]

Finally, on the eve of the midterm elections of 1978, the pressure on the Carter administration to do something about controlling rising inflation and unemployment mounted to extreme levels. As prices skyrocketed 9 percent per year and the jobless multiplied to 6.5 percent of the labor force, Carter announced the creation of a voluntary wage-price controls program on October 16, 1978. A Council on Wage and Price Stability (COWPS) was created to oversee the effort, and quickly enunciated guidelines aimed at holding wage increases to 7 percent a year. Price controls were another matter entirely. Complex standards aimed at limiting businesses' annual price increases to between 6 and 6.5 percent were, however, the general rule.

Guidelines and announcements were all very well. In reality, however, the Carter economic controls program was an exercise in futility aimed at giving the appearance of decisive action. The voluntary price restraints were riddled with so many adminsitrative exemptions that they accomplished nothing. Carter controllers, for example, engaged in a charade with the auto industry aimed at making price increases look smaller than they really were. A 10 percent price increase on 1980 car models was allowed on the convenient assumption that the new designs were "completely new products." In a further effort to help GM stay within its voluntary 6 percent limit for price increases, "federal officials later permitted GM not to count hundreds of dollars of increases that were to cover costs of complying with vehicle-manufacture laws even though car buyers still had to pay them."[27]

Charade or not, the Carter-era controls program produced visceral opposition among traditionalist businessmen and business organizations. The NAM and the U.S. Chamber of Commerce, for example, came out strongly against any form of voluntary wage-price guidelines, fearing that Carter would later ask Congress for the authority to apply mandatory controls to the economy at some future date.

The *cognoscenti* of the Business Council and the Business

Roundtable, however, knew better than to ventilate such fears. Though the members of both organizations were unenthusiastic about controls, they realized that it was politically futile for business-men to oppose controls totally. So, instead of merely saying "no," Business Council and Business Roundtable spokesmen said "yes, but." To the dismay of their ideologically oriented peers, Roundtable and Council leaders played for power. They agreed to support Carter's voluntary wage-price controls program on the conditions that Carter forswear any intention of introducing mandatory con-trols at some later date and that the administration get tougher about controlling federal spending, restricting credit markets via high in-terest rates, reducing deficits, cutting corporate tax rates, and passing legislation aimed at requiring cost-benefit analyses of proposed new regulatory standards. Carter and his administration, facing an emer-gency situation and possessing no more than a weak hold on the affections of any organized interest group in Washington, agreed to the conditions. Agreement made easier by the fact that several of the big businessmen's most important conditions—regulatory and deficit reduction—were key elements of Carter's own legislative agenda. Over the vociferous objections of the liberal wing of the Democratic party, no mandatory controls program was ever sent to Congress by the administration, even though Carter's *pro forma* controls did nothing to halt the worsening conditions that produced 15 percent inflation and 7.5 percent jobless rates by 1980. The Democratic chief executive, likewise, strongly supported regulatory reform (i.e., re-duction) in a Congress two-thirds controlled by Democrats. The deficit reduction and tight-money policies, though complicated by furious infighting on Capitol Hill, were maintained, and at White House urging Roundtable representatives became key actors in ad-ministration efforts to trim existing nondefense programs so as to produce balanced federal budgets in future years.[28]

White House–big business cooperation like this understandably irked defenders of free enterprise as it is taught in elementary eco-nomics textbooks. Editorials in the *Wall Street Journal* in late 1978 and early 1979, for example, blasted the Business Roundtable again and again for its willingness to support the Carter controls. The newspaper did not mention, however, that the leaders of the nation's largest corporations were engaged in a very delicate, even painful, process of pragmatic compromise aimed at protecting their political and pocketbook interests during the most unsettled economic period since the Great Depression. And so, while the *Journal* warned that businessmen were being taken for a ride that could only end in some horrible version of a "planned economy," Irving Shapiro, Reginald Jones, Thomas Murphy, and other corporate political activists like them kept on cutting the deals that they thought necessary.[29]

The remainder of the Carter presidency is perhaps best laid to rest with the observation that it was a sorry political spectacle. With the single exception of the Camp David peace accord signed between Israel and Egypt in September of 1978, Carter and his administration staggered from one disaster to the next. Congress, scenting Carter's growing political predicament, stonewalled every major piece of reform legislation that he sent up to Capitol Hill, passing only a tattered energy-deregulation bill after stripping away most (though not all) of the liberal segments of the proposal. By early 1979, Carter was so discouraged that he was allowing his sense of malaise to show openly. America, he announced in July, was suffering a "crisis of the spirit" and was bogged down in paralysis, stagnation and drift. The fact that Carter shortly afterward proceeded to summarily sack half his Cabinet in a manner redolent of Nixon's throwing his teammates to the wolves following the 1972 elections did nothing to improve Carter's presidential standing. By June of 1979, public opinion polls showed that Carter's popularity had fallen to a point slightly below that that of Nixon immediately preceding his resignation. Carter vainly strove to recover the initiative, but a worsening economy and his inept and self-laudatory handling of the Iranian hostage problem of 1979 and 1980 doomed his political sun to eclipse. Fending off a lackluster challenge by aging war-horse Ted Kennedy, Carter succeeded in obtaining renomination from a party whose leaders edged on to the Carter bandwagon knowing that it would likely crash. By August of 1980, it was so clear that Carter was a dead duck that Business Roundtable leaders ceased their *pro forma* adherence to Carter's economic guidelines program and called for an immediate end to the paper controls effort. As Carter and his diminishing band of faithful supporters hid in the Rose Garden and promised grand things once they achieved a second term, corporate leaders controlled their growing disdain and waited to see what the Republicans might have in store.[30]

THE ROAD
FROM ROOSEVELT
TO REAGAN

THE FIFTY-YEAR SPAN from the onset of the Great Depression to Ronald Reagan's landslide victory in the 1980 elections was an action-packed period for American big business and big businessmen. The half century began inauspiciously enough. Economic chaos unleashed social forces that neither businessmen nor conservative political leaders could control using the established techniques of minimal government and self-regulation by already existent corporate, labor, and agrarian groups. Through the 1930's, business leaders tried again and again to acclimate themselves to changing realities as the federal government grew larger and more powerful by assuming social welfare guarantor responsibilities hitherto left to the private sector and state and local governments. The Business Council occupied a key place in this process of corporate redefinition. It also served as a base from which compromise-minded business political activists, including Gerard Swope and Marion Folsom, kept a corporate presence alive enough in Washington policy councils so that tradition-shattering reforms such as the Social Security Act of 1935 proved to be nowhere near as "radical" or inimical to big businessmen's interests as they might otherwise have been.

When war came in the 1940's, big-business leaders streamed into Washington, and used their presence there to seek to restrain organized labor and other threatening political groups while enjoying the gargantuan profits that went with risk-free war capitalism. Following the war, sophisticated businessmen such as Paul Hoffman, Ralph Flanders, and W. Averell Harriman began a political-damage-control operation in earnest. Using the Committee for Economic Development as a primary organizational tool, such men chose not to essay the potentially expensive and bloody strategy of seeking to roll back federal power. Instead, the CED leaders followed a two-pronged strategy of containing reform drives at home while adding their voices and organizational abilities to the drive to forge the federal government into a powerful military and economic tool to contain communism abroad. By the onset of the Korean "police action," this process of beating down efforts to revive the New Deal at home and ending America's historical tradition of hemispheric military and political isolationism was essentially complete. As the 1950's dawned, the CED again played an important role in accustoming reluctant big businessmen to the potentials of foreign aid and a conservative version of Keynesian economic theory—one that highlighted the virtues of balancing federal budgets over the course of the business cycle. Conservative economics as usual, however, brought an end to the soothing ideological balm of the Eisenhower era.

The 1960's began badly under Kennedy, as the Business Council's disaffiliation from the Commerce Department and the steel-price-hike spat of 1962 amply demonstrated. Kennedy's presidency, however, witnessed the triumph of conservative Keynesianism and set the stage for a regular sequence of corporate and individual tax-rate cuts that have occurred with regularity from that day to this. As Lyndon Baines Johnson assumed the presidential mantle, big businessmen were treated to expert emotional massaging by a high practitioner of the art. Corporate leaders glowed as Johnson gave them the tax cut that Kennedy had promised, and made a separate peace with a wave of social welfare legislation that they, like other conservatives, had no hope of stopping due to the political fallout from Barry Goldwater's failed ideological crusade.

What began in high hope, however, ended in frustration, muddle, and catastrophe. As Vietnam poisoned the wellsprings of the Great Society and undermined the economic foundations of the growth-oriented grand consensus that Johnson had labored so hard to create, corporate leaders returned to their old political dispensation in earnest.

The 1970's, however, provided no return to tradition so far as Richard M. Nixon was concerned. Businessmen's short-lived enthusiasm for peacetime wage and price controls evaporated as it became clear that conservative political forces in the United States were both unwilling and unable to run the political risks involved in keeping powerful unions and consumer activists from taking actions that upset businessmen's instincts and posed varying dangers to their pocketbooks. Realizing at last that the Republicans could not protect them, big-business activists created a powerful political lobbying weapon to protect themselves: the Business Roundtable. The Roundtable, like much leading-edge corporate political activity that preceded it, owed much to the existence and the membership of the Business Council. With the birth of the Roundtable, big business in the United States may at last be said to have come of political age. Roundtable strategy throughout the Carter presidency has clearly demonstrated that the era of grand ideological crusades against "big government" and "socialism"—so evident as late as the 1950's—has been replaced by a period during which businessmen will be considerably more prone to play for power to pursue their concrete collective and individual interests.

Those who believe that Ronald Reagan's election will reverse this trend toward accommodation to the realities of federal power are, I believe, doomed to disappointment. Reagan is more committed to minimal government and pre-Keynesian economic policies than any President since Eisenhower. Presidents, however, come and go—as do broad electoral mandates and the effects of charisma. The political troubles of Kennedy and, later, Nixon are historical cases in point. Corporate leaders such as those active in the affairs of the Business Council and the Business Roundtable may engage in Rotary Club oratory about free enterprise. Such men, however, are exceedingly unlikely to dismantle the political tools for contact, recruitment, research, agenda building, and lobbying that it has taken them half a century and more to create.

There is an additional point to be made here. Reams of ill-informed journalistic and intellectual speculation to the contrary, Reagan is *not* the candidate of some monolithic abstraction called "business" or "big business." Reagan is the candidate of the Taft-Hoover-Goldwater wing of the Republican party—and of an ill-assorted legion of single-interest constituencies angered at the erosion of traditional family, religious, and community loyalties. Big businessmen, we should recall, were not shy about withdrawing their support from Goldwater when he ran in 1964, and the campaign of Goldwater's spiritual successor Reagan produced no delight in the boardrooms of "*Fortune* 500" America. With occasional exceptions, such as "self-made" entrepreneurs from the West and South including Justin Dart (of Dart Industries and more recently the Dart–Kraft Foods combine) and various oil industry executives, the eminences of big business were not numbered among Ronald Reagan's supporters until it became clear that the Democratic party under Jimmy Carter's uncertain leadership was headed for almost certain electoral catastrophe.

Business Roundtable activities since Reagan has assumed the presidency accent some of the difficulties that big businessmen will have in coming to terms with the right wing of the GOP. The Roundtable *has* issued a blanket endorsement of the entire Reagan economic program, and a recent cover story in *Fortune* magazine *has* ventilated the discontents of certain Roundtable members, who maintain that the organization should undertake a grand ideological crusade aimed at dismantling key elements of the federal power structure as a matter of capitalist conscience. These public statements, however, mask a good deal of scrambling for the political high ground that has occurred behind the scenes.[1]

On the crucial matter of taxation, for example, the Roundtable has continued the "yes, but" tactics that worked so well for it during the Carter era. Reagan, we must remember, came to Washington surrounded by libertarian economic ideologues committed, above all else, to two things: Friedmanite monetary policy and massive short-term reductions in *individual* income tax rates (i.e., the Kemp-Roth bill as originally proposed). The tax bill that Reagan eventually passed, however, had attached to it a key item on the Business Roundtable's taxation agenda: a vast decrease in *corporate* tax rates via the agency of an accelerated-depreciation-allowance program that the Roundtable had been backing for at least five years. When a commentator for the *Wall Street Journal* observed recently that the Business Roundtable had enough clout to get a tax bill passed that "included more tax breaks for business [and especially capital-intensive big business] than anyone would have thought imaginable just a couple of years ago," he was referring to the Roundtable's success at political logrolling not only with Democrat-controlled Congresses, but with Republican- and conservative-Democrat-controlled Congresses as well.[2]

The current political dominance of the "New" Right, then, will, I believe, produce no marked changes in the style, strategy, or techniques of corporate political activism. Washington has, after all, recently become a place where there are no permanent political alliances—only permanent political interests. Figuring prominently among the latter are interest groups like big businessmen and institutions that promote their interests like the Business Council and the Business Roundtable.

Big-business influence will, of course, wax and wane. But businessmen, whether they know it or not, will remain indebted for such successes as they have—and they are likely to have plenty in the immediate future—to the half century of institutional history that has been described and analyzed in this book.

Liberals, too, would be well advised to ponder these fifty years of history. For too many years, it seems to me, liberal critics of American business have been guilty of a good deal of intellectual laziness on the subject of the political relationships that exist or have existed between big-business leaders and their opposite numbers in government. I do not mean to suggest that nobody has done a good job of criticism. What I do mean is that left-wing intellectual analysts have too often made the error of not endeavoring to know their enemies well. This is a classic conceptual and political mistake—one that helps account, I think, for the current parlous state of left-wing power and liberal ideology in this country. In coming to the end of this long, and I hope informative, story, the author can only hope that it will help to cut through the layer upon layer of mystification and self-justifying utterance that have surrounded the subject dealt with here. For the rest, it is up to the reader to decide precisely what use to make of it all. Good luck.

A Postscript

REAGANOMICS AND THE CORPORATE ELITE: YEAR ONE

THE CLIMATE OF transcendent emergency that characterizes this country's present political culture makes Americans prey to more than the usual number of spasms of ill-focused concern. Among present anxieties, relationships between corporate and political leaders loom large. The coming into power of Ronald Reagan and the most conservative administration in two decades has brought an avalanche of speculation regarding the operations of big-business interests in official Washington and about the proper role of large corporations in the nation's policymaking councils. A good deal of this conjecture has been characterized by bombast, hyperbole, and a rhetoric of crisis that obscures more than it clarifies. Avoiding such excess, we will make an attempt here to clarify the most important patterns of challenge and response affecting businessmen and bureaucrats alike during a period that may mark an important transition point in the nation's political and economic life.

The New Right Triumvirate for Economic-Policy Making

The United States is a diverse place, and this diversity manifests itself in both the makeup of the Reagan coalition and the efforts of various elements of that coalition to bend it to their particular purposes. In the realm of economic-policy making, three discrete ideological groupings coalesced around the victorious Republican candidate and created that candidate's "new economic policy." These groups are: supply-siders, monetarists, and Republican traditionalists.

Before further discussing what divides these three schools, it is important to understand the single thing that unites them. All New Right ideologues, whatever their loyalties, share a profound hostility to the neoclassical theorist John Maynard Keynes. In particular, they intensely disagree with the Keynesian view that a large and active federal government must maintain a partnership with private business aimed at fostering steady and depression-free economic growth via fine-tuned compensatory taxation and spending policies. In the supply-side view, government not only does not assist capitalism, but is capitalism's main problem. Federal tax rates, in particular, have risen so high that investment and economic growth have been stymied, productivity and competitiveness have decreased, and a huge "underground economy" has been created. The *sine qua non* of New Right economic policy accordingly consists of large-scale tax cuts aimed at freeing the private sector from the federal octopus before it is totally enveloped by it.

Monetarists, for their part, agree with supply-siders that Washington is the villain. Washington, in fact, caused the Great Depression of the 1930's, besides causing all manner of other ills. What the New Right must do, add the monetarists, is to roll back a great many of the regulations about minimum standards and direct governmental provision of services enforced throughout the economy during the 1930's and after. While gradually restoring the virtues of the self-regulating market so beloved of introductory economics textbooks, say monetarist theorists including Milton Friedman, federal policy-makers must very largely confine themselves to steadily controlling the expansion of the total money supply to keep it in approximate synchronization with overall levels of economic growth. Thereby government can stabilize the currency (which these days means, end inflation) and contribute—for a change—to orderly economic and industrial advance as undertaken by businessmen and others in the private sector.

Supply-siders and monetarists, then, know the enemy—government—and have each enunciated a single major cure for the problem. Republican traditionalists, the third element of the New Right triumvirate, however, are less single-issue oriented than their peers. While they agree that Washington has grown too much and too fast, they are less optimistic that tax cuts alone—or strict monetary policy alone—will stem the tide of federal intervention and restore health to the nation's economy. The matter, in the traditionalist view, is more complicated. Taxes must be cut and inflation ended. Deficits, however, pose an additional problem, as does government spending. Unless Washington is forcibly restrained from regularly spending more than it takes in in taxes—and thus running deficits that continually increase the overall size of the federal government's debt— government will have a blank check to grow larger and larger irrespective of the wishes of supply-siders or monetarists. The thing to do, therefore, is to stop payment on the check and force Washington to live within its means. Then and only then will the public threat to private enterprise be well and truly contained.

The Triumvirate in Action

Each of the three anti-Keynesian elements in the New Right coalition pressed for the primacy of its own peculiar version of economic ideology during the Carter-Reagan transition. The result was that in economic policy, as in everything else, Reagan was required to perform a political balancing act of some complexity in order to avoid alienating key constituencies.

As initiated during Reagan's first year in office, the administration's economic program offered something to everybody. Supply-siders got decreases in individual income tax rates, specially tailored to the needs of those in the upper income brackets. Monetarists got assurances that the Federal Reserve Board would not be remiss about throttling back on the expansion of the money supply and crunching the credit markets to reduce the inflation rate. GOP traditionalists and hordes of badly frightened Democrats, for their part, were mollified by large-scale business tax reductions (chiefly the accelerated-depreciation tax provisions known informally as "10-5-3"), and were also promised widespread cuts in the rate of growth of federal spending.

Predictably, none of the major types of ideologues involved particularly liked the compromises that the Reagan White House ended up making. Disagreement was especially intense regarding the revenue side of the budgetary picture. Supply-siders complained that individual tax rates had not been cut far or fast enough, and that the too stringent monetary policy being enforced by the Federal Reserve was keeping interest rates so high that the torrent of investment and resulting fast-paced economic growth so freely predicted by supply-siders was being unfairly penned up or delayed. Monetarists, for their part, responded that the supply-siders were too impatient and that they were forgetting that inflation was *the* key issue for conservatives to address. Unless double-digit inflation and the psychology that went with it were squeezed out of the economy over the long haul, the tax cuts pushed by Arthur Laffer, Congressman Jack Kemp, and other supply-side leading lights would prove illusory due to "bracket creep," and a continued wage-price spiral would unsettle business-men and impede the investment miracle so crucial to the supply-side vision of the world.

While supply-siders and monetarists cleared their throats at one another, Republican traditionalists weighed in with their view of the economic universe. First, the supply-siders had been rash in demand-ing and obtaining large-scale individual tax cuts. The corporate cuts, the argument generally continued, were all right; they only went to businessmen when these businessmen made new investments in plant and equipment (or, to be fully accurate, when corporations on the economic ropes and paying no taxes sold their "refundable tax cred-its" to their better-off brethren). The individual cuts, however, were a case of too much too soon, and might very well increase inflation rates rather than decrease them.

Further, the GOP traditionalists went on, their opponents weren't paying enough attention to balancing the federal budget by cutting federal spending. Fixated on their single issues (tax cutting and money-supply growth, respectively), supply-siders and monetarists tended to forget that cutting tax rates without cutting spending rates would produce huge federal deficits unless the burst of growth in saving, investment, output, employment, and income prophesied by the supply-siders speedily occurred. As no such burst was about to happen, the new Republican administration might find itself in deep trouble. Storm signals on the stock markets throughout the spring and summer of 1981 accented the political dangers involved.

Monetarists, for their part, quickly allied themselves with their traditionalist opposite numbers on this issue of deficits, when no supply-side nirvana immediately appeared. The bigger the deficit, the monetarist logic went, the more money the federal government would need to borrow in private money markets, and the harder it would be for nongovernmental borrowers to avoid being squeezed out and starved of capital that might beef up the endangered private sector.

Increasingly needing somebody or something to blame for the fading away of their economic program, even the supply-siders finally added their voices to the call for spending cuts and balanced budgets. The revenue side of the Reagan administration's budgetary wars might divide conservative ideologues, but the spending side united them. All right-wingers, when push came to shove, found it congenial to equate more federal spending with sin.

The scene then shifted—as it had so often before—to Office of Management and Budget (OMB) chief David Stockman. Stockman, like many of the other New Right ideologues arrayed around Reagan, had initially accepted the supply-side view of the world. By May and June of 1981, however, Wall Street's lack of enthusiasm and a belated resurgence of his own traditionalist Republican instincts caused Stockman to have second thoughts. "I've never believed," he rather too ingenuously told an editor for the *Washington Post* who was then serving as his political amanuensis, "that just cutting taxes alone would cause output and employment to expand." This was another way of saying that the economy wasn't booming far or fast enough to allow the federal treasury to recoup all, or even most of, the revenues it had lost when tax rates were lowered. Now, affirmed Stockman, the crucial thing necessary to save the Administration's anti-Keynesian policy was firm control over federal spending.[1]

Control inevitably meant cuts—even in what was shaping up as a recession. Had the economy boomed, increased revenues from corporate and individual income taxes would have cascaded into federal coffers, financed all expenditures, and eliminated the need for deficits—all with little or no difficulty or expense to anyone. Without the promised short-term boom, federal revenues were falling relative to federal spending (much of which—e.g., Social Security—was mandated to increase by law) and the projected size of federal deficits during the four fiscal years of Reagan's first term were increasing steadily. The only way to keep these deficits under control was to throttle back on spending—or increase taxes—until such time as the delayed boom arrived. Otherwise, Washington would never go on the financial diet that all conservatives agreed to be essential.

Neither spending cuts nor tax increases aimed at balancing the budget, however, proved easy to get through Congress. Conservative congressmen of both parties had initially been sold an uncomplicated, even beatific vision of Reaganomics. If they cut taxes, everybody—including the federal treasury—would win and nobody would lose. Stockman's revised message, however, was decidedly different. Life had become more complicated, Wall Street was balking, and Congress must apportion the short-term pain that was necessary for longer-term economic growth.

First, Stockman tried the tax-increase approach to budget balancing, a gambit that promptly ran into exceedingly choppy seas on Capitol Hill. Supply-siders loudly opposed any effort to cut back substantially on the across-the-board rate reductions they had so recently put front and center on the nation's economic agenda. The best that Stockman was able to do was to delay the onset of some of the cuts by a few months and thus save a few billion dollars. Meanwhile, a congeries of industry groups fought like mad to stonewall Stockman's efforts to cut back on special-interest tax cuts (e.g., the previously mentioned refundable tax credits) that had been grafted onto the Reagan tax bill during its contentious passage through a badly frightened Congress. Stockman's attempts to close various old and new tax loopholes worth many billions of dollars in areas including energy and corporate income statements likewise got nowhere fast. "The hogs," Stockman later recalled, "were really feeding. The greed level, the level of opportunism, just got out of control."[2]

Failing on the tax-increase front, Stockman turned toward expenditure reductions, the only alternative remaining to him. Here, too, his experience was a far from happy one. The fate of the Reagan administration's proposals to substantially reduce the levels of funding for the Export-Import Bank provides instructive evidence of the problems involved.

Since the end of World War II, the Export-Import Bank (Ex-Im Bank for short) has sought to boost American exports by loaning money at subsidized (i.e., below market) rates to foreign borrowers so that those foreigners might use the money to purchase American-made goods. Thus, for example, an airline in Venezuela can go to an arm of the United States government, the Ex-Im Bank, and obtain a loan to buy a Boeing 747 jetliner at a rate substantially below what a domestic American borrower would have to pay for a loan from a privately held American bank. The logic behind such subsidies is that other nations grant them too, and that if American firms are to compete abroad they must be able to steer prospective purchasers to an agency like the Ex-Im Bank or lose sales that, if made, would provide employment to large numbers of American workers. Such subsidization doesn't come free; it is the taxpayer that picks up the

tab for the American portion of the interest rate subsidies estimated
to have cost all developed nations approximately $2 billion in 1978,
$5 billion in 1979, and more today.[3]

One problem with the billions of dollars of subsidized loans made
by the Ex-Im Bank every year is that the overwhelming majority of
them go to purchasers of high-technology American products including jet aircraft, electrical machinery, nuclear reactors, and tele-
communications equipment. Such big-ticket items, in turn, are
manufactured by a handful of the largest corporations in the country.
In 1980, for example, two-thirds of all Ex-Im Bank loans went to
expedite foreign sales made by only seven giant firms: Boeing, General Electric, Westinghouse, McDonnell Douglas, Lockheed, the
Western Electric division of American Telephone and Telegraph,
and Combustion Engineering. Other prominent beneficiaries of
Ex-Im Bank largesse included ITT, Motorola, General Telephone
and Electronics, and Rockwell International.[4]

Noting such facts and figures, Washington *cognoscenti* began
referring to the Ex-Im as "Boeing's Bank." Office of Management
and Budget Director Stockman, for his part, wasn't interested in
insiders' efforts at humor. He argued in favor of a deep reduction in
the level of Export-Import Bank funding. Steep curtailments in assistance to less affluent Americans must, he reasoned, be politically
balanced by cuts that clearly affected big business. Only thus could
the new Republican administration prove to the people that it possessed the intestinal fortitude and determination to reject claims for
special privileges and regard from all interest groups, however powerful or powerless.[5]

But economic power brokers like Stockman hadn't reckoned with
the other voices reaching White House and Capitol Hill ears. Only
weeks after reaching Washington, Reagan's staff was being besieged
by representatives of interested corporations and variously denomi-
nated foreign-trade advisers who held that American companies
desperately needed increases in Ex-Im Bank funding to maintain
their competitive positions in world markets. United States exports,
these advisers told Reagan and his top men, had doubled, in terms
of percentage of GNP, from 6 percent to 12 percent in ten years, and
surely Reagan didn't want to kill geese laying golden eggs?[6]

Reagan, it appeared, had no such intention—particularly after it
became clear to him and any other politician who cared to check that
the corporate giants most heavily dependent upon Ex-Im Bank credits, along with a collection of trade associations including the Na-

tional Foreign Trade Council, were conducting an intensive lobbying campaign on Capitol Hill aimed at getting congressional majorities to restore any cuts in funding that the White House proposed. Eventually the Reagan administration, at Stockman's repeated urging, proposed a 25 percent cutback in Ex-Im Bank funding for a period of five years. As the proposal went through the legislative process on Capitol Hill, rumors began to circulate that the White House might be engaged in a *pro forma* exercise and that the Commerce Department was opposed to the cuts under consideration. Corporate lobbyists from individual companies really got busy. In the end, congressional majorities finally restored most of the proposed funding reductions despite last-minute efforts by Stockman's office, and only about 9 percent—not 25 percent—of the Ex-Im's funds were cut during the first year of Reagan's presidency. Before the end of that same year, a Deputy Treasury Secretary was already warning recalcitrant French officials that any more shenanigans regarding credit subsidy competition on their part might well lead the Reagan administration to double Ex-Im Bank funding to $10 billion to $12 billion annually and use that money to drive French exporters right into the ground.[7]

The problems that Stockman and other New Right enthusiasts faced in connection with the Ex-Im Bank was only one small part of a wider and ultimately more frustrating struggle. Important spending reductions in nondefense areas were made by Reagan and his supporters, often over virulent opposition from liberals and from interest groups possessing particular potency on Capitol Hill. These federal spending cutbacks, however, did not fall upon big businessmen to any significant extent. Stockman's argument that political realism required that every political constituency be forced to tighten its belt in some significant fashion did not end up applying with great force to corporate America, any more than it applied to the military. The businessmen—like the generals—used a crisis atmosphere to equate their continued budgetary support with the survival and security of the nation itself. This strategy has often reaped rich rewards from conservative American politicians, and it did so again.

The Uneasy Agenda

By the end of the Reagan administration's first year in power, then, the New Right triumvirate of supply-siders, monetarists, and GOP traditionalists had strung together economic initiatives of some daring and very little logical coherence. On the taxation front, a 25 percent across-the-board cut in individual income tax rates was to be phased in over three years. The top tax bite on larger incomes was pared from 70 to 50 percent and, over the longer haul, tax rates would be indexed to the inflation rate starting in 1985. Capital gains levies and windfall profits exactions were cut, estate taxes were nearly eliminated, and savers who put their money in various types of accounts in various types of banks were presented with federal tax benefits for doing so. Big businessmen, for their part, received the substantial tax benefits in the form of accelerated depreciation allowances that *Business Week* estimated to be worth $160 billion over the course of the next five years. In addition they got the financial use of refundable tax credits, which basically allow unprofitable companies that aren't paying any taxes at all to sell their tax credits to the behemoth firms that are. Small businessmen, for their part, had to remain content with a ragtag collection of cuts worth only approximately half a billion dollars annually until 1986. Total tax losses from all of the Reagan administration and last-minute congressional cuts were guesstimated by the OMB to run to over $750 billion during the next five years.[8]

Meanwhile the rate of growth of federal expenditures was also scaled back by passage of an initial $35 billion cut in spending for fiscal 1982 in July of 1981 and by the later passage of $4 billion in additional fiscal 1982 cuts (of $12 billion requested) in late December. By January of 1982, Reagan was backing an additional $30 billion in cuts for fiscal 1983, though final congressional action on his proposals remained to be seen.

Thirty-nine billion dollars of cuts in a single fiscal year is hardly petty change. The problem was that the spending cuts the Reaganites pushed through Congress were much smaller than the income cuts they had earlier mandated for the federal treasury in the form of lower taxes. As former Treasury Secretary (under Carter) and Burroughs Corporation CEO W. Michael Blumenthal glumly noted in *Business Week* early in the whole process: "The fundamental problem the President faces is simply that his multiyear tax cutting has created such massive gaps between the Treasury's income and outflow streams that any kind of defense and nondefense budget-cutting sufficient to close this gap is politically and practically well-nigh impossible." Reaganomics, in short, was going to be purchased at the price of soaring federal deficits.[9]

The deficit problem, of course, should never have presented itself. Not, at least, according to the upbeat theories of the supply-side economists of the New Right policymaking coalition. Massive tax cuts were supposed to perk up confidence and expectations, saving and investment levels, productivity, economic growth rates, and federal tax revenues—and all at the same time.

Bankers, brokers, and businessmen, alas, proved more skeptical. On Wall Street, there was much wailing and gnashing of teeth regarding deficits, while bankers were only cautiously optimistic about short-term declines in interest rates and corporate capital-spending budgets did not reveal a supply-side nirvana. By September, 1981, the unwelcome news was there for all to see in the columns of the nation's business press.[10]

This big-business nonresponse to Reaganomics grated on New Right sensibilities. Upon arriving in Washington, the Reaganites had not been chary of suggesting to business representatives that they issue blanket endorsements of the Reagan economic program, as a necessary quid pro quo for the political and economic favors to be rendered to them. Powerful business lobbying groups including the U.S. Chamber of Commerce and the Business Roundtable got the message. Access and acceptability to the government depended upon their providing organizational legitimation to the New Right.

Legitimation was speedily forthcoming. In March of 1981, for example, the Business Roundtable took the unprecedented step of going public in support of an entire administration program. This after spending seven profitable and impressive years gaining an enviable reputation for political clout in Washington by carefully avoiding "ideological" stances and instead concentrating on particular bills, regulations, or elements of the federal tax codes. Once it had grasped the ideological nettle, however, the Roundtable proceeded vigorously. "The business community," it announced, "feels strongly that all four parts of the economic recovery plan [spending cuts, tax cuts, regulatory reduction, and a "stable and consistent monetary policy"] are essential, interrelated, and must be acted upon. . . ." "An economic crisis confronts the American people," another Roundtable report breathlessly began, "and requires far-reaching changes in economic policies," in other words, Reaganomics.[11]

Fulsome oratory like this was aimed at making corporations money. It was also, however, motivated by concern. The big-business leaders of the Business Roundtable knew one thing very well. Reagan's was not a traditional Republican administration in the sense of equating "free enterprise" with whatever businessmen happened to be doing at the moment. The Reaganites' belief in the powers and virtues of marketplace competition as the tool for solving all social ills was more profound, broadly encompassing, and intense than that possessed by many of the corporate politicians who had been involved in practical politics in Washington for years. Reagan's first chief "policy development" adviser, Martin Anderson, reminisced to a *New York Times* reporter midway through the New Right administration's initial year that corporate CEOs had never backed Reagan's presidential candidacy strongly, preferring instead to put their money behind John Connally and others. The reason, Anderson continued, was that "they knew deep down that Reagan meant what he said on free enterprise. CEOs are for free enterprise, but they don't necessarily know what it is." The implication was clear: under Ronald Reagan's tutelage, instruction in Adam Smith's view of the world was going to commence in earnest.[12]

The Businessmen Get Their Marching Orders

A key agent of this instruction was Secretary of the Treasury Donald T. Regan, a Wall Street investment banker who had remained bullish on America. Throughout 1981, Regan traveled the luncheon and dinner circuit bearing a simple and sobering message to business audiences. Corporations and their leaders, the Treasury Secretary reiterated again and again, must be the ones to lead America out of the wilderness and toward the shining capitalist tomorrow. They must do this, moreover, by getting out ahead of the market and the economic indicators and investing a great deal of money in new plant, equipment, research, and product development in a period of double-digit inflation, high interest rates, excess productive capacity, and substantial joblessness.

Regan laid it on the line to his corporate listeners. "Business," he told a meeting of the Chamber of Commerce in March of 1981,

is what produces, and business has to take over. That's going to be the biggest challenge to American business since World War II: How to carry out this program once you're free of the fetters that you've been decrying for so many years.

Business has been saying, "Turn me loose, let me do it." All right, we're going to turn you loose in six months. Are you ready for it? Can you stand the shock of competition?[13]

The answers were not long in coming, and many of them were not to the liking of New Right ideologues. As was already discussed, capital spending did not boom. Weaker investment rates in industries like aerospace, petroleum, and utilities more than offset stronger spending in other industrial sectors such as computers. The economy drifted down into its fourth recession in a decade as the jobless rose to 9 million.

Worse, from the Reaganites' perspective, was the speculative behavior of a handful of giant and high-profile companies including Mobil Oil, Du Pont, and U.S. Steel. Instead of using their tax and other savings to invest in new productive capacity, such corporations began arranging the largest mergers in American corporate history with second-tier energy companies.

Mobil, as so often before, elected to lead with its chin. In August of 1981, only weeks after the Reagan tax cut had been passed, the oil giant tried to stage-manage a multibillion-dollar marriage with Continental Oil Company (Conoco). Mobil was following the principle that it was better to purchase oil reserves than to take the riskier and less convenient course of using its retained tax and other wealth to drill for them.

Unfortunately for Mobil's version of the entrepreneurial dialectic, however, a buy-out of one energy conglomerate's assets by another creates no new jobs. Nor does it please the lawyers of the Antitrust Division of the Justice Department in Washington. For these and other reasons, Conoco's eventual partner in a $6.82 billion marriage was Du Pont, a chemical combine outside of the energy area.

Having failed to gobble up one smaller oil company, Mobil marched farther out into the political wilderness in search of another. This time, the corporation's speculative eye rolled toward Marathon Oil Company of Findlay, Ohio.

But Marathon was not a whit more anxious to seal a pact with Mobil than Conoco had been, and promptly ran off in search of other corporate suitors. Early in the multibillion-dollar bidding war that resulted in November and December of 1981, Marathon began using an old Mobil ploy—using nationally syndicated advertisements to ask inconvenient questions. For instance, wasn't Mobil's "high-handed" and arrogant take-over effort a clear violation of the antitrust acts? And why was Mobil trying to spend $5 billion to buy Marathon's reserves when it could go looking for its own? "Everybody in the U.S. who suffered through the energy shortage," one of Marathon's pithier efforts at public persuasion went, "has got to ask this administration and Congress whether this kind of acquisition is going to increase the nation's oil reserves by a single barrel."[14]

Unfortunately for Mobil, answers to Marathon's prophylactic public queries were hard—indeed, impossible—to find. One of Mobil's own corporate lawyers even went so far as to wonder aloud to the *Wall Street Journal,* "If Section 7 of the Clayton (Antitrust) Act means anything, how can this fly? If this [merger] goes through, what won't go through?"[15]

As it turned out, Mobil's lawyers didn't need to worry about antitrust legislation. Their corporation lost out in the home stretch yet again, this time to U.S. Steel.

The $6 billion marriage between the nation's largest steel producer and Marathon Oil eased around the fringes of the antitrust laws by replacing a "horizontal merger" (i.e., one within a single industry) with a "conglomerate merger" (between companies in unrelated industries). The U.S. Steel–Marathon Oil merger, however, did nothing to increase public esteem for the big-business statesmanship that Reaganites like Secretary of the Treasury Regan were trying to call into being.

U.S. Steel, not to put too fine a point on it, was as politically maladroit as Mobil Oil. For one thing, its leading lights had been loudly complaining for years that their corporation was taxed and regulated by Washington so heavily that it lacked the capital necessary to upgrade its steelmaking facilities to meet the challenge of foreign competitors, who were in the process of seizing 25 percent of the American domestic market. To quell the uproar among steelmakers and their allies in organized labor and elsewhere, Washington doled out largesse. In January of 1978, the Carter administration began the process with a disguised tariff system known (in bureaucratic bafflegab) as the trigger-price mechanism. Trigger prices erased most of the comparative cost advantages enjoyed by foreign (especially Japanese) producers, and helped provide U.S. Steel and other companies with comparative price stability in a period of declining demand for their output. The New Right's ideas proved even more to the steel industry's liking. The accelerated-depreciation and refundable-tax-credit elements of the 1981–1986 tax bill were just the sort of corporate welfare programs that steelmen had been bruiting about in Washington for a decade and more.

It did not look good, however, when U.S. Steel, having received the tax breaks, turned around and spent $6 billion to buy an oil company. Why, asked bemused voices on the banks of the Potomac, didn't U.S. Steel use such an ocean of money to modernize and upgrade its steelmaking facilities? That, after all, was exactly what many congressmen and senators had thought they were buying when they distributed the corporate tax cuts in the first place.

U.S. Steel reacted defensively. Hadn't the legislative spokesmen been aware that the corporation drew up a strategic plan in 1980 that committed it to shrinking the size of its steel assets to less than half of its total capital by 1990? Didn't Washington understand comparative advantage, balance sheets, and basic economic principles?[16]

No, Washington did not. Washington understood politics, and the politics of the situation were outrageous. Having been granted billions in tax breaks, U.S. Steel, like Mobil, appeared to be saying, "To hell with 'em all," and using the money without any sense of social responsibility or quid pro quo whatsoever.[17]

Even some normally circumspect business journals smelled a rat. The acquisition of Marathon Oil by U.S. Steel, *Business Week* announced in a strongly worded editorial,

> is a far cry from the reasons U.S. Steel gave when it asked for government concessions, and it is a far cry from those Congress and the American taxpayer had in mind when they granted the concessions. In the light of this acquisition, and diversification moves embarked on by other steel companies, it is hard to see how the steel industry can expect any further help from Washington. U.S. Steel's decision to acquire Marathon . . . badly tarnishes not only its credibility but also that of the entire steel industry. Unfortunately, in the public mind, confidence in business as a whole is likely to be damaged as well.[18]

Almost as if it wanted to ensure the latter result, Mobil Oil publicly announced its intention of trying to buy up to 25 percent of U.S. Steel in yet another whirl through the speculative jungle. Mobil's effort didn't last long, but by this time, almost nobody in Washington was laughing.[19]

Waiting for the Miracle

As mammoth mergers tarnished the credibility of larger corporations, and as the instantaneous investment miracle initially prophesied by supply-side economists failed to materialize due to the internal contradictions between stimulative tax cuts and a restrictive monetary policy, business leaders were faced with a choice about continuing to provide public support for Reaganomics. Should they abandon ship or stay on board? In fact, few outside of Wall Street headed for the lifeboats. Reaganomics was, after all, providing dollars-and-cents benefits on the tax front—and those benefits had some years yet to run. The benefits, in fact, sometimes (e.g., in the case of the accelerated depreciation provisions) had the characteristic of increasing over time. Better, therefore, to avoid alienating the source of largesse at the start of the process. This logic especially applied to high-profile and panindustrial big-business lobbies like the Business Roundtable, which reiterated their devotion to the varied staples of New Right economic thinking whenever asked. On the level of the individual firm, thought and action was more *ad hoc,* more dependent upon the specific mix of costs and benefits experienced, or expected, by the managerial hierarchy—*vide* Mobil Oil and U.S. Steel. For all this, however, few *"Fortune* 500" chief executive officers polled publicly criticized Reagan for anything. The few who did cavil couched their complaints as questions of degree rather than of underlying policy. Taxes, for instance, had been cut too much, or spending hadn't been pared enough.[20]

On a more private level, it was another story. As early as May of 1981, "corporate public affairs" analysts in Washington began to float warnings that big businessmen might have hitched their wagon too firmly and openly to the Reagan administration's star. As one Washington-based official of a corporate research and advisory organization called the Public Affairs Council put it in an expensive "insider's" newsletter, "The current mood of 'take the shackles off, take the controls off and business will produce,' could leave business holding the bag if there is no genuine improvement in the economy."[21]

Indeed it could. Worse, Reagan might turn on big-business-as-usual elements of the corporate world in the event that his economic policies failed to achieve what he hoped of them. The bag that business could one day be left holding, therefore, might be handed to it by a New Right president anxious to maintain the political initiative by assigning blame to somebody other than himself.

All this businessmen sensed, and more besides. In the long run, things tend to become more complicated in politics. In the short run, however, businessmen, like the Reagan administration itself, waited for a miracle. Promises of almost instantaneous economic recovery by the spring of 1982 were replaced by more cautious presidential rhetoric that eased around problems by promising the country would be "on the road to prosperity and stable growth by the latter half of the year." "Difficult moments," however, would occur in the months ahead.[22]

Indeed they would. Advancing into the void left by a disorganized and dispirited Democratic party, the Reaganites and their big-business allies pursued their alliance of mutual convenience. They had won great victories together—offensive victories, not defensive ones. Now the furious economic action of the preceding year halted as Reagan sought to shift the political agenda toward his proposals for a "New Federalism." The opposing forces waited—liberals for the speedy unraveling of the neoconservative grand design, the New Right for the gradual achievement of its pre-Keynesian vision. In the relative political silence, capitalists occasionally wondered whether they might have bitten off more than they could chew. Their present circumstances, unfortunately, provided no easy answer to the question.

NOTES

Prologue

1. Myron Taylor to Edward R. Stettinius, Jr., June 11, 1938, Box 63, Edward R. Stettinius, Jr., Papers, Alderman Library, University of Virginia, Charlottesville, Va.

2. Ibid.

3. "Washington Conferences" memo, July 4, 1938, p. 4., in bound volume entitled "Washington Notes," Box 64, Stettinius Papers.

4. All quotes are taken from Stettinius' typescript "Interview with President Roosevelt," ibid.

5. "Washington Notes, September, 1938," pp. 2–15, and "Washington Notes, October 6, 1938," ibid.

6. John Kenneth Galbraith, *American Capitalism,* 2nd rev. ed. (Boston: Houghton Mifflin, 1956), pp. 56–57.

Chapter One

1. For the full text of the Swope Plan, see J. George Frederick, ed., *The Swope Plan: Details, Criticisms, Analysis* (New York: Business Bourse, 1931).

2. U.S. Congress, Senate, Committee on Manufactures, *"Hearings on a Bill to Establish a National Economic Council—S. 6215"* (Washington, D.C.: Government Printing Office, 1932), passim. The Sloan quote is on pp. 380–81.

3. Henry S. Dennison, *Ethics and Modern Business* (Boston: Houghton Mifflin, 1932), pp. 58–59.

4. Quote on p. 185 of Robert F. Himmelberg, *The Origins of the National Recovery Administration: Business, Government, and the Trade Association Issue, 1921–1933* (New York: Fordham University Press, 1976). Chapter 10 of the Himmelberg book is very informative about corporate activities during and immediately after the 1932 elections, and is heavily relied upon in the remainder of this section.

5. For Hoover's negative comments, see *The Memoirs of Herbert Hoover: The Great Depression, 1929–1941* (New York: Macmillan, 1952), pp. 334–35, 420.

6. Broadus Mitchell, *Depression Decade: From the New Era Through the New Deal, 1929–1941* (New York: Harper Torchbooks, 1969), p. 324.

7. Harriman quote from Thomas E. Vadney, *The Wayward Liberal: A Political Biography of Donald Richberg* (Louisville, Ky.: University Press of Kentucky, 1970), p. 119.

8. Daniel C. Roper, *Fifty Years of Public Life* (Durham, N.C.: University of North Carolina Press, 1941), p. 284.

9. "History of the Industrial Advisory Board," bound typescript, Vol. 1, p. 1, Record Group 9, Series 37, National Recovery Administration Records, Miscellaneous Report and Documents Series, Box 8336, National Archives (hereafter designated "History of the IAB" and NRA Records); Charles F. Roos, *NRA Economic Planning* (Bloomington, Ind.: Principia Press, 1937), pp. 68, 74; Leverett S. Lyon et al., *The National Recovery Administration* (Washington, D.C.: Brookings Institution, 1935), pp. 100–102, 148, 156; "History of Code Making" typescript, March 2, 1935, pp. 1–4, NRA Records Box 8784 (hereafter cited as "History of Code Making"); William Leuchtenburg, "The New Deal and the Analogue of War," in John Braeman et al., eds., *Change and Continuity in Twentieth Century America* (Columbus, Ohio: Ohio State University Press, 1964), pp. 123, 128–29; Donald Richberg, *The Rainbow* (Garden City, N.Y.: Doubleday, 1936), pp. 115–16; Hugh S. Johnson, *The Blue Eagle From Egg to Earth* (Garden City, N.Y.: Doubleday, 1935), pp. 216, 238, 293; *"Hearings on the Proposed Code for the Lumber and Timber Products Industry,"* p. 212, NRA Records, Box 7161; "History of the IAB," Vol. 1, pp. 6–7, 111–12; "Industrial Advisory Board, Minutes of Regular Meetings, 1933–1934" file, meetings of August 22, 1933, and October 31, 1933, NRA Records, Box 8415 (hereafter cited as IAB Regular Meetings File); "Industrial Advisory Board, Minutes of the Dinner Meetings, June, 1934–June, 1935" file, meeting of November 16, 1933, NRA Records, Box 8416 (hereafter cited as IAB Dinner Meetings File).

10. The history of the SCC is covered in U.S. Congress, Senate, "Hearings Before a Subcommittee of the Committee on Education and Labor: Violations of the Right of Free Speech and Assembly and Interference With the Right of Labor to Organize and Bargain Collectively," Part 45, "Supplementary Exhibits, The Special Conference Committee," 76th Congress (Washington, D.C.: Government Printing Office, 1939), pp. 16777–800. (This government report is more familiarly known as the LaFollette labor spy investigation or the LaFollette Committee report.)

11. According to Frances Perkins, Gerard Swope told her and Franklin D. Roosevelt (then governor of New York) in 1926 that his corporation had "no objection to a trade union if [it] could have one trade union. But the company simply could not deal with twenty different crafts unions and have jurisdictional disputes between them." Roosevelt and Perkins (then the industrial commissioner of New York State) thereupon advised New York AFL leaders to consider beginning industrial-union-organizing drives in the state's electrical manufacturing industry. The AFL, however, had no interest in proceeding in such a fashion. See Frances Perkins, *The Roosevelt I Knew* (New York: Viking Press, 1946), p. 309; David Loth, *Swope of G.E.* (New York: Simon and Schuster, 1958), p. 309.

Federated Department Stores' Louis Kirstein was another businessman who had had long experience with labor leaders, in particular Sidney Hillman of the Amalgamated Clothing Workers Union. Throughout the 1920's, Kirstein was a force in the development of nationwide conciliation and arbitration techniques developed for the clothing industry, and this brought him into close and continuing contact with

ACWU leaders. In March of 1930, for example, Kirstein wrote a man whom he was trying to recruit as an arbitrator that his respect for Hillman was quite sincere. "I think," he wrote, "that [Hillman] was one of the first [labor leaders] to realize that the workers of an industry succeeded (as the owners of that industry did) and, it was naturally up to them to help toward bringing about such a situation." (Kirstein to Horace Stern, March 28, 1930, Case 4, Louis Kirstein Papers, Baker Library, Harvard Business School. See also Jacob S. Potofsky to Kirstein, November 10, 1937, and Kirstein to unidentified correspondent, January 13, 1959, both Case 7, Kirstein Papers.)

12. Lewis Lorwin and C. Wubnig, *Labor Relations Boards* (Washington, D.C.: Brookings Institution, 1935), pp. 87–91; IAB Regular Meetings File, "Minutes of the Joint Meeting of the Industrial Advisory Board and the Labor Advisory Board held at the Shoreham, August 3, 1933," pp. 1–6; ibid., p. 7. Swope's relations with Green and the AFL are covered in David Loth, *Swope of G.E.,* pp. 166–72; IAB Regular Meetings File, "Meeting of IAB and LAB, August 3, 1933," pp. 6–7; IAB Regular Meetings File, "Combined Meeting of the Industrial Advisory Board and the Labor Advisory Board, Friday, August 4, 1933, in the Department of Commerce," pp. 1–4; F. W. McCulloch and T. Bornstein, *The National Labor Relations Board* (New York: Praeger, 1974), p. 11.

13. David Brody, "The Rise and Decline of Welfare Capitalism," in John Braeman et al., eds., *Change and Continuity,* p. 147ff.; Irving Bernstein, *The Turbulent Years* (Boston: Houghton Mifflin, 1970), passim; Lewis Lorwin and C. Wubnig, *Labor Relations Boards,* p. 92 (n. 8); Irving Bernstein, *The New Deal Collective Bargaining Policy* (Berkeley: University of California Press, 1950), pp. 58–59; Lewis Lorwin and C. Wubnig, *Labor Relations Boards,* pp. 93–94, 106.

14. Irving Bernstein, *The New Deal Collective Bargaining Policy,* pp. 61–62; Lewis Lorwin and C. Wubnig, *Labor Relations Boards,* pp. 97–98; Frances Perkins, *The Roosevelt I Knew,* pp. 238–39. See also Frances Perkins, "Eight Years as Madame Secretary," *Fortune,* September, 1941, p. 79.

15. Louis Adamic, *My America: 1928–1938* (New York: Harper and Brothers, 1938), pp. 358–59.

16. *New York Times,* January 7, 1934, p. 13; ibid., March 9, 1934, p. 9.

17. Robert Wood to Louis Kirstein, September 27, 1933, "NIRA—P-2" file, Box 7, Kirstein Papers; Alfred Sloan to Pierre du Pont, December 15, 1933, and Du Pont to Sloan, January 4, 1934, "NLB—1933" and "NLB—January–April, 1934" files, Record Group 10, Series A, File 1173–5, Pierre S. du Pont Papers, Eleutherian Mills–Hagley Foundation Library, Wilmington, Del.

18. J. J. Huthmacher, *Senator Robert F. Wagner and the Rise of Urban Liberalism* (New York: Pantheon, 1968), pp. 161–63; Irving Bernstein, *The New Deal Collective Bargaining Policy,* pp. 57–58; Lewis Lorwin and C. Wubnig, *Labor Relations Boards,* pp. 102–10; Pierre du Pont to National Labor Board, February 19, 1943, and the resulting exchange of letters between Du Pont and Lincoln Filene in the "NLB—1934" file, File 1173–5, Du Pont Papers.

19. Gerard Swope to Pierre du Pont, February 26, 1934, and Walter Teagle to Du Pont, February 21, 1934, "NLB—1934" file, File 1173–3, Du Pont Papers; Teagle to Kirstein, March 1, 1934, "NIRA—Walter C. Teagle" file, Case 7, Kirstein Papers; James A. Gross, *The Making of the National Labor Relations Board: A Study in Economics, Politics, and the Law,* Vol. 1, *1933–1937* (Albany, N.Y.: State University of New York Press, 1974), pp. 44–62.

20. J. J. Huthmacher, *Senator Robert F. Wagner,* pp. 163ff.; Lewis Lorwin and C. Wubnig, *Labor Relations Boards,* pp. 110–19; Louis Kirstein to Walter Teagle,

March 26, 1934, Teagle to Kirstein, March 27, 1934, and April 8, 1934, all in "NIRA—Walter Teagle" file, Case 7, Kirstein Papers.

21. James A. Gross, *The Making of the National Labor Relations Board,* pp. 111–12; Irving Bernstein, *The New Deal Collective Bargaining Policy,* pp. 81, 87.

22. "Views on the Wagner National Labor Relations Bill—S. 1958" report, ca. February, 1935, Box 47, Donald Richberg Papers, Library of Congress.

23. James A. Gross, *The Making of the National Labor Relations Board,* p. 144; Lewis Lorwin and C. Wubnig, *Labor Relations Boards;* Irving Bernstein, *The Turbulent Years;* Arthur Schlesinger, Jr., *The Coming of the New Deal,* pp. 400–406; *The Politics of Upheaval* (Boston: Houghton Mifflin, 1960), pp. 292–93.

24. Hugh S. Johnson, *The Blue Eagle,* p. 272; Ellis W. Hawley, *The New Deal and the Problem of Monopoly* (Princeton, N.J.: Princeton University Press, 1968), pp. 97, 102; Arthur Schlesinger, Jr., *The Coming of the New Deal,* pp. 132–35; William Leuchtenburg, *FDR and the New Deal, 1932–1940* (New York: Harper and Row, 1963), pp. 67–68; Thomas E. Vadney, *The Wayward Liberal,* pp. 120–31; Franklin D. Roosevelt, "Address . . . at the General Conference of Code Authorities . . . , March 5, 1934," NRA Records, Box 8385.

25. IAB Dinner Meetings File, meeting of October 12, 1933; IAB Regular Meetings File, meeting of March 23, 1934; IAB Dinner Meetings File, meeting of July 12, 1934.

26. IAB Monthly Meetings File, meetings of July 12, 1934, and July 26, 1934.

27. "History of the Industrial Advisory Board," Vol. 1, pp. 11, 14, 149–50 and Vol. 4, pp. 26–27, 60–62, NRA Records, Box 8336; "Industrial Advisory Board: Minutes of the IAB as Reorganized, July, 1934–May, 1935, passim, NRA Records, Box 8416; Bernard Bellush, *The Failure of the NRA* (New York: W. W. Norton, 1975), pp. 140–55; Herman Krooss, *Executive Opinion* (Garden City, N.Y.: Doubleday, 1970), pp. 162, 176, 183–90; U.S. Congress, House of Representatives, "Hearings on the Extension of the National Industrial Recovery Act," 74th Congress, 1st session (Washington, D.C.: Government Printing Office, 1935), passim.

28. Swope's lack of fear regarding the growth of federal power was not a New Deal or post-Depression phenomenon. In the spring of 1938, former socialist Robert W. Bruere reported to a friend that he had had an interesting conversation on public ownership with GE's president. In private, Swope "said, for example, that he believed that all economic institutions and services whose techniques had been fully worked out should be publicly owned, and he matched my references to the water systems of our great municipalities by saying that he believed that life insurance companies had reached the state of development that warranted placing them in this category." By the late 1930's, Swope had become an advocate of national health insurance. See Bruere to Morris L. Cooke, April 25, 1928, Box 2, Morris L. Cooke Papers, Franklin D. Roosevelt Library, Hyde Park, New York, and Swope to Donald Richberg, March 1, 1949, Box 2, Richberg Papers.

29. "History of the IAB," Vol. 1, pp. 115, 226–34; IAB Monthly Meetings File, meetings of January 17, 1935, and February 28, 1935; Business Advisory Council reports on labor policy dated January 15, March 3, and May 2, 1935, in Franklin D. Roosevelt Papers, Official File 3-Q, FDR Library.

30. The custom continued even after this time. As late as March of 1943, the executive secretary of the Business Council wrote a Council member who wished to invite a congressman to a Council meeting: "It has been the policy of the Council not to invite members of Congress to our functions except on rare occasions." In 1940, even prominent senators like James F. Byrnes, a member of the Senate Appropriations Committee, expressed almost total ignorance of the makeup or

activities of the organization. See Walter White to R. C. Patterson, March 9, 1943, and Byrnes to Jesse Jones, September 5, 1940, both in Box 786, General Records of the Department of Commerce, National Archives.

31. Businessmen's lack of understanding of the nuances of federal politics is attested to by a letter that Henry Kendall, Gerard Swope's successor as chairman of the Business Council, wrote (in vain) to Pierre du Pont in 1935. "I very much hope and fully expect," Kendall began, "that the next Chairman [of the Council] will pick things up where I left off and enable the Council to be a more influential factor in advising on next year's legislation before it gets fully drafted, or before administrative minds are definitely committed." The Council's mainstream did not quickly learn the simple truth that those who arrive early and propose consistently during the subcommittee and committee stages of the legislative process are those to whom such laurels as exist are generally distributed. (Kendall to Pierre du Pont, undated, "BAC—1935" file, File 1173-3, Du Pont Papers.)

32. Edwin E. Witte, *The Development of the Social Security Act* (Madison, Wis.: University of Wisconsin Press, 1963), p. 50; Edward Berkowitz and Kim McQuaid, *Creating the Welfare State: The Political Economy of Twentieth Century Reform* (New York: Praeger Special Studies, 1980), chapter 6.

33. Edwin E. Witte, *The Development of the Social Security Act,* p. 50.

34. U.S. Congress, Senate, Select Committee on Unemployment Insurance, "Hearings on . . . S.R. n. 483," 72nd Congress, 1st session (Washington, D.C.: Government Printing Office, 1932), pp. 21–51, especially pp. 29–30. For Teagle's views, see "In Retrospect—June 13, 1934—Walter C. Teagle," "NRA—Industrial Advisory Board—1934" file, File 1173-3, Du Pont Papers.

35. Daniel Nelson, *Unemployment Insurance: The American Experience, 1915–1935* (Madison, Wis.: University of Wisconsin Press, 1969) provides excellent coverage of the business position in these regards.

36. Unemployment insurance legislation was changed in the early 1960's to allow supplementary federal grants to the jobless in emergency situations. Swope and Teagle would not have been pleased.

For the statistics about "experience rating," see Marion B. Folsom, "Stabilization of Employment and Income," *Conference Board Management Record,* February, 1939, copy in Box 73, Stettinius Papers.

37. Gaston V. Rimlinger, *Welfare Policy and Industrialization in Europe, America, and Russia* (New York: John Wiley and Sons, 1971), p. 4; "If Money," *Saturday Evening Post,* Vol. 208 (March 11, 1935), pp. 12–13, 121–27; Nicholas Roosevelt, *The Townsend Plan* (Garden City, N.Y.: Doubleday, 1936), passim.

38. Arthur Altmeyer, *The Formative Years of Social Security* (Madison, Wis.: University of Wisconsin Press, 1968), p. 3; Arthur Schlesinger, Jr., *The Coming of the New Deal,* pp. 302–303; William Leuchtenburg, *FDR and the New Deal,* pp. 130–33; J. Douglas Brown, *An American Philosophy of Social Security: Evolution and Issues* (Princeton, N.J.: Princeton University Press, 1972), pp. 10–12.

39. J. Douglas Brown, *An American Philosophy of Social Security,* pp. 21–22. The last-minute concerns regarding financing that are referred to here resulted from the fact that Social Security's retirement program was not identical to private programs. Workers who retired after contributing to Social Security for only a few years during the early years of the program were paid more in pensions than they had contributed in taxes. This, in turn, increased the burden on later generations of Social Security–tax payers. Realizing that this was the case, Committee on Economic Security experts, anxious to limit the combined tax rate paid by employers and employees to 5 percent of the payroll, proposed that if and when that limit

was reached, the federal government should start making contributions into the Social Security retirement fund.

Secretary of the Treasury Morgenthau and President Roosevelt would have none of it. Both wanted the Social Security pension system put on a *strictly* self-financing basis. To insure this, Morgenthau, with Roosevelt's approval, boosted Social Security tax rates and decreased the annuities received by retirees to keep the program self-supporting. Opponents of this decision included Marion Folsom, who wrote Senator Wagner at the time that "the increased rates of taxation now proposed would unnecessarily drain consumers of purchasing power and thus produce deflationary tendencies harmful to the whole economy." Folsom was right. For all that, the deflationary aspects remained. (J. J. Huthmacher, *Senator Robert F. Wagner,* pp. 185–86.)

40. For the White House meeting, see *New York Times,* May 9, 1935, p. 2.

That Swope and other pro–Social Security Act Business Council members had some persuading to do is testified to by the fact that the Business Council continued to argue that unemployment insurance should be financed by employer *and employee* contributions throughout the rest of the Depression decade.

The unreceptivity of the Business Council mainstream to the social welfare initiatives of the Roosevelt administration is also attested to by the following letter a high General Motors executive sent to Edward Stettinius three weeks after Roosevelt was first elected:

"Public unemployment insurance through public agencies would no doubt enormously increase the cost to industry, by setting up new bureaucratic functions and a new army of public employees . . . and of course the result would be to recognize and provide for a permanent army of unemployed—all to be paid for by employers. . . .

"You and I," this resolutely reactionary corporate official continued, "have repeatedly discussed the only real economic remedies for this approaching [*sic*] [unemployment] menace, namely (1) drastic reduction in all public expenditures; and (2) a definite cooperative effort to rehabilitate the land through subsistence-farming great numbers of those now unemployed who will undoubtedly be without any reasonably continuous work for many years to come." (Edmond E. Lincoln to Stettinius, November 21, 1932, Box 550, Stettinius Papers.)

41. Charles McKinley and Robert W. Fraser, *Launching Social Security: A Capture and Record Account* (Madison, Wis.: University of Wisconsin Press, 1970), pp. 346–56.

42. Gerard Swope to FDR, May 25, 1937, President's Personal File 2943, FDR Library.

43. See FDR to Gerard Swope, May 28, 1937 and other letters in President's Personal File 2943, FDR Library. Edward D. Berkowitz and Kim McQuaid, *Creating the Welfare State* covers disagreements between corporate and noncorporate social welfare experts during the 1930's, 1940's, and 1950's; Martha Derthick, *Policymaking for Social Security* (Washington, D.C.: Brookings Institution, 1979), especially chapter 11, dismisses the businessmen as tangential to the policy process, an opinion I emphatically do not share.

44. Politicians' reciprocal appreciation of corporate realists is not hard to find. Gerard Swope, for one, was privately complimented by Roosevelt on many occasions. In October of 1935, for example, relations between most businessmen and the White House were at their lowest point since Roosevelt had entered office. For all that, he penned a sprightly note to Swope's brother Herbert (a well-known newspaper reporter and Democratic party insider) to the effect that "you and Gerard

should rate not as twins but as quintuplets! And, strictly between ourselves, you amount to a whole lot more than the Dionnes." (FDR to Herbert Bayard Swope, October 29, 1935, President's Personal File 2943, FDR Library.) Swope's relations with Secretary of Labor Frances Perkins and Secretary of the Interior Harold Ickes were also exceedingly warm. Ickes, in fact, tried to hire Swope for his department after Swope's first retirement from GE in 1939. Unfortunately for Ickes, New York's liberal Mayor Fiorello LaGuardia snapped up Swope first, and promptly put him to work designing the first large-scale municipal public-housing program in the nation. See Frances Perkins, *The Roosevelt I Knew,* pp. 234–35; Harold Ickes, *The Secret Diary of Harold Ickes,* Vol. 3, *1939–1941* (New York: Simon and Schuster, 1954), pp. 72, 92; J. J. Huthmacher, *Senator Robert F. Wagner,* p. 206ff.

Chapter Two

1. Owen D. Young, "Courage for the Future," *Vital Speeches,* Vol. 1 (April 22, 1935), pp. 459–60.

2. The public-opinion poll results are from Ralph Levering's excellent *The Public and American Foreign Policy, 1918–1978* (New York: Foreign Policy Association and McGraw-Hill, 1978), p. 74.

3. See Robert Emmet Sherwood, *Roosevelt and Hopkins: An Intimate History* (New York: Harper and Brothers, 1948), pp. 104–11.

4. W. Averell Harriman, "Remarks to the Sun Valley Conference . . . [of the Business Council] . . . April 3–5, 1938," Box 72, Stettinius Papers; "Address by W. Averell Harriman . . . November 11, 1938," Box 73, Stettinius Papers.

5. Robert Emmet Sherwood, *Roosevelt and Hopkins,* p. 111; interview with W. Averell Harriman, November 4, 1975.

6. Robert Emmet Sherwood, *Roosevelt and Hopkins,* p. 107.

7. W. Averell Harriman to Business Council members, December 20, 1938, and Edward Stettinius to Harriman, December 29, 1938, Box 73, Stettinius Papers; interview with Harriman, November 5, 1975.

8. *New York Times,* January 7, 1939, p. 2; ibid., March 4, 1939, p. 1; ibid., May 12, 1938, p. 17.

9. Walter White to Business Council members, May 18, 1939, Box 73, Stettinius Papers; William Batt to W. Averell Harriman, March 13, 1940, Box 585, Stettinius Papers.

10. This proposal to balance federal budgets over the course of the business cycle became a centerpiece of the economic thinking of the Committee for Economic Development after its founding in 1942–1943 (see chapter 5). This was, as we shall see, due largely to the fact that Business Council members including Ralph Flanders were the moving spirits behind the CED's early research efforts. Businessmen like Henry Dennison and Ralph Flanders did not enunciate a watered-down version of Keynesian thinking overnight. According to John Kenneth Galbraith, Dennison greeted Galbraith's conversion to Keynesian theory in 1936–1937 with no great shock or disdain. "One evening," Galbraith has written in a chapter of an as yet unpublished autobiography, "I told Dennison that Keynes' argument (in the *General Theory of Employment, Interest, and Money*) bore out his own view. Dennison expressed no surprise; he thought that some day some economist would see things as they were. He had always been impressed by Keynes' independence of mind." (Galbraith to author, December 18, 1973. For further details of the John Kenneth

Galbraith–Henry Dennison relationship, see Kim McQuaid, "Henry S. Dennison and a 'Science' of Industrial Reform, 1900–1950," *American Journal of Economics and Sociology,* Vol. 36 [January, 1977], pp. 91–93.)

As for Flanders, his views were clear in a letter that he wrote to Dean Wallace H. Donham of the Harvard Business School in 1931:

"I feel that the [federal] Government must come to long-time budgeting instead of trying to balance the budget in a given fiscal year. The latter practice is pernicious.

"In the course of a business cycle there is a time to tax and a time to expand expenditures and a time to contract them. There is a time to expand currency and credit and a time to contract them. One of our most urgent lines of action will be to get this viewpoint understood and acted upon by Congress and the administration." (Flanders to Donham, December 15, 1931, Wallace B. Donham Papers, Baker Library, Harvard Business School.) For a later statement of Flanders' views, see his *Platform for America* (New York: Harper and Row, 1936). The Ralph Flanders Papers deposited at the Syracuse University Library are the best single source for the motivations behind Ralph Flanders et al., *Toward Full Employment* (New York: Whittlesey House, 1938).

11. Eliot Janeway, *The Struggle for Survival: A Chronicle of Economic Mobilization During World War II* (New Haven, Conn.: Yale University Press, 1951), pp. 53–60.

12. Eliot Janeway, *The Struggle for Survival,* pp. 62, 65; Hugh Johnson to Edward Stettinius, August 21, 1939, Box 74, Stettinius Papers.

13. Ralph Levering, *The Public and American Foreign Policy, 1918–1978,* pp. 77–78.

14. I. F. Stone, *Business as Usual: The First Year of Defense* (New York: Modern Age, 1941), pp. 13–14.

15. For the shift in business opinion on mobilization in the period from 1939 to 1940, see Roland N. Stromberg, "American Business and the Approach of War, 1935–1941," *Journal of Economic History,* Vol. 12 (Winter, 1953), pp. 69, 72–75.

16. Bruce Catton, *The War Lords of Washington* (New York: Harcourt, Brace, 1948), p. 101.

17. For Swope's cynicism, see Irving S. Michelman, *The Crisis Meeters: Business Response to Social Crises* (Clifton, N.J.: A. M. Kelley, 1973), pp. 268–69.

18. David Lilienthal, *The Journals of David Lilienthal: The TVA Years, 1939–1945* (New York: Harper and Row, 1964), pp. 218–19. See also C. E. Pickett to Gerard Swope, July 27, 1934, and Owen Young to Swope, June 2, 1936, and August 10, 1936, Box 8, Owen D. Young Papers, Van Hornesville, N.Y.; for the prevalence of Jewish entrepreneurs among FDR's political backers, see Herman Krooss, *Executive Opinion,* p. 185.

Financier and longtime Business Council activist Sidney Weinberg was another prominent Jewish businessman who broke with Roosevelt in 1940 after voting for him in 1932 and 1936. See Studs Terkel, *Hard Times: An Oral History of the Great Depression* (New York: Avon, 1971), p. 94.

19. David Lilienthal, *The Journals of David Lilienthal: The Venturesome Years, 1950–1955* (New York: Harper and Row, 1964), pp. 329–30; Joseph Barnes, *Wendell Willkie* (New York: Simon and Schuster, 1952), pp. 319–20.

20. Owen Young to Wendell Willkie, July 30, 1940, and November (*sic:* October) 15, 1940, Box 34, Young Papers; William O. Douglas, *Go East Young Man, The Early Years: The Autobiography of William O. Douglas* (New York: Simon and Schuster, 1974), p. 423; Joseph Barnes, *Wendell Willkie,* pp. 157–58; Samuel

Crowther to Donaldson Brown, August 16, 1940, and Brown to Crowther, August 20, 1940, Box 119, Stettinius Papers.

21. For the "socialist" fears even among the corporate *cognoscenti,* see, for example, John Hancock to Edward Stettinius, October 18, 1939, Box 74, Stettinius Papers. For less cogent corporate critiques, see the comments in Herman Krooss, *Executive Opinion.* For the "fringe" efforts to forward public power, and for the White House and congressional squelching of same, see Gerald T. White, *Billions for Defense: Government Financing by the Defense Plant Corporation During World War II* (University, Ala.: University of Alabama Press, 1980), pp. 36, 160.

22. For the lackadasical nature of America's World War I industrial mobilization, see Robert D. Cuff, *The War Industries Board: Business-Government Relations during World War I* (Baltimore: Johns Hopkins University Press, 1973), pp. 133–34, 204–19.

23. Bruce Catton, *The War Lords of Washington,* p. 46.

24. I. F. Stone, *Business as Usual,* pp. 161–67; "Report of the Committee on the Renegotiation of War Contracts . . . , January 14, 1943" and the accompanying Business Council minutes of that date, Box 76, Lou Holland Papers, Harry S. Truman Library, Independence, Mo.

25. Blair Bolles, *How to Get Rich in Washington* (New York: W. W. Norton, 1952), pp. 243–44, 247, 256; Gerald T. White, *Billions for Defense,* p. 7.

26. Stimson quote in John Morton Blum, *V was for Victory: Politics and American Culture during World War II* (New York: Harcourt Brace Jovanovich, 1976), p. 122; Blair Bolles, *How to Get Rich in Washington,* p. 47.

27. Quote in Gerald T. White, *Billions for Defense,* pp. 1–2.

28. Gerald T. White, *Billions for Defense,* passim, especially pp. 10, 132, 141; I. F. Stone, *Business as Usual,* p. 183; Eliot Janeway, *The Struggle for Survival,* pp. 1–46.

29. I. F. Stone, *Business as Usual,* pp. 129–30.

30. William Batt to Edward Stettinius, May 20, 1940, Box 627, Stettinius Papers.

31. Alan S. Milward, *War, Economy, and Society, 1939–1945* (Berkeley, Calif.: University of California Press, 1979), p. 104; Eliot Janeway, *The Struggle for Survival,* pp. 266–68.

32. For background on Nelson, see the statements of Nelson's friend and supporter Bruce Catton in his *The War Lords of Washington,* pp. 40–110.

33. Alan S. Milward, *War, Economy, and Society, 1939–1945,* p. 104. For the Controlled Materials Plan, see Alfred D. Chandler, Jr., "The Large Industrial Corporation," in Stephen E. Ambrose, ed., *Institutions in Modern America* (Baltimore: Johns Hopkins University Press, 1967), pp. 92–94; Eliot Janeway, *The Struggle for Survival,* pp. 315–17.

34. Bruce Catton, *The War Lords of Washington,* p. 115; Eliot Janeway, *The Struggle for Survival,* p. 296.

35. Bruce Catton, *The War Lords of Washington,* pp. 200–201.

36. Ibid.

37. For the "super-umpire" quote, and for Nelson's fall from grace, see Bruce Catton, *The War Lords of Washington,* pp. 202–207.

38. The author here owes a debt—as have many historians before him—to William Leuchtenburg's essay "The New Deal and the Analogue of War," in John Braeman et al., eds., *Change and Continuity,* pp. 81–143.

39. "Minutes of the Business Council Meeting of November 14–16, 1941," Box 627, Stettinius Papers.

Chapter Three

1. John Morton Blum, *V was for Victory,* p. 123.

2. "Remarks of Jesse Jones and R. R. Deupree . . . , January 30, 1943," File A-24, Kirstein Papers.

3. For Business Council statements opposing the Wagner Act and its elaborations, see "Report on Labor Policy . . . February 7, 1938," Box 72, Stettinius Papers; "Minutes of the General Council Meeting . . . June 1–2, 1939," Box 73, Stettinius Papers (where opposition to the LaFollette Oppressive Labor Practices Act of 1939 was expressed); *New York Times,* June 3, 1939, p. 1 (where an impatient Harry Hopkins told a Council delegation that "the success of the Council does not require that government should meet business half way"); undated memo from Benjamin V. Chen to Harry Hopkins (ca. March, 1940), detailing objections to proposed Council amendments to the National Labor Relations Act and the Fair Labor Standards Act, Harry Hopkins Papers, FDR Library; "Minutes of the Council Meeting of August 27, 1940" file, Box 92, Stettinius Papers (for Council reluctance to accept Sidney Hillman's request to come out with a clear statement on industrial unionism of some kind); and "Report of the Labor Policy Committee . . . November 14, 1941," File A-24, Kirstein Papers (where the Council came out, yet again, against trade union "coercion" on the eve of Pearl Harbor).

For the wide-ranging corporate efforts to eviscerate the Wagner Act via the judicial system, see James A. Gross, *The Making of the National Labor Relations Board,* pp. 3, 198–203 and Harry A. Millis and Emily C. Brown, *From the Wagner Act to Taft-Hartley: A Study of National Labor Policy and Labor Relations* (Chicago: University of Chicago Press, 1950), pp. 33, 79–88, 106.

4. In recent years, a good deal of nonsense has been written about this 1937 agreement between U.S. Steel and the CIO. Libertarian and neo-Marxist scholars alike tend to view the signing as indicative of a wide-ranging rapprochement between the nation's big-business and labor leaderships. For a succinct and devastating critique of such views, see Melvyn Dubovsky and Warren Van Tine, *John L. Lewis: A Biography* (New York: Quadrangle/New York Times Books, 1977), pp. 273–77. For internal U.S. Steel materials confirming Dubovsky and Van Tine's analysis, see "Agreement between U.S. Steel [Carnegie-Illinois Steel Corporation] and Steelworkers Organizing Committee . . . , March 17, 1937," in "Labor Policy: General Instructions for Procedure . . . June 15, 1937" file, Box 51, Stettinius Papers; editorial in the *Daily Metal Trade* of July 10, 1937, copy in Box 50, Stettinius Papers; John Elting, "How U.S. Steel Works With the Union," *Forbes,* March 15, 1938, p. 12ff.; unsigned memorandum detailing U.S. Steel's collective bargaining policy in "Finance Committee Matter . . . , April 11, 1939" file, Box 66, Stettinius Papers.

5. Swope was particularly active in efforts to formulate nationwide mediation and conciliation procedures and to end the internecine warfare that was occurring between the crafts leaders of the AFL and the industrial unionists of the CIO. In June of 1938, for example, Swope and two other Council members (Henry Harriman and Charles Hook of Armco Steel) were appointed to a presidential commission that traveled to Sweden and England to investigate those nations' arbitration and collective-bargaining procedures. Swope, the chairman of the group, returned to America and made complimentary comments about Sweden's experience. The report his

commission wrote, however, had no substantial effect. Swope was somewhat more successful in his attempts to mediate AFL and CIO frictions. On October 8, 1938, presidential assistant James Early wrote Roosevelt that Swope had just called him to say that he had had "very satisfactory" conversations with John L. Lewis and Sidney Hillman of the CIO. Swope believed, Early added, that "if the AF of L selected three or four men and the CIO selected three or four and at least two neutrals from the outside . . . this group could sit about the table right now and have an excellent chance to work out a solution to the whole labor dispute problem." For all of Swope's entree with CIO leaders, his optimism in this matter, too, was decidedly misplaced. (For the Sweden-England visit, see Arthur Krock, "In the Nation: The Swope Commission," *New York Times,* June 24, 1938, p. 18; Gerard Swope, "Much Merit Seen in Swedish Employer-Employee Agreements," ibid., May 21, 1939; ibid., October 27, 1938, p. 15; David Loth, *Swope of G.E.,* pp. 230–31ff.; For Swope's efforts to ameliorate the AFL-CIO feud, see Stephen Early to FDR, October 8, 1938, President's Personal File 2943, FDR Library. For a good summary of the intensity of AFL-CIO frictions during the late 1930's, see Harry A. Millis and Emily C. Brown, *From the Wagner Act to Taft-Hartley,* pp. 204–5.

6. James MacGregor Burns, *Roosevelt: The Soldier of Freedom* (New York: Harcourt Brace Jovanovich, 1970), p. 117; *New York Times,* December 11, 1941, p. 34; ibid., December 31, 1941, p. 16; *Time,* December 22, 1941, p. 35.

7. James MacGregor Burns, *Roosevelt: The Soldier of Freedom,* pp. 194–96; Geoffrey Perrett, *Days of Sadness, Years of Triumph: The American People, 1939–1945* (Baltimore: Penguin, 1974), pp. 265–66.

8. For the depth of the animosity between AFL and CIO affiliates in this period, see, for example, Harry A. Millis and Emily C. Brown, *From the Wagner Act to Taft-Hartley,* pp. 204–12.

9. Joel Seidman, *American Labor From Defense to Reconversion* (Chicago: University of Chicago Press, 1953), p. 94.

10. National War Labor Board, *Termination Report,* Vol. 2 (Washington, D.C.: Government Printing Office, 1946), pp. 2, 4. Later, the U.S. Chamber of Commerce and the NAM were asked to help supply the industrial members of the Board as late as January of 1944; however, Business Council minutes recorded that neither organization was providing the Business Council very much help in this regard ("Minutes of the Council Meeting of January 12–13, 1944," Box 160, Holland Papers.)

Professor Howell J. Harris of the University of Durham will shortly publish a book on businessmen and labor policy during the 1940's with the University of Wisconsin Press. On the basis of draft chapters that the author has read, the book should be well worth the attention of readers interested in the subject.

11. The three Council members on the NDMB were: Cyrus Ching, Walter Teagle, and Roger Lapham. Council members George Mead and Rolland J. Hamilton were the alternate employer delegates. William Marx Wolff, Jr., "Peak Business Associations in National Politics: The Business Council and the Committee for Economic Development," (Ph.D. thesis, Tufts University, 1978), p. 176.

12. "Minutes of the General [Council] . . . Meeting of October 9, 1941," File A-24, Kirstein Papers.

13. All quotes are from the Council statement of March 20, 1942, entitled "Compulsory Maintenance of Union Membership," copy in File A-24, Kirstein Papers.

14. The standard source for wartime labor-relations policy is Joel Seidman, *American Labor from Defense to Reconversion.*

15. Joel Seidman, *American Labor from Defense to Reconversion,* pp. 94–102, 106; William H. Davis, "Aims and Policies of the National War Labor Board," *Annals of the American Academy of Political and Social Science,* Vol. 224 (November, 1942), pp. 141–45; *Time,* May 4, 1942, p. 13.

16. Unions had enrolled 10.5 million members in December of 1941. Almost four years later, their rolls had swelled to 14.7 million (Joel Seidman, *American Labor from Defense to Reconversion,* p. 195).

17. "Minutes of the Council Meeting of May 12–13, 1944," Box 160, Holland Papers.

18. Otis L. Graham, *Toward a Planned Society: From Roosevelt to Nixon* (New York: Oxford University Press, 1976), pp. 52–58.

19. Charles E. Merriam, "The National Resources Planning Board: A Chapter in American Planning Experience," *American Political Science Review,* Vol. 38 (December, 1944), p. 1080.

20. For the effect of the Beveridge report, see Alan S. Milward, *War, Economy, and Society, 1939–1945,* pp. 340–41. More complete treatments are provided in Walter Trattner, *From Poor Law to Welfare State* (New York: Free Press, 1974) and Richard Titmuss, *Essays on the Welfare State* (Boston: Beacon Press, 1969).

21. The full text of the Economic Bill of Rights message is in *The Public Papers of Franklin D. Roosevelt,* Vol. 13, *1944–1945* (Washington, D.C.: Government Printing Office, 1946), p. 32 and in Henry Steele Commager, ed., *Documents in American History,* 7th ed. (New York: Appleton-Century-Crofts, 1963), pp. 483–85.

22. William Benton to Paul Hoffman, October 14, 1941, Paul Hoffman Papers, Box 40, Truman Library.

23. Benton and Hoffman's early organizational efforts are covered in Robert M. Collins, "Positive Business Responses to the New Deal: The Roots of the Committee for Economic Development, 1933–1942," *Business History Review,* Vol. 52 (Autumn, 1978), pp. 384–88 and Karl Schriftgeisser, *Business Comes of Age: The Story of the Committee for Economic Development and its Impact Upon the Economic Policies of the United States, 1940–1960* (New York: Harper and Row, 1960), pp. 1–22.

24. Karl Schriftgeisser, *Business Comes of Age,* p. 19.

25. Jesse Jones, *Fifty Billion Dollars: My Thirteen Years with the FRC, 1932–1935* (New York: Macmillan, 1951), pp. 257ff.; Grace Tully, *F.D.R.—My Boss* (New York: Viking Press, 1949), pp. 188–91; Robert M. Collins, "Positive Business Responses to the New Deal," *Business History Review,* Vol. 52 (Autumn, 1978), p. 386.

26. Karl Schriftgeisser, *Business Comes of Age,* pp. 18–22; "Minutes of the General Council Meeting of April 9, 1942," File A-24, Kirstein Papers; see also the correspondence between Jesse Jones and Council leaders in File 102517/36, Record Group 40, National Archives.

27. Jesse Jones to S. Clay Williams, June 25, 1942, File 102517/36, Record Group 40, National Archives.

28. Other members of the CED Research Committee during its crucial early years were: Donald David, president of Harvard Business School (who was made a member of the Business Council in 1944); Max Epstein, chairman of the General American Transportation Company of Chicago; Eric Johnston, who became the president of the United States Chamber of Commerce in 1942 and a Business Council member in 1943; and S. Bayard Colgate, chairman of the Colgate-Palmolive Company. See Karl Schriftgeisser, *Business Comes of Age,* p. 62.

29. Robert A. Brady, "The CED: What Is It and Why?," *Antioch Review,* Vol. 4 (Spring, 1944), p. 24.

30. James M. Kemper (Commerce Trust Company, Kansas City, Mo.) to Carroll

L. Wilson and Jesse Jones, June 24, 1942, File 102517/36, Record Group 40, National Archives. (Kemper was the son of a man who had been a Business Council member from its formation in 1933 until his death in 1938.)

31. The "New Deal ploy" phrase was used by Jesse Jones, among others. See Karl Schriftgeisser, *Business Comes of Age,* pp. 18–19.

32. The closeness of the cooperation between CED and the Commerce Department is attested to by the fact that Jesse Jones allowed the new business organization to have free office space in the Commerce Department building in Washington for the first several years of its existence. For this and other data regarding CED–Commerce Department interlocks, see David Eakins, "The Development of Corporate Liberal Policy Research in the United States, 1885–1965," (Ph.D. thesis, University of Wisconsin, 1966), pp. 330–58.

33. Owen Young, by then recently retired as chairman of General Electric, was among those who also proposed a centralized approach. Young wanted, in effect, the Commerce Department to establish a tripartite business-labor-agriculture body that operated very much along the lines of GE President Swope's National Chamber of Commerce and Industry plan, first enunciated in 1933–1934. Young's proposal got nowhere, and he was not included on the roster of CED leaders. This despite the fact that Secretary of Commerce Jones had initially wanted Young to become the first chairman of the new organization. See David Eakins' thesis, p. 346; see also William Marx Wolff's thesis, pp. 261–62.

Proof that the process of structuring the CED reflected a conscious effort to cooperate with the Chamber of Commerce and the NAM is provided by the following excerpts from a letter that Business Council member S. Clay Williams wrote to Jesse Jones on July 2, 1942:

"I was glad to learn . . . last week that the new [CED] plan includes, in addition to the broad purposes disclosed at [the Business Council meeting] at Hot Springs, specific features [for cooperation with the NAM and Chamber of Commerce, and that it] includes the opportunity of availing indirectly of the forces they represent.

"Your thinking was way ahead of mine in another respect, too, in that I had not seen the definite advantages of attempting this tie-in through the new organization [CED] instead of with the Business . . . Council." (Clayton to Jones, July 2, 1942, Record Group 40, File 102517/36, National Archives.)

34. Robert A. Brady, "The CED: What Is It and Why?," *Antioch Review,* Vol. 4 (Spring, 1944), pp. 28–29; Karl Schriftgeisser, *Business and Public Policy: The Role of the Committee for Economic Development, 1942–1967* (Englewood Cliffs, N.J.: Prentice-Hall, 1967), p. 2

35. David Eakins' thesis, pp. 344–45; Karl Schriftgeisser, *Business and Public Policy,* p. 2.

36. Karl Schriftgeisser, *Business Comes of Age,* pp. 48–49.

37. William B. Benton, "The Economics of a Free Society: A Declaration of American Economic Policy," *Fortune,* October, 1944, pp. 162–65.

38. Ralph Levering, *The Public and American Foreign Policy, 1918–1978,* p. 97.

Chapter Four

1. "Minutes of the General Council Meeting . . . January 14, 143," copy in Box 76, Holland Papers.

2. Ralph Flanders to Robert F. Lenhart, March 6, 1945, "CED—1945" file, Donald K. David Papers, Baker Library, Harvard Business School.

3. Stephen Bailey, *Congress Makes a Law: The Story Behind the Employment Act of 1946* (New York: Columbia University Press, 1950), pp. 57–58; G. William Domhoff, *The Powers That Be* (New York: Alfred A. Knopf, 1978), pp. 109–10.

4. Stephen Bailey, *Congress Makes a Law*, pp. 4–5, 133–41. The U.S. Chamber of Commerce, though opposed to the full-employment bill, did not testify for or against the legislation before Congress. This inactivity was due to the fact that Chamber President Eric Johnston did not oppose the bill as it was eventually "modified" by conservative interests including the CED.

5. Ralph Flanders to Robert Wagner, June 14, 1945, copy in Box 40, William S. Clayton Papers, Truman Library.

6. Donald David to George Humphrey, July 12, 1945, "BAC—1945" file, David Papers. (Underlining in original.)

7. Paul Hoffman to Donald David, July 19, 1945, "CED—1945" file, David Papers.

8. Quoted in Karl Schriftgeisser, *Business Comes of Age*, pp. 96–97.

9. Stephen Bailey, *Congress Makes a Law*, p. 123.

10. Ibid., pp. 117, 134–49; David Eakins' thesis, pp. 391–98.

11. "Minutes of the Council Meeting of October 26–27, 1945" and Donald David to H. E. Babcock, October 18, 1945, in "BAC—1945" file, David Papers.

12. Stephen Bailey, *Congress Makes a Law*, p. 163.

13. Ibid., p. 166.

14. William Marx Wolff's thesis, pp. 325–30, especially p. 326.

15. Donald David to Walter White, February 13, 1946, "BAC—1946" file, David Papers.

16. Otis L. Graham, Jr., *Toward a Planned Society*, pp. 88–90; Daniel Patrick Moynihan, *The Politics of a Guaranteed Income: The Nixon Administration and the Family Assistance Plan* (New York: Random House, 1973), pp. 94–95; Karl Schriftgeisser, *Business Comes of Age*, pp. 96–97; Alonzo Hamby, *Beyond the New Deal: Harry S. Truman and American Liberalism* (New York: Columbia University Press, 1973), pp. 63–69.

To keep abreast of developments within the Council of Economic Advisers after its creation, the Business Council appointed a Committee on Economic Policy to cooperate with the new research body. Marion Folsom became chairman, and Donald David vice-chairman. Both had done yeoman service in the battle against the full-employment bill.

17. Karl Schriftgeisser, *Business Comes of Age*, pp. 73–75. For the NAM's conservative postwar shift, see Philip H. Burch, Jr., "The NAM as an Interest Group," *Politics and Society*, Fall, 1973, pp. 97–130.

18. Joel Seidman, *American Labor From Defense to Reconversion*, pp. 109–17.

19. Elias Lieberman, *Unions Before the Bar* (New York: Harper and Row, 1950), pp. 305–306; Melvin Dubovsky and Warren Van Tine, *John L. Lewis*, pp. 423–40.

20. E.g., "Between January, 1941 and July, 1945, the cost of living rose by about one-third. During this period basic wage rates [exclusive of overtime] in manufacturing increased by 24 per cent and urban wages by 32 per cent, while the weekly earnings of manufacturing employees rose 70 per cent [largely as a result of overtime employment]." During approximately the same period, after-tax corporate profits rose from $6.4 billion (in 1940) to $10.8 billion (in 1944)—an increase of 60 percent. (Joel Seidman, *American Labor From Defense to Reconversion*, pp. 128–29).

21. Eric F. Goldman, *The Crucial Decade and After: America, 1945–1960* (New York: Vintage 1960), p. 25; Joel Seidman, *American Labor From Defense to Reconversion*, p. 221; D. W. Crowther et al., "Work Stoppages Caused by Labor-

Management Disputes in 1946," *Monthly Labor Review,* Vol. 64 (April, 147), pp. 780ff.

22. Edward O'Connell to Matthew J. Connelly, August 23, 1945, quoted in Robert J. Donovan, *Conflict and Crisis: The Presidency of Harry S. Truman, 1945–1948* (New York: W. W. Norton, 1977), p. 111.

23. Robert J. Donovan, *Conflict and Crisis,* p. 119; Robert H. Ferrell, ed., *Off the Record: The Private Papers of Harry S. Truman* (New York: Harper and Row, 1980), p. 68 (entry for September 20, 1945). See also Eben A. Ayers diary, Truman Library.

24. "Labor-Management Conference on Industrial Relations," *Monthly Labor Review,* Vol. 62 (January, 1946), p. 37.

25. Ibid., pp. 38–39 (for the full membership of all the delegations to the Conference).

26. R. Alton Lee, *Truman and Taft-Hartley: A Question of Mandate* (Lexington, Ky.: University of Kentucky Press, 1966), pp. 23–26; *New York Times,* December 1, 1946, pp. 1, 10–11; Harry A. Millis and Emily C. Brown, *From the Wagner Act to Taft-Hartley,* pp. 306–11; Joel Seidman, *American Labor From Defense to Reconversion,* pp. 222–23

27. Bert Cochran, *Harry S. Truman and the Crisis Presidency* (New York: E. P. Dutton, 1973), pp. 199–200; Harry A. Millis and Emily C. Brown, *From the Wagner Act to Taft-Hartley,* pp. 253–54.

28. "Report of Committee on Labor Policy," October, 1945, Box 786, General Records of the Department of Commerce, National Archives, passim; "BAC— Membership of Committees, May, 1946," Box 17, Alfred Schindler Papers, Truman Library.

Members of the Business Council's Labor Policy Committee when the committee was "reorganized" in August of 1945 were, in addition to Chairman Hook of Armco and Vice-Chairman Prentis of Armstrong Cork: Cyrus S. Ching (U.S. Rubber), John L. Collyer (B. F. Goodrich), James D. Francis (Island Creek Coal Company), Reuben B. Robertson (Champion Paper Company), Charles Edward Wilson (General Electric), and Roger Williams (vice-president, Newport News Shipbuilding and Drydock Company). It is perhaps not without interest that long-time corporate labor-relations specialist Cyrus Ching became the first head of the Federal Mediation and Conciliation Service, which was one of the institutional creations of the Taft-Hartley Act.

29. "Report of the Committee on Labor Policy," pp. 5–8.

30. See, for example, William Green, "The Taft-Hartley Act: A Critical View," *Annals of the American Academy,* Vol. 274 (March, 1951), p. 203; Robert J. Donovan, *Conflict and Crisis,* pp. 110–20.

31. "Minutes of the General Council Meeting, December 12–13, 1945," Box 40, Clayton Papers; *New York Times,* December 1, 1945, pp. 10–12; Howell Harris, "Getting Everybody Back on the Same Team: An Interpretation of the Industrial Relations Policies of American Business in the 1940's," (Ph.D. thesis, Oxford University, 1979), pp. 178–85.

32. Harry A. Millis and Emily C. Brown, *From the Wagner Act to Taft-Hartley,* pp. 284–92. Eric Johnston, president of the U.S. Chamber of Commerce from 1942 until May of 1946, wanted to move beyond this conservative strategy and essay cooperative relationships with the AFL and CIO. Johnston was unable, however, to carry his organization with him in this effort—and so it was left to the CED and Business Council to enunciate the "moderate" business alternative by themselves. See Howell Harris' thesis, pp. 172–73.

33. Henry Ford II, "The Challenge of Human Engineering," an address to the Society of Automotive Engineers, January, 1946 (quoted in Howell Harris' thesis, p. 230).

34. Howell Harris' thesis. Chapters 5 and 6 provide an exceedingly useful summary of the full scope of these varied efforts.

35. David Eakins' thesis, p. 415.

36. Robert J. Donovan, *Conflict and Crisis,* pp. 212–13; Robert S. Ferrell, *Off the Record,* pp. 103–104.

37. "Minutes of the General Council Meeting, January 16–17, 1946," Box 53, Clayton Papers; Henry Wallace to Charles Hook, June 6, 1946, "BAC—1946" file, David Papers; "Minutes of the General Council Meeting, June 20–21, 1946," Box 17, Schindler Papers; Harry A. Millis and Emily C. Brown, *From the Wagner Act to Taft-Hartley,* p. 361 (for a summary of the Case Bill that Truman vetoed—and the Business Council supported).

38. John Morton Blum, ed., *The Price of Vision: The Diary of Henry A. Wallace, 1942–1946* (Boston: Houghton Mifflin, 1973), p. 581. Democratic urgings for compromise on labor law reform may have had some tangential effect upon the leadership of the CED. In February of 1947, as the fight over what became the Taft-Hartley Act was beginning in earnest, the CED came out with an innocuous policy statement entitled "Collective Bargaining: How to Make It More Effective." This statement, after making general declarations regarding CED opposition to jurisdictional strikes, the unionization of foremen, and boycotts, went on to support the voluntary mediation of labor-management disputes and suggested other noncompulsory means by which unions and management could make collective bargaining more effective on a day-to-day basis. This CED statement promised that the vexing questions of "industry-wide bargaining, the closed shop, secondary boycotts, [and] the monopolistic power of unions" would be addressed in a later policy statement. This promised report was never completed, and CED's preliminary statement regarding collective-bargaining policy apparently did not exercise any important influence during the period when the Taft-Hartley Act was in process of completion. Important CED research adviser Sumner H. Slichter eventually enunciated support for Taft-Hartley when the bill was passed by Congress. See Harry A. Millis and Emily C. Brown, *From the Wagner Act to Taft-Hartley,* p. 291; Karl Schriftgeisser, *Business and Public Policy,* pp. 161–62; "Collective Bargaining: How to Make It More Effective" (New York: Committee for Economic Development, 1947), *passim;* R. Alton Lee, *Truman and Taft-Hartley,* p. 91.

39. Harry A. Millis and Emily C. Brown, *From the Wagner Act to Taft-Hartley,* pp. 365–71; Howell Harris' thesis, pp. 193–95.

40. Harry A. Millis and Emily C. Brown, *From the Wagner Act to Taft-Hartley,* p. 385.

41. Joel Seidman, *American Labor From Defense to Reconversion,* pp. 265–67; Elias Lieberman, *Unions before the Bar,* pp. 312–30; Harry A. Millis and Emily C. Brown, *From the Wagner Act to Taft-Hartley,* pp. 588–89, 613, 640, 649; Walter M. Daniels, ed., *The American Labor Movement* (New York: H. W. Wilson, 1958), pp. 118–29. Nineteen Western and Southern states passed so-called "right to work" laws that banned the union shop.

42. One indication of the lack of popular awareness regarding the issues involved in conservative attempts to modify national labor law is that "a Gallup poll in January, 1947, reported that only 19 per cent of the population had a generally correct idea of the provisions of the Wagner Act, 12 per cent gave completely wrong

answers, and 69 per cent said that they simply did not know." (Harry A. Millis and Emily C. Brown, *From the Wagner Act to Taft-Hartley*, p. 262).

43. R. Alton Lee, *Truman and Taft-Hartley*, pp. 107ff.; Howell Harris' thesis, p. 198; "Report on Labor-Management Relations Act of 1947," January 27, 1949, p. 4, Box 77, Holland Papers.

44. Ralph Levering, *The Public and American Foreign Policy, 1918–1978*, p. 97.

45. Stephen E. Ambrose, *Rise to Globalism: American Foreign Policy, 1938–1980*, 2nd rev. ed. (New York: Penguin, 1980), pp. 139–40.

46. John Morton Blum, ed., *The Price of Vision*, pp. 560–61.

47. Ibid., pp. 626–28.

48. *New York Times*, June 23, 1947, pp. 1, 5; "Eight Men Who Will Find How Much U.S. Can Spare for Europe," *U.S. News and World Report*, Vol. 23 (September 9, 1947), pp. 52–55; David Eakins' thesis, p. 382.

The Harriman Committee was joined in its work by two other committees of government representatives that drafted specialized reports on United States natural resources and the effects of a foreign aid program on the domestic American economy. The Harriman Committee, however, was *primus inter pares.* Business Council members on the Harriman Committee included—besides Harriman himself —Hiland Batcheller (Allegheny-Ludlum Steel), John L. Collyer (B. F. Goodrich), Chester C. Davis (a former New Deal agricultural-policy administrator who had recently retired as the chairman of the Federal Reserve Bank of St. Louis), R. R. Deupree (Procter and Gamble), and Paul Hoffman (Studebaker Motors). All but Batcheller and Harriman were also CED trustees. Also affiliated with CED was Owen Young, the recently retired chairman of General Electric. Harriman, Batcheller, Collyer, Davis, Hoffman, and Young chaired six of the eight subcommittees that did the detailed work of the President's Committee on Foreign Aid.

49. Robert J. Donovan, "Harriman Committee Scales Down Europe Aid, Says That Czar Should Run It," *New York Herald Tribune*, November 9, 1947, pp. 1, 3; Karl Schriftgeisser, *Business and Public Policy*, pp. 118–19. For the initial hesitancy of some businessmen regarding aid for socialist regimes, see Owen Young to W. Averell Harriman, September 12, 1947, Box 483, Young Papers. (Young was afraid that West German socialists—unlike their opposite numbers in England— would not prove stable enough to contain the spread of communist political power.)

50. Quoted in David Eakins' thesis, p. 381; and David Eakins, "Business Planners and America's Postwar Expansion," in David Horowitz, *Corporations and the Cold War* (New York: Monthly Review Press, 1970), p. 164.

John Gimbel argues in his *The Origins of the Marshall Plan* (Stanford, Calif.: Stanford University Press, 1976) that the tone of the economic and geopolitical crisis enunciated by the Harriman Committee, Clayton, and numerous others, was, in substantial part, a conscious technique used by State Department planners and their allies to "ride the Marshall Plan home safely on the high tide of anti-Communist rhetoric and opinion (which it had helped to further)" in order to "sell" the idea of rehabilitating postwar West Germany along lines that they themselves favored. (John Gimbel, *The Origins of the Marshall Plan*, pp. 267–68, 259–60.) While elements of political calculation were not absent in the remarks of a State Department eminence like Clayton, it is important to remember that his fears of radicalism of any kind were profound. Clayton had, in fact, been an early and enthusiastic member of the American Liberty League when it was organized in 1934 to battle the "Roosevelt Revolution." I am inclined, therefore, to give more weight than Gimbel does to the view that business politicians like Clayton, Harriman, and Paul Hoffman were quite genuinely afraid of the alarming prospects that they warned of.

It is also relevant to point out that Clayton's influence in postwar Washington was very great, due largely to his close personal relations with conservative Southern Democrats who occupied strategic positions on Capitol Hill. Truman, for example, intended to offer the position of Secretary of State to Clayton in 1946 if George Marshall refused the post. When Marshall retired in 1949, Truman again tried to recruit Clayton for the post, but later told his White House aides that the opposition of Clayton's wife to his remaining in Washington had led Clayton to withdraw his name from consideration. Even John Kenneth Galbraith liked Clayton. See John Kenneth Galbraith, *A Life in Our Times* (Boston: Houghton Mifflin, 1981), pp. 39–40, 168–69, 240–41; William Benton to Clayton, August 22, 1947, Box 61, Clayton Papers; and Ayers Diary, p. 72 (April 21, 1949).

51. Truman's message to Congress requesting the Marshall Plan hit at the same economic points that Clayton had, before going on to address the ideological and political rationales for such assistance. See Barton J. Bernstein and Allen J. Matusow, *The Truman Administration: A Documentary History* (New York: Torchbooks, 1966), pp. 266–67.

52. David S. McLelland and Clark E. Woodhouse, "The Business Elite and Foreign Policy," *Western Political Quarterly,* Vol. 13 (1960), pp. 175–78.

53. James Marion Jones, *The Fifteen Weeks: February 21–June 5, 1947* (New York: Harcourt, Brace and World, 1964), pp. 117–25; Karl Schriftgeisser, *Business and Public Policy,* p. 119; Owen Young to Arthur Vandenberg, March 9, 1948, Box 483, Young Papers.

54. Robert H. Ferrell, *Off the Record,* p. 129; David Eakins' thesis, pp. 384–85.

55. Owen Young to Paul Hoffman, April 9, 1948, and Young to W. Averell Harriman, April 22, 1948, Box 483, Young Papers; Paul F. Douglass, *Six Upon the World: An American Culture for an Industrial Age* (Boston: Little, Brown, 1954), p. 35.

56. David Eakins' thesis, pp. 385–86.

57. Theodore A. Wilson, *The Marshall Plan: An Atlantic Venture of 1947–1951 and How It Shaped Our World* (New York: Foreign Policy Association, 1977), p. 38. Harriman, Philip D. Reed of GE, and other corporate political activists came in for some censure regarding their willingness to tolerate the continued existence of cartels, particularly in West Germany. See, for example, James Stewart Martin, *All Honorable Men* (Boston: Little, Brown, 1950), especially pp. 264–300.

58. Cabell Phillips, "Truman's New Romance: The Businessman," *Collier's,* Vol. CXXV (June 3, 1950), p. 11.

59. For a discussion of Keyserling's beliefs, see Alonzo L. Hamby, *Beyond the New Deal,* pp. 295–303. See also Leon Keyserling's Oral History Memoir at the Truman Library.

60. Cabell Phillips, "Truman's New Romance: The Businessman," *Collier's,* Vol. CXXV (June 3, 1950), p. 12–13.

61. A. E. Holmans, *United States Fiscal Policy, 1945–1959: Its Contribution to Economic Stability* (London: Oxford University Press, 1961), p. 184; Bert Cochran, *Harry Truman and the Crisis Presidency,* pp. 340–41.

62. "Summary Notes on Special Meeting of the Business Advisory Council . . . , July 26, 1950," Box 76, Holland Papers; "Report of Council Activities for the Year 1950," Box 38-S, Winthrop W. Aldrich Papers, Baker Library, Harvard Business School; Fred Lazarus, Jr., to Walter White, January 20, 1951, Box 89, Clayton Papers; *New York Times,* October 17, 1950, p. 53; ibid., November 6, 1950, p. 1; ibid., November 5, 1950, p. 20; A. E. Holmans, *United States Fiscal Policy,*

1945–1959, pp. 144–45; Gerald T. White, *Billions for Defense,* pp. 140–43; Blair Bolles, *How to Get Rich in Washington,* passim.

63. *New York Times,* January 13, 1951, p. 10; ibid., May 19, 1951, p. 7; ibid., May 29, 1951, p. 14.

64. Edward S. Flash, Jr., *Economic Advice and Presidential Leadership: The Council of Economic Advisers* (New York: Columbia University Press, 1965), pp. 66–67; Alonzo Hamby, *Beyond the New Deal,* pp. 446–49; Craufurd D. Goodwin, ed., *Exhortation and Controls: The Search for a Wage-Price Policy, 1945–1971* (Washington, D.C.: Brookings Institution, 1975), pp. 76–79.

65. "Draft of Tax Policy Statement, Committee on Taxation [Business Advisory Council, February, 1951]," p. 3, Box 77, Holland Papers.

66. Ibid., p. 4.

67. Ibid., p. 1; see also *New York Times,* March 16, 1951, p. 41.

68. Karl Schriftgeisser, *Business and Public Policy,* pp. 50–51; A. E. Holmans, *United States Fiscal Policy, 1945–1959,* pp. 161–77.

69. A. E. Holmans, *United States Fiscal Policy, 1945–1959,* p. 170; Hubert H. Humphrey, *The Education of a Public Man: My Life in Politics* (Garden City, N.Y.: Doubleday, 1976), p. 139.

70. *New York Times,* May 12, 1951, p. 13; ibid., May 13, 1951, p. 26; ibid., September 14, 1951, pp. 37, 40; ibid., August 26, 1951, Section 6, pp. 9ff.; ibid., December 2, 1951, p. 65; ibid., March 14, 1952, p. 9; ibid., May 20, 1952, p. 30; ibid., June 4, 1952, p. 19; see also "Minutes of the General Council Meeting of May 9–10, 1952," Box 77, Holland Papers.

Chapter Five

1. Robert H. Ferrell, ed., *The Eisenhower Diaries* (New York: W. W. Norton, 1981), p. 161.

2. A convenient summary of Taft's very often conflicting views is contained in Ronald Radosh, *Prophets of the Right: Profiles of Conservative Critics of American Globalism* (New York: Simon and Schuster, 1975), pp. 160–90; see also Arthur Larson, *Eisenhower: The President Nobody Knew* (New York: Charles Scribner's Sons, 1968), pp. 68–69.

3. Robert H. Ferrell, ed., *The Eisenhower Diaries,* pp. 197–98, 203–204.

4. For Clay's importance in the draft-Ike effort see the numerous letters in Box 24 of the Prepresidential Papers, Name File, Dwight D. Eisenhower Library, Abilene, Kans.

Clay became an active member of the Business Council in 1950 and served an initial term of five years. He was reappointed to the Council in 1956, and served a second term until 1961. From 1961 until 1968, Clay enjoyed honorary membership in the organization. Marshall's involvement was apparently a good deal less extensive than Clay's. He joined the Council in 1949, served until 1955, and assumed honorary status in 1957. On one occasion, Marshall (then serving as Secretary of Defense for Truman) briefed the Business Council on defense mobilization policy at the Pentagon. The available record shows no other Council-related activity on Marshall's part. (John W. Burke [executive secretary, Business Council] to author, April 24, 1981; "Remarks of the Secretary of Defense at the BAC Conference, January 18, 1951," copy in the Ralph Flanders Papers, Syracuse University.)

5. John Bartlow Martin, *Adlai Stevenson of Illinois* (Garden City, N.Y.: Doubleday, 1976), pp. 125, 165, 169, 540, 611, 637–38.

6. Bernard Sternsher, "Liberalism in the Fifties: The Travail of Redefinition," *Antioch Review,* Vol. XXII (September, 1952), pp. 315–31; John Fischer, "The Lost Liberals: Can They Find a Road Map?," *Harper's,* Vol. 194 (May, 1947), pp. 385–95; James A. Wechsler, *Reflections of an Angry Middle-aged Editor* (New York: Random House, 1960), pp. 47–67; Karl Kaysen, "Big Business and the Liberals: Then and Now," *The New Republic,* Vol. 131 (November 22, 1954), pp. 118–20; David Lilienthal, *Big Business: A New Era* (New York: Harper and Brothers, 1953), passim; Robert B. Westbrook, "Tribune of the Technostructure: The Popular Economics of Stuart Chase," *American Quarterly,* Vol. 32 (Fall, 1980), pp. 387–408; Leonard and Mark Silk, *The American Establishment* (New York: Basic Books, 1981), p. 65.

7. The "ambulatory quorum" phrase is Bryce Harlow's. Harlow served as Eisenhower's main contact man with Congress throughout his presidency. (Harlow to author, March 28, 1980.)

8. Hobart Rowen, "America's Most Powerful Private Club," *Harper's,* Vol. 221 (September, 1960), pp. 79–84; Lucius Clay confirms the accuracy of Rowen's observations in his oral history project memoir deposited at the Eisenhower Library, pp. 50–59; the "gold mine" quote is from Ralph Flanders' autobiography, *Senator from Vermont* (Boston: Houghton Mifflin, 1961), p. 183.

Lucius Clay's role in selecting George Humphrey as Secretary of the Treasury is confirmed by another Washington reporter of the period who went on to edit Humphrey's official papers. Humphrey, the reporter notes, first met Clay when Clay was American military chief in defeated postwar Germany and Humphrey was one of the legion of corporate CEOs recruited by Paul Hoffman and W. Averell Harriman to assist in the work of the Economic Cooperation Administration. Robert Stevens and Charles Wilson of GM probably met Clay in a similar fashion. See Nathaniel R. Howard, ed., *The Basic Papers of George M. Humphrey as Secretary of the Treasury, 1953–1957* (Cleveland: Western Reserve Historical Society, 1965), p. xxvii..

9. Herbert S. Parmet, *Eisenhower and the American Crusades* (New York: Macmillan, 1972), pp. 157, 159, 295–97.

10. For a useful overview of recruitment patterns in the various Cabinet-level agencies, see John McDonald, "The Businessman in Government," *Fortune* (July, 1954), pp. 68–70, 158. For the efficiency analogies applied to the administration's social welfare programs, see Edward D. Berkowitz and Kim McQuaid, "Welfare Reform in the 1950's," *The Social Service Review,* Vol. 54 (March, 1980), pp. 45–58.

11. *Public Papers of the Presidents: Dwight D. Eisenhower, 1953* (Washington, D.C.: Government Printing Office, 1954), pp. 100–103. For the Business and Defense Services Administration, see Michael D. Reagan, "The BDSA, 1953–1957," *The Western Political Quarterly,* Vol. 14 (June, 1961), pp. 570–81. Commerce Department leaders hoped to expand the scope of the Business Council model to include no less than twenty industry-specific councils with nongovernmental chairmen, agendas set by industry rather than government, and privately financed staffs. Opposition from the Department of Justice short-circuited the creation of most of these councils. However, one industry-specific council, the National Petroleum Council established on the eve of the Second World War, was allowed to function along Business Council lines. For congressional concern regarding these matters, see U.S. Congress, House Judiciary Committee, Antitrust Subcommittee, "Interim Re-

port on WOCs and Government Advisory Groups," 84th Congress, 2nd session (Washington, D.C.: Government Printing Office, 1956), pp. 7–8.

12. "Minutes of the General Council Meeting, April 30–May 1, 1948," p. 5, "BAC—1948" file, David Papers.

13. Bert Cochran, *Harry S. Truman and the Crisis Presidency,* p. 290; Robert H. Ferrell, *The Eisenhower Diaries,* pp. 209, 212–13; Geoffrey Perrett, *A Dream of Greatness: The American People, 1945–1963* (New York: Coward, McCann and Geoghegan, 1980), pp. 168, 406–407.

14. *Historical Statistics of the United States: Colonial Times to 1970,* Vol. 2 (Washington, D.C.: Government Printing Office, 1976), p. 1114.

15. Nathaniel R. Howard, ed., *The Basic Papers of George M. Humphrey,* p. 41.

16. Arthur Larson, *Eisenhower: The President Nobody Knew,* p. 23.

17. David Lilienthal, *The Journals of David E. Lilienthal: The Venturesome Years, 1950–1955,* p. 449.

18. Richard M. Fried, *Men Against McCarthy* (New York: Columbia University Press, 1976), pp. 91, 200–217, 295–313, 362 (n. 112).

19. Ralph M. Flanders Oral History Project Memoir, Eisenhower Library, pp. 1–15; Charles J. V. Murphy, "McCarthy and the Businessman," *Fortune* (April, 1954), pp. 156ff.

20. Richard M. Fried, *Men Against McCarthy,* pp. 279–80; Fred Cook, *The Nightmare Decade: The Life and Times of Senator Joe McCarthy* (New York: Random House, 1971), pp. 494–508.

21. Hobart Rowen, "America's Most Powerful Private Club," *Harper's,* Vol. 221 (September, 1960), p. 84.

22. Mira Wilkins, *The Maturing of Multinational Enterprise: American Business Abroad from 1914 to 1970* (Cambridge: Harvard University Press, 1970), p. 289.

23. Thomas V. DiBacco, "American Business and Foreign Aid: The Eisenhower Years," *Business History Review,* Vol. XLI (Spring, 1967), pp. 23–25; Lucius D. Clay, Sr., Oral History Memoir, Eisenhower Library, p. 95; Nathaniel R. Howard, ed., *The Basic Papers of George M. Humphrey,* p. 83.

24. "Report of Committee on Foreign Economic Policy—October 23, 1954," quoted in U.S. Congress, House Judiciary Committee, Antitrust Subcommittee, "Hearings on WOC's and Government Advisory Groups," Part II (Washington, D.C.: Government Printing Office, 1955), pp. 1093–94; Clarence B. Randall, *A Foreign Economic Policy for the United States* (Chicago: University of Chicago Press, 1954), pp. 8, 20–24. Contrast Randall's book with Paul G. Hoffman, *World Without Want* (New York: Harper and Row, 1960), passim.

25. David S. McLellan and Charles E. Woodhouse, "The Business Elite and Foreign Policy," *Western Political Quarterly,* Vol. 13 (1960), pp. 182–83; David A. Baldwin, *Economic Development and American Foreign Policy, 1943–1962* (Chicago: University of Chicago Press, 1966), pp. 64 65, 148–52, 214–16.

26. Thomas V. DiBacco, "American Business and Foreign Aid: The Eisenhower Years," *Business History Review,* Vol. XLI (Spring, 1967), p. 26.

27. Dwight D. Eisenhower, *Waging Peace: The White House Years, 1956–1961* (Garden City, N.Y.: Doubleday, 1965), pp. 132–47.

28. Dwight Eisenhower to Harold Boeschenstein, November 1, 1957, and Boeschenstein to Eisenhower, November 4, 1957, Official File 2-B, White House Central Files, Box 17, Eisenhower Library; Harold Boeschenstein Oral History Project Memoir, Eisenhower Library, passim.

29. Thomas V. DiBacco, "American Business and Foreign Aid: The Eisenhower Years," *Business History Review,* Vol. XLI (Spring, 1967), p. 30; Clarence B. Ran-

dall to Robert B. Anderson et al., February 2, 1959, Official File 2-B, White House Central Files, Box 17, Eisenhower Library; Philip E. Taylor to R. J. Saulnier, November 25, 1957, Box 6, Council of Economic Advisers, Office of, Records, 1953–1961, Eisenhower Library; Frederick H. Mueller to Business Council, September 15, 1959, and George A. Wyeth to Mueller, May 20, 1959, Box 1, Frederick H. Mueller Papers, Eisenhower Library.

30. David S. McLelland and Charles E. Woodhouse, "The Business Elite and Foreign Policy," *Western Political Quarterly,* Vol. 13 (1960), pp. 186–90. Businessmen particularly prominent in the affairs of CED and the Business Council in the foreign aid struggle included Beardsley Ruml, Philip Reed, Harvey Firestone, Eric Johnston, and J. Peter Grace in addition to the men listed in the text.

31. Eisenhower became a trustee of the CED in May of 1950, while he was briefly president of Columbia University. Though he told one CED official that he was "deeply impressed" by the first CED policy statements he read and stated that he was "heartily in accord with their tenor," he was completely inactive in the affairs of the organization after he returned to Europe to head American and Allied forces there. See Prepresidential Papers (especially Eisenhower to James F. Brownlee, March 17, 1950), Name File, Box 130, Eisenhower Library.

32. Herman Krooss, *Executive Opinion,* p. 243.

33. Ralph Flanders to Wallace B. Donham, December 15, 1931, Donham Papers.

34. See Ralph Flanders, Henry S. Dennison, Lincoln Filene, and Morris Leeds, *Toward Full Employment.* For Dennison's views, see Kim McQuaid, "Henry S. Dennison and the 'Science' of Industrial Reform, 1900–1950," *American Journal of Economics and Sociology,* January, 1977, pp. 79–98.

35. Marion B. Folsom Oral History Memoir, Eisenhower Administration Vol., Columbia University Oral History Project Library, New York, pp. 30ff.; Herbert Stein, *The Fiscal Revolution in America* (Chicago: University of Chicago Press, 1969), pp. 220–40.

36. Arthur Larson, *Eisenhower: The President Nobody Knew,* p. 25.

37. Herbert Stein, *The Fiscal Revolution in America,* pp. 287–91.

38. Ibid., p. 306.

39. John Kenneth Galbraith, *American Capitalism,* pp. 80–81.

40. Robinson Newcomb to Arthur F. Burns, July 24, 1953, "CED—Depression Study—1953" file, Box 17, Arthur F. Burns Papers, Eisenhower Library.

41. Herbert Stein, "Budget Policy to Maintain Stability—October 15, 1953," "Interdepartmental Committees—CED—October, 1953" file, Box 9, Burns Papers.

42. Karl Schriftgeisser, *Business Comes of Age,* p. 103.

43. U.S. Bureau of the Census, *Historical Statistics of the United States: Colonial Times to 1957* (Washington, D.C.: Government Printing Office, 1960), pp. 710, 713, 736.

44. Herman Kroos, *Executive Opinion,* p. 243.

45. Herbert Stein, *The Fiscal Revolution in America,* pp. 222, 306–308.

46. *Newsweek,* November 19, 1956, pp. 93–94; *New York Times,* November 11, 1956, p. 56. Democratic eminences were as disgruntled with the election as were the corporate leaders of the Business Council. Truman, for example, so despised Stevenson that he backed Business Council pioneer W. Averell Harriman for the Democratic presidential nomination. Liberal economist Paul Samuelson, for his part, noted that "the joke was in 1956, there was only one man in the country who was really worried about deficit spending in his viscera and that was candidate Steven-

son." Harriman, after losing the nomination to Stevenson, wrote Truman that Stevenson had at long last accepted the New Deal. "Now," he continued, "we have to see that he accepts the [Truman] Fair Deal and moves on from there." (Oral History Interview with Walter Heller, Kermit Gordon, James Tobin, Gardiner Ackley, and Paul Samuelson, John F. Kennedy Library, Boston, p. 76; Harriman to Truman, August 31, 1956, Postpresidential Papers, Name File, Box 37, Truman Library.

47. Robert H. Ferrell, *The Eisenhower Diaries,* pp. 288–89; Arthur Larson, *Eisenhower: The President Nobody Knew,* pp. 40–41; Charles E. Alexander, *Holding the Line: The Eisenhower Era, 1952–1961* (Bloomington, Ind.: Indiana University Press, 1975), pp. 31–32; Norton Long, "American Business and American Liberals: Slogans or Responsibility?," *Political Quarterly,* Vol. 29 (April–June, 1958), pp. 173–74.

48. Herbert Stein, *The Fiscal Revolution in America,* pp. 327–57, especially p. 341.

49. Edwin L. Dale, *Conservatives in Power: A Study in Frustration* (Garden City, N.Y.: Doubleday, 1960), pp. 143–45; Dwight D. Eisenhower, *Waging Peace,* pp. 239–57; Herbert Stein, *The Fiscal Revolution in America,* pp. 316, 358–60.

50. *New York Times,* May 12, 1957, p. 70; ibid., October 26, 1957, p. 11; Paul W. McCracken to R. J. Saulnier, May 1, 1958, and Langbourne M. Williams to Paul C. Cabot, April 2, 1958, "BAC—Committee Report on Tax Policy and Foreign Investment" file, Box 6, Council of Economic Advisers, Office of, Records, Eisenhower Library; "Report of the Committee on Taxation—October 30, 1959," Box 1, Mueller Papers.

51. *New York Times,* May 15, 1960, p. 43.

52. Richard M. Nixon, *Six Crises* (Garden City, N.Y.: Doubleday, 1962), pp. 309–11.

53. *Newsweek,* May 16, 1960, p. 89.

Chapter Six

1. Don Oberdorfer and Walter Pincus, "Businessmen in Politics: Luther Hodges and Edward Day," in Lester Tanzer, ed., *The Kennedy Circle* (Washington, D.C.: Robert B. Luce, 1961), pp. 237–54.

2. Hobart Rowen, *The Free Enterprisers: Kennedy, Johnson, and the Business Establishment* (New York: G. P. Putnam's Sons, 1964), pp. 63–64; Luther H. Hodges Oral History Project Memoir, JFK Library, pp. 16–17; Luther Hodges, "BAC Memo—Tentative—Confidential," February 23, 1961, Papers of President John F. Kennedy, President's Office Files, Departments and Agencies, Box 72, JFK Library.

3. "Suggestions for Improvement of BAC" memo, January 16, 1961, Box 126, John W. Snyder Papers, Truman Library.

4. Thomas J. Watson, Jr., Oral History Project Memoir, JFK Library, p. 4.

5. "Advantages and Disadvantages of BAC" memo, January 16, 1961, and "Observations of a BAC Wife" memo, January 16, 1961, both in Box 126, Snyder Papers.

6. Hobart Rowen, *The Free Enterprisers,* pp. 65–66; *Newsweek,* April 17, 1961, p. 90; Edward Gudeman Oral History Memoir, JFK Library, pp. 6–8.

7. Luther Hodges Oral History Project Memoir, p. 17.

8. *Washington Post,* June 9, 1961; John W. Burke to Business Council members, July 12, 1961, Box 126, Snyder Papers.

9. Hobart Rowen, *The Free Enterprisers,* pp. 68–69.

10. *Toledo Blade,* July 7, 1961, p. 1; *Toledo Times,* editorial, July 11, 1961; both in Box 126, Snyder Papers.

11. Luther Hodges Oral History Project Memoir, p. 18.

12. Hobart Rowen, *The Free Enterprisers,* p. 70.

13. *Newsweek,* October 23, 1961, p. 73; Hobart Rowen, *The Free Enterprisers,* pp. 69–73; Ralph Dungan to author, September 9, 1975; Myer Feldman to author, August 5, 1975.

14. Interview with W. Averell Harriman, November 4, 1975.

15. John W. Snyder to Luther Hodges, July 8, 1961; J. Spencer Love to Hodges, June 14, 1961, and July 11, 1961; Love to Snyder, July 12, 1961, all in Box 126, Snyder Papers; Hobart Rowen, *The Free Enterprisers,* pp. 73–75.

16. Edwin L. Dale, Jr., *Conservatives in Power,* p. 172; Dwight D. Eisenhower, *Waging Peace,* pp. 458–59; Roy Hoopes, *The Steel Crisis* (New York: John Day, 1963), pp. 270–71.

17. W. W. Rostow, *The Diffusion of Power, 1957–1972* (New York: Macmillan, 1972), pp. 136–45.

18. William J. Barber, "The Kennedy Years: Purposeful Pedagogy," in Craufurd D. Goodwin, ed., *Exhortation and Controls,* pp. 166–70.

19. For Blough's views, see Roger Blough, "My Side of the Steel Price Story," *Look,* Vol. 27 (January 29, 1963), pp. 19–23 and Blough, *The Washington Embrace of Business* (Pittsburgh: Carnegie-Mellon University Press, 1975), passim. Blough's statement on p. 20 of his *Look* article that Kennedy's was an effort to predetermine steel industry prices that was "unprecedented in peacetime" was absolute claptrap.

20. Theodore Sorensen, *Kennedy* (New York: Harper and Row, 1965), p. 449.

21. Quoted in Bruce Miroff, *Pragmatic Illusions: The Presidential Politics of John F. Kennedy* (New York: David McKay, 1976), p. 178.

22. The rumor that Kennedy called all businessmen SOBs has continued to be one of the most often retold stories regarding Kennedy's domestic presidency. The fact that JFK's father, Joseph Kennedy, a self-made banker and movie entrepreneur, was a businessman himself leads me to agree with Kennedy's right-hand man Theodore Sorensen that Kennedy's statement was substantially misquoted. See Sorensen, *Kennedy,* pp. 449–50.

23. Roy Hoopes, *The Steel Crisis,* pp. 180–92.

24. William Robinson to Eisenhower, April 13, 1962, Box 4, William Robinson Papers, Eisenhower Library.

25. Roy Hoopes, *The Steel Crisis,* pp. 80, 106; Lee Loevinger Oral History Memoir, JFK Library, p. 19.

26. Roy Hoopes, *The Steel Crisis,* pp. 219ff.; Bruce Miroff, *Pragmatic Illusions,* p. 180; Roger Blough, *The Washington Embrace of Business,* p. 153. Business Council members understood that Adam Smith's capitalist world was a thing of the past, and had long been trying to replace the neoclassical model of price competition with alternative views. In 1952, for example, the Council sponsored a report prepared by Edward S. Mason of Harvard which argued that technological and product competition was at least as important as price competition in determining how free the market was. Size per se was also stated to be an unjustifiable criterion for antitrust prosecution. "Effective competition," the report concluded, "exists where there is business rivalry, existing and potential, with reasonable opportunities for freedom of choice of goods and services; and not restricting the opportunity for

others to engage in such competition." This attempted resolution of the free-market, free-enterprise issue in a fashion congenial to big business was not greatly persuasive to the Justice Departments of the Eisenhower and subsequent administrations. See U.S. Congress, House of Representatives, Judiciary Committee, Antitrust Subcommittee, "Hearings on WOC's and Government Advisory Groups," Part II, pp. 1059–76.

27. Walter Heller to JFK, May 13, 1962, Box 31, Theodore Sorensen Papers, JFK Library.

28. Roy Hoopes, *The Steel Crisis,* pp. 236–37; Council of Economic Advisers Oral History Memoir, JFK Library, pp. 427–28.

29. Roswell Gilpatric Oral History Memoir, JFK Library, p. 96; Hugh Sidey Oral History Memoir, JFK Library, pp. 30–32.

30. Theodore Sorensen, "The Kennedy Administration and Business, June 20, 1962," Box 29, Sorensen Papers.

31. T. Reardon to Cabinet member, July 26, 1962; Theodore Sorensen, "The Administration and Business, Talking Paper, Cabinet Meeting, July 26, 1962"; Sorensen to Edward Gudeman, November 9, 1962; and Gudeman to Sorensen, November 13, 1962, all in Box 29, Sorensen Papers; Robert Stevens to Myer Feldman, June 6, 1962, Box 25, Myer Feldman Papers, JFK Library.

32. Herbert Stein, *The Fiscal Revolution in America,* pp. 387–88.

33. Hobart Rowen, *The Free Enterprisers,* pp. 46–60; Herbert Stein, *The Fiscal Revolution in America,* pp. 391–93.

34. Herbert Stein, *The Fiscal Revolution in America,* pp. 395, 399–401.

35. Council of Economic Advisers Oral History Memoir, pp. 32, 34, 219, 373, Appendix-Footnote 7-F.

36. Ibid., pp. 433–35; Roy Hoopes, *The Steel Crisis,* pp. 245–46.

37. Walter Heller to JFK, July 14, 1962, Box 29, Sorensen Papers.

38. Herbert Stein, *The Fiscal Revolution in America,* pp. 420–21, 415–17; Hobart Rowen, *The Free Enterprisers,* pp. 234–35.

39. Herbert Stein, *The Fiscal Revolution in America,* pp. 417–19.

40. Bernard Nossiter, *The Mythmakers: An Essay on Power and Wealth* (Boston: Houghton Mifflin, 1964), pp. 34–36; Hobart Rowen, *The Free Enterprisers,* pp. 233–43; Council of Economic Advisers Oral History Memoir, pp. 433–39.

41. Bernard Nossiter, *The Mythmakers,* p. 35; Bruce Miroff, *Pragmatic Illusions,* pp. 211–12; Herbert Stein, *The Fiscal Revolution in America,* pp. 438–39; Hobart Rowen, *The Free Enterprisers,* p. 243.

42. Hobart Rowen, *The Free Enterprisers,* p. 234; Herbert Stein, *The Fiscal Revolution in America,* pp. 451–53; *New York Times,* October 19, 1963, p. 2; ibid., October 21, 1963, p. 1.

43. John Kenneth Galbraith to author, August 31, 1979; Council of Economic Advisers Oral History Memoir, pp. 371–72.

44. Thomas J. Watson, Jr., Oral History Memoir, pp. 8–10.

45. John F. Kennedy, "Remarks to the White House Conference on National Economic Issues—May 21, 1962," copy in Box 29, Sorensen Papers.

46. Council of Economic Advisers Oral History Memoir, pp. 51, 206, 266; David McDonald Oral History Memoir, JFK Library, pp. 1–9; Edward S. Flash, *Economic Advice and Presidential Leadership: The Council of Economic Advisers* (New York: Columbia University Press, 1965), pp. 208–209; Hobart Rowen, *The Free Enterprisers,* p. 286; Henry Fairlie, *The Kennedy Promise* (Garden City, N.Y.: Doubleday, 1972), p. 151; Bernard Nossiter, *The Mythmakers,* pp. 220–21; John Kenneth Galbraith to JFK, April 17, 1962, Box 76, John Kenneth Galbraith Papers, JFK

Library; James Tobin to JFK, March 13, 1962, Box 31, Sorensen Papers.

47. William L. O'Neill, *Coming Apart: An Informal History of America in the 1960's* (New York: Quadrangle, 1976), p. 62.

48. William Robinson to Dwight Eisenhower, December 12, 1962, Box 4, Robinson Papers.

49. Ibid.

Chapter Seven

1. *Public Papers of the Presidents: Lyndon Baines Johnson, 1963–1964* (Washington, D.C.: Government Printing Office, 1965), pp. 22–25; Hobart Rowen, *The Free Enterprisers,* p. 280. For businessmen's reactions to the President's early symbolic gestures, see the letters in Box 426 of the White House Central Files, Federal Government—Organizations, Lyndon B. Johnson Library, Austin, Tex.

2. Norman Mailer, *Some Honorable Men* (Boston: Little, Brown, 1972), pp. 22–24.

3. Alexander Trowbridge Oral History Memoir, LBJ Library, Reel 1, pp. 25–27.

4. Walter Heller to LBJ, April 13, 1964, Box 42, Walter Heller Papers, JFK Library. Heller also advised LBJ during this period to pay attention to CED leaders as well, to find some "new faces" who weren't "Bourbons," and to recruit more bankers. The Business Council usually had one, two, or three of New York City's largest bankers on its membership rolls at any given time during the 1960's.

5. Hobart Rowen, "That Man [LBJ] Made a Lot of Friends," *Newsweek,* January 20, 1964, pp. 63–64.

6. John Connor to LBJ, January 8, 1964, LBJ Presidential Papers, White House Central Files, Federal Government—Organizations (hereafter designated LBJ/WHCF/FGO), Box 426, LBJ Library.

7. *Newsweek,* January 20, 1964, p. 63.

8. Eric F. Goldman, *The Tragedy of Lyndon Baines Johnson* (New York: Alfred A. Knopf, 1969), pp. 25, 46; Kermit Gordon to LBJ, February 20, 1964, LBJ/WHCF/FGO, Box 246; Walter Heller to LBJ, January 7, 1964, LBJ Presidential Papers, Appointment File (Diary Backup), (hereafter designated LBJ/Diary Backup), Box 3, LBJ Library; Robert B. Anderson Oral History Memoir, LBJ Library, pp. 21–24.

9. *New York Times,* May 9, 1964, p. 1; ibid., May 10, 1964, p. 43.

10. *New York Times,* May 9, 1964, p. 30; C. Douglas Dillon to LBJ and Mac Kilduff to Jack Valenti, January 7, 1964, LBJ/WHCF/FGO, Box 426; Valenti to LBJ, December 21, 1964, and Walter Heller to LBJ, April 13, 1964, LBJ Presidential Papers, White House Central Files, Business and Economics (hereafter designated "LBJ/WHCF/BE"), Box 8, LBJ Library. The other members of the Business Council's White House liaison committee, in addition to Stanton of CBS, were: Henry Ford II, Thomas J. Watson, Jr., William A. Hewitt (Deere and Company), Juan Trippe (Pan American), Frederick Kappel (AT&T), and George R. Brown (Brown and Root). All save Kappel (who was replaced by Albert Nickerson of Mobil Oil when Kappel's term as Business Council chairman concluded) stayed on in these posts throughout LBJ's presidency.

11. Clarence J. Francis, "Breakfast with Herbert Hoover, June 29, 1962" typescript, Box 4, Clarence J. Francis Papers, Eisenhower Library.

12. Theodore H. White, *The Making of the President, 1964* (New York:

Atheneum, 1965), p. 71; Robert B. Anderson Oral History Memoir, LBJ Library, pp. 21–24.

13. Theodore H. White, *The Making of the President, 1964*, pp. 182ff.

14. David T. Bazelon, *Power in America: The Politics of a New Class* (New York: New American Library, 1964), pp. 100–101; Theodore H. White, *The Making of the President, 1964*, pp. 351–52; Eric F. Goldman, *The Tragedy of Lyndon Baines Johnson*, pp. 224–25; Sidney Weinberg to Marvin Watson, November 30, 1966, LBJ Presidential Papers, White House Central Files, Name File, LBJ Library.

15. Edwin M. Epstein, *The Corporation in American Politics* (Englewood Cliffs, N.J.: Prentice-Hall, 1969), p. 96; David T. Bazelon, *Power in America*, pp. 97–98.

16. "M" to Jack Valenti, August 17, 1964, LBJ/WHCF/BE, Box 8; "Remarks by the President at the Businessmen's Luncheon, October 6, 1964," LBJ/Diary Backup, Box 10.

17. Marion B. Folsom Oral History Memoir—Eisenhower Administration, pp. 56–58.

18. Eric F. Goldman, *The Tragedy of Lyndon Baines Johnson*, pp. 264–65. Henry Fowler had first surfaced as a Council employee in 1955, when Congressman Emanuel Celler had futilely attempted to subpoena Council records in a short-lived investigation that the Eisenhower administration stonewalled. See U.S. Congress, House of Representatives, Judiciary Committee, Antitrust Subcommittee, "Hearings on WOCs and Government Advisory Groups," Part II, passim.

19. Jack Valenti to LBJ, December 21, 1964 and Thomas J. Watson, Jr., to LBJ, December 21, 1964, LBJ/WHCF/BE, Box 8; C. Douglas Dillon to LBJ, May 7, 1964 LBJ/WHCF/FGO, Box 426; Alfred C. Neal to LBJ, February 5, 1964, LBJ/WHCF/FGO, Box 420.

20. Jack Valenti to LBJ, February 1, 1965, LBJ/WHCF/FGO, Box 426; *Public Papers of the Presidents: Lyndon Baines Johnson, 1963–1964*, Pt. 1 (Washington, D.C.: Government Printing Office, 1965), pp. 1628–31; *New York Times,* December 3, 1964, p. 1.

21. Henry Fowler to LBJ, May 15, 1965, and Fowler to David Packard, ca. July, 1968, LBJ/WHCF/FGO, Box 416; Roger Blough Oral History Memoir, LBJ Library, pp. 3–4, 28. The Business Council committee for liaison with the Treasury Department consisted of Harold Boeschenstein (chairman) (Owens-Corning Fiberglass), Henry C. Alexander (Morgan Guaranty Trust), G. Keith Funston (New York Stock Exchange), David Packard (Hewlett-Packard), Henry S. Wingate (International Nickel), Sidney Weinberg, Frederick Donner (GM), Roger Blough, Paul L. Davies (FMC Corporation), W. B. Murphy (Campbell's Soup), Eugene Beesley (Eli Lilly), and Frank Milliken (Kennecott Copper).

22. *New York Times,* February 10, 1965, p. 25; ibid., May 8, 1965, p. 1; ibid., May 9, 1965, pp. 1, 36; *Newsweek,* May 17, 1965, pp. 73–74.

23. Norman MacRae, *The Neurotic Trillionaire* (New York: Harcourt Brace Jovanovich, 1970), pp. 20–30; W. W. Rostow, *The Diffusion of Power, 1959–1972*, pp. 330–32 (for a useful categorization of Johnson-era reform legislation).

24. W. B. Murphy to LBJ, ca. October, 1965, and "Notes on a Dinner Meeting . . . [of the Business Council], October 4, 1965," LBJ/WHCF/FGO, Box 426.

25. Gardner Ackley to LBJ, March 30, 1966, LBJ/Diary Backup, Box 32.

26. For a well-written and pungent version of these events to which I am very heavily indebted, see James L. Cochrane, "The Johnson Administration: Moral Suasion Goes to War," in Craufurd D. Goodwin, ed., *Exhortation and Controls,* pp. 193–244. The Ackley quote is on p. 244. See also Lawrence McQuade Oral History Memoir, LBJ Library, pp. 9–11. Secretary of Commerce Connor's refusal

to assist LBJ in maintaining the controls "cost him very heavily with the President and the White House" in McQuade's estimation. McQuade was Connor's assistant at the time.

27. Joseph Califano to LBJ, April 15, 1966, LBJ/Diary Backup, Box 32.

28. U.S. Bureau of the Census, *Historical Statistics of the United States, Colonial Times to 1970,* Vol. 2 (Washington, D.C.: Government Printing Office, 1976), p. 1116.

29. Roger Blough Oral History Memoir, pp. 22–25.

30. *New York Times,* October 24, 1966, p. 1.

31. Theodore Levitt, "The Johnson Treatment," *Harvard Business Review,* Vol. XLV (January–February, 1967), pp. 114, 121.

32. Theodore Levitt, "Why Business Always Loses," *Harvard Business Review,* Vol. XLVI (March–April, 1968), p. 83.

33. James L. Cochrane, "The Johnson Administration: Moral Suasion Goes to War," in Craufurd D. Goodwin, ed., *Exhortation and Controls,* pp. 263–64; Norman MacRae, *The Neurotic Trillionaire,* pp. 46–49; Godfrey Hodgson, *America in Our Time* (New York: Random House, 1976), pp. 392–93.

34. Joseph Califano to LBJ, October 13, 1966, and Gardner Ackley to LBJ, October 11, 1966, Box 16, Joseph Califano Papers, LBJ Library; Armand Hammer to LBJ, October 7, 1966, and Henry Fowler to LBJ, November 5, 1966, LBJ/WHCF/BE, Box 31; *New York Times,* October 24, 1966, p. 1; Craufurd D. Goodwin, ed., *Exhortation and Controls,* p. 264.

35. *New York Times,* October 22, 1966, p. 36; Gardner Ackley to LBJ, "Meeting with the Business Council Liaison Committee, December 9, 1966," LBJ/WHCF/FGO, Box 426.

36. Gardner Ackley to LBJ, January 4, 1967, LBJ/Diary Backup, Box 52.

37. Gardner Ackley to LBJ, February 27, 1967, LBJ/WHCF/BE, Box 1; Fred Panzer to LBJ, February 24, 1967, LBJ/WHCF/BE, Box 31.

38. Gardner Ackley to LBJ, "Report from Business Council Meeting, May 15, 1967," LBJ/WHCF/FGO, Box 426. At the same time that Business Council CEOs opposed a tax hike, Council *economists* favored one. (*New York Times,* May 13, 1967, p. 1.)

39. "Notes of the Luncheon Meeting of the President with Business Leaders: In the Mansion, August 10, 1967," LBJ/Diary Backup, Box 73, passim.

40. "Statement of Principles," ca. September, 1967, Box 52, Califano Papers.

41. Alexander Trowbridge to LBJ, November 20, 1967, and Joseph Califano to Marvin Watson, October 7, 1967, LBJ/Diary Backup, Box 84; *New York Times,* October 21, 1967, p. 1.

42. "Statement of Chairman Wilbur Mills (D. Ark.) on the Necessity for Establishing Controls Over the Future Course of Federal Spending—October 6, 1967" copy in Box 52, Califano Papers.

43. Harry McPherson to Joseph Califano, October 25, 1965, LBJ/WHCF/BE, Box 1.

44. *Public Papers of the Presidents: Lyndon Baines Johnson, 1968–1969,* Part I (Washington, D.C.: Government Printing Office, 1970), pp. 593–97; *New York Times,* May 12, 1968, p. 1.

45. Joseph Califano to LBJ, May 17, 1968, LBJ/WHCF/FGO, Box 426.

46. Arthur Okun to Joseph Califano, May 13, 1968, Box 54, Califano Papers; Califano to LBJ, May 17, 1968, LBJ/WHCF/FGO, Box 426; Henry Fowler to LBJ, June 10, 1968, LBJ/WHCF/BE, Box 7.

47. Leo C. Beebe Oral History Memoir, LBJ Library, Reel 2, p. 18.

48. Eric F. Goldman, *The Tragedy of Lyndon Baines Johnson,* p. 197; Hubert H. Humphrey, *The Education of a Public Man,* pp. 293, 375; Edwin M. Epstein, *The Corporation in American Politics,* pp. 54–55.

49. Arthur Okun to LBJ, October 21, 1968, LBJ/WHCF/FGO, Box 426.

50. *Public Papers of the Presidents: Lyndon Baines Johnson, 1968–1969,* Part II (Washington, D.C.: Government Printing Office, 1970), pp. 1165–68; *New York Times,* December 5, 1968, p. 1.

Chapter Eight

1. Thomas E. Mann, "Elections and Change in Congress," in Thomas E. Mann and Norman Ornstein, eds., *The New Congress* (Washington, D.C.: American Enterprise Institute, 1981), pp. 34–35; A. James Reichley, *Conservatives in an Age of Change: The Nixon and Ford Administrations* (Washington, D.C.: Brookings Institution, 1981), p. 2.

2. Richard M. Nixon, *RN: The Memoirs of Richard Nixon* (New York: Grosset and Dunlap, 1978), pp. 351–52.

3. A. James Reichley, *Conservatives in an Age of Change,* p. 73; Rowland Evans and Robert Novak, *Nixon in the White House: The Frustration of Power* (New York: Random House, 1971), pp. 25–26.

4. Norman MacRae, *The Neurotic Trillionaire,* pp. 50–53.

5. Rowland Evans and Robert Novak, *Nixon in the White House,* pp. 178, 190.

6. *Statistical Abstract of the United States, 1980* (Washington, D.C.: Government Printing Office, 1981), pp. 258–59; A. James Reichley, *Conservatives in an Age of Change,* p. 172.

7. Leonard Silk, *Nixonomics: How the Dismal Science of Free Enterprise Became the Black Art of Controls* (New York: Praeger, 1972), pp. 3–11.

8. Rowland Evans and Robert Novak, *Nixon in the White House,* pp. 188–89.

9. *New York Times,* May 10, 1969, p. 1; ibid., May 11, 1969, p. 8; ibid., October 18, 1969, p. 19; ibid., February 12, 1970, p. 27; ibid., February 13, 1970, p. 53.

10. Ibid., May 9, 1970, p. 1.

11. Leonard Silk, *Nixonomics,* pp. 12–13.

12. *New York Times,* October 18, 1970, p. 1; Neil De Marchi, "The First Nixon Administration: Prelude to Controls," in Craufurd D. Goodwin, ed., *Exhortation and Controls,* pp. 317–26.

13. Leonard Silk, *Nixonomics,* pp. 36–47; *New York Times,* May 10, 1970, p. 39; Arnold Weber, *In Pursuit of Price Stability: The Wage-Price Freeze of 1971* (Washington, D.C.: Brookings Institution, 1973), pp. 6–7.

14. Theodore H. White, *The Making of the President, 1972* (New York: Atheneum, 1973), p. 51.

15. A. James Reichley, *Conservatives in an Age of Change,* p. 218; Leonard Lurie, *The Running of Richard Nixon* (New York: Coward, McCann and Geoghegan, 1972), pp. 324ff.

16. A. James Reichley, *Conservatives in an Age of Change,* p. 220; Rowland Evans and Robert Novak, *Nixon in the White House,* pp. 204–209.

17. *Congress and the Nation,* Vol. 3, *1969–1972: A Review of Government and Politics* (Washington, D.C.: Congressional Quarterly, 1973), pp. 106–108.

18. *New York Times,* August 12, 1971, p. 27; ibid., August 15, 1971, p. 30; ibid., August 11, 1971, p. 36.

19. William Safire, *Before the Fall: An Inside View of the Pre-Watergate White House* (Garden City, N.Y.: Doubleday, 1975), pp. 507–17; Leonard Silk, *Nixonomics*, pp. 17–18.

20. *Congress and the Nation*, Vol. 3, pp. 77ff., 111, 113–14.

21. *New York Times*, August 17, 1971, pp. 1, 17; ibid., August 19, 1971, pp. 1, 22; *Business Week*, September 25, 1971, pp. 36–37.

22. Craufurd D. Goodwin, ed., *Exhortation and Controls*, pp. 74–75.

23. *New York Times*, August 25, 1971, p. 1; ibid., September 14, 1971, pp. 1, 26. There is no strong indication that the Business Council had any well-formulated agenda regarding wage-price controls before Nixon enunciated his program. As late as May of 1971, a suggestion by a Council member (J. Irwin Miller of Cummins Engine) that a controls program be introduced caused "many" Council members to dispute his views. The Council's full membership did, however, take the unusual step of having a public straw vote on the issue. (*New York Times*, May 9, 1971, p. 25; Neil De Marchi, "The First Nixon Administration: Prelude to Controls," in Craufurd D. Goodwin, ed., *Exhortation and Controls*, p. 340.)

24. *New York Times*, September 14, 1971, p. 26.

25. *Weekly Compilation of Presidential Documents: October 25, 1971* (Washington, D.C.: Government Printing Office, 1971), pp. 1438–39.

26. Craufurd D. Goodwin, ed., *Exhortation and Controls*, p. 75; *Congress and the Nation*, Vol. 3, pp. 112–13.

27. *New York Times*, October 13, 1971, pp. 1, 18; ibid., October 18, 1971, p. 1.

28. "How the Unions Will Get Around Wage Controls," *Business Week*, January 22, 1972, p. 74.

29. Leonard Silk, *Nixonomics*, pp. 77–78; *Business Week*, August 28, 1971, pp. 52–55; ibid., September 11, 1971, pp. 71ff; T. Wendell Butler, Frederick W. Allen, and Charles B. Stockdale, "Congress and Controls" in Department of the Treasury, Office of Economic Stabilization, *Historical Working Papers on the Economic Stabilization Program, August 15, 1971, to April 30, 1974,* Part I (Washington, D.C.: Government Printing Office, 1974), pp. 119–24.

30. *Historical Working Papers on the Economic Stabilization Program,* Part I, p. 124; Leonard Silk, *Nixonomics*, pp. 79–80.

31. "Productivity: The Pay Board Versus Nixon," *Business Week*, March 25, 1972, pp. 68ff.

32. *New York Times*, January 5, 1972, p. 1; ibid., January 6, 1972, p. 36; ibid., February 8, 1972, p. 18; ibid., March 23, 1972, pp. 1, 34; ibid., March 24, 1972, p. 1. The Pay Board had first gotten tough with the Aerospace Workers Union in January, but the March, 1972, longshoremen decision provided the flash point for AFL-CIO dissent on the productivity issue.

33. C. Jackson Grayson and Louis Neeb, *Confessions of a Price Controller* (New York: Dow Jones, 1974), passim; Jack W. Duvall and John B. Gussman, "Compliance and Enforcement," *Historical Working Papers on the Economic Stabilization Program,* Part I, pp. 806–807; Donald B. Johnson, *The Republican Party and Wendell Willkie* (Urbana, Il.: University of Illinois Press, 1960), p. 311.

34. "Phase Two Honeymoon Is Over," *Business Week*, January 29, 1972, pp. 23–24.

35. *Congress and the Nation*, Vol. 3, pp. 115–17; George P. Schultz and Kenneth W. Dam, *Economic Policy Behind the Headlines* (New York: W. W. Norton, 1977), p. 74.

36. *Business Week*, November 13, 1971, p. 39; Neil De Marchi, "The First Nixon Administration: Prelude to Controls," in Craufurd D. Goodwin, ed., *Exhortation*

and Controls, p. 344; "Congress and Controls," *Historical Working Papers on the Economic Stabilization Program,* Part I, pp. 119–65.

37. Edward R. Tufte, *Political Control of the Economy* (Princeton, N.J.: Princeton University Press, 1978), pp. 48–49; A. James Reichley, *Conservatives in an Age of Change,* pp. 226–27.

38. Michael Harrington, *Decade of Decision: The Crisis of the American System* (New York: Simon and Schuster, 1980), p. 47; *New York Times,* February 18, 1972, p. 1; ibid., May 13, 1972, p. 39.

39. Arnold R. Weber to author, October 22, 1979; *Business Week,* August 26, 1972, pp. 23–24; ibid., November 18, 1972, pp. 15–16; *New York Times,* May 14, 1972, p. 14; ibid., October 21, 1972, p. 43; ibid., October 22, 1972, p. 48; A. James Reichley, *Conservatives in an Age of Change,* pp. 227–28; Patrick Buchanan, *Conservative Votes, Liberal Victories* (New York: Pantheon, 1975), pp. 119–20; *Historical Working Papers on the Economic Stabilization Program,* Part I, pp. 139–43.

40. "Foggier Phase III Threatens the Outlook," *Business Week,* March 3, 1973, pp. 15–16; Michael Harrington, *Decade of Decision,* p. 48; *New York Times,* May 12, 1973, p. 41; ibid., May 13, 1973, p. 40; George P. Schultz and Kenneth W. Dam, *Economic Policy Behind the Headlines,* pp. 74–75.

41. *New York Times,* May 12, 1973, p. 41.

Chapter Nine

1. Henry Kissinger was among those strenuously opposed to naming Connally to the GOP ticket in 1972. For his views and Nixon's reactions to them, see Richard Nixon, *RN: The Memoirs of Richard Nixon,* p. 591.

2. Bryce Harlow to author, January 18, 1979; Andrew Buchsbaum, "Lords of the Chamber, Knights of the Roundtable: A Study of Business Lobbying Associations" (undergraduate thesis, Harvard University, 1979), p. 33.

3. Bryce Harlow to author, January 18, 1979; interview with Bryce Harlow, March 28, 1980.

4. The episodic nature of CEO involvement in legislative affairs in Washington in the period immediately preceding the organization of the March Group is detailed in Paul W. Cherington and Ralph L. Gillen, *The Business Representative in Washington* (Washington, D.C.: Brookings Institution, 1962), especially pp. 69–71.

5. Interview with Bryce Harlow, March 28, 1980.

6. The academic literature regarding industry-specific regulatory problems is voluminous and unusually dull. For well-written popular treatments, see Mark Green et al., *The Closed Enterprise System* (New York: Grossman, 1972) and Louis M. Kohlmeier, *The Regulators: Watchdog Agencies in the Public Interest* (New York: Harper and Row, 1969). For an example of how industry-specific regulatory bodies can be captured by their industrial clientele, see U.S. Congress, House of Representatives, Committee on Government Operations, "Report on Problems in the Relationship Between the Commerce Department's Maritime Administration and the National Maritime Council, a Trade Organization" (Washington, D.C.: Government Printing Office, 1978).

7. Murray Weidenbaum, *Business, Government, and the Public,* 1st ed. (Englewood Cliffs, N.J.: Prentice-Hall, 1977), pp. 13–16; David Vogel, "Businessmen Unite," *Wall Street Journal,* January 14, 1980, p. 18.

8. *New York Times,* May 13, 1967, p. 35; ibid., October 10, 1969, p. 43; ibid., October 17, 1970, p. 58; ibid., May 8, 1971, p. 12; ibid., May 9, 1970, p. 11; interview with Arthur Newmyer, March 26, 1980.

9. David Vogel, "How Business Responds to Opposition: Corporate Political Strategies During the 1970's," paper read at the 1979 annual meeting of the American Political Science Association, Washington, D.C., pp. 27–29, 41–45.

10. Craufurd D. Goodwin, ed., *Exhortation and Controls,* pp. 256–62, 310–40; Andrew Buchsbaum's thesis, pp. 29–30; Arnold Weber, *In Pursuit of Price Stability,* pp. 6–7.

11. Interview with Bryce Harlow; Interview with Arthur Newmyer; Interview with John Post (Executive Director, Business Roundtable), September 8, 1981; Andrew Buchsbaum's thesis, pp. 30–31; Mark Green and Andrew Buchsbaum, *The Corporate Lobbies: Political Profiles of the Business Roundtable and the Chamber of Commerce* (Washington, D.C.: Public Citizen, 1980), pp. 80–82.

12. Interview with Andrew Buchsbaum, July 25, 1978; Interview with Peter Slavin, July 22, 1978.

13. Elizabeth Drew, *Washington Journal: The Events of 1973–1974* (New York: Vintage, 1976), pp. 133–34, 140.

14. Convenient summaries of the legislative changes alluded to here can be found in Norman Ornstein and Shirley Elder, *Interest Groups, Lobbying, and Policy-Making* (Washington, D.C.: Congressional Quarterly, 1978) and Walter J. Oleszek, *Congressional Procedures and the Policy Process* (Washington, D.C.: Congressional Quarterly, 1978).

15. *Public Papers of the Presidents: Gerald R. Ford, 1974* (Washington, D.C.: Government Printing Office, 1975), p. 733.

16. Here the paper trail very largely runs out on big businessmen's political action in Washington. All of the specifics regarding the nuts and bolts of Roundtable organization detailed above came to me as a result of a series of interviews with present and former Roundtable hands and with longtime congressional committee staffers. Of particular importance were interviews with Walter Hasty (April 8, 1980), James Keogh (April 24, 1980), Bryce Harlow (March 28, 1980), John Podesta (March 20, 1980), Robert Nichols (January 21, 1980), James Graham (February 5, 1980), Janet Potts (January 28, 1980), Edward A. Merlis (January 10, 1980), Alan F. Coffey, Jr. (January 30, 1980), Michael Pertschuk (December 14, 1979), and John Post (March 13, 1981). Any reader is free to doubt the accuracy of unpublished sources like these. He or she should also consider, however, that the research detailed here was thoroughly checked by the editorial staff of the *Harvard Business Review* before they published my article "The Roundtable: Learning How to Win in Washington" in their May–June, 1981, issue. I will, however, be glad to listen to informed protests about anything I have written at any time.

17. *New York Times,* November 16, 1975, pp. 1, 74; ibid., March 7, 1976, Section III, p. 7; Peter Slavin, "The Business Roundtable: New Lobbying Arm of Big Business," *Business and Society Review,* No. 16 (Winter, 1975–1976), pp. 28–32; Barry M. Hager, "Business Roundtable: New Lobbying Force," *Congressional Quarterly,* September 17, 1977, pp. 1964–68.

18. For a summary of the deregulation views of the Carter administration, see an early statement by the man whom Carter selected to be his chairman of the Council of Economic Advisers: Charles L. Schultze, "The Public Use of the Private Interest," *Harper's,* May, 1977, pp. 43–62.

19. *New York Times,* November 2, 1976, p. 16. A readable overview of the 1976

campaign is Elizabeth Drew, *American Journal: The Events of 1976* (New York: Random House, 1977). For those who prefer the "horse race" or "who's ahead now?" school of journalism, see Jules Witcover, *Marathon: The Pursuit of the Presidency, 1972–1976* (New York: Viking, 1977).

20. James W. Singer, "Business and Government: A New 'Quasi-Public' Role," *National Journal,* April 15, 1978, pp. 596–99; "Business' Most Powerful Lobby in Washington," *Business Week,* December 20, 1976, pp. 60–63; Martin Tolchin, "Carter's Corporate Brain Trust," *New York Times,* July 24, 1978, pp. D-1, D-4; John A. Roberts, "Business Takes On a New Approach to Public Issues," *Du Pont Context,* Vol. 7, No. 1 (1978), pp. 10–13; Agis Salpukas, "How Big Business Grappled With the Arab Boycott," *New York Times,* August 21, 1977, Section III, pp. 1, 5; Edgar M. Bronfman, "How To Succeed in Business by Really Trying: The Arab Boycott," *New Republic,* June 4, 1977, pp. 17–19; Adam Clymer, "Like Carter, Potomac Power is Ambiguous," *New York Times,* January 8, 1978, Section XII, pp. 26, 30.

21. Haynes Johnson, *In the Absence of Power: Governing America* (New York: Viking, 1980), pp. 217, 226.

22. Carter's lack of attention to the legislative branch of government is detailed in Gary M. Fink, *Prelude to the Presidency: The Political Character and Legislative Leadership Style of Governor Jimmy Carter* (Westport, Conn.: Greenwood Press, 1980). For Carter's apparent inability to avoid confusing politics and administration, see Joseph Califano, *Governing America: An Insider's Report From the White House and the Cabinet* (New York: Simon and Schuster, 1981), especially chapter 10.

23. George Schwartz, "The Successful Fight Against a Federal Consumer Protection Agency," *Michigan State University Business Topics,* Summer, 1979, pp. 45–57; "Business Lobbying: Threat to the Public Interest," *Consumer Reports,* September, 1978, pp. 526–31.

24. *Wall Street Journal,* May 17, 1978, p. 1; Thomas Ferguson and Joel Rogers, "Labor Law Reform and Its Enemies," *Nation,* January 6–13, 1979, pp. 1, 17–20; D. Quinn Mills, "Flawed Victory in Labor Law Reform," *Harvard Business Review,* Vol. 79 (May–June, 1979), pp. 92–102.

25. William T. Moye, "Presidential Labor-Management Committees: Productive Failures," *Industrial and Labor Relations Review,* Vol. 34 (October, 1980), pp. 64–65; John T. Dunlop to author, December 14, 1978.

26. "Policies Necessary to Reduce the Rate of Inflation, June, 1978" (New York and Washington, D.C.: Business Roundtable, 1978), passim.

27. Robert L. Simison, "Detroit Runs Risk of Reviving Industry Critics," *Wall Street Journal,* August 25, 1981, p. 28.

28. "An Odd Alliance for Budget Balance," *Business Week,* May 19, 1980, p. 159; *Wall Street Journal,* October 20, 1978, p. 24; *New York Times,* June 2, 1979, pp. 1, 12; plus articles in the *Wall Street Journal* for October 16 and 19, 1980, and the transcript of the PBS news program *The McNeil-Lehrer Report* for October 25, 1978.

29. The *Wall Street Journal* editorials attacking the Roundtable are: "The Short View" (December 29, 1978), "Mr. Bosworth's Enemies List" (January 12, 1979), "Down With Big Business" (April 18, 1979), "More on Big Business" (April 26, 1979), and "Economic Education" (October 3, 1979). GM's Murphy responded to *Journal* attacks for the Roundtable on January 9, 1979, April 23, 1979, and April 30, 1979.

30. Joseph Califano, *Governing America,* pp. 418–30; "The Roundtable Asks For

an End to Guidelines," *Business Week,* August 11, 1980, pp. 28–29; Philip Shabe-coff, "Big Business on the Offensive," *New York Times Magazine,* December 6, 1979, pp. 134ff.

Conclusion

1. "An Economic Strategy For the 1980's . . . , March, 1981," (New York and Washington, D.C.: Business Roundtable, 1981), passim; Walter Guzzardi, Jr., "A New Public Face for Big Business," *Fortune,* June 30, 1980, pp. 48–52.
2. Norman C. Miller, "The Political Danger of New Mega-Corporations," *Wall Street Journal,* August 20, 1981, p. 20.

A Postscript

1. William Greider, "The Education of David Stockman," *Atlantic,* Vol. 248 (December, 1981).
2. Ibid., p. 51.
3. *Wall Street Journal,* November 21, 1980, p. 4.
4. *Electronic Engineering Times,* May 25, 1981, pp. 1, 17.
5. *Business Week,* February 23, 1981, p. 35.
6. *Business Week,* December 1, 1980, p. 145; ibid., January 26, 1981, p. 135; *Wall Street Journal,* November 13, 1980, p. 48.
7. *Wall Street Journal,* May 22, 1981; ibid., June 15, 1981; *New York Times Magazine,* October 25, 1981, p. 95; *Atlantic,* Vol. 248, p. 38 (Stockman); *Wall Street Journal,* July 22, 1981, p. 20.
8. Robert W. Merry, "Congress Clears Reagan's Tax Cut Plan: Rejecting Tradi-tional Economic Policies," *Wall Street Journal,* July 30, 1981, p. 3; *Business Week,* December 21, 1981, p. 36; Thomas B. Edsall, "Small Business Left Out of Taxes Horse Trading," *Washington Post,* August 7, 1981, pp. E-1, E-2; *Atlantic,* Vol. 248, p. 47 (Stockman).
9. W. Michael Blumenthal, "What Ronald Reagan Can Learn From Jimmy Carter," *Business Week,* October 26, 1981, p. 19.
10. *Wall Street Journal,* September 1, 1981, p. 27; ibid., January 14, 1982, p. 3; ibid., January 13, 1982, p. 25; "Capital Spending Refuses to Budge," *Business Week,* November 16, 1981, p. 47; "The Capital Spending Bust," *Newsweek,* December 28, 1981, p. 55.
11. *Roundtable Report,* May, 1981, p. 1; "An Economic Strategy for the Eigh-ties," (New York: Business Roundtable, 1981), p. 1.
12. Sidney Blumenthal, "Whose Side Is Business on, Anyway?" *New York Times Magazine,* October 25, 1981, p. 95.
13. "What You Can Do for Your Country: Treasury Secretary Regan Throws Down the Gauntlet to Business," *Nation's Business,* April, 1981, p. 52.
14. Henry F. Myers et al., "Another Dry Hole," *Wall Street Journal,* January 8, 1982, p. 12.
15. Ibid., p. 1.
16. For U.S. Steel's diversification plans, see Richard J. Kirkland, Jr., "Big Steel Recasts Itself," *Fortune,* April 6, 1981, pp. 29–34.

17. "Business Disappoints Congress," *Business Week,* December 21, 1981, pp. 36–37.

18. "The Steel Industry's Tarnished Credibility," *Business Week,* December 7, 1981, p. 144.

19. *Wall Street Journal,* January 13, 1982, p. 31.

20. Frank Allen, "Corporate Leaders Strongly Support Reagan's Handling of the Economy," *Wall Street Journal,* October 7, 1981, Section 2, p. 1; Frank Allen, "President Has Confidence of Most Bosses," *Wall Street Journal,* January 21, 1982, Section II, p. 1.

21. *Business and Public Affairs Fortnightly,* Vol. 111, No. 6 (May 15, 1981), p. 1.

22. *Wall Street Journal,* January 27, 1982, p. 3.

BIBLIOGRAPHY

Private Papers and Document Collections

Aldrich, Winthrop W. Baker Library, Harvard Business School, Boston.
Ayers, Eben A. Harry S. Truman Library, Independence, Mo.
Burns, Arthur F. Dwight D. Eisenhower Library, Abilene, Kans.
Califano, Joseph. Lyndon B. Johnson Library, Austin, Tex.
Clayton, William S. Harry S. Truman Library, Independence, Mo.
Commerce, Department of. General Records. National Archives, Washington, D.C.
Cooke, Morris L. Franklin D. Roosevelt Library, Hyde Park, N.Y.
Council of Economic Advisers. Office of, Records. Dwight D. Eisenhower Library, Abilene, Kans.
David, Donald K. Baker Library, Harvard Business School, Boston.
Donham, Wallace B. Baker Library, Harvard Business School, Boston.
du Pont, Pierre S. Eleutherian Mills–Hagley Foundation Library, Wilmington, Del.
Eisenhower, Dwight D. Prepresidential Papers. Dwight D. Eisenhower Library, Abilene, Kans.
———. Presidential Papers. White House Central Files. Dwight D. Eisenhower Library, Abilene, Kans.
Flanders, Ralph. Syracuse University, Syracuse, N.Y.
Francis, Clarence J. Dwight D. Eisenhower Library, Abilene, Kans.
Galbraith, John Kenneth. John F. Kennedy Library, Boston.
Heller, Walter. John F. Kennedy Library, Boston.
Hoffman, Paul. Harry S. Truman Library, Independence, Mo.
Holland, Lou. Harry S. Truman Library, Independence, Mo.
Hopkins, Harry. Franklin D. Roosevelt Library, Hyde Park, N.Y.
Johnson, Lyndon B. Presidential Papers. Appointment File (Diary Backup). Lyndon B. Johnson Library, Austin, Tex.
———. Presidential Papers. White House Central Files. Business and Economics. Lyndon B. Johnson Library, Austin, Tex.
———. Presidential Papers. White House Central Files. Federal Government—Organizations. Lyndon B. Johnson Library, Austin, Tex.
———. Presidential Papers. White House Central Files. Name File. Lyndon B. Johnson Library, Austin, Tex.

362

Kennedy, John F. President's Office Files. Departments and Agencies. John F. Kennedy Library, Boston.

Kirstein, Louis. Baker Library, Harvard Business School, Boston.

Mueller, Frederick H. Dwight D. Eisenhower Library, Abilene, Kans.

National Archives. Washington, D.C.

National Recovery Administration. Records. National Archives, Washington, D.C.

———. Records. Miscellaneous Report and Document Series. National Archives, Washington, D.C.

Richberg, Donald. Library of Congress, Washington, D.C.

Robinson, William. Dwight D. Eisenhower Library, Abilene, Kans.

Roosevelt, Franklin D. Franklin D. Roosevelt Library, Hyde Park, N.Y.

Schindler, Alfred. Harry S. Truman Library, Independence, Mo.

Snyder, John W. Harry S. Truman Library, Independence, Mo.

Sorensen, Theodore. John F. Kennedy Library, Boston.

Stettinius, Edward R., Jr. Alderman Library, University of Virginia, Charlottesville, Va.

Truman, Harry S. Postpresidential Papers. Harry S. Truman Library, Independence, Mo.

Young, Owen D. Privately held. Van Hornesville, N.Y.

United States Government Reports

Bureau of the Census. *Historical Statistics of the United States: Colonial Times to 1957.* Washington, D.C.: Government Printing Office, 1960.

———. *Historical Statistics of the United States: Colonial Times to 1970.* Vol. 2. Washington, D.C.: Government Printing Office, 1976.

Congress. House. Committee on Government Operations. *Report on Problems in the Relationships Between the Commerce Department's Maritime Administration and the National Maritime Council, a Trade Organization.* Washington, D.C.: Government Printing Office, 1978.

———. House. *Hearings on the Extension of the National Industrial Recovery Act.* 74th Congress, 1st session. Washington, D.C.: Government Printing Office, 1935.

———. House. Judiciary Committee. Antitrust Subcommittee. *Hearings on WOCs and Government Advisory Groups.* Part II. Washington, D.C.: Government Printing Office, 1955.

———. House. Judiciary Committee. Antitrust Subcommittee. *Interim Report on WOCs and Government Advisory Groups.* 84th Congress, 2nd session. Washington, D.C.: Government Printing Office, 1956.

———. Senate. Committee on Manufactures. *Hearings on a Bill to Establish a National Economic Council.* Washington, D.C.: Government Printing Office, 1932.

——— Senate. *Hearings of a Subcommittee of the Committee on Education and Labor: Violations of the Right of Free Speech and Assembly and Interference With the Right of Labor to Organize and Bargain Collectively.* Part 45. *Supplementary Exhibits, the Special Conference Committee.* 76th Congress. Washington, D.C.: Government Printing Office, 1939.

———. Senate. Select Committee on Unemployment Insurance. *Hearings.* 72nd Congress, 1st session. Washington, D.C.: Government Printing Office, 1932.

Department of the Treasury. Office of Economic Stabilization. *Historical Working Papers on the Economic Stabilization Program, August 15, 1971, to April 30, 1974.* Part I. Washington, D.C.: Government Printing Office, 1974.

National War Labor Board. *Termination Report.* Vol. 2. Washington, D.C.: Government Printing Office, 1946.

The Public Papers of Franklin D. Roosevelt: 1944–1945. Vol. 13. Washington, D.C.: Government Printing Office, 1946.

Public Papers of the Presidents: Dwight D. Eisenhower, 1953. Washington, D.C.: Government Printing Office, 1954.

Public Papers of the Presidents: Lyndon Baines Johnson, 1963–1964. Part I. Washington, D.C.: Government Printing Office, 1965.

Public Papers of the Presidents: Lyndon Baines Johnson, 1968–1969. Part I. Washington, D.C.: Government Printing Office, 1970.

Public Papers of the Presidents: Lyndon Baines Johnson, 1968–1969. Part II. Washington, D.C.: Government Printing Office, 1970.

Public Papers of the Presidents: Gerald R. Ford, 1974. Washington, D.C.: Government Printing Office, 1975.

Statistical Abstract of the United States, 1980. Washington, D.C.: Government Printing Office, 1981.

Weekly Compilation of Presidential Documents: October 25, 1971. Washington, D.C.: Government Printing Office, 1971.

Books

Adamic, Louis. *My America: 1928–1938.* New York: Harper and Brothers, 1938.

Alexander, Charles E. *Holding the Line: The Eisenhower Era, 1952–1961.* Bloomington, Ind.: University of Indiana Press, 1975.

Altmeyer, Arthur. *The Formative Years of Social Security.* Madison, Wis.: University of Wisconsin Press, 1968.

Ambrose, Stephen E. *Rise to Globalism: American Foreign Policy, 1938–1980.* Second Revised Edition. New York: Penguin, 1980.

Bailey, Stephen. *Congress Makes a Law: The Story Behind the Employment Act of 1946.* New York: Columbia University Press, 1950.

Baldwin, David A. *Economic Development and American Foreign Policy, 1943–1962.* Chicago: Chicago University Press, 1966.

Barnes, Joseph. *Wendell Willkie.* New York: Simon and Schuster, 1952.

Bazelon, David T. *Power in America: The Politics of a New Class.* New York: New American Library, 1964.

Bellush, Bernard. *The Failure of the NRA.* New York: W. W. Norton, 1975.

Berkowitz, Edward, and Kim McQuaid. *Creating the Welfare State: The Political Economy of Twentieth-Century Reform.* New York: Praeger Special Studies, 1980.

Bernstein, Barton J., and Allen J. Matosow. *The Truman Administration: A Documentary History.* New York: Harper Torchbooks, 1966.

Berstein, Irving. *The New Deal Collective Bargaining Policy.* Berkeley, Calif.: University of California Press, 1950.

———. *The Turbulent Years.* Boston: Houghton Mifflin, 1970.

Blough, Roger. *The Washington Embrace of Business.* Pittsburgh: Carnegie-Mellon University Press, 1975.

Blum, John Morton, ed. *The Price of Vision: The Diary of Henry A. Wallace, 1942–1946.* Boston: Houghton Mifflin, 1973.
————. *V was for Victory: Politics and American Culture During World War II.* New York: Harcourt Brace Jovanovich, 1976.
Bolles, Blair. *How To Get Rich in Washington.* New York: W. W. Norton, 1952.
Brown, J. Douglas. *An American Philosophy of Social Security: Evolution and Issues.* Princeton, N.J.: Princeton University Press, 1972.
Buchanan, Patrick. *Conservative Votes, Liberal Victories.* New York: Pantheon, 1975.
Buchsbaum, Andrew. "Lords of the Chamber, Knights of the Roundtable: A Study of Business Lobbying Associations." Undergraduate Thesis. Harvard University, 1979.
Burns, James McGregor. *Roosevelt: The Soldier of Freedom.* New York: Harcourt Brace Jovanovich, 1970.
Califano, Joseph. *Governing America: An Insider's Report From the White House and the Cabinet.* New York: Simon and Schuster, 1981.
Catton, Bruce. *The War Lords of Washington.* New York: Harcourt, Brace and Company, 1948.
Cherington, Paul W., and Ralph L. Gillen. *The Business Representative in Washington.* Washington, D.C.: Brookings Institution, 1962.
Cochran, Bert. *Harry S. Truman and the Crisis Presidency.* New York: E. P. Dutton, 1973.
Commager, Henry Steele, ed. *Documents in American History.* Seventh Edition. New York: Appleton-Century-Crofts, 1963.
Congress and the Nation. Vol. 3. *1969–1972: A Review of Government and Politics.* Washington, D.C.: Congressional Quarterly, 1973.
Cook, Fred. *The Nightmare Decade: The Life and Times of Senator Joe McCarthy.* New York: Random House, 1971.
Cuff, Robert D. *The War Industries Board: Business Government Relations During World War I.* Baltimore, Md.: Johns Hopkins University Press, 1973.
Dale, Edwin L. *Conservatives in Power: A Study in Frustration.* Garden City, N.Y.: Doubleday, 1960.
Daniels, Walter M., ed. *The American Labor Movement.* New York: H. W. Wilson, 1958.
Dennison, H. S. *Ethics and Modern Business.* Boston: Houghton Mifflin, 1932.
Derthick, Martha. *Policymaking for Social Security.* Washington, D.C.: Brookings Institution, 1979.
Domhoff, G. William. *The Powers That Be.* New York: Alfred A. Knopf, 1978.
Donovan, Robert J. *Conflict and Crisis: The Presidency of Harry S. Truman, 1945–1948.* New York: W. W. Norton, 1977.
Douglas, William O. *Go East Young Man, The Early Years: The Autobiography of William O. Douglas.* New York: Random House, 1974.
Douglass, Paul F. *Six Upon the World: An American Culture for an Industrial Age.* Boston: Little, Brown, 1954.
Drew, Elizabeth. *American Journals: The Events of 1976.* New York: Random House, 1977.
————. *Washington Journal: The Events of 1973–1974.* New York: Vintage, 1976.
Dubovsky, Melvin, and Warren Van Tine. *John L. Lewis: A Biography.* New York: Quadrangle/New York Times, 1977.
Eakins, David. "The Development of Corporate Liberal Policy Research in the United States, 1885–1965." Ph.D. Thesis. University of Wisconsin, 1966.

An Economic Strategy for the 1980's—March, 1981. New York and Washington, D.C.: Business Roundtable, 1981.

Eisenhower, Dwight David. *Waging Peace: The White House Years, 1956–1961.* Garden City, N.Y.: Doubleday, 1965.

Epstein, Edwin M. *The Corporation in American Politics.* Englewood Cliffs, N.J.: Prentice-Hall, 1969.

Evans, Rowland, and Robert Novak. *Nixon in the White House: The Frustration of Power.* New York: Random House, 1971.

Ferrell, Robert H., ed. *The Eisenhower Diaries.* New York: W. W. Norton, 1981.

———. *Off the Record: The Private Papers of Harry S. Truman.* New York: Harper and Row, 1980.

Fink, Gary M. *Prelude to the Presidency: The Political Character and Legislative Leadership Style of Governor Jimmy Carter.* Westport, Conn.: Greenwood, 1980.

Flanders, Ralph. *Platform for America.* New York: Harper and Row, 1936.

———. *Senator from Vermont.* Boston: Houghton Mifflin, 1961.

Flanders, Ralph, Henry S. Dennison, and Lincoln Filene. *Toward Full Employment.* New York: Whittlesey House, 1938.

Flash, Edward S., Jr. *Economic Advice and Presidential Leadership: The Council of Economic Advisers.* New York: Columbia University Press, 1965.

Frederick, George, ed. *The Swope Plan: Details, Criticisms, Analysis.* New York: Business Bourse, 1931.

Fried, Richard M. *Men Against McCarthy.* New York: Columbia University Press, 1976.

Galbraith, John Kenneth. *American Capitalism.* Second Revised Edition. Boston: Houghton Mifflin, 1956.

———. *A Life in Our Times.* Boston: Houghton Mifflin, 1981.

Gimbel, John. *The Origins of the Marshall Plan.* Stanford, Calif.: Stanford University Press, 1976.

Goldman, Eric F. *The Crucial Decade and After: America, 1945–1960.* New York: Vintage, 1960.

———. *The Tragedy of Lyndon Baines Johnson.* New York: Alfred A. Knopf, 1969.

Graham, Otis L. *Toward a Planned Society: From Roosevelt to Nixon.* New York: Oxford University Press, 1976.

Grayson, C. Jackson, and Louis Neeb. *Confessions of a Price Controller.* New York: Dow Jones, 1974.

Green, Mark, and Andrew Buchsbaum. *The Corporate Lobbies: Political Profiles of the Business Roundtable and the Chamber of Commerce.* Washington, D.C.: Public Citizen, 1980.

Gross, James A. *The Making of the National Labor Relations Board: A Study in Economics, Politics, and the Law.* Vol. 1. *1933–1937.* Albany, N.Y.: State University of New York Press, 1974.

Hamby, Alonzo. *Beyond the New Deal: Harry S. Truman and American Liberalism.* New York: Columbia University Press, 1973.

Harrington, Michael. *Decade of Decision: The Crisis of the American System.* New York: Simon and Schuster, 1980.

Harris, Howell. "Getting Everybody Back on the Same Team: An Interpretation of the Industrial Relations Policies of American Business in the 1940's." Ph.D. Thesis. Oxford University, 1979.

Hawley, Ellis W. *The New Deal and the Problem of Monopoly.* Princeton, N.J.: Princeton University Press, 1968.

Himmelberg, F. *The Origins of the National Recovery Administration: Business, Government, and the Trade Association Issue, 1921–1933.* New York: Fordham University Press, 1976.

Hodgson, Godfrey. *America in Our Time.* New York: Random House, 1976.

Hoffman, Paul G. *World Without Want.* New York: Harper and Row, 1960.

Holmans, A. E. *United States Fiscal Policy, 1945–1959: Its Contribution to Economic Stability.* London: Oxford University Press, 1961.

Hoopes, Roy. *The Steel Crisis.* New York: John Day, 1963.

Hoover, Herbert. *The Memoirs of Herbert Hoover: The Great Depression, 1929–1941.* New York: Macmillan, 1952.

Howard, Nathaniel R., ed. *The Basic Papers of George M. Humphrey as Secretary of the Treasury, 1953–1957.* Cleveland: Western Reserve Historical Society, 1965.

Humphrey, Hubert H. *The Education of a Public Man: My Life in Politics.* Garden City, N.Y.: Doubleday, 1976.

Huthmacher, J. J. *Senator Robert F. Wagner and the Rise of Urban Liberalism.* New York: Atheneum, 1968.

Ickes, Harold. *The Secret Diary of Harold Ickes.* Vol. 3. *1939–1941.* New York: Simon and Schuster, 1954.

Janeway, Eliot. *The Struggle for Survival: A Chronicle of Economic Mobilization During World War II.* New Haven, Conn.: Yale University Press, 1951.

Johnson, Donald B. *The Republican Party and Wendell Willkie.* Urbana, Ill: University of Illinois Press, 1960.

Johnson, Haynes. *In the Absence of Power: Governing America.* New York: Viking, 1980.

Johnson, Hugh S. *The Blue Eagle From Egg to Earth.* Garden City, N.Y.: Doubleday, 1935.

Johnston, Eric. *America Unlimited.* Garden City, N.Y.: Doubleday, 1944.

Jones, James Marion. *The Fifteen Weeks: February 21–June 5, 1947.* New York: Harcourt, Brace and World, 1964.

Jones, Jesse. *Fifty Billion Dollars: My Thirteen Years With the RFC, 1932–1935.* New York: Macmillan, 1951.

Kroos, Herman. *Executive Opinion.* Garden City, N.Y.: Doubleday, 1970.

Larson, Arthur. *Eisenhower: The President Nobody Knew.* New York: Charles Scribner's Sons, 1968.

Lee, R. Alton. *Truman and Taft-Hartley: A Question of Mandate.* Lexington, Ky.: University of Kentucky Press, 1966.

Leuchtenburg, William. *FDR and the New Deal, 1932–1940.* New York: Harper and Row, 1963.

Levering, Ralph. *The Public and American Foreign Policy, 1918–1978.* New York: Foreign Policy Association and McGraw-Hill, 1978.

Lieberman, Elias. *Unions Before the Bar.* New York: Harper and Brothers, 1950.

Lilienthal, David. *Big Business: A New Era.* New York: Harper and Brothers, 1953.

———. *The Journals of David Lilienthal: The TVA Years, 1939–1945.* New York: Harper and Row, 1964.

———. *The Journals of David Lilienthal: The Venturesome Years, 1950–1955.* New York: Harper and Row, 1964.

Lorwin, Lewis, and C. Wubnig. *Labor Relations Boards.* Washington, D.C.: Brookings Institution, 1935.

Loth, David. *Swope of G.E.* New York: Simon and Schuster, 1958.

Lurie, Leonard. *The Running of Richard Nixon.* New York: Coward, McCann and Geoghegan, 1972.

Lyon, Leverett S., et al. *The National Recovery Administration.* Washington, D.C.: Brookings Institution, 1935.

MacRae, Norman. *The Neurotic Trillionaire: A Survey of Mr. Nixon's America.* New York: Harcourt Brace Jovanovich, 1970.

Mailer, Norman. *Some Honorable Men.* Boston: Little, Brown, 1972.

Martin, James Stewart. *All Honorable Men.* Boston: Little, Brown, 1950.

Martin, John Bartlow. *Adlai Stevenson of Illinois.* Garden City, N.Y.: Doubleday, 1976.

McCulloch, F. W., and T. Bornstein. *The National Labor Relations Board.* New York: Praeger, 1974.

McKinley, Charles, and Robert W. Fraser. *Launching Social Security: A Capture and Record Account.* Madison, Wis.: University of Wisconsin Press, 1970.

Michelman, Irving S. *The Crisis Meeters: Business Response to Social Crises.* Clifton, N.J.: A. M. Kelley, 1973.

Millis, Harry A., and Emily C. Brown. *From the Wagner Act to Taft-Hartley: A Study of National Labor Policy and Labor Relations.* Chicago: University of Chicago Press, 1950.

Milward, Alan S. *War, Economy and Society, 1939–1945.* Berkeley, Calif.: University of California Press, 1979.

Miroff, Bruce. *Pragmatic Illusions: The Presidential Politics of John F. Kennedy.* New York: David McKay, 1976.

Mitchell, Brodus. *Depression Decade: From the New Era Through the New Deal, 1929–1941.* New York: Harper Torchbooks, 1969.

Moynihan, Daniel Patrick. *The Politics of a Guaranteed Income: The Nixon Administration and the Family Assistance Plan.* New York: Random House, 1973.

Nelson, Daniel. *Unemployment Insurance: The American Experience, 1915–1935.* Madison, Wis.: University of Wisconsin Press, 1979.

Nixon, Richard M. *RN: The Memoirs of Richard Nixon.* New York: Grosset and Dunlap, 1978.

———. *Six Crises.* Garden City, N.Y.: Doubleday, 1962.

Nossiter, Bernard. *The Mythmakers: An Essay on Power and Wealth.* Boston: Houghton Mifflin, 1964.

Oleszek, Walter J. *Congressional Procedures and the Policy Process.* Washington, D.C.: Congressional Quarterly, 1978.

Ornstein, Norman, and Shirley Elder. *Interest Groups, Lobbying, and Policy-Making.* Washington, D.C.: Congressional Quarterly, 1978.

Parmet, Herbert S. *Eisenhower and the American Crusades.* New York: Macmillan, 1972.

Perkins, Frances. *The Roosevelt I Knew.* New York: Viking, 1946.

Perret, Geoffrey. *Days of Sadness, Years of Triumph: The American People, 1939–1945.* Baltimore, Md.: Penguin, 1974.

———. *A Dream of Greatness: The American People, 1945–1963.* New York: Coward, McCann and Geoghegan, 1980.

Policies Necessary to Reduce the Rate of Inflation: June, 1978. New York and Washington, D.C.: Business Roundtable, 1978.

Radosh, Ronald. *Prophets of the Right: Profiles of Conservative Critics of American Globalism.* New York: Simon and Schuster, 1975.

Randall, Clarence B. *A Foreign Economic Policy for the United States.* Chicago, Ill.: University of Chicago Press, 1954.

Reichley, A. James. *Conservatives in an Age of Change: The Nixon and Ford Administrations.* Washington, D.C.: Brookings Institution, 1981.

Richberg, Donald. *The Rainbow.* Garden City, N.Y.: Doubleday, 1936.

Rimlinger, Gaston V. *Welfare Policy and Industrialization in Europe, America and Russia.* New York: John Wiley and Sons, 1971.

Roos, Charles F. *NRA Economic Planning.* Bloomington, Ind.: Principia Press, 1937.

Roosevelt, Nicholas. *The Townsend Plan.* Garden City, N.Y.: Doubleday, 1936.

Roper, Daniel C. *Fifty Years of Public Life.* Durham, N.C.: University of North Carolina Press, 1941.

Rostow, W. W. *The Diffusion of Power, 1957–1972.* New York: Macmillan, 1972.

Rowen, Hobart. *The Free Enterprisers: Kennedy, Johnson, and the Business Establishment.* New York: G. P. Putnam's Sons, 1964.

Safire, William. *Before the Fall: An Inside View of the Pre-Watergate White House.* Garden City, N.Y.: Doubleday, 1975.

Schlesinger, Arthur, Jr. *The Coming of the New Deal.* Boston: Houghton Mifflin, 1959.

———. *The Politics of Upheaval.* Boston: Houghton Mifflin, 1960.

Schriftgeisser, Karl. *Business and Public Policy: The Role of the Committee for Economic Development, 1942–1967.* Englewood Cliffs, N.J.: Prentice-Hall, 1967.

———. *Business Comes of Age: The Story of the Committee for Economic Development and Its Impact Upon the Economic Policies of the United States, 1940–1960.* New York: Harper and Row, 1960.

Schultz, George P., and Kenneth W. Dam. *Economic Policy Behind the Headlines.* New York: W. W. Norton, 1977.

Seidman, Joel. *American Labor From Defense to Reconversion.* Chicago: Chicago University Press, 1953.

Sherwood, Robert Emmet. *Roosevelt and Hopkins: An Intimate History.* New York: Harper and Brothers, 1948.

Silk, Leonard. *The American Establishment.* New York: Basic Books, 1981.

———. *Nixonomics: How the Dismal Science of Free Enterprise Became the Black Art of Controls.* New York: Praeger, 1972.

Sorensen, Theodore. *Kennedy.* New York: Harper and Row, 1965.

Stein, Herbert. *The Fiscal Revolution in America.* Chicago, Ill.: University of Chicago Press, 1969.

Stone, I. F. *Business as Usual: The First Year of Defense.* New York: Modern Age, 1941.

Terkel, Studs. *Hard Times: An Oral History of the Great Depression.* New York: Avon, 1971.

Titmuss, Richard. *Essays on the Welfare State.* Boston: Beacon, 1969.

Trattner, Walter. *From Poor Law to Welfare State.* New York: Free Press, 1974.

Tufte, Edward R. *Political Control of the Economy.* Princeton, N.J.: Princeton University Press, 1978.

Tully, Grace. *F.D.R.—My Boss.* New York: Viking Press, 1949.

Vadney, Thomas E. *The Wayward Liberal: A Political Biography of Donald Richberg.* Louisville, Ky.: 1970.

Weber, Arnold. *In Pursuit of Price Stability: The Wage-Price Freeze of 1971.* Washington, D.C.: Brookings Institution, 1973.

Wechsler, James A. *Reflections of an Angry Middle-aged Editor.* New York: Random House, 1960.

Weidenbaum, Murray. *Business Government and the Public.* First Edition. Englewood Cliffs, N.J.: Prentice-Hall, 1977.
White, Gerald T. *Billions for Defense: Government Financing by the Defense Plant Corporation During World War II.* University, Ala.: University of Alabama Press, 1980.
White, Theodore H. *The Making of the President, 1964.* New York: Atheneum, 1965.
―――. *The Making of the President, 1972.* New York: Atheneum, 1973.
Wilkins, Mira. *The Maturing of Multinational Enterprise: American Business Abroad From 1914 to 1970.* Cambridge, Mass.: Harvard University Press, 1970.
Wilson, Theodore A. *The Marshall Plan: An Atlantic Venture of 1947–1951 and How It Shaped Our World.* New York: Foreign Policy Association, 1977.
Witcover, Jules. *Marathon: The Pursuit of the Presidency, 1972–1976.* New York: Viking, 1977.
Witte, Edwin E. *The Development of the Social Security Act.* Madison, Wis.: University of Wisconsin Press, 1963.
Wolff, William Marx, Jr. "Peak Business Associations in National Politics: The Business Council and the Committee for Economic Development." Ph.D. Thesis. Tufts University, 1978.

Articles

Benton, William B. "The Economics of a Free Society: A Declaration of American Economic Policy." *Fortune* (October, 1944).
Berkowitz, Edward D., and Kim McQuaid. "Welfare Reform in the 1950's." *The Social Service Review,* Vol. 54 (March, 1980).
Blough, Roger. "My Side of the Steel Price Story." *Look,* Vol. 27 (January, 1963).
Brady, Robert A. "The CED: What Is It and Why?" *Antioch Review,* Vol. 4 (Spring, 1944).
Bronfman, Edgar M. "How to Succeed in Business by Really Trying: The Arab Boycott." *New Republic* (June 4, 1977).
Burch, Philip H., Jr. "The NAM as an Interest Group." *Politics and Society* (Fall, 1973).
Clymer, Adam. "Like Carter, Potomac Power Is Ambiguous." *New York Times,* Sec. XII (January 8, 1978).
Collins, Robert M. "Positive Business Responses to the New Deal: The Roots of the Committee for Economic Development, 1933–1942." *Business History Review,* Vol. 52 (Autumn, 1978).
Crowther, D. W., et al. "Work Stoppages Caused by Labor-Management Disputes in 1946." *Monthly Labor Review,* Vol. 64 (April, 1947).
Davis, William H. "Aims and Policies of the National War Labor Board." *Annals of the American Academy of Political and Social Science,* Vol. 224 (November, 1942).
DiBacco, Thomas V. "American Business and Foreign Aid: The Eisenhower Years." *Business History Review,* Vol. XLI (Spring, 1967).
Donovan, Robert J. "Harriman Committee Scales Down Europe Aid, Says That Czar Should Run It." *New York Herald Tribune* (November 9, 1947).
Ferguson, Thomas, and Joel Rogers. "Labor Law Reform and Its Enemies." *Nation* (January 6–13, 1979).

Fischer, John. "The Lost Liberals: Can They Find a Road Map?" *Harper's,* Vol. 194 (May, 1947).

Green, William. "The Taft-Hartley Act: A Critical View." *Annals of the American Academy of Political and Social Science,* Vol. 274 (March, 1951).

Guzzardi, Walter, Jr. "A New Public Face for Big Business." *Fortune* (June 30, 1980).

Hager, Barry M. "Business Roundtable: New Lobbying Force." *Congressional Quarterly* (September 17, 1977).

Kaysen, Karl. "Big Business and the Liberals: Then and Now." *New Republic,* Vol. 131 (November 22, 1954).

Krock, Arthur. "In the Nation: The Swope Commission." *New York Times* (June 24, 1938).

Levitt, Theodore. "The Johnson Treatment." *Harvard Business Review,* Vol. XLV (January-February, 1967).

———. "Why Business Always Loses." *Harvard Business Review,* Vol. XLVI (March–April, 1968).

Long, Norton. "American Business and American Liberals: Slogans or Responsibility." *Political Quarterly,* Vol. 29 (April–June, 1958).

McDonald, John. "The Businessman in Government." *Fortune* (July, 1954).

McLelland, David S., and Clark E. Woodhouse. "The Business Elite and Foreign Policy." *Western Political Quarterly,* Vol. 13 (1960).

Merriam, Charles E. "The National Resources Planning Board: A Chapter in American Planning Experience." *American Political Science Review,* Vol. 38 (December, 1944).

Miller, Norman C. "The Political Danger of New Mega-Corporations." *Wall Street Journal* (August 20, 1981).

Mills, D. Quinn. "Flawed Victory in Labor Law Reform." *Harvard Business Review,* Vol. 79 (May–June, 1979).

Moye, William T. "Presidential Labor-Management Committees: Productive Failures." *Industrial and Labor Relations Review,* Vol. 34 (October, 1980).

Murphy, Charles J. V. "McCarthy and the Businessman." *Fortune* (April, 1954).

Perkins, Frances. "Eight Years as Madame Secretary." *Fortune* (1941).

Phillips, Cabell. "Truman's New Romance: The Businessman." *Collier's,* Vol. CXXV (June 3, 1950).

Reagan, Michael D. "The BDSA, 1953–1957." *The Western Political Review,* Vol. 14 (June, 1961).

Roberts, John A. "Business Takes On a New Approach to Public Issues." *Du Pont Context,* Vol. 7, no. 1 (1978).

Rowen, Hobart. "America's Most Powerful Private Club." *Harper's,* Vol. 221 (September, 1960).

———. "That Man [LBJ] Made a Lot of Friends." *Newsweek,* Vol. 63 (January 20, 1964).

Salpukas, Agis. "How Big Business Grappled With the Arab Boycott." *New York Times,* Sec. III (August 21, 1977).

Schultze, Charles L. "The Public Use of the Private Interest." *Harper's* (May, 1977).

Schwartz, George. "The Successful Fight Against a Federal Consumer Protection Agency." *Michigan State University Business Topics* (Summer, 1979).

Shabecoff, Philip. "Big Business on the Offensive." *New York Times Magazine* (December 6, 1979).

Simison, Robert L. "Detroit Runs Risk of Reviving Industry Critics." *Wall Street Journal* (August 25, 1981).

Singer, James W. "Business and Government: A New 'Quasi-Public' Role." *National Journal* (April 15, 1978).

Slavin, Peter. "The Business Roundtable: New Lobbying Arm of Big Business." *Business and Society Review,* no. 16 (Winter 1975–1976).

Sternsher, Bernard. "Liberalism in the Fifties: The Travail of Redefinition." *Antioch Review,* Vol. XXII (September, 1952).

Stromberg, Roland N. "American Business and the Approach of War, 1935–1941." *Journal of Economic History,* Vol. 12 (Winter, 1953).

Swope, Gerard. "Much Merit Seen in Swedish Employer-Employee Agreements." *New York Times* (May 21, 1939).

Tolchin, Martin. "Carter's Corporate Brain Trust." *New York Times* (July 24, 1978).

Vogel, David. "Businessmen Unite." *Wall Street Journal* (January 14, 1980).

———. "How Business Responds to Opposition: Corporate Political Strategies During the 1970's." Paper read at the 1979 annual meeting of the American Political Science Association, Washington, D.C.

Westbrook, Robert B. "Tribune of the Technostructure, the Popular Economics of Stuart Chase." *American Quarterly,* Vol. 32 (Fall, 1980).

Young, Owen D. "Courage for the Future." *Vital Speeches,* Vol. 1 (April 22, 1935).

Essays

Barber, William J. "The Kennedy Years: Purposeful Pedagogy." *Exhortations and Controls: The Search for a Wage-Price Policy, 1945–1971.* Ed. Craufurd D. Goodwin. Washington, D.C.: Brookings Institution, 1975.

Brody, David. "The Rise and Decline of Welfare Capitalism." *Change and Continuity in Twentieth-Century America.* Ed. John Braeman et al. Columbus, Ohio: Ohio State University Press, 1964.

Chandler, Alfred D., Jr. "The Large Industrial Corporation." *Institutions in Modern America.* Ed. Stephen E. Ambrose. Baltimore, Md.: John Hopkins University Press, 1967.

Cochrane, James L. "The Johnson Administration: Moral Suasion Goes to War." *Exhortation and Controls: The Search for a Wage-Price Policy, 1945–1971.* Ed. Craufurd D. Goodwin. Washington, D.C.: Brookings Institution, 1975.

Eakins, David. "Business Planners and America's Postwar Expansion." *Corporations and the Cold War.* Ed. David Horowitz. New York: Monthly Review Press, 1970.

Leuchtenburg, William. "The New Deal and the Analogue of War." *Change and Continuity in Twentieth-Century America.* Ed. John Braeman et al. Columbus, Ohio: Ohio State University Press, 1964.

Mann, Thomas E. "Elections and Change in Congress." *The New Congress.* Ed. Thomas E. Mann and Norman Ornstein. Washington, D.C.: American Enterprise Institute, 1981.

Oberdorfer, Don, and Walter Pincus. "Businessmen in Politics: Luther Hodges and Edward Day." *The Kennedy Circle.* Ed. Lester Tanzer. Washington, D.C.: Robert B. Luce, 1961.

Memoirs

Anderson, Robert B. "Oral History Memoir." Lyndon B. Johnson Library, Austin, Tex.

Beebe, Leo C. "Oral History Memoir." Lyndon B. Johnson Library, Austin, Tex.

Blough, Roger. "Oral History Memoir." Lyndon B. Johnson Library, Austin, Tex.

Boeschenstein, Harold. "Oral History Project Memoir." Dwight D. Eisenhower Library, Abilene, Kans.

Clay, Lucius D., Sr. "Oral History Memoir." Dwight D. Eisenhower Library, Abilene, Kans.

Council of Economic Advisers. "Oral History Memoir." John F. Kennedy Library, Boston.

Flanders, Ralph M. "Oral History Project Memoir." Dwight D. Eisenhower Library, Abilene, Kans.

Folsom, Marion B. "Oral History Memoir—Eisenhower Administration." Columbia University Oral History Project Library, New York.

Gilpatric, Roswell. "Oral History Memoir." John F. Kennedy Library, Boston.

Gudeman, Edward. "Oral History Memoir." John F. Kennedy Library, Boston.

Heller, Walter, Kermit Gordon, James Tobin, Gardiner Ackley, and Paul Samuelson. "Oral History Interview." John F. Kennedy Library, Boston.

Hodges, Luther H. "Oral History Project Memoir." John F. Kennedy Library, Boston.

Keyserling, Leon. "Oral History Memoir." Harry S. Truman Library, Independence, Mo.

McDonald, David. "Oral History Memoir." John F. Kennedy Library, Boston.

McQuade, Lawrence. "Oral History Memoir." Lyndon B. Johnson Library, Austin, Tex.

Trowbridge, Alexander. "Oral History Memoir." Lyndon B. Johnson Library, Austin, Tex.

Watson, Thomas J., Jr. "Oral History Project Memoir." John F. Kennedy Library, Boston.

Interviews

Buchsbaum, Andrew. July 25, 1978.

Coffey, Alan F., Jr. January 30, 1980.

Graham, James. February 5, 1980.

Harlow, Bryce N. March 28, 1980.

Harriman, W. Averell. November 4, 1975.

———. November 5, 1975. Washington, D.C.

Hasty, Walter. April 8, 1980.

Keogh, James. April 24, 1980.

Merlis, Edward A. January 10, 1980.

Newmyer, Arthur. March 26, 1980.

Nichols, Robert. January 21, 1980.

Pertschuk, Michael. December 14, 1979.

Podesta, John. March 20, 1980.
Post, John. March 13, 1978.
————. September 8, 1981. Washington, D.C.
Potts, Janet. January 28, 1980.
Slavin, Peter. July 22, 1978.

Letters to Author

Burke, John W. April 24, 1981.
Dungan, Ralph. September 9, 1975.
Dunlop, John T. December 14, 1978.
Feldman, Myer. August 5, 1975.
Galbraith, John Kenneth. December 18, 1973.
————. August 31, 1979.
Harlow, Bryce N. January 18, 1979.
————. March 28, 1980.

List of Acronyms

AAA: Agricultural Adjustment Act
AFL-CIO: American Federation of Labor–Congress of Industrial Organizations
AT&T: American Telephone and Telegraph

CBS: Columbia Broadcasting System
CEA: Council of Economic Advisers
CED: Committee for Economic Development
CEO: Chief Executive Officer
CES: Committee on Economic Security
CIA: Central Intelligence Agency
Conoco: Continental Oil Company
COWPS: Council on Wage and Price Stability
CUAR: Construction Users Anti-Inflation Roundtable

DPC: Defense Plant Corporation

ECA: Economic Cooperation Administration
Ex-Im Bank: Export-Import Bank

GE: General Electric
GM: General Motors
GNP: Gross National Product
GOP Grand Old Party (Republican Party)

IAB: Industrial Advisory Board
IBM: International Business Machines
ITT: International Telephone and Telegraph

LLSC: Labor Law Study Committee
LTV: Ling-Temco-Vought

MIT: Massachusetts Institute of Technology

NAB: National Alliance of Businessmen
NAM: National Association of Manufacturers
NATO: North Atlantic Treaty Organization
NDAC: National Defense Advisory Commission
NIRA: National Industrial Recovery Act
NLB: National Labor Board
NLRB: National Labor Relations Board
NRA: National Recovery Administration
NRPB: National Resources Planning Board
NWLB: National War Labor Board

OMB: Office of Management and Budget
OPEC: Organization of Petroleum Exporting Countries
OPM: Office of Production Management

RFC: Reconstruction Finance Corporation

SCC: Special Conference Committee
SPAB: Supply Priorities and Allocations Board

TNEC: Temporary National Economic Committee
TVA: Tennessee Valley Authority

UAW: United Automobile Workers

WIN buttons: Whip Inflation Now
WPB: War Production Board
WRB: War Resources Board

375

INDEX

ABOUT THE AUTHOR

KIM MCQUAID grew up in rural Maine. He received his B.A. from Antioch College in 1970 and his Ph.D. in history from Northwestern University in 1975. His previous work includes a book, *Creating the Welfare State,* and articles about business-government relations that have appeared in such publications as the *Harvard Business Review,* the *Anti-Trust Law and Economics Review,* and the *New England Quarterly.* Kim McQuaid teaches history at Lake Erie College in Painesville, Ohio.